PHILOSOPHY AND RELIGION

Some Contemporary Perspectives

Edited by
JERRY H. GILL
Department of Philosophy
Southwestern at Memphis
Memphis, Tennessee

Burgess Publishing Company

426 South Sixth Street • Minneapolis, Minn. 55415

DEDICATED
TO
ROBERT A. TRAINA

i

INTRODUCTION

Generally speaking there are three ways of approaching the philosophical consideration of religion. There is, to begin with, the historical approach which seeks to trace the development of religious questions and theories through their long ancestry. Secondly, there is the topical approach which organizes the main themes of religious philosophy according to logically ordered topics and considers them one by one. Thirdly, there is the "school of thought," or perspectives approach which groups various contributions in the field according to a similarity of method and/or content.

Each of these three ways of studying the relation between philosophy and religion has its values and its limitations. By and large most books of readings in the philosophy of religion are constructed according to one or the other of the first two ways, or according to some combination of the two. The present book of readings is designed according to the third, or perspectives approach, in order to provide a useful source book for those who prefer this approach. The primary limitation of such an arrangement is that it is notoriously difficult to define a school of thought and/or to choose representative writings which others working in the field will agree are, in fact, representative. Although this difficulty is acknowledged to be great, it is also believed to be surmountable, and the following choice and groupings of essays is offered in substantiation of this belief.

Within recent years there has been a great increase of interest in the relation of philosophy to religion, and this interest has given rise to a variety of contemporary perspectives. Moreover, it is possible to make a case for introducing students to a given field by means of an encounter with those thinkers who most strongly influence the contemporary climate. With this in mind, the present book has been organized exclusively around contemporary perspectives. While no claim is made for the exhaustiveness of this list of perspectives, it is hoped that the list is representative of those movements which are exerting a forceful influence on the thought of our day.

In addition to its exclusive contemporary focus, the present volume is characterized by the inclusion of a number of essays which are as rare in books as they are important in contemporary philosophy of religion. These include the essays by Martin Heidegger (previously unpublished), Albert Camus, Frederick Ferré, John Wisdom, and Bernard Lonergan. There are also a number of essays which are worthy of being classified as "classic" in stature, such as those by Paul Tillich, Gabriel Marcel, and Bertrand Russell. Finally, there are a number of essays which are both sound and representative of the contemporary scene, including those by John Macquarrie, Charles Hartshorne, Ian Ramsey, and Michael Novak.

For purposes of integration it may prove helpful to provide a brief discussion of some of the more important themes and problems which are common to many of the writers represented. Space will only permit an introduction of four such considerations, each of which plays a crucial role in nearly all of the following chapters. Both the students and professors making use of this book are urged to give some attention to such topical considerations.

First, there is the question of the relationship between philosophy and religion. This question is sometimes viewed in terms of the relation between reason and faith. Each of the traditional positions on this question can be found within the following selections. There are those who maintain that philosophy and religion have essentially nothing to do with one another. This position has its historical roots in the likes of Tertullian, Pascal, Hume, Kant, and Kierkegaard. It is interesting to note that this position has been used both as a defense and as criticism of theistic belief! At the opposite end of the continuum are those who maintain some form of synthesis between philosophy and religion, and whose heritage includes such thinkers as Augustine, Anselm, Descartes, Spinoza, and Hegel. In between stand those who hold out for some sort of functional relationship between philosophy and religion, as did Aquinas, Locke, William James, and Alfred North Whitehead.

Second, there is the question of the reasons which can be given for and against religious and/or theistic belief. Here, too, the field is divided amongst a variety of approaches. There are those who would focus on rational analysis, either to argue in favor of religious belief, or to argue against it. In addition, there have always been thinkers who have appealed to various aspects of human experience—psychological, sociological, historical—in order to establish the reasonableness or unreasonableness of religious belief. Finally, in line with the distinctions made in the first part of the preceding paragraph, there have been those who maintain that any form of reasoning about religion is a waste of time and effort. Although these positions are not without their historical representatives, it is difficult to divide them according to such rubrics, since many make use of more than one approach.

Third, another key issue which has recently come to the center of the stage, but which has always been present in the wings, is that of the structure or meaning of the religious use of language. Today this issue is often known as "the God-talk debate," and it has become central as a result of contemporary philosophy's concern with language and meaning. Historically there have been those who proceeded on the assumption that God-talk is essentially the same as metaphysical and/or scientific language. Over against these have stood those who maintain that although religious language seeks to function in a manner similar to the language of science, it fails in this effort and can only be regarded as unintelligible. In between these extremes have stood thinkers who argue that while God-talk is not to be understood as some sort of "super" scientific language, it by no means follows that it must be regarded as unintelligible. These thinkers generally argue for viewing religious language as analogical or metaphorical in nature.

Fourth, one of the basic issues in the philosophy of religion has always been that of providing a fruitful and coherent model by means of which to understand the essential nature of reality and/or human experience. Some have opted for a monolithic model which would provide for a maximum of stability and a minimum of multiplicity. Others have sought to construct a view which involves a good deal of plurality and change without giving way to chaos. Within each of these two main approaches there have always been a number of different possibilities, from pantheism through dualism to evolutionism. Most of these options are still viable today, as the selections which follow clearly indicate.

These, then, are some of the historical and topical concerns which ought to be kept in mind when coming to grips with various contemporary perspectives. Nearly all of the essays in this book exhibit characteristics which can be related to the above mentioned concerns, and to many others as well. While it is of immense importance to trace out these relationships with the past and with traditional topical divisions, it should also be borne in mind that, in the final analysis, the primary concern of such study must be to come to grips with the intellectual developments of one's own time. One begins where one is, or one never begins at all!

CONTENTS

Introduction

Part One: The Existentialist Perspective

Part Two: The Humanist Perspective

Part Three: The Process Perspective

Part Four: The Analytic Perspective

Part Five: The Neo-Catholic Perspective

PART ONE:

THE
EXISTENTIALIST
PERSPECTIVE

INTRODUCTION

Though it has certain historical predecessors, existentialism is, strictly speaking, a twentieth century phenomenon. Nietzsche, Pascal, Dostoyevsky, and Kierkegaard all share in the existentialist heritage, but it has only been in our time that the emphases which these thinkers have in common have exerted a profound influence in the philosophical and religious worlds. The thinkers represented in this section all reflect the themes of earlier existentialist thinkers, but in a way which is particularly appropriate to our century. This introduction will limit itself to a brief survey of some of the main emphases given expression in the following selections. It should also be noted that the authors included represent a wide spectrum, both geographically and ideologically, within the existentialist perspective.

First off, it can be said that existentialist thinkers share a common concern for the priority of human values. It is this concern which gives rise to the affinity between existentialism and religious questions. Whereas philosophy has often concerned itself with other questions—such as those of a scientific and logical nature—existentialist thinkers are agreed that the first job of philosophy is to come to grips with the value structure of human existence. Clearly, this concern is of primary importance to religious thinkers as well. Although there are "atheistic" existentialists as well as theistic ones, even these find it necessary to define themselves and their positions in relation to the traditional religious posture.

It is on the basis of their concern with the values of human existence that the writers in question have been grouped together, for good or for ill, under the heading "existentialist." The questions of the nature of human existence, the proper mode of existence, and the basis of responsibility are all central to these thinkers. In all of these questions emphasis is placed upon the ultimacy of personal integrity and individuality. Moreover, there is a strong concern to develop a stance toward life which takes full cognizance of the stark realities of human existence, such as anxiety, absurdity, and death. Thus, there is a constant protest against what might be called the naive optimism of all forms of Idealism, religious and non-religious.

Secondly, the other side of this positive concern for human, existential values is a negative appraisal of the importance of empirical or scientific reason. While some existentialists have actually taken what must be labeled an "irrationalist" approach, most have been content to mark out the limitations of what might be termed "critical reason" with respect to questions of ethics and religion. By and large existentialist writers maintain a strict dichotomy between the factual and the valuational dimensions of human existence. Thus, critical reason, which is appropriate to factual considerations, is thought to be essentially irrelevant to valuational considerations. It is claimed that critical reason, with its stress upon objectivity, alienates the knower from the known and systematically avoids all questions of decision and commitment as hopelessly "subjective." Thus, the existentialist claims, all of the truly important considerations of human existence are set aside. For these reasons it is thought useless and harmful to subject valuational issues to the structures of critical reason.

Among those existentialists who address themselves to a philosophical consideration of religion, nearly all are agreed that the foregoing remarks apply with equal force to religious questions. Religion is seen as a subdivision within the valuational domain, and thus outside of the scope of critical reason. Here again it is to be noted that this is not an irrationalist claim, since it is maintained both that critical reason has other, more appropriate concerns, and that there are other means available for coming to an understanding of the valuational and religious aspects of existence. The mention of these "other means" leads directly to the next main theme of the existentialist perspective.

The final emphasis that will be discussed in this introduction is that which is placed upon the importance of ontology, or metaphysics. This emphasis, as well as that placed on human values, brings existentialism into direct relationship with religion. On the one hand, there is a concrete effort made by nearly all those writing from within this perspective to analyze the nature of existence in general, or as it is usually put, to understand "Being itself." This effort is often confined to a focus on the "existentials" of human experience, such as anxiety, fear, absurdity, and death, by way of carving out a meaningful place to stand in daily life. On the other hand, there is often an interest among existentialist thinkers in constructing a rather full-blown metaphysical position in order to interrelate the various aspects of experience in a stable and coherent worldview. This interest is in harmony with the Idealist tradition extending from Plato down through Hegel. Thus, it is that the concepts of God, nature, the self, immortality, and the like play a role in both religion and existentialist philosophy.

The connection between this concern for ontology and previously mentioned negative appraisal of critical reason is to be found by zeroing in on the method by means of which existentialist ontology is to be developed. While these thinkers are against the application of critical reason in the valuational and religious realms, they are in favor of the application of what is often termed "speculative reason." Most often philosophy is identified with that enterprise which seeks to draw all the data of human experience and knowledge together by way of making generalizations about the nature of reality as a whole. Sometimes this methodology is equated with some form of intuition or introspection. In the latter case, existentialism is transformed into what is known today as "Phenomenology." Perhaps the most important characteristic of speculative reason, as contrasted with critical reason, is its attempt to "get inside of" reality, rather than to objectively describe it. The methods of doing this are as varied as the thinkers who advocate this approach.

Bearing these emphases in mind, the student's best bet for coming to an understanding of the existentialist perspective is to wrestle firsthand with the selections which follow. There will, of course, be a number of other obviously common themes in addition to those which have been introduced above. There will also be a good number of themes which are unique to each individual writer. As much can be learned from contrasting these thinkers as from comparing them, and there is no time like the present in which to begin.

Paul Tillich's essay, "Reason and the Quest for Revelation," reflects most of the issues discussed above. He argues a classic case for what might be termed "ontological existentialism" in that he synthesizes Germanic Idealism and the twentieth century search for personal meaning. On the basis of this synthesis, Tillich goes on to build an impressive and complex philosophical theology. Gabriel Marcel, in his "On the Ontological Mystery," is content to make a distinction (between a problem and a mystery) which is essentially similar to that of Tillich without building any sort of system upon it. The short, but highly compact, essay by Martin Heidegger presents an altogether different facet of existentialist thought. Previously unpublished, this piece is a prize and rare expression of Heidegger's later philosophy, which has been described as something of a "poetic mysticism." John Macquarrie, who has learned a great deal from both Heidegger and Rudolph Bultmann, represents English speaking existentialism at its best. His short essay serves as an excellent summary of the existentialist application of existentialism philosophy to theology. These essays as a group represent the main geographical divisions of the existentialist approach to religion: German (Heidegger), French (Marcel), British (Macquarrie) and American (Tillich).

CHAPTER ONE

REASON AND THE QUEST
FOR REVELATION*

by Paul Tillich

A. THE STRUCTURE OF REASON

1. The Two Concepts of Reason

Epistemology, the "knowledge" of knowing, is a part of ontology, the knowledge of being, for knowing is an event within the totality of events. Every epistemological assertion is implicitly ontological. There-fore, it is more adequate to begin an analysis of existence with the ques-tion of being rather than with the problem of knowledge. Moreover, it is in line with the predominant classical tradition. But there are situations in which the opposite order ought to be followed, namely, when an on-tological tradition has become doubtful and the question arises whether the tools used in the creation of this tradition are responsible for its failure. This was the situation of ancient probabilism and skepticism in relation to the struggle between the philosophical schools. It was the situation of Descartes in the face of the disintegrating medieval traditions. It was the situation of Hume and Kant with respect to the traditional metaphysics. It is the perennial situation of theology, which always must give an account of its paths to knowledge because they seem to deviate radically from all ordinary ways. Although epistemology precedes ontology in these instances, it is an error to assume that epistemology is able to provide the foundation of the philosophical or theological system. Even if it precedes the other parts of the system, it is dependent on them in such a way that it can be elaborated only by anticipating them explicitly and implicitly. Recent Neo-Kantian philos-

*Used with permission from *Systematic Theology*, Vol. I, University of Chicago Press, Chicago, Illinois, 1951.

ophers recognized the dependence of epistemology on ontology and contributed to the fall of the epistemological tidal wave which arose in the second half of the nineteenth century. Classical theology always has been aware that a doctrine of revelation presupposes doctrines of God, man, Christ, etc. It has known that the epistemological "preamble" is dependent on the whole of the theological system. Recent attempts to make epistemological and methodological considerations an independent basis for theological work have been futile.[1] Therefore, it is necessary that the systematic theologian, when he begins with the epistemological part (the doctrine of Reason and Revelation), should indicate clearly the anticipations he makes both with respect to Reason and with respect to Revelation.

One of the greatest weaknesses of much theological writing and of much religious talk is that the word "reason" is used in a loose and vague way, which is sometimes appreciative but usually depreciatory. While popular talk can be excused for such unpreciseness (although it has religious dangers), it is inexcusable if a theologian uses terms without having defined or exactly circumscribed them. Therefore, it is necessary to define from the very beginning the sense in which the term "reason" will be used.

We can distinguish between an ontological and a technical concept of reason. The former is predominant in the classical tradition from Parmenides to Hegel; the latter, though always present in pre-philosophical and philosophical thought, has become predominant since the breakdown of German classical idealism and in the wake of English empiricism.[2] According to the classical philosophical tradition, reason is the structure of the mind which enables the mind to grasp and to transform reality. It is effective in the cognitive, aesthetic, practical, and technical functions of the human mind. Even emotional life is not irrational in itself. *Eros* drives the mind toward the true (Plato). Love for the perfect form moves all things (Aristotle). In the "apathy" of the soul the *logos* manifests its presence (Stoics). The longing for its origin elevates soul and mind toward the ineffable source of all meaning (Plotinus). The *appetitus* of everything finite drives it toward the good-itself (Aquinas). "Intellectual love" unites intellect and emotion in the most rational state of the mind (Spinoza). Philosophy is "service of God;" it is a thinking which is at the same time life and joy in the "absolute truth" (Hegel), etc. Classical reason is Logos, whether it is understood in a more intuitive or in a more critical way. Its cognitive nature is one element in addition to others; it is cognitive and aesthetic, theoretical and practical, detached and passionate, subjective and objective. The denial of reason in the classical sense is antihuman because it is antidivine.

But this ontological concept of reason always is accompanied and sometimes replaced by the technical concept of reason. Reason is reduced to the capacity for "reasoning." Only the cognitive side of the classical concept of reason remains, and within the cognitive realm only those cognitive acts which deal with the discovery of means for ends. While reason in the sense of Logos determines the ends and only in the second place the means, reason in the technical sense determines the means while accepting the ends from "somewhere else." There is no danger in this situation as long as technical reason is the companion of ontological reason and "reasoning" is used to fulfil the demands of reason. This situation prevailed in most pre-philosophical as well as philosophical periods of human history, although there always was the threat that "reasoning" might separate itself from reason. Since the middle of the nineteenth century this threat has become a dominating reality. The consequence is that the ends are provided by nonrational forces, either by positive traditions or by arbitrary decisions serving the will to power. Critical reason has ceased to exercise its controlling function over norms and ends. At the same time the noncognitive sides of reason have been consigned to the irrelevance of pure subjectivity. In some forms of logical positivism the philosopher even refuses to "understand" anything that transcends technical reason, thus making his philosophy completely irrelevant for questions of existential concern. Technical reason, however refined in logical and methodological respects, dehumanizes man if it is separated from ontological reason. And, beyond this, technical reason itself is impoverished and corrupted if it is not continually nourished by ontological reason. Even in the means-ends structure of "reasoning" assertions about the nature of things are presupposed which themselves are not based on technical reason. Neither structures, Gestalt processes, values, nor meanings can be grasped without ontological reason. Technical reason can reduce them to something less than their true reality. But, by reducing them to this status, it has deprived itself of insights which are decisive for the means-ends relationship. Of course one knows many *aspects* of human nature by analyzing physiological and psychological processes and by using the elements provided by this analysis for physicotechnical or psychotechnical purposes. But if one claims to know man in this way, one misses not only the nature of man but even decisive truths about man within a means-ends relationship. This is true of every realm of reality. Technical reason always has an important function, even in systematic theology. But technical reason is adequate and meaningful only as an expression of ontological reason and as its companion. Theology need not make a decision for or against one of these two concepts of reason. It uses the methods of technical reason, the means-ends relation, in establishing a consistent, logical, and correctly derived organism of thought. It accepts the refinements of the cognitive methods applied by technical reason. But it rejects the confusion of technical with ontological reason. For instance, theology cannot accept the support of technical reason in "reasoning" the existence of a God. Such a God would belong to the means-ends relationship. He would be less than God. On the other hand, theology is not perturbed by the attack on the Christian message made by technical reason, for these attacks do not reach the level on which religion stands. They may destroy superstitions, but they do not even touch faith. Theology is (or should be) grateful for the critical function of the type of technical reason which shows that there is no such "thing" as a God within the context of means-ends relationships. Religious objects, seen in terms of the universe of discourse constituted by technical reason, are objects of superstition subject to destructive criticism. Wherever technical reason dominates, religion is superstition and is either foolishly supported by reason or rightly removed by it.

Although theology invariably uses technical reason in its systematic work, it cannot escape the question of its relation to ontological reason. The traditional question of the relation of reason to revelation should not be discussed on the level of technical reason, where it constitutes no genuine problem, but on the level of ontological reason, of reason in the sense of *logos*. Technical reason is an instrument, and, like every instrument, it can be more or less perfect and can be used more or less skilfully. But no existential problem is involved in its use. The situation is quite different with respect to ontological reason. It was the mistake of idealistic philosophy that it identified revelation with ontological reason while rejecting the claims of technical reason. This is the very essence of the idealistic philosophy of religion. In opposition to idealism, theology must show that, although the essence of ontological reason, the universal *logos* of being, is identical with the content of revelation, still reason, if actualized in self and world, is dependent on the destructive structures of existence and the saving structures of life (Parts III and IV); it is subjected to finitude and separation, and it can participate in the "New Being." Its actualization is not a matter of technique but of "fall" and "salvation." It follows that the theologian must consider reason from several different perspectives. In theology one must distiguish not only ontological from technical reason but also ontological reason in its essential perfection from its predicament in the different stages of its actualization in existence, life, and history. The religious judgment that reason is "blind," for instance, neither refers to technical reason, which can see most things in its own realm quite well, nor to ontological reason in its essential perfection, namely, in unity with being-itself. [3] The judgment that reason is blind refers to reason under the conditions of existence; and the judgment that reason is weak—partly liberated from blindness, partly held in it—refers to reason within life and history. If these distinctions are not made, every statement about reason is incorrect or dangerously ambiguous.

2. Subjective and Objective Reason

Ontological reason can be defined as the structure of the mind which enables it to grasp and to shape reality. From the time of Parmenides it has been a common assumption of all philosophers that the *logos*, the word which grasps and shapes reality, can do so only because reality itself has a *logos* character. There have been widely differing explanations of the relation between the *logos* structure of the grasping-and-shaping-self and the *logos* structure of the grasped-and-shaped-world. But the necessity of an explanation has been acknowledged almost unanimously. In the classical descriptions of the way in which subjective reason and objective reason—the rational structure of the mind and the rational structure of reality—are related, four main types appear. The first type considers subjective reason as an effect of the whole of reality on a part of it, namely, on the mind. It presupposes that reality has the power of producing a reasonable mind through which it can grasp and shape itself. Realism, whether naive, critical, or dogmatic (materialism), takes this stand, often without recognizing its basic presupposition. The second type considers objective reason as a creation of subjective reason on the basis of an unstructured matter in which it actualizes itself. Idealism, whether in the restricted forms of ancient philosophy or in the unrestricted forms of modern philosophy, makes this assertion, often without any explanation of the fact that matter is receptive to the structural power of reason. The third type affirms the ontological independence and the functional interdependence of subjective and objective reason, pointing to the mutual fulfilment of the one in the other. Dualism or pluralism, whether metaphysical or epistemological, takes this position, often without asking the question of an underlying unity of subjective and objective reason. The fourth type affirms an underlying identity which expresses itself in the rational structure of reality. Monism, whether it describes the identity in terms of being or in terms of experience (pragmatism), takes this position, often without explaining the difference between subjective and objective reason.

The theologian is not obligated to make a decision about the degree of truth of these four types. However, he must consider their common presuppositions when he uses the concept of reason. Implicitly theologians always have done this. They have spoken of creation through the Logos or of the spiritual presence of God in everything real. They have called man the image of God because of his rational structure and have charged him with the task of grasping and shaping the world.

Subjective reason is the structure of the mind which enables it to grasp and to shape reality on the basis of a corresponding structure of reality (in whatever way this correspondence may be explained). The description of "grasping" and "shaping" in this definition is based on the fact that subjective reason always is actualized in an individual self which is related to its environment and to its world in terms of reception and reaction. The mind receives and reacts. In receiving reasonably, the mind grasps its world; in reacting reasonably, the mind shapes its world. "Grasping," in this context, has the connotation of penetrating into the depth, into the essential nature of a thing or an event, of understanding and expressing it. "Shaping," in this context, has the connotation of transforming a given material into a Gestalt, a living structure which has the power of being.

The division between the grasping and the shaping character of reason is not exclusive. In every act of reasonable reception an act of shaping is involved, and in every act of reasonable reaction an act of grasping is involved. We transform reality according to the way we see it, and we see reality according to the way we transform it. Grasping and shaping the world are interdependent. In the cognitive realm this has been clearly expressed in the Fourth Gospel, which speaks of knowing the truth by doing the truth. [4] Only in the active realization of the true does truth become manifest. In a similar way Karl Marx called every theory which is not based on the will to transform reality an "ideology," that is, an attempt to preserve existing evils by a theoretical construction which justifies them. Some of the impact of instrumentalist thinking on our contemporaries stems from its emphasis on the unity of action and knowledge.

While the cognitive side of "receiving rationality" demands special discussion, what has been said makes it possible to survey the entire field of ontological reason. In both types of rational acts, the grasping and the shaping, a basic polarity is visible. This is due to the fact that an emotional element is present in every rational act. On the receptive side of reason we find a polarity between the cognitive and the aesthetic elements. On the reactive side of reason we find a polarity between the organizational and the organic elements. But this description of the "field of reason" is only preliminary. Each of the four functions mentioned includes transitional stages on the path to its opposite pole. Music is further removed from the cognitive function than the novel, and technical science is further removed from the aesthetic realm than biography or ontology. Personal communion is further removed from organization than national community, and commercial law is further removed from the organic realm than government. One should not try to construe a static system of the rational functions of the human mind. There are no sharp limits between them, and there is much historical change in their growth and in their relationships. But all of them are functions of ontological reason, and the fact that in some of them the emotional element is more decisive than in others does not make them less rational. Music is no less rational than mathematics. The emotional element in music opens a dimension of reality which is closed to mathematics. Communion is no less rational than law. The emotional element in communion opens a dimension of reality which is closed to law. There is, of course, an implicit mathematical quality in music and a potential legal quality in all communal relations. But this is not their essence. They have their own rational structures. This is the meaning of Pascal's sentence about the "reasons of the heart which reason cannot comprehend." [5] Here "reason" is used in a double sense. The "reasons of the heart" are the structures of aesthetic and communal experience (beauty and love); the reason "which cannot comprehend them" is technical reason.

Subjective reason is the rational structure of the mind, while objective reason is the rational structure of reality which the mind can grasp and according to which it can shape reality. Reason in the philosopher grasps the reason in nature. Reason in the artist grasps the meaning of things. Reason in the legislator shapes society according to the structures of social balance. Reason in the leaders of a community shapes communal life according to the structure of organic interdependence. Objective reason is rational if, in the twofold process of reception and reaction, it expresses the rational structure of reality. This relation, whether it is described in ontological or epistemological terms, is not static. Life being itself, reason unites a dynamic with a static element in an indissoluble amalgamation. This refers not only to subjective but also to objective reason. Both the rational structure of reality and the rational structure of the mind possess duration within change and change in duration. The problem of actual reason, therefore, is not only to avoid errors and failures in the grasping and shaping of reality but also to make the dynamics of reason effective in every act of subjective reason and in every moment of objective reason. The danger involved in this situation is that the dynamics of rational creativity may be confused with the distortions of reason in existence. The dynamic element of reason forces the mind to take this risk. In every rational act three elements inhere: the static element of reason, the dynamic element of reason, and the existential distortion of both of them. Therefore, it is possible for the mind to defend something as a static element of reason which is a distortion of it or for the mind to attack something as distorted which is a dynamic element of reason. Academic art defends the static element of aesthetic reason, but in much academic art there is a distortion of something which was creative and new when if first arose and which was attacked at its inception as a distortion of former academic ideals. Social conservatism is a distortion of something which once was a dynamic creation, attacked at the time of its appearance as a distortion of former conservative ideals. These risks are unavoidable in all processes of actual reason, in mind as well as in reality.

One must ask what the dynamic element in objective reason means. It is a problem whether one can speak about a changing element within the structure of reality. Nobody doubts that reality changes, but many people believe that change is possible only because the structure of reality is unchangeable. If this were so, the rational structure of the mind itself would be unchangeable, and the rational process would have only two elements—the static element and the failure to grasp and to shape it adequately. One would have to dismiss the dynamic element of reason altogether if subjective reason alone were dynamic. Reality itself creates structural possibilities within itself. Life, as well as mind, is creative. Only those things can live which embody a rational structure. Living beings are successful attempts of nature to actualize itself in accordance with the demands of objective reason. If nature does not follow these demands, its products are unsuccessful trials. The same is true of legal forms and social relations. New products of the historical process are attempts which can succeed only if they follow the demands of objective reason. Neither nature nor history can create anything that contradicts reason. The new and the old in history and nature are bound together in an overwhelming rational unity which is static and dynamic at the same time. The new does not break this unity; it cannot because objective reason is the structural possibility, the *logos* of being.

3. The Depth of Reason

The depth of reason is the expression of something that is not reason but which precedes reason and is manifest through it. Reason in both its objective and its subjective structures points to something which appears in these structures but which transcends them in power and meaning. This is not another field of reason which could progressively be discovered and expressed, but it is that which is expressed through every rational expression. It could be called the "substance" which appears in the rational structure, or "being-itself" which is manifest in the *logos* of being, or the "ground" which is creative in every rational creation, or the "abyss" which cannot be exhausted by any creation or by any totality of them, or the "infinite potentiality of being and meaning" which pours into the rational structures of mind and reality, actualizing and transforming them. All these terms which point to that which "precedes" reason have a metaphorical character. "Preceding" is itself metaphorical. This is necessarily so, because if the terms were used in their proper sense, they would belong to reason and would not precede it.

While only a metaphorical description of the depth of reason is possible, the metaphors may be applied to the various fields in which reason is actualized. In the cognitive realm the depth of reason is its quality of pointing to truth-itself, namely, to the infinite power of being and of the ultimately real, through the relative truths in every field of knowledge. In the aesthetic realm the depth of reason is its quality of pointing to "beauty-itself," namely, to an infinite meaning and an ultimate significance, through the creations in every field of aesthetic intuition. In the legal realm the depth of reason is its quality of pointing to "justice-itself," namely, to an infinite seriousness and an ultimate dignity, through every structure of actualized justice. In the communal realm the depth of reason is its quality of pointing to "love-itself," namely, to an infinite richness and an ultimate unity, through every form of actualized love. This dimension of reason, the dimension of depth, is an essential quality of all rational functions. It is their own depth, making them inexhaustible and giving them greatness.

The depth of reason is that characteristic of reason which explains two functions of the human mind, the rational character of which can neither be affirmed nor denied because they demonstrate an independent structure which can neither be reduced to other functions of reason nor be derived from prerational psychological or sociological elements. Myth is not primitive science, nor is cult primitive morality. Their

content, as well as the attitude of people toward them, disclose elements
which transcend science as well as morality—elements of infinity which
express ultimate concern. These elements are essentially implicit in every
rational act and process, so that in principle they do not require separate expression. In every act of grasping truth, truth-itself is grasped
implicitly, and in every act of transforming love, love-itself transforms
implicitly, etc. The depth of reason is essentially manifest in reason.
But it is hidden in reason under the conditions of existence. Because
of these conditions reason in existence expresses itself in myth and cult
as well as in its proper functions. There should be neither myth nor
cult. They contradict essential reason; they betray by their very existence
the "fallen" state of a reason which has lost immediate unity with its
own depth. It has become "superficial," cutting itself off from its
ground and abyss. Christianity and the Enlightenment agree in the
judgment that there should be neither myth nor cult, but from different
presuppositions. Christianity envisages a state without myth and cult,
potentially in the "beginning," actually in the "end," fragmentarily and
by anticipation in the flux of time. Enlightenment sees the end of myth
and cult in a new future when rational knowledge has vanquished myth
and rational morals have conquered cult. Enlightenment and rationalism confuse the essential nature of reason with the predicament of
reason in existence. Essentially reason is transparent toward its depth
in each of its acts and processes. In existence this transparency is opaque
and is replaced by myth and cult. Therefore, both of these are utterly
ambiguous from the point of view of existential reason. Innumerable
theories defining them, explaining them, and explaining them away are
a token of this situation. If we ignore the merely negative theories,
most of which are based on psychological and sociological explanations
and which are consequences of the rationalistic understanding of reason, we are driven to the following alternative: either myth and cult are
special realms of reason along with the others, or they represent the
depth of reason in symbolic form. If they are considered to be special
rational functions in addition to the others they are in a never ending
and insoluble conflict with the other functions. They are swallowed by
them, placed into the category of irrational feelings, or maintained as
strange bodies, heteronomous and destructive, within the structure of
reason. If, however, myth and cult are considered to be the expressions
of the depth of reason in symbolic form, they lie in a dimension where
no interference with the proper functions of reason is possible. Wherever the ontological concept of reason is accepted and the depth of
reason is understood no conflicts between myth and knowledge, between cult and morals, are necessary. Revelation does not destroy reason, but reason raises the question of revelation.[6]

B. REASON IN EXISTENCE

4. The Finitude and the Ambiguities of Actual Reason

Reason as the structure of mind and reality is actual in the processes of being, existence, and life. Being is finite, existence is self-contradictory, and life is ambiguous (see Parts II-IV). Actual reason participates in these characteristics of reality. Actual reason moves through finite categories, through self-destructive conflicts, through ambiguities, and through the quest for what is unambiguous, beyond conflict, and beyond bondage to the categories.

The nature of finite reason is described in classical form by Nicolaus Cusanus and Immanuel Kant. The former speaks of the *docta igno-rantia*, the "learned ignorance," which acknowledges the finitude of man's cognitive reason and its inability to grasp its own infinite ground. But, in recognizing this situation, man is at the same time aware of the infinite which is present in everything finite, though infinitely transcending it. This presence of the inexhaustible ground in all beings is called by Cusanus the "coincidence of the opposites." In spite of its finitude, reason is aware of its infinite depth. It cannot express it in terms of rational knowledge (ignorance), but the knowledge that this is impossible is real knowledge (learned). The finitude of reason does not lie in the fact that it lacks perfection in grasping and shaping reality. Such imperfection is accidental to reason. Finitude is essential for reason, as it is for everything that participates in being. The structure of this finitude is described in the most profound and comprehensive way in Kant's "critiques."[7] The categories of experience are categories of finitude. They do not enable human reason to grasp reality-in-itself; but they do enable man to grasp his world, the totality of the phenomena which appear to him and which constitute his actual experience. The main category of finitude is time. Being finite means being temporal. Reason cannot break through the limits of temporality and reach the eternal, just as it cannot break through the limits of causality, space, substance, in order to reach the first cause, absolute space, universal substance. At this point the situation is exactly the same as it is in Nicolaus Cusanus: by analyzing the categorical structure of reason, man discovers the finitude in which he is imprisoned. He also discovers that his reason does not accept this bondage and tries to grasp the infinite with the categories of finitude, the really real with the categories of experience, and that it necessarily fails. The only point at which the prison of finitude is open is the realm of moral experience, because in it something unconditional breaks into the whole of temporal and causal conditions. But this point which Kant reaches is nothing more than a point, an unconditional command, a mere awareness of the depth of reason.

Kant's "critical ignorance" describes the finitude of reason as clearly as the "learned ignorance" of Nicolaus Cusanus. The difference, however, is that, in Cusanus, Catholic mysticism points to an intuitive union with the ground and abyss of reason, while, in Kant, Protestant criticism restricts reason to the acceptance of the unconditional imperative as the only approach to reality-itself. In post-Kantian metaphysics reason forgot its bondage to the categories of finitude. But this self-elevation to divine dignity brought on dethronement and contempt of reason and made the victory of one of its functions over all the others possible. The fall of a deified reason after Hegel contributed decisively to the enthronement of technical reason in our time and to the loss of the universality and the depth of ontological reason.

But reason is not merely finite. It is true that reason, along with all things and events, is subject to the conditions of existence. It contradicts itself and is threatened with disruption and self-destruction. Its elements move against each other. But this is only the one side of the picture. In the actual life of reason its basic structure is never completely lost. If it were lost, mind as well as reality would have been destroyed in the very moment of their coming into existence. In the actual life of reason essential and existential forces, forces of creation and forces of destruction, are united and disunited at the same time. These conflicts in actual reason supply the content for a justifiable theological criticism of reason. But an accusation of reason *as such* is a symptom either of theological ignorance or of theological arrogance. On the other hand, an attack on theology *as such* in the name of reason is a symptom of rationalistic shallowness or rationalistic *hybris*. An adequate description of the inner conflicts of ontological reason should replace the popular religious and half-popular theological lamentations about reason as such. And it should, at the same time, force reason to acknowledge its own existential predicament out of which the quest for revelation arises.

5. The Conflict within Actual Reason and the Quest for Revelation

(a) *Autonomy against heteronomy.* — Under the conditions of existence the structural elements of reason move against each other. Although never completely separated, they fall into self-destructive conflicts which cannot be solved on the basis of actual reason. A description of these conflicts must replace the popular religious or theological attacks on the weakness or blindness of reason. The self-criticism of reason in the light of revelation penetrates much deeper and is considerably more rational than these inarticulate and often merely emotional attacks. The polarity of structure and depth within reason produces a conflict between autonomous and heteronomous reason under the conditions of existence. Out of this conflict arises the quest for theonomy. The polarity of the static and the dynamic elements of reason produces a conflict between absolutism and relativism of reason under the conditions of existence. This conflict leads to the quest for the concrete-absolute. The polarity of the formal and the emotional elements of reason produces the conflict between formalism and irrationalism of reason under the conditions of existence. Out of this conflict arises the quest for the union of form and mystery. In all three cases reason is driven to the quest for revelation.

Reason which affirms and actualizes its structure without regarding its depth is autonomous. Autonomy does not mean the freedom of the individual to be a law to himself, as theological writers often have asserted, establishing in this way an easy scapegoat for their attacks on an independent culture. Autonomy means the obedience of the individual to the law of reason, which he finds in himself as a rational being. The *nomos* ("law") of *autos* ("self") is not the law of one's personality structure. It is the law of subjective-objective reason; it is the law implied in the *logos* structure of mind and reality. Autonomous reason, in affirming itself in its different functions and their structural demands, uses or rejects that which is merely an expression of an individual's situation within him and around him. It resists the danger of being conditioned by the situation of self and world in existence. It considers these conditions as the material which reason has to grasp and to shape according to its structural laws. Therefore, autonomous reason tries to keep itself free from "ungrasped impressions" and "unshaped strivings." Its independence is the opposite of wilfulness; it is obedience to its own essential structure, the law of reason which is the law of nature within mind and reality, and which is divine law, rooted in the ground of being itself. This is true of all functions of ontological reason.

Historically, autonomous reason has liberated and maintained itself in a never ending fight with heteronomy. Heteronomy imposes a strange *(heteros)* law *(nomos)* on one or all of the functions of reason. It issues commands from "outside" on how reason should grasp and shape reality. But this "outside" is not merely outside. It represents, at the same time, an element in reason itself, namely, the depth of reason. This makes the fight between autonomy and heteronomy dangerous and tragic. It is, finally, a conflict in reason itself. As long as reason is pre-rational, a confusing mass of sense impressions, a chaotic mass of instincts, strivings, compulsions, no genuine heteronomy has appeared. All this is outside reason, but it is not a law to which reason is asked to subject itself; it is not law in any rational sense. The problem of heteronomy is the problem of an authority which claims to represent reason, namely, the depth of reason, against its autonomous actualization. The basis of such a claim is not the superiority in rational power which many traditions, institutions, or personalities obviously have. The basis of a genuine heteronomy is the claim to speak in the name of the ground of being and therefore in an unconditional and ultimate way. A heteronomous authority usually expresses itself in terms of myth and cult because these are the direct and intentional expressions of the depth of reason. It is also possible for nonmythical and nonritual forms to gain power over the mind (e.g., political ideas). Heteronomy in this sense is usually a reaction against an autonomy which has lost its depth and has become empty and powerless. But as a reaction it is destructive, denying to reason the right of autonomy and destroying its structural laws from outside.

Autonomy and heteronomy are rooted in theonomy, and each goes astray when their theonomous unity is broken. Theonomy does not mean the acceptance of a divine law imposed on reason by a highest authority; it means autonomous reason united with its own depth. In a theonomous situation reason actualizes itself in obedience to its structural laws and in the power of its own inexhaustible ground. Since God *(theos)* is the law *(nomos)* for both the structure and the ground of reason, they are united in him, and their unity is manifest in a theonomous situation. But there is no complete theonomy under the conditions of existence. Both elements which essentially are united in it struggle with each other under the conditions of existence .and try to destroy each other. In this struggle they tend to destroy reason itself. Therefore, the quest for a reunion of what is always split in time and space arises *out* of reason and not in opposition to reason. This quest is the quest for revelation.

Seen in a world historical perspective the conflict between autonomy and heteronomy is the key to any theological understanding of the Greek as well as of the modern development and of many other problems of the spiritual history of mankind. The history of Greek philosophy, for example, can be written as a curve which starts with the still theonomous pre-philosophical period (mythology and cosmology), the slow elaboration of the autonomous structures of reason (pre-Socratic), the classical synthesis of structure and depth (Plato), the rationalization of this synthesis in the different schools (after Aristotle), the despair of reason in trying autonomously to create a world to live in (skepticism), the mystical transcending of reason (neo-Platonism), the questioning of authorities in past and present (philosophical schools and religious sects), the creation of a new theonomy under Christian influence (Clement and Origen), and the intrusion of heteronomous elements (Athanasius and Augustine). During the high Middle Ages a theonomy (Bonaventura) was realized under the preponderance of heteronomous elements (Thomas). Toward the end of the medieval period heteronomy became all-powerful (Inquisition), partly as a reaction against autonomous tendencies in culture and religion (nominalism), and destroyed the medieval theonomy. In the period of Renaissance and Reformation the conflict grew to new intensity. The Renaissance, which showed a theonomous character in its Neo-Platonic beginnings (Cusanus, Ficino), became increasingly autonomous in its later development (Erasmus, Galileo). Conversely, the Reformation, which in its early years united a religious with a cultural emphasis on autonomy (Luther's reliance on his conscience, and Luther and Zwingli's connection with the humanists), very soon developed a heteronomy which surpassed even that of the later Middle Ages in some respects (Protestant orthodoxy). In the eighteenth and nineteenth centuries, in spite of some heteronomous remnants and reactions, autonomy won an almost complete victory. Orthodoxy and fundamentalism were pushed into the corners of cultural life, sterile and ineffective. Classical and Romantic attempts to re-establish theonomy with autonomous means (Hegel, Schelling) did not succeed, producing radical autonomous reactions (post-Hegelians, on the one hand, and strong heteronomous reactions (revivalism), on the other hand. Under the guidance of technical reason autonomy conquered all reactions but completely lost the dimension of depth. It

became shallow, empty, without ultimate meaning, and produced
conscious or unconscious despair. In this situation powerful heter-
onomies of a quasi-political character entered the vacuum created by
an autonomy which lacked the dimension of depth. The double fight
against an empty autonomy and a destructive heteronomy makes the
quest for a new theonomy as urgent today as it was at the end of the
ancient world. The catastrophe of autonomous reason is complete.
Neither autonomy nor heteronomy, isolated and in conflict, can give
the answer.

(b) *Relativism against absolutism.*—Essentially, reason unites a static
and a dynamic element. The static element preserves reason from losing its identity within the life-process. The dynamic element is the
power of reason to actualize itself rationally in the process of life, while
without the static element reason could not be the structure of life.
Under the conditions of existence the two elements are torn from each
other and move against each other.

The static element of reason appears in two forms of absolutism—
the absolutism of tradition and the absolutism of revolution. The dynamic element of reason appears in two forms of relativism—positivistic
relativism and cynical relativism. The absolutism of tradition identifies
the static element of reason with special traditions, such as socially accepted morals, established political forms, "academic" aesthetics, and
unquestioned philosophical principles. This attitude is usually called
"conservative." But conservatism can mean two things. It can mean the
readiness to defend the static side of reason against an exclusive emphasis on the dynamic side, and it can mean the fanaticism which considers dynamic structures of reason as static and elevates them to absolute
validity. However, in any special case it is impossible to separate the
static from the dynamic element, and every attempt to do so leads
finally to a destruction of the absolutized forms through the attack of
other forms which emerge in the process of actual reason. Such attacks
are made in the power of another type of absolutism, the revolutionary.
But after one absolutism is destroyed by a revolutionary attack, the
victor establishes itself in equally absolute terms. This is almost unavoidable, because the attack was victorious through the strength of an
absolute claim, often of a utopian character. Revolutionary reason
believes just as deeply as traditionalism that it represents unchangeable
truth, but it is being more inconsistent in this belief. The absolutism of
tradition can point to past ages, with the claim that it is saying what
always has been said. Revolutionary absolutism, however, has experienced at least in one case the breakdown of such a claim, namely, the
breaching of tradition involved in its own victory; and it should envisage the possibility of its own end. But it does not. [8] This shows
that the two types of absolutism are not exclusive; they elicit each other.

Both are contradicted by different forms of relativism. Relativism
denies a static element in the structure of reason or emphasizes the
dynamic element so much that no definite place is left for actual reason.

Relativism can be positivistic or cynical, the former parallel to the absolutism of tradition, the second to the absolutism of revolution. Positivistic relativism takes what is "given" (posited) without applying absolute criteria to its valuation. In practice, therefore, it can become as conservative as any kind of absolutism of tradition, but on another basis and with other implications. For instance, the positivism of law in the middle of the nineteenth century was a reaction against the revolutionary absolutism of the eighteenth century. But it was not absolutistic itself. It accepted the positive law of different nations and periods as "merely given," but it did not allow critical attacks from the side of the natural law, nor did it establish current positive law as eternal law. Similarly, the aesthetic relativism of this period placed all previous styles on the same level without giving any of them preference in terms of a classical ideal. In the sphere of social relations local traditions were praised and their divergent developments were accepted without a critical norm. More important than all these is philosophical positivism. From the time of David Hume it has developed in many directions and has replaced absolute norms and criteria in all realms of life by pragmatic tests. Truth is relative to a group, to a concrete situation, or to an existential predicament. In this respect the recent forms of existentialism agree with the principles of pragmatic relativism and with some forms of the European *Lebensphilosophie* ("philosophy of life") to a surprising degree. It is the tragedy of this positivism that it either transforms itself into a conservative absolutism or into the cynical type of relativism. Only in countries where the remnants of former absolutisms are still powerful enough to delay such developments are the self-destructive implications of positivism hidden (England, the United States).

Cynical relativism usually is a result of a disappointment over utopian absolutism. It employs skeptical arguments against absolute principles, but it does not draw either of the two possible consequences of radical skepticism. It neither turns to revelation nor leaves the realm of thought and action altogether as ancient skepticism often did. Cynicism is an attitude of superiority over, or indifference toward, any rational structure, whether static or dynamic. Cynical relativism uses reason only for the sake of denying reason—a self-contradiction which is "cynically" accepted. Rational criticism, which presupposes some valid structures, is not the basis of cynical relativism. Its basis is disbelief in the validity of any rational act, even if it is merely critical. Cynical relativism is not wrecked by its self-contradictions. Its nemesis is the empty space it produces, the complete vacuum into which new absolutisms pour.

"Criticism" is an attempt to overcome the conflict between absolutism and relativism. It is an attitude which is not restricted to so-called critical philosophy. It is present in the whole history of philosophy, nor is it restricted to philosophy. It is effective in all spheres of ontological reason. It is the attempt to unite the static and the dynamic elements of reason by depriving the static element of content and by reducing it to a pure form. An example is the "categorical imperative," which denies special demands and which surrenders concrete details to the contingencies of the situation. Criticism combines a positivistic with a revolutionary element, excluding traditionalism as well as cynicism. Socrates and Kant are representative of the critical attitude in philosophy. But the development of their schools proves that the critical attitude is more a demand than a possibility. In both schools either the static or the dynamic element prevailed, frustrating the critical attempt. Although Plato's earlier dialogues were critical, Platonism grew in the direction of absolutism. In spite of their acceptance of the rationalism of Socrates, hedonism and cynicism grew in the direction of absolutism. Kant's classical followers became pure absolutists, while the Neo-Kantian school emphasized the relativism of an infinite process. This is not accidental. The critical attitude, by establishing absolute though assumedly empty criteria, deceived itself about their emptiness. These criteria always mirrored a special situation, for example, the situation of Athens in the Peloponnesian War, or the victory of the bourgeois mind in western Europe. The principles established by critical philosophy were too concrete and consequently too relative for their absolute claim. But their application was too absolutistic; it represented a special form of life which claimed more than relative validity. Therefore, in the ancient as well as in the modern world, criticism was unable to overcome the conflict between absolutism and relativism. Only that which is absolute and concrete at the same time can overcome this conflict. Only revelation can do it.

(c) *Formalism against emotionalism.*—In its essential structure reason unites formal and emotional elements. There is a predominance of the formal element in the cognitive and the legal functions of reason and of the emotional element in its aesthetic and communal functions. But in all its activities essential reason unites both elements. Under the conditions of existence the unity is disrupted. The elements move against each other and produce conflicts as deep and destructive as are the conflicts already discussed.

Formalism appears in the exclusive emphasis on the formal side of every rational function and in the separation of the functions from each other. Controlling knowledge and the corresponding formalized logic, if taken as the pattern of all knowledge, represent formalism in the cognitive realm. Controlling knowledge is one side of cognitive reason and an essential element in every cognitive act. But its attempt to monopolize the whole cognitive function and to deny that any other avenue is knowledge and can attain truth shows its existential disruption. It keeps cognitive reason from digging into those strata of things and events which can be grasped only with *amor intellectualis* ("intellectual love"). Formalism in the cognitive realm is intellectualism, the use of the cognitive intellect without *erōs*. Emotional reactions against intellectualism forget the obligation of strict, serious, and technically correct thinking in all matters of knowledge. But they are right in demanding a knowledge which not only controls but also unites.[9]

In the aesthetic realm formalism is an attitude, expressed in the phrase "art for art's sake," which disregards the content and meaning of artistic creations for the sake of their form. Aestheticism deprives art of its existential character by substituting detached judgments of taste and a refined connoisseurship for emotional union. No artistic expression is possible without the creative rational form, but the form, even in its greatest refinement, is empty if it does not express a spiritual substance. Even the richest and most profound artistic creation can be destructive for spiritual life if it is received in terms of formalism and aestheticism.[10] The emotional reactions of most people against aestheticism are wrong in their aesthetic judgment but right in their fundamental intention.

Formalism in the realm of legal reason places exclusive emphasis on the structural necessities of justice without asking the question of the adequacy of a legal form to the human reality which it is supposed to shape. The tragic alienation between law and life which is a subject of complaint in all periods is not caused by bad will on the part of those who make and enforce the law; it is a consequence of the separation of form from emotional participation. Legalism in the sense of legal formalism can become, like certain types of logic, a kind of play with pure forms, consistent in itself, detached from life. If applied to life, this play can turn into a destructive reality. Form armed with power can become a terrible organ of suppression in a social group. From our point of view, legal formalism and totalitarian suppression are intimately related. Emotional reactions against legal formalism misunderstand the structural necessities of law, but they realize instinctively the inadequacy of legal formalism for meeting the demands of life.

In the communal function of reason, formalism preserves, applies, and defends the conventional forms which have shaped social and personal life. Conventionalism, as this attitude can be called, must not be confused with traditionalism. The latter makes an absolute claim for special traditions or conventions because of their content and meaning. Conventionalism makes no absolute claim for the conventions it defends, nor does it value them because of their content and meaning. Conventionalism affirms the social and personal forms as forms. Automatic obedience to the accepted ways of behavior is demanded by conventional formalism. Its tremendous power in social relations, in education, and in self-discipline makes it a tragic force in all human history. It tends to destroy the inborn vitality and creativity of every new being and of every new generation. It cripples life and replaces love by rule. It shapes personalities and communities by suppressing the spiritual and emotional substance which it is supposed to shape. The form destroys the meaning. Emotional reactions against conventional formalism are especially explosive and catastrophic. They have a "blind spot" with regard to the supporting, preserving, and directing power of convention and habit; but they are right in opposing its formalistic distortion with passion and sacrifice.

Formalism appears not only in every function of ontological reason but also in the relation of the functions to each other. The unity of reason is disrupted by its division into departments each of which is controlled by a special set of structural forms. This refers to the grasping and to the shaping functions of reason as well as to their interrelationship. The cognitive function, deprived of its aesthetic element, is separated from the aesthetic function, deprived of its cognitive element. In essential reason these two elements are united in various degrees, as reflected in functions like historical and ontological intuition, on the one hand, psychological novels and metaphysical poetry, on the other hand. The union of the cognitive and aesthetic functions is fully expressed in mythology, the womb out of which both of them were born and came to independence and to which they tend to return. The Romanticists of the early nineteenth century, philosophers and artists, tried to re-establish the unity of the cognitive and the aesthetic functions (this attempt has been continued by many recent artists and philosophers—expressionism, new realism, existentialism). They turned away from cognitive and aesthetic formalism and consequently from the separation of the two functions. They even tried to unite both in a new myth. But in this they failed. No myth can be created, no unity of the rational functions can be reached, on the basis of reason in conflict. A new myth is the expression of the reuniting power of a new revelation, not a product of formalized reason.

The shaping functions of reason also are separated from each other by the formalization of reason and its separation from emotion. The organizational function, deprived of an organic basis, is separated from the organic function, deprived of an organizational structure. In essential reason these two elements are united in various degrees and with various transitions, in a way analogous to the life of free organizations within an embracing legal structure. The union of legal and communal functions is fully expressed in the cult community which is the mother of both of them and to which they try to return. Old and new romanticists long for a state which represents the Christian "body" of the idealized Middle Ages, or, if this cannot be re-established, national or racial bodies, or the "body" of mankind. They look for an organism which can become the bearer of a nonformalized law.[11] But neither mankind as an organism nor a common cult as the function of a religious world community can unite in itself law and communion. This unity can be created neither by a formalized constitution nor by unorganized sympathies, desires, and movements. The quest for a new and universal communion, in which organization and organism are united, is the quest for revelation.

Finally, the formalization of reason separates its grasping from its shaping functions. This conflict is usually described as the conflict between theory and practice. A grasping which has lost the element of shaping and a shaping which has lost the element of grasping are in conflict with each other. In essential reason the two elements are united.

The much-abused word "experience" has *one* connotation which points to this unity: experience unites insight with action. In the relation of myth and cult no separation is even imaginable. Cult includes the myth on the basis of which it acts out the divine-human drama, and myth includes the cult of which it is the imaginary expression. It is, therefore, understandable that there is a continuous struggle for the reunion of theory and practice. In his description of the "poverty of philosophy" Marx challenged a philosophy which interprets the world without changing it. Nietzsche in his attack on historism challenged a historiography which is not related to our historical existence. Religious socialism took over the insight of the Fourth Gospel that truth must be done, and it took over the insight of the whole biblical tradition that without active participation in the "new reality" its nature cannot be known. Instrumentalism points to the intimate relation between action and knowledge, though it remains predominantly on the level of technical reason. Nevertheless, the conflicts remain. Practice resists theory, which it considers inferior to itself; it demands an activism which cuts off every theoretical investigation before it has come to its end. In practice one cannot do otherwise, for one must act before one has finished thinking. On the other hand, the infinite horizons of thinking cannot supply the basis for any concrete decision with certainty. Except in the technical realm where an existential decision is not involved, one must make decisions on the basis of limited or distorted or incomplete insights. Neither theory nor practice in isolation can solve the problem of their conflict with each other. Only a truth which is present in spite of the infinity of theoretical possibilities and only a good which is present in spite of the infinite risk implied in every action can overcome the disruption between the grasping and the shaping functions of reason. The quest for such a truth and such a good is the quest for revelation.

The functional splits of reason are consequences of the formalization of reason, of the conflict between formalism and emotionalism. The consequences of the formalization of reason are manifest. Emotion reacts against them and against formal reason in all realms. But this reaction is futile because it is merely "emotional," that is, minus structural elements. Emotion is powerless against intellectualism and aestheticism, against legalism and conventionalism, if it remains mere emotion. But, although powerless over reason, it can have great power of destruction over the mind, personally and socially. Emotion without rational structure (in the sense, of course, of ontological reason) becomes irrationalism. And irrationalism is destructive in two respects. If it attacks formalized reason, it must have some rational content. This content, however, is not subjected to rational criticism and gets its power from the strength of the emotion which carries it. It is still reason, but irrationally promoted reason, and therefore blind and fanatical. It has all the qualities of the demonic, whether it is expressed in religious or secular terms. If, on the other hand, irrationalism empties itself of any content and becomes mere subjective feeling, a vacuum is produced,

into which distorted reason can break without a rational check.[12] If
reason sacrifices its formal structures, and with them its critical power,
the result is not an empty sentimentality but the demonic rise of anti-
rational forces, which often are supported by all the tools of technical
reason. This experience drives men to the quest for the reunion of form
and emotion. This is a quest for revelation. Reason does not resist
revelation. It asks for revelation, for revelation means the reintegration
of reason.

C. THE COGNITIVE FUNCTION OF REASON
AND THE QUEST FOR REVELATION

6. The Ontological Structure of Knowledge

Systematic theology must give special consideration to the cognitive
function of ontological reason in developing the concept of revelation,
for revelation is the manifestation of the ground of being for human
knowledge. While theology as such cannot produce an epistemology of
its own, it must refer to those characteristics of cognitive reason which
are relevant for the cognitive character of revelation. In particular, theology must give a description of cognitive reason under the conditions
of existence. But a description of the conflicts of existential cognition
presupposes an understanding of its ontological structure, for it is the
polar structure of cognitive reason which makes its existential conflicts
possible and drives it to the quest for revelation.

Knowing is a form of union. In every act of knowledge the knower
and that which is known are united; the gap between subject and object
is overcome. The subject "grasps" the object, adapts it to itself, and, at
the same time, adapts itself to the object. But the union of knowledge
is a peculiar one; it is a union through separation. Detachment is the
condition of cognitive union. In order to know, one must "look" at a
thing, and, in order to look at a thing, one must be "at a distance."
Cognitive distance is the presupposition of cognitive union. Most philosophers have seen both sides. The old dispute whether the equal
recognizes the equal or whether the unequal recognizes the unequal is
a classical expression of the insight that union (which presupposes some
equality) and distance (which presupposes some inequality) are polar
elements in the process of cognition. The unity of distance and union is
the ontological problem of knowledge. It drove Plato to the myth of
an original union of the soul with the essences (ideas), of the separation
of soul from the truly real in temporal existence, of the recollection of
the essences, and of reunion with them through the different degrees of
cognitive elevation. The unity is never completely destroyed; but there
is also estrangement. The particular object is strange as such, but it contains essential structures with which the cognitive subject is essentially
united and which it can remember when looking at things. This motif
runs through the whole history of philosophy. It explains the titanic
attempts of human thought in all periods to make the cognitive relation understandable—the strangeness of subject and object and, in spite

of it, their cognitive union. While skepticism despaired of the possibility of uniting the object with the subject, criticism removed the object as a thing-in-itself from the realm of actual knowledge without explaining how knowledge can grasp reality and not only appearance. While positivism completely removed the difference between subject and object, and idealism decreed their identity, both of them failed to explain the estrangement of subject and object and the possibility of error. Dualism postulated a transcendent unity of subject and object in a divine mind or substance, without explaining man's participation in it. Yet each of these attempts was aware of the ontological problem of knowledge: the unity of separation and union.

The epistemological situation is confirmed existentially by certain aspects of personal and social life as they are related to knowledge. The passion of knowing for the sake of knowing, which frequently can be found in primitive as well as in refined forms, indicates that a want, a vacuum, is filled by successful cognition. Something which was strange, but which nevertheless belongs to us, has become familiar, a part of us. According to Plato, the cognitive *erōs* is born out of poverty and abundance. It drives us toward reunion with that to which we belong and which belongs to us. In every act of knowledge want and estrangement are conquered.

But knowledge is more than a fulfilling; it also transforms and heals; this would be impossible if the knowing subject were only a mirror of the object, remaining in unconquered distance from it. Socrates was aware of this situation when he made the assertion that out of the knowing of the good the doing of the good follows. It is, of course, as easy as it is cheap to state that one may know the good without doing it, without being able to do it. One should not confront Socrates with Paul in order to show how much more realistic Paul was. It is at least probable that Socrates knew what every schoolboy knows—that some people act against their better knowledge. But he also knew something of which even philosophers and theologians are ignorant—that true knowledge includes union and, therefore, openness to receive that with which one unites. This is the knowledge of which Paul also speaks, the *gnosis* which in New Testament Greek means cognitive, sexual, and mystical union at the same time. In this respect there is no contrast between Socrates and Paul. He who knows God or the Christ in the sense of being grasped by him and being united with him does the good. He who knows the essential structure of things in the sense of having received their meaning and power acts according to them; he does the good, even if he has to die for it.

Recently the term "insight" has been given connotations of *gnosis*, namely, of a knowledge which transforms and heals. Depth psychology attributes healing powers to insight, meaning not a detached knowledge of psychoanalytic theory or of one's own past in the light of this theory but a repetition of one's actual experiences with all the pains and horrors of such a return. Insight in this sense is a reunion with one's own past

and especially with those moments in it which influence the present de-
structively. Such a cognitive union produces a transformation just as
radical and as difficult as that presupposed and demanded by Socrates
and Paul. For most of the Asiatic philosophies and religions the uniting,
healing, and transforming power of knowledge is a matter of course.
Their problem—never completely solved—is the element of distance,
not that of union.

Another existential confirmation of the interpretation of knowledge
as a unity between distance and union is the social valuation of knowledge in all integrated human groups. Insight into the principles on
which the life of the group is based, and acceptance of them, is considered an absolute precondition for the life of the group. There is no
difference in this respect between religious or secular, democratic or
totalitarian, groups. It is impossible to understand the emphasis in all
social groups on the knowledge of the dominating principles, if the
uniting character of knowledge is not recognized. Much criticism of so-
called dogmatism, often made by people who are unaware of their own
dogmatic assumptions, is rooted in the misinterpretation of knowledge
as a detached cognizance of objects separated from the subject. Dogmatism with respect to such knowledge is indeed meaningless. But if
knowledge unites, much depends on the object with which it unites.
Error becomes dangerous if it means union with distorted and deceiving
elements of reality, with that which is not really real but which only
claims to be. Anxiety about falling into error or about the error into
which others might fall or have fallen, the tremendous reactions against
error in all cohesive social groups, the interpretation of error as demonic
possession—all this is understandable only if knowledge includes union.
Liberalism, the protest against dogmatism, is based on the authentic
element of detachment which belongs to knowledge and which demands
openness for questions, inquiries, and new answers, even to the point of
the possible disintegration of a social group. Under the conditions of
existence no final solution for this conflict can be found. As reason generally is drawn into the conflict between absolutism and relativism, so
cognitive reason is subject to the conflict between union and detachment in every act of knowledge. Out of this conflict the quest arises for
a knowledge which unites the certainty of existential union with the
openness of cognitive detachment. This quest is the quest for the knowledge of revelation.

7. Cognitive Relations

The element of union and the element of detachment appear in different proportions in the different realms of knowledge. But there is no
knowledge without the presence of both elements. Statistical indexes
are material for physical or sociological knowledge, but they are not
themselves knowledge. Devotional meditations imply cognitive elements,
but they are not themselves knowledge.

The type of knowledge which is predominantly determined by the element of detachment can be called "controlling knowledge."[13] Controlling knowledge is the outstanding, though not the only, example of technical reason. It unites subject and object for the sake of the control of the object by the subject. It transforms the object into a completely conditioned and calculable "thing." It deprives it of any subjective quality. Controlling knowledge looks upon its object as something which cannot return its look. Certainly, in every type of knowledge subject and object are logically distinguished. There is always an object, even in our knowledge of God. But controlling knowledge "objectifies" not only logically (which is unavoidable) but also ontologically and ethically. No thing, however, is merely a thing. Since everything that is participates in the self-world structure of being, elements of self-relatedness are universal. This makes union with everything possible. Nothing is absolutely strange. Speaking in a metaphorical manner, one could say that as we look at things so things looks at us with the expectation of being received and the offer of enriching us in cognitive union. Things indicate that they might be "interesting" if we enter their deeper levels and experience their special power of being.[14] At the same time, this does not exclude the fact that they are objects in the technical sense, things to be used and formed, means for ends which are strange to their inner meaning (*telos*). A metal is "interesting;" it has elements of subjectivity and self-relatedness. It is, on the other hand, material for innumerable tools and purposes. While the nature of metals admits of an overwhelming amount of objectifying knowledge and technical use, the nature of man does not. Man resists objectification, and if his resistance to it is broken, man himself is broken. A truly objective relation to man is determined by the element of union; the element of detachment is secondary. It is not absent; there are levels in man's bodily, psychic, and mental constitution which can and must be grasped by controlling knowledge. But this is neither the way of knowing human nature nor is it the way of knowing any individual personality in past or present, including one's self. Without union there is no cognitive approach to man. In contrast to controlling knowledge this cognitive attitude can be called "receiving knowledge." Neither actually nor potentially is it determined by the means-ends relationship. Receiving knowledge takes the object into itself, into union with the subject. This includes the emotional element, from which controlling knowledge tries to detach itself as much as possible. Emotion is the vehicle for receiving cognition. But the vehicle is far from making the content itself emotional. The content is rational, something to be verified, to be looked at with critical caution. Nevertheless, nothing can be received cognitively without emotion. No union of subject and object is possible without emotional participation.

The unity of union and detachment is precisely described by the term "understanding." Its literal meaning, to stand under the place where the object of knowledge stands, implies intimate participation. In ordinary use it points to the ability to grasp the logical meaning of something. Understanding another person or a historical figure, the life of an animal or a religious text, involves an amalgamation of controlling and receiving knowledge, of union and detachment, of participation and analysis.

Most cognitive distortions are rooted in a disregard of the polarity which is in cognitive reason. This disregard is not simply an avoidable mistake; it is a genuine conflict under the conditions of existence. One side of this conflict is the tension between dogmatism and criticism within social groups. But there are other sides to it. Controlling knowledge claims control of every level of reality. Life, spirit, personality, community, meanings, values, even one's ultimate concern, should be treated in terms of detachment, analysis, calculation, technical use. The power behind this claim is the preciseness, verifiability, the public approachability of controlling knowledge, and, above all, the tremendous success of its application to certain levels of reality. It is impossible to disregard or even to restrain this claim. The public mind is so impregnated with its methodological demands and its astonishing results that every cognitive attempt in which reception and union are presupposed encounters utter distrust. A consequence of this attitude is a rapid decay of spiritual (not only of the Spiritual) life, an estrangement from nature, and, most dangerous of all, a dealing with human beings as with things. In psychology and sociology, in medicine and philosophy, man has been dissolved into elements out of which he is composed and which determine him. Treasures of empirical knowledge have been produced in this way, and new research projects augment those treasures daily. But man has been lost in this enterprise. That which can be known only by participation and union, that which is the object of receiving knowledge, is disregarded. Man actually has become what controlling knowledge considers him to be, a thing among things, a cog in the dominating machine of production and consumption, a dehumanized object of tyranny or a normalized object of public communications. Cognitive dehumanization has produced actual dehumanization.

Three main movements have tried to resist the tidal wave of controlling knowledge: romanticism, philosophy of life, and existentialism. They all have had instantaneous success, but they have lost out in the long run because they could not solve the problem of the criterion of the false and the true. The Romantic philosophy of nature confused poetry and symbolic intuition with knowledge. It ignored the strangeness of the world of objects, the strangeness not only of the lower but also of the higher levels of nature toward man. If Hegel called nature "estranged spirit," his emphasis was not on "estranged" but on "spirit," which gave him the possibility of approaching nature with receiving knowledge, with attempts to participate in it and to unite with it. But Hegel's philosophy of nature was a failure of world-wide significance. A Romantic philosophy of nature cannot escape this defeat. Neither can a philosophy of life which tries to create cognitive union with the dynamic process of life. Such a philosophy recognizes that life is not an object of controlling knowledge; that life must be killed in order to be subjected to the means-ends structure; that life in its dynamic creativity, in its *élan vital* (Bergson), is open only to receiving knowledge, to intuitive participation and mystical union. This, however, raises the question which life-philosophy never was able to answer: How can the intuitive union in which life is aware of itself be verified? If it is unexpressible, it is not knowledge. If it can be expressed, it falls under the criterion of cognitive reason, and its application demands detachment, analysis, and objectification. The relation between receiving and controlling knowledge is not explained by Bergson or by any other of the life-philosophers. Existentialism tries to save the freedom of the individual self from the domination of controlling knowledge. But this freedom is described in terms which not only lack any criterion but also any content. Existentialism is the most desperate attempt to escape the power of controlling knowledge and of the objectified world which technical reason has produced. It says "No" to this world, but, in order to say "Yes" to something else, it has either to use controlling knowledge or to turn to revelation. Existentialism, like romanticism and philosophy of life, must either surrender to technical reason or ask the question of revelation. Revelation claims to create complete union with that which appears in revelation. It is receiving knowledge in its fulfilment. But, at the same time, it claims to satisfy the demands of controlling knowledge, of detachment and analysis.

8. Truth and Verification

Every cognitive act strives for truth. Since theology claims to be true, it must discuss the meaning of the term "truth," the nature of revealed truth, and its relation to other forms of truth. In the absence of such a discussion the theological claim can be dismissed by a simple semantic device, often used by naturalists and positivists. According to them, the use of the term "truth" is restricted to empirically verifiable statements. The predicate "true" should be reserved either for analytic sentences or for experimentally confirmed propositions. Such a terminological limitation of the terms "true" and "truth" is possible and is a matter of convention. But, whenever it is accepted, it means a break with the whole Western tradition and necessitates the creation of another term for what has been called *alēthēs* or *verum* in classical, ancient, medieval, and modern literature. Is such a break necessary? The answer ultimately depends not on reasons of expediency but on the nature of cognitive reason.

Modern philosophy usually speaks of true and false as qualities of judgments. Judgments can grasp or fail to grasp reality and can, accordingly, be true or false. But reality in itself is what it is and it can neither be true nor false. This certainly is a possible line of arguing, but it is also possible to go beyond it. If the question is asked, "What makes a judgment true?" something must be said about reality itself. There must be an explanation of the fact that reality can give itself to the cognitive act in such a way that a false judgment can occur and in

such a way that many processes of observation and thought are necessary in order to reach true judgments. The reason is that things hide
their true being; it must be discovered under the surface of sense impressions, changing appearances, and unfounded opinions. This discovery is made through a process of preliminary affirmations, consequent
negations, and final affirmations. It is made through "yes and no" or
dialectically. The surface must be penetrated, the appearance undercut,
the "depth" must be reached, namely, the *ousia*, the "essence" of things,
that which gives them the power of being. This is their truth, the "really
real" in difference from the seemingly real. It would not be called
"true," however, if it were not true for someone, namely, for the mind
which in the power of the rational word, the *logos*, grasps the level of
reality in which the really real "dwells." This notion of truth is not
bound to its Socratic-Platonic birthplace. In whatever way the terminology may be changed, in whatever way the relation between true and
seeming reality may be described, in whatever way the relation of mind
and reality may be understood, the problem of the "truly real" cannot
be avoided. The seemingly real is not unreal, but it is deceptive if it is
taken to be really real.

One could say that the concept of true being is the result of disappointed expectations in our encounter with reality. For instance, we
meet a person, and the impressions we receive of him produce expectations in us about his future behavior. Some of these expectations will
be deceptive and will provoke the desire for a "deeper" understanding
of his personality, in comparison with which the first understanding
was "superficial." New expectations arise and prove again to be partially
deceptive, driving us to the question of a still deeper level of his personality. Finally we may succeed in discovering his real, true personality
structure, the essence and power of his being, and we will not be deceived any longer. We may still be surprised; but such surprises are to
be expected if a personality is the object of knowledge. The truth of
something is that level of its being the knowledge of which prevents
wrong expectations and consequent disappointments. Truth, therefore,
is the essence of things as well as the cognitive act in which their essence is grasped. The term "truth" is, like the term "reason," subjective-
objective. A judgment is true because it grasps and expresses true being;
and the really real becomes truth if it is grasped and expressed in a true
judgment.

The resistance of recent philosophy against the ontological use of
the term has been aroused by the assumption that truth can be verified
only within the realm of empirical science. Statements which cannot
be verified by experiment are considered tautologies, emotional self-
expressions, or meaningless propositions. There is an important truth in
this attitude. Statements which have neither intrinsic evidence nor a way
of being verified have no cognitive value. "Verification" means a
method of deciding the truth or falsehood of a judgment. Without such
a method, judgments are expressions of the subjective state of a person

but not acts of cognitive reason. The verifying test belongs to the nature of truth; in this positivism is right. Every cognitive assumption (hypothesis) must be tested. The safest test is the repeatable experiment. A cognitive realm in which it can be used has the advantage of methodological strictness and the possibility of testing an assertion in every moment. But it is not permissible to make the experimental method of verification the exclusive pattern of all verification. Verification can occur within the life-process itself. Verification of this type (experiential in contradistinction to experimental) has the advantage that it need not halt and disrupt the totality of a life-process in order to distil calculable elements out of it (which experimental verification must do). The verifying experiences of a nonexperimental character are truer to life, though less exact and definite. By far the largest part of all cognitive verification is experiential. In some cases experimental and experiential verification work together. In other cases the experimental element is completely absent.

It is obvious that these two methods of verification correspond to the two cognitive attitudes, the controlling and the receiving. Controlling knowledge is verified by the success of controlling actions. The technical use of scientific knowledge is its greatest and most impressive verification. Every working machine is a continuously repeated test of the truth of the scientific assumptions on the basis of which it has been constructed. Receiving knowledge is verified by the creative union of two natures, that of knowing and that of the known. This test, of course, is neither repeatable, precise, nor final at any particular moment. The life-process itself makes the test. Therefore, the test is indefinite and preliminary; there is an element of risk connected with it. Future stages of the same life-process may prove that what seemed to be a bad risk was a good one and vice versa. Nevertheless, the risk must be taken, receiving knowledge must be applied, experiential verification must go on continually, whether it is supported by experimental tests or not.

Life-processes are the object of biological, psychological, and sociological research. A large amount of controlling knowledge and experimental verification is possible and actual in these disciplines; and, in dealing with life-processes, scientists are justified in striving to extend the experimental method as far as possible. But there are limits to these attempts which are imposed not by impotence but by definition. Life-processes have the character of totality, spontaneity, and individuality. Experiments presuppose isolation, regularity, generality. Therefore, only separable elements of life-processes are open to experimental verification, while the processes themselves must be received in a creative union in order to be known. Physicians, psychotherapists, educators, social reformers, and political leaders deal with that side of a life-process which is individual, spontaneous, and total. They can work only on the basis of a knowledge which unites controlling and receiving elements. The truth of their knowledge is verified partly by experimental test, partly by a participation in the individual life with which they deal. If this "knowledge by participation" is called "intuition," the cognitive approach to every individual life-process is intuitive. Intuition in this sense is not irrational, and neither does it by-pass a full consciousness of experimentally verified knowledge.

Verification in the realm of historical knowledge also unites an experimental with an experiential element. The factual side of historical research is based on sources, traditions, and documents which test one another in a way comparable to experimental methods athough no historical event can be repeated). The selective and interpretative side, however, without which no historiography ever has been written, is based on participation in terms of understanding and explanation. Without a union of the nature of the historian with that of his object, no significant history is possible. But *with* this union the same period and the same historical figure have received many different historically significant interpretations on the basis of the same verified material. Verification in this respect means to illuminate, to make understandable, to give a meaningful and consistent picture. The historian's task is to "make alive" what has "passed away." The test of his cognitive success, of the truth of his picture, is whether or not he is able to do this. This test is not final, and every historical work is a risk. But it is a test, an experiential, though not an experimental, verification.

Principles and norms, which constitute the structure of subjective and objective reason, are the cognitive object of philosophy. Rationalism and pragmatism discuss the question of their verification in such a way that both of them by-pass the element of cognitive union and receiving knowledge. Rationalism tries to develop principles and norms in terms of self-evidence, universality, and necessity. Categories of being and thinking, principles of aesthetic expression, norms of law and communion, are open to critical analysis and to a priori knowledge. The analogy of mathematical evidence, which needs neither the tests of controlling nor those of receiving knowedge, is used for the derivation of the rational principles, categories, and norms. Analytic thought can make decisions about the rational structure of mind and reality.

Pragmatism asserts just the opposite. It takes the so-called principles of reason, the categories and norms, to be results of accumulated and tested experience, open for radical changes by future experience and subject to ever repeated tests. They must prove their power of explaining and judging a given material of empirical knowledge, of aesthetic expression, of legal structures and communal forms. If they are able to do this, they are pragmatically verified.

Neither rationalism nor pragmatism sees the element of participation in knowledge. Neither of them distinguishes receiving from controlling knowledge. Both are largely determined by the attitude of controlling knowledge and tied up with the alternatives implied in it. Against both of them it must be said that the verification of the principles of ontological reason has the character neither of rational self-evidence nor of a pragmatic test. Rational self-evidence cannot be attributed to a principle which contains more than the mere form of rationality, as, for instance, Kant's categorical imperative. Every concrete principle, every category and norm, which expresses more than pure rationality is subject to experimental or experiential verification. It is not self-evident, even if it contains a self-evident element (which, however, cannot be abstracted from it). Pragmatism is in no better position. It lacks a criterion. If the successful working of the successful working of the principles is called the "criterion," the question arises, "What is the criterion of success?" This question cannot be answered again in terms of success, that is, pragmatically. Neither can it be answered rationally except in a completely formalistic way.

The way in which philosophical systems have been accepted, experienced, and verified points to a method of verification beyond rationalism and pragmatism. These systems have forced themselves upon the mind of many human beings in terms of receptive knowledge and ~~~ ~~~~ ~~~~~. In terms of controlling knowledge, rational criticism, or pragmatic tests, they have been refuted innumerable times. But they live. Their verification is their efficacy in the life-process of mankind. They prove to be inexhaustible in meaning and creative in power. This method of verification is certainly not precise and not definite, but it is permanent and effective. It throws out of the historical process what is exhausted and powerless and what cannot stand in the light of pure rationality. Somehow it combines the pragmatic and the rational elements without falling into the fallacies of either pragmatism or rationalism. Nevertheless, even this way of verification is threatened by the possibility of final meaninglessness. It is more true to life than the competing methods. But it carries with it the radical risk of life. It is significant in what it tries to verify, but it is not secure in its verification.

This situation mirrors a basic conflict in cognitive reason. Knowledge stands in a dilemma; controlling knowledge is safe but not ultimately significant, while receiving knowledge can be ultimately significant, but it cannot give certainty. The threatening character of this dilemma is rarely recognized and understood. But if it is realized and not covered up by preliminary and incomplete verifications, it must lead either to a desperate resignation of truth or to the quest for revelation, for revelation claims to give a truth which is both certain and of ultimate concern—a truth which includes and accepts the risk and uncertainty of every significant cognitive act, yet transcends it in accepting it.

FOOTNOTES

1. See the Introduction.

2. See Max Horkheimer, *The Eclipse of Reason* (New York and Oxford: Oxford University Press, 1947).

3. Cf. Plato's myth of the soul in its original state seeing the "ideas" or eternal essences.

4. John 3:21.

5. Blaise Pascal, *Pensées*, Selection 277.

6. For extensive discussions of the concepts "symbol," "myth," and "cult" see chaps. iii and iv.

7. It is unfortunate that Kant often is interpreted only as an epistemological idealist and an ethical formalist—and consequently rejected. Kant is more than this. His doctrine of the categories is a doctrine of human finitude. His doctrine of the categorical imperative is a doctrine of the unconditional element in the depth of practical reason. His doctrine of the teleological principle in art and nature enlarges the concept of reason beyond its cognitive technical sense toward what we have called "ontological reason."

8. Protestant orthodox absolutism is less consistent than Catholic ecclesiastical absolutism. Schleiermacher's statement that "the Reformation continues" is the only consistent Protestant attitude. It is an astonishing, though anthropologically rather revealing, fact that in America groups representing a most radical absolutism of tradition call themselves "Daughters" or "Sons" of the American Revolution. Russian communism not only has maintained the absolutism of its revolutionary attack but has developed partially into an absolutism of tradition by relating itself consciously to the traditions of the pre-revolutionary past. Marx himself in his emphasis on the transitory character of every stage of the revolutionary process was much more consistent in this respect. He could have said: "The revolution continues."

9. See the following sections.

10. Every public performance of Bach's *Passion of St. Matthew* carries with it the risk of making the gospel story more meaningless for people who admire the great art of Bach's music without being grasped by its infinite meaning.

11. This is the real problem of the world organization toward which mankind is striving today and which is prematurely anticipated by the movement for a world government.

12. The empty irrationalism of the German youth movement was fertile soil for the rational irrationalism of the Nazis.

13. Cf. Max Scheler, *Versuche zu einer Soziologie des Wissens* (Munich, 1924).

14. Goethe asks us to consider how "being" (*seiend*) things are, pointing to the unique structure which is their power of being.

CHAPTER TWO

ON THE ONTOLOGICAL MYSTERY*
by Gabriel Marcel

The title of this essay is likely to annoy the philosopher as much as to startle the layman, since philosophers are inclined to leave mystery either to the theologians or else to the vulgarisers, whether of mysticism or of occultism, such as Maeterlinck. Moreover, the term *ontological*, which has only the vaguest meaning for the layman, has become discredited in the eyes of Idealist philosophers; while the term *mystery* is reserved by those thinkers who are imbued with the ideas of Scholasticism for the revealed mysteries of religion.

Thus my terminology is clearly open to criticism from all sides. But I can find no other which is adequate to the body of ideas which I intend to put forward and on which my whole outlook is based. Readers of my *Journal Métaphysique* will see that they represent the term of the whole spiritual and philosophical evolution which I have described in that book.

Rather than to begin with abstract definitions and dialectical arguments which may be discouraging at the outset, I should like to start with a sort of global and intuitive characterisation of the man in whom the sense of the ontological—the sense of being—is lacking, or, to speak more correctly, of the man who has lost the awareness of this sense. Generally speaking, modern man is in this condition; if ontological demands worry him at all, it is only dully, as an obscure impulse. Indeed I wonder if a psychoanalytical method, deeper and more discerning than any that has been evolved until now, would not reveal the morbid effects of the repression of this sense and of the ignoring of this need.

*Used with permission from *The Philosophy of Existence*, the Philosophical Library, New York, New York, 1949

The characteristic feature of our age seems to me to be what might be called the misplacement of the idea of function, taking function in its current sense which includes both the vital and the social functions.

The individual tends to appear both to himself and to others as an agglomeration of functions. As a result of deep historical causes, which can as yet be understood only in part, he has been led to see himself more and more as a mere assemblage of functions, the hierarchical interrelation of which seems to him questionable or at least subject to conflicting interpretations.

To take the vital functions first. It is hardly necessary to point out the role which historical materialism on the one hand, and Freudian doctrines on the other, have played in restricting the concept of man.

Then there are the social functions—those of the consumer, the producer, the citizen, etc.

Between these two there is, in theory, room for the psychological functions as well; but it is easy to see how these will tend to be interpreted in relation either to the social or the vital functions, so that their independence will be threatened and their specific character put in doubt. In this sense, Comte, served by his total incomprehension of psychical reality, displayed an almost prophetic instinct when he excluded psychology from his classification of sciences.

So far we are still dealing only with abstractions, but nothing is easier than to find concrete illustrations in this field.

Travelling on the Underground, I often wonder with a kind of dread what can be the inward reality of the life of this or that man employed on the railway—the man who opens the doors, for instance, or the one who punches the tickets. Surely everything both within him and outside him conspires to identify this man with his functions—meaning not only with his functions as worker, as trade union member or as voter, but with his vital functions as well. The rather horrible expression 'time table' perfectly describes his life. So many hours for each function. Sleep too is a function which must be discharged so that the other functions may be exercised in their turn. The same with pleasure, with relaxation; it is logical that the weekly allowance of recreation should be determined by an expert on hygiene; recreation is a psycho-organic function which must not be neglected any more than, for instance, the function of sex. We need go no further; this sketch is sufficient to suggest the emergence of a kind of vital schedule; the details will vary with the country, the climate, the profession, etc., but what matters is that there is a schedule.

It is true that certain disorderly elements—sickness, accidents of every sort—will break in on the smooth working of the system. It is therefore natural that the individual should be overhauled at regular intervals like a watch (this is often done in America). The hospital plays the part of the inspection bench or the repair shop. And it is from this same standpoint of function that such essential problems as birth control will be examined.

As for death, it becomes, objectively and functionally, the scrapping of what has ceased to be of use and must be written off as total loss.

I need hardly insist on the stifling impression of sadness produced by this functionalised world. It is sufficient to recall the dreary image of the retired official, or those urban Sundays when the passers-by look like people who have retired from life. In such a world, there is something mocking and sinister even in the tolerance awarded to the man who has retired from his work.

But besides the sadness felt by the onlooker, there is the dull, intolerable unease of the actor himself who is reduced to living as though he were in fact submerged by his functions. This uneasiness is enough to show that there is in all this some appalling mistake, some ghastly misinterpretation, implanted in defenceless minds by an increasingly inhuman social order and an equally inhuman philosophy (for if the philosophy has prepared the way for the order, the order has also shaped the philosophy).

I have written on another occasion that, provided it is taken in its metaphysical and not its physical sense, the distinction between the *full* and the *empty* seems to me more fundamental than that between the *one* and the *many*. This is particularly applicable to the case in point. Life in a world centered on function is liable to despair because in reality this world is *empty*, it rings hollow; and if it resists this temptation it is only to the extent that there come into play from within it and in its favour certain hidden forces which are beyond its power to conceive or to recognise.

It should be noted that this world is, on the one hand, riddled with problems and, on the other, determined to allow no room for mystery. I shall come back to this distinction between problem and mystery which I believe to be fundamental. For the moment I shall only point out that to eliminate or to try to eliminate mystery is (in this functionalist world) to bring into play in the face of events which break in on the course of existence—such as birth, love and death— that psychological and pseudo-scientific category of the 'purely natural' which deserves a study to itself. In reality, this is nothing more than the remains of a degraded rationalism from whose standpoint cause explains effect and accounts for it exhaustively. There exist in such a world, nevertheless, an infinity of problems, since the causes are not known to us in detail and thus leave room for unlimited research. And in addition to these theoretical puzzles there are innumerable technical problems, bound up with the difficulty of knowing how the various functions, once they have been inventoried and labelled, can be made to work together without doing one another harm. These theoretical and technical questions are interdependent, for the theoretical problems arise out of the different techniques while the technical problems cannot be solved without a measure of pre-established theoretical knowledge.

In such a world the ontological need, the need of being, is exhausted in exact proportion to the breaking up of personality on the one hand and, on the other, to the triumph of the category of the 'purely natural' and the consequent atrophy of the faculty of *wonder*.

But to come at last to the ontological need itself; can we not approach it directly and attempt to define it? In reality this can only be done to a limited extent. For reasons which I shall develop later, I suspect that the characteristic of this need is that it can never be wholly clear to itself.

To try to describe it without distorting it we shall have to say something like this:

Being is—or should be—necessary. It is impossible that everything should be reduced to a play of successive appearances which are inconsistent with each other ('inconsistent' is essential), or, in the words of Shakespeare, to 'a tale told by an idiot.' I aspire to participate in this being, in this reality—and perhaps this aspiration is already a degree of participation, however rudimentary.

Such a need, it may be noted, is to be found at the heart of the most inveterate pessimism. Pessimism has no meaning unless it signifies: it would surely be well if there were being, but there is no being, and I, who observe this fact, am therefore nothing.

As for defining the word 'being,' let us admit that it is extremely difficult. I would merely suggest this method of approach being is what withstands—or what would withstand—an exhaustive analysis bearing on the data of experience and aiming to reduce them step by step to elements increasingly devoid of intrinsic or significant value. (An analysis of this kind is attempted in the theoretical works of Freud.)

When the pessimist Besme says in *La Ville* that *nothing is*, he means precisely this, that there is no experience that withstands this analytical test. And it is always towards death regarded as the manifestation, the proof of this ultimate nothingness that the kind of inverted apologetic which arises out of absolute pessimism will inevitably gravitate.

A philosophy which refuses to endorse the ontological need is, nevertheless, possible; indeed, generally speaking, contemporary thought tends towards this abstention. But at this point a distinction must be made between two different attitudes which are sometimes confused: one which consists in a systematic reserve (it is that of agnosticism in all its forms), and the other, bolder and more coherent, which regards the ontological need as the expression of an outworn body of dogma liquidated once and for all by the Idealist critique.

The former appears to me to be purely negative: it is merely the expression of an intellectual policy of 'not raising the question.'

The latter, on the contrary, claims to be based on a positive theory of thought. This is not the place for a detailed critical study of this philosophy. I shall only note that it seems to me to tend towards an unconscious relativism, or else towards a monism which ignores the personal in all its form, ignores the tragic and denies the transcendent, seeking to reduce it to its caricatural expressions which distort its essential character. I shall also point out that, just because this philosophy continually stresses the activity of verification, it ends by ignoring *presence*—that inward realisation of presence through love which infinitely transcends all possible verification because it exists in an immediacy beyond all conceivable mediation. This will be clearer to some extent from what follows.

Thus I believe for my part that the ontological need cannot be silenced by an arbitrary dictatorial act which mutilates the life of the spirit at its roots. It remains true, nevertheless, that such an act is possible, and the conditions of our life are such that we can well believe that we are carrying it out; this must never be forgotten.

These preliminary reflections on the ontological need are sufficient to bring out its indeterminate character and to reveal a fundamental paradox. To formulate this need is to raise a host of questions: Is there such a thing as being? What is it? etc. Yet immediately an abyss opens under my feet: I who ask these questions about being, how can I be sure that I exist?

Yet surely I, who formulate this *problem*, should be able to remain *outside* it—*before* or *beyond* it? Clearly this is not so. The more I consider it the more I find that this problem tends inevitably to invade the proscenium from which it is excluded in theory: it is only by means of a fiction that Idealism in its traditional form seeks to maintain on the margin of being the consciousness which asserts it or denies it.

So I am inevitably forced to ask: Who am I—I who question being? How am I qualified to begin this investigation? If I do not exist, how can I succeed in it? And if I do exist, how can I be sure of this fact?

Contrary to the opinion which suggests itself at this point, I believe that on this plane the *cogito* cannot help us at all. Whatever Descartes may have thought of it himself, the only certainty with which it provides us concerns only the epistemological subject as organ of objective cognition. As I have written elsewhere, the *cogito* merely guards the threshold of objective validity, and that is strictly all; this is proved by the indeterminate character of the *I*. The *I am* is, to my mind, a global statement which it is impossible to break down into its component parts.

There remains a possible objection; it might be said: Either the being designated in the question 'What am I?' concerns the subject of cognition, and in this case we are on the plane of the *cogito;* or else that which you call the ontological need is merely the extreme point (or perhaps only the fallacious transposition) of a need which is, in reality, vital and with which the metaphysician is not concerned.

But is it not a mistake arbitrarily to divide the question, *Who am I?* from the ontological 'problem' taken as a whole? The truth is that neither of the two can be dealt with separately, but that when they are taken together, they cancel one another out *as problems*.

It should be added that the Cartesian position is inseparable from a form of dualism which I, for my part, would unhesitatingly reject. To raise the ontological problem is to raise the question of being as a whole and of oneself seen as a totality.

But should we not ask ourselves if we must not reject this dissociation between the intellectual and the vital, with its resultant over- or under-estimation of the one or the other? Doubtless it is legitimate to establish certain distinctions within the unity of the being who thinks and who endeavours to *think himself;* but it is only beyond such distinctions that the ontological problem can arise and it must relate to that being seen in his all-comprehensive unity.

To sum up our reflections at this point, we find that we are dealing with an urge towards an affirmation—yet an affirmation which it seems impossible to make, since it is not until it has been made that I can regard myself as qualified to make it.

It should be noted that this difficulty never arises at a time when I am actually faced with a problem to be solved. In such a case I work on the data, but everything leads me to believe that I need not take into account the *I* who is at work—it is a factor which is presupposed and nothing more.

Here, on the contrary, what I would call the ontological status of the investigator assumes a decisive importance. Yet so long as I am concerned with thought itself I seem to follow an endless regression. But by the very fact of recognising it as endless I transcend it in a certain way: I see that this process takes place within an affirmation of being—an affirmation which I *am* rather than an affirmation which I *utter:* by uttering it I break it, I divide it, I am on the point of betraying it.

It might be said, by way of an approximation, that my inquiry into being presupposes an affirmation in regard to which I am, in a sense, passive, *and of which I am the stage rather than the subject.* But this is only at the extreme limit of thought, a limit which I cannot reach without falling into contradiction. I am therefore led to assume or to recognise a form of participation which has the reality of a subject; this participation cannot be, by definition, an *object* of thought; it cannot serve as a solution—it appears beyond the realm of problems: it is meta-problematical.

Conversely, it will be seen that, if the meta-problematical can be asserted at all, it must be conceived as transcending the opposition between the subject who asserts the existence of being, on the one hand, and being *as asserted by that subject,* on the other, and as underlying it in a given sense. To postulate the meta-problematical is to postulate the primacy of being over knowledge (not of being as *asserted,* but of being as *asserting itself*); it is to recognise that knowledge is, as it were, environed by being, that it is interior to it in a certain sense—a sense perhaps analogous to that which Paul Claudel tried to define in his *Art Poétique.* From this standpoint, contrary to what epistemology seeks vainly to establish, there exists well and truly a mystery of cognition; knowledge is contingent on a participation in being for which no epistemology can account because it continually presupposes it.

At this point we can begin to define the distinction between mystery and problem. A mystery is a problem which encroaches upon its own data, invading them, as it were, and thereby transcending itself as a simple problem. A set of examples will help us to grasp the content of this definition.

It is evident that there exists a mystery of the union of the body and the soul. The indivisible unity always inadequately expressed by such phrases as *I have a body, I make use of my body, I feel my body*, etc., can be neither analysed nor reconstituted out of precedent elements. It is not only data, I would say that it is the basis of data, in the sense of being my own presence to myself, a presence of which the act of self-consciousness is, in the last analysis, only an inadequate symbol.

It will be seen at once that there is no hope of establishing an exact frontier between problem and mystery. For in reflecting on a mystery we tend inevitably to degrade it to the level of a problem. This is particularly clear in the case of the problem of evil.

In reflecting upon evil, I tend, almost inevitably, to regard it as a disorder which I view from outside and of which I seek to discover the causes or the secret aims. Why is it that the 'mechanism' functions so defectively? Or is the defect merely apparent and due to a real defect of my vision? In this case the defect is in myself, yet it remains objective in relation to my thought, which discovers it and observes it. But evil which is only stated or observed is no longer evil which is suffered: in fact, it ceases to be evil. In reality, I can only grasp it as evil in the measure in which it *touches* me—that is to say, in the measure in which I am *involved*, as one is involved in a law-suit. Being 'involved' is the fundamental fact; I cannot leave it out of account except by an unjustifiable fiction, for in doing so, I proceed as though I were God, and a God who is an onlooker at that.

This brings out how the distinction between what is *in me* and what is only *before me* can break down. This distinction falls under the blow of a certain kind of thought: thought at one remove.

But it is, of course, in love that the obliteration of this frontier can best be seen. It might perhaps even be shown that the domain of the meta-problematical coincides with that of love, and that love is the only starting point for the understanding of such mysteries as that of body and soul, which, in some manner, is its expression.

Actually, it is inevitable that, in being brought to bear on love, thought which has not thought itself—unreflected reflection—should tend to dissolve its meta-problematical character and interpret it in terms of abstract concepts, such as the will to live, the will to power the *libido*, etc. On the other hand, since the domain of the problematical is that of the objectively valid, it will be extremely difficult—if not impossible—to refute these interpretations without changing to a new ground: a ground on which, to tell the truth, they lose their meaning. Yet I have the assurance, the certainty—and it envelops me like a protective cloak—that for as much as I really love I must not be concerned with these attempts at devaluation.

It will be asked: What is the criterion of true love? It must be answered that there is no criteriology except in the order of the objective and the problematical; but we can already see at a distance the eminent ontological value to be assigned to fidelity.

Let us take another illustration, more immediate and more particular, which may shed some light on the distinction between problem and mystery.

Say that I have made an encounter which has left a deep and lasting trace on all my life. It may happen to anyone to experience the deep spiritual significance of such a meeting—yet this is something which philosophers have commonly ignored or disdained, doubtless because it effects only the particular person as person—it cannot be universalised, it does not concern rational being in general.

It is clear that such a meeting raises, if you will, a problem; but it is equally clear that the solution of this problem will always fall short of the only question that matters. Suppose that I am told, for instance: 'The reason you have met this person in this place is that you both like the same kind of scenery, or that you both need the same kind of treatment for your health'—the explanation means nothing. Crowds of people who apparently share my tastes were in the Engadine or in Florence at the time I was there; and there are always numbers of patients suffering from the same disease as myself at the health resort I frequent. But neither this supposed identity of tastes nor this common affliction has brought us together in any real sense; it has nothing to do with that intimate and unique affinity with which we are dealing. At the same time, it would be transgression of this valid reasoning to treat this affinity as if it were itself the cause and to say: 'It is precisely this which has determined our meeting.'

Hence I am in the presence of a mystery. That is to say, of a reality rooted in what is beyond the domain of the problematical properly so called. Shall we avoid the difficulty by saying that it was after all nothing but a coincidence, a lucky chance? But the whole of me immediately protests against this empty formula, this vain negation of what I apprehend with the deepest of my being. Once again we are brought back to our first definition of a mystery as a problem which encroaches upon its own data: I who inquire into the meaning and the possibility of this meeting, I cannot place myself outside it or before it; I am engaged in this encounter, I depend upon it, I am inside it in a certain sense, it envelops me and it comprehends me—even if it is not comprehended by me. Thus it is only by a kind of betrayal or denial that I can say: 'After all, it might not have happened, I would still have been what I was, and what I am to-day.' Nor must it be said: I have been changed by it as by an outward cause. No, it has developed me from within, it has acted in me as an inward principle.

But this is very difficult to grasp without distortion. I shall be inevitably tempted to react against this sense of the inwardness of the encounter, tempted by my probity itself, by what from a certain standpoint I must judge to be the best—or at least the safest—of myself.

There is a danger that these explanations my strengthen in the minds of my readers a preliminary objection which must be stated at once.

It will be said: The meta-problematical of which you speak is after all a content of thought; how then should we not ask ourselves what is its mode of existence? What assures us of its existence at all? Is it not itself problematical in the highest degree?

My answer is categorical: To think, or, rather, to assert, the meta-problematical is to assert it as indubitably real, as a thing of which I cannot doubt without falling into contradiction. We are in a sphere where it is no longer possible to dissociate the idea itself from the certainty or the degree of certainty which pertains to it. Because this idea *is* certainty, it *is* the assurance of itself; it is, in this sense, something other and something more than an idea. As for the term *content of thought* which figured in the objection, it is deceptive in the highest degree. For content is, when all is said and done, derived from experience; whereas it is only by a way of liberation and detachment from experience that we can possibly rise to the level of the meta-problematical and of mystery. This liberation must be *real;* this detachment must be *real;* they must not be an abstraction, that is to say a fiction recognised as such.

And this at last brings us to recollection, for it is in recollection and in this alone that this detachment is accomplished. I am convinced, for my part, that no ontology—that is to say, no apprehension of ontological mystery in whatever degree—is possible except to a being who is capable of recollecting himself, and of thus proving that he is not a living creature pure and simple, a creature, that is to say, which is at the mercy of its life and without a hold upon it.

It should be noted that recollection, which has received little enough attention from pure philosophers, is very difficult to define—if only because it transcends the dualism of being and action or, more correctly, because it reconciles in itself these two aspects of the antinomy. The word means what it says—the act whereby I re-collect myself as a unity; but this hold, this grasp upon myself, is also relaxation and abandon. *Abandon to . . . relaxation in the presence of . . .*—yet there is no noun for these prepositions to govern. The way stops at the threshold.

Here, as in every other sphere, problems will be raised, and it is the psychologist who will raise them. All that must be noted is that the psychologist is no more in a position to shed light on the metaphysical bearing of recollection than on the noetic value of knowledge.

It is within recollection that I take up my position—or, rather, I become capable of taking up my position—in regard to my life; I withdraw from it in a certain way, but not as the pure subject of cognition; *in this withdrawal I carry with me that which I am and which perhaps my life is not.* This brings out the gap between my being and my life. I am not my life; and if I can judge my life—a fact I cannot deny without falling into a radical scepticism which is nothing other than despair —it is only on condition that I encounter myself within recollection beyond all possible judgment and, I would add, beyond all representation. Recollection is doubtless what is least spectacular in the soul; it does not consist in looking at something, it is an inward hold, an inward reflection, and it might be asked in passing whether it should not be seen as the ontological basis of memory—that principle of effective and non-representational unity on which the possibility of remembrance rests. The double meaning of 'recollection' in English is revealing.

It may be asked: is not recollection identical with that dialectical moment of the turning to oneself (*retour sur soi*) or else with the *fuer sich sein* which is the central theme of German Idealism?

I do not think so. To withdraw into oneself is not to be for oneself nor to mirror oneself in the intelligible unity of subject and object. On the contrary. I would say that here we come up against the paradox of that actual mystery whereby the I into which I withdraw ceases, for as much, to belong to itself. 'You are not your own'—this great saying of St. Paul assumes in this connection its full concrete and ontological significance; it is the nearest approach to the reality for which we are groping. It will be asked: is not this reality an object of intuition? Is not that which you term 'recollection' the same as what others have termed 'intuition?'

But this again seems to me to call for the utmost prudence. If intuition can be mentioned in this content at all, it is not an intuition which is, or can be, given as such.

The more an intuition is central and basic in the being whom it illuminates, the less it is capable of turning back and apprehending itself.

Moreover, if we reflect on what an intuitive knowledge of being could possibly be, we see that it could never figure in a collection, a procession of simple experiences of *Erlebnisse,* which all have this characteristic that they can be at times absorbed and at others isolated and, as it were, uncovered. Hence, any effort to remember such an intuition, to represent it to oneself, is inevitably fruitless. From this point of view, to be told of an intuitive knowledge of being is like being invited to play on a soundless piano. Such an intuition cannot be brought out into the light of day, for the simple reason that we do not possess it.

We are here at the most difficult point of our whole discussion. Rather than to speak of intuition in this context, we should say that we are dealing with an assurance which underlies the entire development of thought, even of discursive thought; it can therefore be approached only by a second reflection—a reflection whereby I ask myself how and from what starting point I was able to proceed in my initial reflection, which itself postulated the ontological, but without knowing it. This second reflection is recollection in the measure in which recollection can be self-conscious.

It is indeed annoying to have to use such abstract language in a matter which is not one of dialectics *ad usum philosophorum*, but of what is the most vital and, I would add, the most dramatic moment in the rhythm of consciousness seeking to be conscious of itself.

It is this dramatic aspect which must now be brought out.

Let us recall what we said earlier on: that the ontological need, the need of being, can deny itself. In a different context we said that being and life do not coincide; my life, and by reflection all life, may appear to me as for ever inadequate to something which I carry within me, which in a sense I am, but which reality rejects and excludes. Despair is possible in any form, at any moment and to any degree, and this betrayal may seem to be counselled, if not forced upon us, by the very structure of the world we live in. The deathly aspect of this world may, from a given standpoint, be regarded as a ceaseless incitement to denial and to suicide. It could even be said in this sense that the fact that suicide is always possible is the essential starting point of any genuine metaphysical thought.

It may be surprising to find in the course of this calm and abstract reasoning such verbal star turns—words so emotionally charged—as 'suicide' and 'betrayal.' They are not a concession to sensationalism. I am convinced that it is in drama and through drama that metaphysical thought grasps and defines itself *in concreto*. Two years ago, in a lecture on the 'Problem of Christian Philosophy' which he delivered at Louvain, M. Jacques Maritain said: 'There is nothing easier for a philosophy than to become tragic, it has only to let itself go to its human weight.' The allusion was doubtless to the speculation of a Heidegger. I believe, on the contrary, that the natural trend of philosophy leads it into a sphere where it seems that tragedy has sinply vanished—evaporated at the touch of abstract thought. This is borne out by the work of many contemporary Idealists. Because they ignore the person, offering it up to I know not what ideal truth, to what principle of pure inwardness, they are unable to grasp those tragic factors of human existence to which I have alluded above; they banish them, together with illness and everything akin to it, to I know not what disreputable suburb of thought outside the ken of any philosopher worthy of the name. But, as I have stressed earlier on, this attitude is intimately bound up with the rejection of the ontological need; indeed, it is the same thing.

If I have stressed despair, betrayal and suicide, it is because these are the most manifest expressions of the will to negation as applied to being.

Let us take despair. I have in mind the act by which one despairs of reality as a whole, as one might despair of a person. This appears to be the result, or the immediate translation into other terms, of a kind of balance sheet. Inasmuch as I am able to evaluate the world of reality (and, when all is said and done, what I am unable to evaluate is for me as if it were not) I can find nothing in it that withstands that process of dissolution at the heart of things which I have discovered and traced. I believe that at the root of despair there is always this affirmation: 'There is nothing in the realm of reality to which I can give credit — no security, no guarantee.' It is a statement of complete insolvency.

As against this, hope is what implies credit. Contrary to what was thought by Spinoza, who seems to me to have confused two quite distinct notions, fear is correlated to desire and not to hope, whereas what is negatively correlated to hope is the act which consists in putting things at their worst — an act which is strikingly illustrated by what is known as defeatism, and which is ever in danger of being degraded into the desire of the worst. Hope consists in asserting that there is at the heart of being, beyond all data, beyond all inventories and all calculations, a mysterious principle which is in connivance with me, which cannot but will that which I will, if what I will deserves to be willed and is, in fact, willed by the whole of my being.

We have now come to the centre of what I have called the ontological mystery, and the simplest illustrations will be the best. To hope against all hope that a person whom I love will recover from a disease which is said to be incurable is to say: It is impossible that I should be alone in willing this cure; it is impossible that reality in its inward depth should be hostile or so much as indifferent to what I assert is in itself a good. It is quite useless to tell me of discouraging *cases* or *examples:* beyond all experience, all probability, all statistics, I assert that a given order shall be re-established, that reality *is* on my side in willing it to be so. I do not wish: I assert; such is the prophetic tone of true hope.

No doubt I shall be told: 'In the immense majority of cases this is an illusion.' But it is of the essence of hope to exclude the consideration of cases; moreover, it can be shown that there exists an ascending dialectic of hope, whereby hope rises to a plane which transcends the level of all possible empirical disproof — the plane of salvation as opposed to that of success in whatever form.

It remains true, nevertheless, that the correlation of hope and despair subsists until the end; they seem to me inseparable. I mean that while the structure of the world we live in permits — and may even seem to counsel — absolute despair, yet it is only such a world that can give rise to an unconquerable hope. If only for this reason, we cannot be sufficiently thankful to the great pessimists in the history of thought; they have carried through an inward experience which needed to be made and of which the radical possibility no apologetics should disguise; they have prepared our minds to understand that despair can be what it was for Nietzsche (though on an infra-ontological level and in a domain fraught with mortal dangers) the springboard to the loftiest affirmation.

At the same time, it remains certain that, for as much as hope is a mystery, its mystery can be ignored or converted into a problem. Hope is then regarded as a desire which wraps itself up in illusory judgments to distort an objective reality which it is interested in disguising from itself. What happens in this case is what we have already observed in connection with encounter and with love; it is because mystery can — and, in a sense, logically must — be degraded into a problem that an interpretation such as that of Spinoza, with all the confusion it implies, had to be put forward sooner or later. It is important and must be stressed that this attitude has nothing against it so long as our standpoint is on the hither-side of the realm of the ontological. Just as long as my attitude towards reality is that of someone who is not involved in it, but who judges it his duty to draw up its minutes as exactly as possible (and this is by definition the attitude of the scientist), I am justified in maintaining in regard to it a sort of principle of mistrust, which in theory is unlimited in its application; such is the legitimate standpoint of the workman in the laboratory, who must in no way prejudge the result of his analysis, and who can all the better envisage *the worst*, because at this level the very notion of worst is empty of meaning. But an investigation of this sort, which is just like that of an accountant going through the books, takes place on the hither-side of the order of mystery, an order in which the problem encroaches upon its own data.

It would indeed be a profound illusion to believe that I can still maintain this same attitude when I undertake an inquiry, say, into the value of life; it would be a paralogism to suppose that I can pursue such an inquiry as though my own life were not at issue.

Hence, between hope — the reality of hope in the heart of the one whom it inhabits — and the judgment brought to bear upon it by a mind chained to objectivity there exists the same barrier as that which separates a pure mystery from a pure problem.

This brings us to a nodal point of our subject, where certain intimate connections can be traced.

The world of the problematical is the world of fear and desire, which are inseparable; at the same time, it is that world of the functional — or of what can be functionalised — which was defined at the beginning of this essay; finally, it is the kingdom of technics of whatever sort. Every technique serves, or can be made to serve, some desire or some fear; conversely, every desire as every fear tends to invent its appropriate technique. From this standpoint, despair consists in the recognition of the ultimate inefficacy of all technics, joined to the inability or the refusal to change over to a new ground — a ground where all technics are seen to be incompatible with the fundamental nature of being, which itself escapes our grasp (in so far as our grasp is limited to the world of objects and to this alone). It is for this reason that we seem nowadays to have entered upon the very era of despair; we have not ceased to believe in technics, that is to envisage reality as a complex of problems; yet at the same time the failure of technics *as a whole* is as discernible to us as its *partial* triumphs. To the question: what can man achieve? we continue to reply: He can achieve as much as his technics; yet we are obliged to admit that these technics are unable *to save man himself,* and even that they are apt to conclude the most sinister alliance with the enemy he bears with him.

I have said that man is *at the mercy of his technics.* This must be understood to mean that he is increasingly incapable of controlling his technics, or rather of *controlling his own control.* This control of his own control, which is nothing else than the expression on the plane of active life of what I have called thought at one remove, cannot find its centre or its support anywhere except in recollection.

It will be objected that even those whose faith in technics is strongest are bound to admit that there exist enormous realms which are outside man's control. But what matters is the spirit in which this admission is made. We have to recognise that we have no control over meteorological conditions, but the question is: do we consider it desirable and just that we should have such control? The more the sense of the ontological tends to disappear, the more unlimited become the claims of the mind which has lost it to a kind of cosmic governance, because it is less and less capable of examining its own credentials to the exercise of such dominion.

It must be added that the more the disproportion grows between the claims of the technical intelligence on the one hand, and the persisting fragility and precariousness of what remains its material substratum on the other, the more acute becomes the constant danger of despair which threatens this intelligence. From this standpoint there is truly an intimate dialectical correlation between the optimism of technical progress and the philosophy of despair which seems inevitably to emerge from it—it is needless to insist on the examples offered by the world of to-day.

It will perhaps be said: This optimism of technical progress is animated by great hope. How is hope in this sense to be reconciled with the ontological interpretation of hope?

I believe it must be answered that, *speaking metaphysically, the only genuine hope is hope in what does not depend on ourselves,* hope springing from humility and not from pride. This brings us to the consideration of another aspect of the mystery—a mystery which in the last analysis, is one and unique—on which I am endeavouring to throw some light.

The metaphysical problem of pride—*hubris*—which was perceived by the Greeks and which has been one of the essential themes of Christian theology, seems to me to have been almost completely ignored by modern philosophers other than theologians. It has become a domain reserved for the moralist. Yet from my own standpoint it is an essential —if not the vital—question. It is sufficient to recall Spinoza's definition of *superbia* in his *Ethics* (III, def. XXVIII) to see how far he was from grasping the problem: 'Pride is an exaggeratedly good opinion of ourselves which arises from self-love.' In reality, this is a definition of vanity. As for pride, it consists in drawing one's strength solely from oneself. The proud man is cut off from a certain form of communion with his fellow men, which pride, acting as a principle of destruction, tends to break down. Indeed, this destructiveness can be equally well directed against the self; pride is in no way incompatible with self-hate; this is what Spinoza does not seem to have perceived.

An important objection may be raised at the point we have now reached.

It will perhaps be said: Is not that which you are justifying ontologically in reality a kind of moral quietism which is satisfied by passive acceptance, resignation and inert hope? But what, then, becomes of man as man, as active being? Are we to condemn action itself inasmuch as it implies a self-confidence which is akin to pride? Can it be that action itself is a kind of degradation?

This objection implies a series of misunderstandings.

To begin with, the idea of inert hope seems to me a contradiction in terms. Hope is not a kind of listless waiting; it underpins action or it runs before it, but it becomes degraded and lost once the action is spent. Hope seems to me, as it were, the prolongation into the unknown of an activity which is central—that is to say, rooted in being. Hence it has affinities, not with desire, but with the will. The will implies the same refusal to calculate possibilities, or at any rate it suspends this calculation. Could not hope therefore be defined as the will when it is made to bear on what does not depend on itself?

The experimental proof of this connection is that it is the most active saints who carry hope to its highest degree; this would be inconceivable if hope were simply an inactive state of the soul. The mistake so often made here comes from a stoical representation of the will as a stiffening of the soul, whereas it is on the contrary relaxation and creation.

The term 'creation,' which occurs here for the first time, is, nevertheless, decisive. Where there is creation there can be no degradation, and to the extent that technics are creative, or imply creativity, they are not degrading in any way. Degradation begins at the point where creativeness falls into self-imitation and self-hypnotism, stiffening and falling back on itself. This may, indeed, bring out the origin of the confusion which I denounced in the context of recollection.

Great is the temptation to confuse two distinct movements of the soul, whose opposition is blurred by the use of spacial metaphors. The stiffening, the contraction, the falling back on the self which are inseparable from pride, and which are indeed its symbol, must not be confused with the humble withdrawal which befits recollection and whereby I renew my contact with the ontological basis of my being.

There is every reason to think that such withdrawal in recollection is a presupposition of aesthetic creativity itself. Artistic creation, like scientific research, excludes the act of self-centering and self-hypnotism which is, ontologically speaking, pure negation.

It may perhaps seem that my thesis comes so near to that of Bergson as to coincide with it, but I do not think that this is the case. The terms almost invariably used by Bergson suggest that for him the essential character of creativity lay in its inventiveness, in its spontaneous innovation. But I wonder if by limiting our attention to this aspect of creation we do not lose sight of its ultimate significance, which is its deep-rootedness in being. It is at this point that I would bring in the notion of *creative fidelity;* it is a notion which is the more difficult to grasp and, above all, to define conceptually, because of its underlying and unfathomable paradox, and because it is at the very centre of the realm of the meta-problematical.

It is important to note that the idea of fidelity seems difficult to maintain in the context of Bergsonian metaphysics, because it will tend to be interpreted as a routine, as an observance in the pejorative sense of the word, as an arbitrary safeguard *against* the power of renewal which is the spirit itself.

I am inclined to think that there is something in this neglect of the values of fidelity which deeply vitiates the notion of static religion as it is put forward in *Les Deux Sources de la Morale et de la Religion.* It may perhaps be useful to devote some thought to creative fidelity in order to elucidate this point.

Faithfulness is, in reality, the exact opposite of inert conformism. It is the active recognition of something permanent, not formally, after the manner of a law, but ontologically; in this sense, it refers invariably to a presence, or to something which can be maintained within us and before us as a presence, but which, *ipso facto,* can be just as well ignored, forgotten and obliterated; and this reminds us of that menace of betrayal which, to my mind, overshadows our whole world.

It may perhaps be objected that we commonly speak of fidelity to a principle. But it remains to be seen if this is not an arbitrary transposition of the notion of fidelity. A principle, in so far as it is a mere abstract affirmation, can make no demands upon me because it owes the whole of its reality to the act whereby I sanction it or proclaim it. Fidelity to a principle as a principle is idolatry in the etymological sense of the word; it might be a sacred duty for me to deny a principle from which life has withdrawn and which I know that I no longer accept, for by continuing to conform my actions to it, it is myself—myself as presence—that I betray.

So little is fidelity akin to the inertia of conformism that it implies an active and continuous struggle against the forces of interior dissipation, as also against the sclerosis of habit. I may be told: This is nevertheless no more than a sort of active conservation which is the opposite of creation. We must, I think, go much further into the nature of fidelity and of presence before we can reply to this point.

If presence were merely an *idea* in us whose characteristic was that it was nothing more than itself, then indeed the most we could hope would be to maintain this idea in us or before us, as one keeps a photograph on a mantelpiece or in a cupboard. But it is of the nature of presence as presence to be uncircumscribed; and this takes us once again beyond the frontier of the problematical. Presence is mystery in the exact measure in which it is presence. Now fidelity is the active perpetuation of presence, the renewal of its benefits—of its virtue which consists in a mysterious incitement to create. Here again we may be helped by the consideration of aesthetic creativeness; for if artistic creation is conceivable, it can only be on condition that the world *is* present to the artist in a certain way—present to his heart and to his mind, present to his very being.

Thus if creative fidelity is conceivable, it is because fidelity is ontological in its principle, because it prolongs presence which itself corresponds to a certain kind of hold which being has upon us; because it multiplies and deepens the effect of this presence almost unfathomably in our lives. This seems to me to have almost inexhaustible consequences, if only for the relationships between the living and the dead.

I must insist once again: A presence to which we are faithful is not at all the same thing as the carefully preserved effigy of an object which has vanished; an effigy is, when all is said and done, nothing but a likeness; metaphysically it is *less* than the object, it is a diminution of the object. Whereas presence, on the contrary, is *more* than the object, it exceeds the object on every side. We are here at the opening of a vista at whose term death will appear as the *test of presence*. This is an essential point and we must consider it carefully.

It will no doubt be said: What a strange way of defining death! Death *is* a phenomenon definable in biological terms; it *is not* a test.

It must be answered: It is what it signifies and, moreover, what it signifies to a being who rises to the highest spiritual level to which it is possible for us to attain. It is evident that if I read in the newspaper of the death of Mr. So-and-so, who is for me nothing but a name, this event *is* for me nothing more than the subject of an announcement. But it is quite another thing in the case of a being who has been granted to me as a presence. In this case, everything depends on me, on my inward attitude of maintaining this presence which could be debased into an effigy.

It will be objected: This is nothing more than a description in recondite and unnecessarily metaphysical terms of a common psychological fact. It is evident that it depends upon us in a certain measure to enable the dead to survive in our memory, but this existence is no more than subjective.

I believe that the truth is altogether different and infinitely more mysterious. In saying, 'It depends upon us that the dead should live on in our memory,' we are still thinking of the idea in terms of a diminution or an effigy. We admit that the object has disappeared, but that there remains a likeness which it is in our power to keep, as a daily woman 'keeps' a flat or a set of furniture. It is all too evident that this manner of keeping can have no ontological value whatsoever. But it is altogether different in the case where fidelity is creative in the sense which I have tried to define. A presence is a reality; it is a kind of influx; it depends upon us to be permeable to this influx, but not, to tell the truth, to call it forth. Creative fidelity consists in maintaining ourselves actively in a permeable state; and there is a mysterious interchange between this free act and the gift granted in response to it.

An objection which is the converse of the preceding one may be expected at this point. I will be told: 'All right. You have now ceased to decorate a psychological platitude with metaphysical ornaments, but only to make a gratuitous assertion which is unproved and which is beyond all possible experimental proof; this was inevitable as soon as you replaced the ambiguous and neutral term "presence" by the much more compromising term "influx."'

To reply to this objection, we must refer again to what I have already said of mystery and of recollection. Indeed, it is only on the meta-problematical level that the notion of influx can possibly be accepted. If it were taken in its objective sense, as an accretion of strength, we would indeed be faced with a thesis, not of metaphysics, but of physics, which would be open to every possible objection. When I say that a being is granted to me as a presence or as a being (it comes to the same, for he is not a being for me unless he is a presence), this means that I am unable to treat him as if he were merely placed in front of me; between him and me there arises a relationship which, in a sense, surpasses my awareness of him; he is not only before me, he is also within me—or, rather, these categories are transcended, they have no longer any meaning. The word influx conveys, though in a manner which is far too physical and spacial, the kind of interior accretion, of accretion from within, which comes into being as soon as presence is effective. Great and almost invincible is the temptation to think that such effective presence can be only that of an object; but if we believed this we would fall back to the level of the problematical and remain on the hither-side of mystery; and against this belief fidelity raises up its voice: 'Even if I cannot see you, if I cannot touch you, I feel that you are with me; it would be a denial of you not to be assured of this.' *With* me: note the metaphysical value of this word, so rarely recognised by philosophers, which corresponds neither to a relationship of inherence or immanence nor to a relationship of exteriority. It is of the essence of genuine *coesse*—I must use the Latin word—that is to say, of genuine intimacy, to lend itself to the decomposition to which it is subjected by critical thought; but we already know that there exists another kind of thought, a thought which bears upon that thought itself, and is related to a bottled up yet efficacious underlying intuition, of which it suffers the attraction.

It must be added (and this brings us to the verge of another sphere) that the value of such intimacy, particularly in regard to the relation between the living and the dead, will be the higher and the more assured the more this intimacy is grounded in the realm of total spiritual availability (*disponibilité*)—that is to say, of pure charity; and I shall note in passing that an ascending dialectic of creative fidelity corresponds to the dialectic of hope to which I have already referred.

The notion of availability is no less important for our subject than that of presence, with which it is bound up.

It is an undeniable fact, though it is hard to describe in intelligible terms, that there are some people who reveal themselves as 'present'— that is to say, at our disposal—when we are in pain or in need to confide in someone, while there are other people who do not give us this feeling, however great is their goodwill. It should be noted at once that the distinction between presence and absence is not at all the same as that between attention and distraction. The most attentive and the most conscientious listener may give me the impression of not being present; he gives me nothing, he cannot make room for me in himself, whatever the material favours which he is prepared to grant me. The truth is that there is a way of listening which is a way of giving, and another way of listening which is a way of refusing, of refusing *oneself;* the material gift, the visible action, do not necessarily witness to presence. We must not speak of proof in this connection; the word would be out of place. Presence is something which reveals itself immediately and unmistakably in a look, a smile, an intonation or a handshake.

It will perhaps make it clearer if I say that the person who is at my disposal is the one who is capable of being with me with the whole of himself when I am in need; while the one who is not at my disposal seems merely to offer me a temporary loan raised on his resources. For the one I am a presence; for the other I am an object. Presence involves a reciprocity which is excluded from any relation of subject to object or of subject to subject-object. A concrete analysis of unavailability (*indisponibilité*) is no less necessary for our purpose than that of betrayal, denial or despair.

Unavailability is invariably rooted in some measure of alienation. Say, for instance, that I am told of some misfortune with which I am asked to sympathise: I understand what I am told; I admit in theory that the sufferers deserve my sympathy; I see that it is a case where it would be logical and just for me to respond with sympathy; I even offer my sympathy, but only with my mind; because, when all is said and done, I am obliged to admit that I feel absolutely nothing. Indeed, I am sorry that this should be so; the contradiction between the indifference which I feel in fact and the sympathy which I know I ought to feel is humiliating and annoying; it diminishes me in my own eyes. But it is no use; what remains in me is the rather embarrassing awareness that, after all, these are people I do not know—if one had to be touched by every human misfortune life would not be possible, it would indeed be too short. The moment I think: After all, this is only a case, No. 75,627, it is no good, I can feel nothing.

But the characteristic of the soul which is present and at the disposal of others is that it cannot think in terms of *cases;* in its eyes there are *no cases at all.*

And yet it is clear that the normal development of a human being implies an increasingly precise and, as it were, automatic division between what concerns him and what does not, between things for which he is responsible and those for which he is not. Each one of us becomes the centre of a sort of mental space arranged in concentric zones of decreasing interest and participation. It is as though each one of us secreted a kind of shell which gradually hardened and imprisoned him; and this sclerosis is bound up with the hardening of the categories in accordance with which we conceive and evaluate the world.

Fortunately, it can happen to anyone to make an encounter which breaks down the framework of this egocentric topography; I know by my own experience how, from a stranger met by chance, there may come an irresistible appeal which overturns the habitual perspectives just as a gust of wind might tumble down the panels of a stage set— what had seemed near becomes infinitely remote and what had seemed distant seems to be close. Such cracks are repaired almost at once. But it is an experience which leaves us with a bitter taste, an impression of sadness and almost of anguish; yet I think it is beneficial, for it shows us as in a flash all that is contingent and—yes—artificial in the crystallised pattern of our personal system.

But it is, above all, the sanctity realised in certain beings which reveals to us that what we call the normal order is, from a higher point of view, from the standpoint of a soul rooted in ontological mystery, merely the subversion of an order which is its opposite. In this connection, the study of sanctity with all its concrete attributes seems to me to offer an immense speculative value; indeed, I am not far from saying that it is the true introduction to ontology.

Once again a comparison with the soul which is not at the disposal of others will throw light on our subject.

To be incapable of presence is to be in some manner not only occupied but encumbered with one's own self. I have said in some manner; the immediate object of the preoccupation may be one of any number; I may be preoccupied with my health, my fortune, or even with *my inward perfection.* This shows that to be occupied with oneself is not so much to be occupied with *a particular object* as to be occupied in *a particular manner.* It must be noted that the contrary of this state is not a state of emptiness or indifference. The real contrast is rather between the being who is opaque and the being who is transparent. But this inward opacity remains to be analysed. I believe that it consists in a kind of obduracy or fixation; and I wonder if, by generalising and adapting certain psychoanalytical data, we would not find that it is the fixation in a given zone or in a given key of a certain disquiet which, in itself, is something quite different. But what is remarkable is that the disquiet persists within this fixation and gives it that character of constriction which I mentioned in connection with the degradation of the will. There is every reason to believe that this indefinite disquiet should be identified with the anguish of temporality and with that aspiration of man not towards, but *by* death, which is at the heart of pessimism.

Pessimism is rooted in the same soil as the inability to be at the disposal of others. If the latter grows in us as we grow old, it is only too often because, as we draw near to what we regard as the term of our life, anxiety grows in us almost to the point of choking us; to protect itself, it sets up an increasingly heavy, exacting and, I would add, vulnerable mechanism of self-defence. The capacity to hope diminishes in proportion as the soul becomes increasingly chained to its experience and to the categories which arise from it, and as it is given over more completely and more desperately to the world of the problematical.

Here at last can be brought together the various motifs and thematic elements which I have had to bring out one by one. In contrast to the captive soul we have described, the soul which is at the disposal of others is consecrated and inwardly dedicated; it is protected against suicide and despair, which are interrelated and alike, because it knows that it is not its own, and that the most legitimate use it can make of its freedom is precisely to recognise that it does not belong to itself; this recognition is the starting point of its activity and creativeness.

The difficulties of a philosophy of this sort must not be disguised. It is inevitably faced by a disquietening alternative: Either it will try to solve these difficulties—to give all the answers; in that case it will fall into the excesses of a dogmatism which ignores its vital principles and, I would add, into those of a sacrilegious theodicy, or else it will allow these difficulties to subsist, labelling them as mysteries.

Between these two I believe that there exists a middle way—a narrow, difficult and dangerous path which I have tried to discover. But, like Karl Jaspers in his *Philosophy of Existence,* I can only proceed in this kind of country by calling out to other travellers. If, as it occasionally happened, certain minds respond—not the generality, but this being and that other—then there is a way. But, as I believe Plato perceived with incomparable clarity, it is a way which is undiscoverable except through love, to which alone it is visible, and this brings us to what is perhaps the deepest characteristic of that realm of the metaproblematical of which I have tried to explore certain regions.

A serious objection remains to be mentioned. It will perhaps be said: All that you have said implies an unformulated reference to the data of Christianity and can only be understood in the light of these data. Thus we understand what you mean by presence if we think of the Eucharist and what you mean by creative fidelity if we think of the Church. But what can be the value of such a philosophy for those who are a-Christian—for those who ignore Christianity or who do not ac-

cept it? I would answer: it is quite possible that the existence of the
fundamental Christian data may be necessary *in fact* to enable the mind
to conceive some of the notions which I have attempted to analyse; but
these notions cannot be said to depend on the data of Christianity, and
they do not presuppose it. On the other hand, should I be told that
the intellect must leave out of account anything which is not a universal data of thinking as such, I would say that this claim is exagger-
ated and in the last analysis, illusory. Now, as at any other time, the
philosopher is placed in a given historical situation from which he is
most unlikely to abstract himself completely; he would deceive himself
if he thought that he could create a complete void both within and
around himself. Now this historical situation implies as one of its essential data the existence of the Christian fact—quite independently of
whether the Christian religion is accepted and its fundamental assertions
are regarded as true or false. What appears to me evident is that we
cannot reason to-day as though there were not behind us centuries of
Christianity, just as, in the domain of the theory of knowledge, we
cannot pretend that there have not been centuries of positive science.
But neither the existence of Christianity nor that of positive science
plays in this connection more than the role of a fertilising principle.
It favours the development of certain ideas which we might not have
conceived without it. This development may take place in what I would
call para-Christian zones; for myself, I have experienced it more than
twenty years before I had the remotest thought of becoming a Catholic.

Speaking more particularly to Catholics, I should like to note that
from my own standpoint the distinction between the natural and the
supernatural must be rigorously maintained. It will perhaps be objected that there is a danger that the word 'mystery' might confuse this
very issue.

I would reply that there is no question of confusing those mysteries
which are enveloped in human experience as such with those mysteries
which are revealed, such as the Incarnation or Redemption, and to
which no effort of thought bearing on experience can enable us to attain.

It will be asked: why then do you use the same word for two such
distinct notions? But I would point out that no revelation is, after all,
conceivable unless it is addressed to a being who is *involved—committed*—in the sense which I have tried to define—that is to say, to a
being who participates in a reality which is non-problematical and
which provides him with his foundation as subject. Supernatural life
must, when all is said and done, find a hold in the natural—which is
not to say that it is the flowering of the natural. On the contrary it
seems to me that any study of the notion of *created Nature,* which is
fundamental for the Christian, leads to the conclusion that there is in
the depth of Nature, as of reason which is governed by it, a fundamental principle of inadequacy to itself which is, as it were, a restless anticipation of a different order.

To sum up my position on this difficult and important point, I would say that the recognition of the ontological mystery, in which I perceive as it were the central redoubt of metaphysics, is, no doubt, only possible through a sort of radiation which proceeds from revelation itself and which is perfectly well able to affect souls who are strangers to all positive religion of whatever kind; that this recognition, which takes place through certain higher modes of human experience, in no way involves the adherence to any given religion; but it enables those who have attained to it to perceive the possibility of a revelation in a way which is not open to those who have never ventured beyond the frontiers of the realm of the problematical and who have therefore never reached the point from which the mystery of being can be seen and recognised. Thus, a philosophy of this sort is carried by an irresistible movement towards the light which it perceives from afar and of which it suffers the secret attraction.

CHAPTER THREE

THE PROBLEM OF A NON-OBJECTIFYING THINKING AND SPEAKING IN CONTEMPORARY THEOLOGY*

by Martin Heidegger

What in this problem merits inquiry?

So far as I see there are *three themes* which need to be thought through.

1. It is obligatory to determine above everything else *what* theology as a mode of thinking and speaking has to discuss. That *'what'* is the Christian faith and what is believed. Only when this is clearly in view can it be inquired how thinking and speaking must be constituted so that they correspond to the meaning and claim of faith and so avoid introducing concepts into faith which are foreign to it.

2. It is indispensable to set out what is meant by *objectifying* thinking and speaking *prior to* a discussion of non-objectifying thinking and speaking. The question is thereby raised whether every thinking as thinking and every speaking as speaking are already objectifying or not.

   Should it become evident that thinking and speaking are not already objectifying in and of themselves, this then leads to a third theme.

3. It is obligatory to decide to what extent the problem of a non-objectifying thinking and speaking is a genuine problem at all, whether something is not inquired after here, the interrogation of which only thinks past the subject matter, distracts from the theme of theology and unnecessarily complicates it. In this case the theological consultation now being held would have the task of making

*Used with permission of the author. Previously unpublished. Originally a position paper at the Second Drew University Consultation on Hermeneutics, 1964.

it clear that it is on a trail with its problem that leads nowhere. This would be, so it appears, only a negative outcome of the consultation. But it only appears to be so. For in reality the unavoidable consequence would be that theology would gain final and decisive clarity about the necessity of its central task, viz., not to derive the categories of its thinking and the mode of its language from philosophy and the sciences on loan, but rather to think and speak in accordance with the subject matter out of faith for faith. If this faith by its own conviction concerns man as man in his very being, then genuine theological thinking and speaking does not require special preparation in order to encounter men and get their ear.

The three themes mentioned above should now be developed more precisely in detail. I myself can give some suggestions concerning the second theme from the standpoint of philosophy. For the discussion of the first theme, which must be the basis of the entire consultation, if it is not to take place in a vacuum, is the task of theology. The third theme comprises the theological consequence to be drawn from the adequate treatment of the first and second themes. I attempt here to give some suggestions for the treatment of the second theme, and even these only in the form of some questions. To be avoided is the impression that it were a matter of an articulation of dogmatic theses on the basis of a Heideggerian philosophy—which does not exist.

APROPOS OF THE SECOND THEME

Prior to any discussion of the question of a *non*-objectifying thinking and speaking in theology, it remains necessary to reflect upon what one understands by an *objectifying* thinking and speaking, when the problem is posed in the context of a theological consultation. This reflection calls for the question:

Is objectifying thinking and speaking a special mode of thinking and speaking, or must every thinking as thinking, every speaking as speaking, of necessity be objectifying?

The question may only be resolved when the following questions have first been clarified and answered:

(a) What does it mean to objectify?

(b) What does thinking mean?

(c) What does speaking mean?

(d) Is every thinking in itself a speaking and every speaking in itself a thinking?

(e) In what sense are thinking and speaking objectifying, in what sense are they not?

It lies in the nature of the thing that these questions interlock in the discussion of them. The full weight of these questions, however, underlies the problem of your theological consultations. These same questions, developed in a more or less clear and adequate fashion, constitute at the same time the as yet hidden center of those endeavors at which contemporary "philosophy" aims from its extreme counter-positions (Carnap <—> Heidegger). Today these positions are called: the techno-logical-scientistic view of language and the speculative-hermeneutical experience of language. Both positions are determined by unfathomably diverse tasks. The first position wants to bring all thinking and speaking, even that of philosophy, under the jurisdiction of a system of signs which can be construed as a technical-logical system. That means, to restrict it as an instrument of science. The second position has grown out of the question of what is to be experienced as the subject matter itself for the thinking of philosophy and how this subject matter (being as being) is to be expressed. In neither position is it a question of the separate sphere of a philosophy of language (analogous to a philosophy of nature or of art), but rather language is recognized as the realm within which every thinking of philosophy and every mode of thinking and saying dwell and move.

To the extent that the being of man is determined by the Western tradition in such a way that man is that animal which "has language" ($\zeta\omega o\nu$ $\lambda o\gamma o\nu$ $\epsilon\chi o\nu$)—even man as acting being is such only as the one which "has language"—nothing less is at stake in the dispute between the two positions than the question of the existence of man and his destiny.

In what way and to what limits theology can and must allow itself to be involved in this dispute is to be determined by theology itself.

The following brief clarifications of questions (a) through (e) may be prefaced by an observation which has probably occasioned the "prob-lem of a non-objectifying thinking and speaking in contemporary the-ology." It is the widespread opinion which has been uncritically ac-cepted, viz., that every thinking as conceiving, every speaking as audible articulation, is already objectifying. It is impossible here to investigate the origin of this opinion in detail. Decisive is the distinction between the rational and irrational, which has long ago been advanced without clarification. This distinction on its part is put forward on the authority of a rational thinking which itself remains unclarified. More recently, however, the teachings of Nietzsche, Bergson, and the philosophies of life became decisive for the assertion of the objectifying character of every thinking and speaking. Insofar as we say "is"—expressly or not —everywhere in speaking, insofar as being means presence, however, and this presence is construed in modern times as objectivity [*Gegen-standlichkeit* und *Objektivitat*], thinking as representation [*Vor-stellen*] and speaking as audible articulation unavoidably carry with them a crystallization of the "stream of life," which is in itself in flux, and thereby a falsification of it. On the other hand, the establishment of the permanent, although it falsifies, is indispensable for the main-tenance and subsistence of human life. The following text from Nietzs-che may serve as evidence for this opinion, which has been advanced in various forms: "The media of language are unsuitable to express 'becoming': it belongs to our indispensable need for maintenance perpetually to posit a more substantial world of the permanent, of things, etc. [i.e. of objects]" (*The Will to Power*, n. 715 [1887 88]).

The following suggestions with respect to questions (a) through (e) intend themselves to be understood as questions and thought through as such. For the mystery of language, on which the entire reflection must collect, remains that phenomenon which is most worthy of inquiry and thought, expecially when the insight dawns that language is not a work of man: language speaks. Man speaks only as he cor-responds to language. These assertions are not the offspring of a chimerical "mysticism." Language is a primal phenomenon, whose properties can not be established by data, but can only be sighted in an unpredisposed experience of language. Man can invent artificial vocables and signs, but he can do so only with reference to and out of a language already articulated. Thinking remains critical even in view of the primal phenomenon. For critical thinking means: perpetually to distinguish (χρινειν) between that which demands a proof for its justification and that which requires simple perceiving and receiving for its confirmation. It is always easier to provide a proof in the given case than in the case differently situated to enter in upon the receptive perception.

Ad (a) What does it mean to objectify? It means to make something into an Object[1], to posit it as Object and to represent it only as Object. And what does Object mean? In the Middle Ages the *obiectum* denoted that which is thrown against, held against perception, imagination, judgment, wishing and beholding. On the other hand, *subiectum* denoted υποχειμενον, that which is there of itself (not brought there by means of representation), that which is present [*das Anwesende*], e.g., the things. The meaning of the words *subiectum* and *obiectum*, in comparison with common usage today, is precisely the reverse: *subiectum* is that which exists (objectively) in itself, *obiectum* that which is only (subjectively) represented [*Vorgestellte*]. As a consequence of the transformation of the conception of *subiectum* by Descartes (cf. *Holzwege* 98ff.), the concept of Object also took on an altered meaning. For Kant Object signifies: the existing object [*Gegenstand*] of scientific experience. Every Object [*Objekt*], but not every Gegenstand [object] (e.g., the thing in itself [*Ding an sich*]) is a possible Object [*Objekt*]. The categorical imperative, the ethical ought, duty are not Objects of scientific experience. When they are reflected upon, when they are intended in one's acting, they are not thereby objectified. The everyday experience of the things in the wider sense is neither objectifying nor a reification [*Vergegenständlichung*]. If we are sitting in a garden, for example, and are enjoying the blooming roses, we do not make the rose into an Object, not even into a *Gegenstand* [object], i.e., into something represented [*Vorgestellten*] thematically. When I am now given over in my silent speaking to the radiant red of the rose, and meditate on the redness of the rose, this redness is then neither an Object [*Objekt*], nor a thing, nor a *Gegenstand* [object] like the blooming rose. The rose stands in the garden, perhaps swaying to and

1. [Object with capital 'O' represents Objekt, object with small 'o' Gegenstand, following the convention established by Macquarrie and Robinson in Being and Time.]

fro in the breeze. The redness of the rose, on the other hand, neither stands in the garden nor can it sway to and fro in the breeze. Nevertheless I think it and speak of it in that I name it. Accordingly, there is a thinking and saying which in no way objectifies nor reifies [*vergegenstandlicht*].

I can indeed conceive the statue of Apollo in the museum at Olympia as an Object of the scientific mode of representation [*Vorstellen*]; I can calculate the marble physically with respect to its weight; I can investigate the marble with respect to its chemical composition. But this objectifying thinking and speaking does not catch sight of Apollo as he shows himself in his beauty and in this appears as the vision of the god.

Ad (b) What does thinking mean? If we heed what has just been set out, it then becomes clear that thinking and speaking are not exhausted in theoretical-scientific representation [*Vorstellen*] and assertion. Thinking is rather the comportment permitting that which shows itself and how it shows itself to give to it what it has to say of that which appears. Thinking is not necessarily a representation [*Vorstellen*] of something as Object. Only scientific thinking and speaking are objectifying. If all thinking as such were already objectifying, the shaping of works of art would then remain meaningless, for they could never show themselves to man because he would forthwith turn that which appears into an Object and so deny appearing to the work of art.

The assertion that all thinking as thinking is objectifying is groundless. It rests on a disregard for the phenomena and betrays a deficiency in critical judgment.

Ad (c) What does speaking mean? Does language consist only in transforming what is thought into sounds, which one perceives only as objectively ascertainable tones and sounds? Or is the audible articulation of speaking (in conversation) already something quite different from a sequence of acoustically objectifiable tones, which are charged with a meaning by means of which Objects are discussed? Is speaking in its ownmost being not a saying, a manifold showing of that which hearing, i.e., the obedient attention to that which appears, lets be said? If we only bring this painstakingly into view, can one then still uncritically assert that speaking as speaking is already objectifying and always so? If we offer [*zusprechen*] consolation to one who is ill and touch [*ansprechen*] him in his inmost self, do we turn this person into an Object? Is language really only an instrument which we use to manipulate Objects? Does language stand at man's disposal at all? Is language only a work of man? Is man that being who has language in his possession? Or is it language, which "has" man insofar as language is where he belongs, which first discloses world to him and simultaneously his dwelling in the world?

Ad (d) Is every thinking a speaking and every speaking a thinking? On the basis of the questions discussed thus far we have already been directed toward the supposition that this conjunction (identity) of thinking and speaking is actual. This identity is attested from antiquity in that λογος and λεγειν at once mean: talking and thinking. But this identity is even not yet adequately discerned and appropriately experienced. A major obstacle lurks in the fact that the Greek interpretation of language, viz., the grammatical, was oriented to the assertion about the things. The things were later re-interpreted as Objects by modern metaphysics. The erroneous opinion thereby suggested itself that thinking and speaking refer to Objects and only to Objects.

If, however, we catch sight of the true state of affairs, viz., that thinking in every instance is a letting-be-said of that which shows itself and is accordingly a cor-responding [*Entsprechen*] (saying) to that which shows itself, then it must become evident in how far even poetizing is a thinking saying, an insight which, however, can not be determined in its own being by the traditional logic of the assertion about Objects. It is precisely the insight into the conjunction of thinking and saying that permits the recognition of the untenability and arbitrariness of the thesis that thinking and speaking as such of necessity are objectifying.

Ad (e) In what sense are thinking and speaking objectifying, in what sense are they not?

Thinking and speaking are objectifying, i.e., positing something given as Object in the field of scientific-technological representing [*Vorstellen*]. In this context they are necessary because this mode of perception is forced to posit its theme in advance as a calculable, causally explicable object [*Gegenstand*], i.e., as Object [*Objekt*] in the Kantian sense. Outside of this field thinking and speaking are by no means objectifying.

Today, however, the danger exists and is growing that the scientific-technological mode of thinking is expanding to all areas of life. The false impression that all thinking and speaking were objectifying is thereby enhanced. The thesis in which this is maintained dogmatically and without basis on its part aids and abets the fateful tendency to represent everything solely in a technological-scientific way as an Object of possible control and manipulation. At the same time language itself and its destiny is now affected by this process of unbounded technological objectification. Language is distorted into an instrument of reporting and calculable information. It is treated like a manipulatable Object, to which the mode of thinking must conform itself. But the saying of language is not necessarily an expression of statements *about* Objects. In its ownmost nature it is a saying *of* that which reveals and addresses itself to man in multifarious ways, to the extent that he does not close himself to that which shows itself, by restricting himself to the predominance of objectifying thinking.

That thinking and speaking are objectifying only in a derivative and delimited sense can never be scientifically deduced by means of proofs. The very being of thinking and saying can only be apprehended in an unbiased sighting of the phenomena.

Thus it may very well be an error to think that being can be attributed only to that which can be calculated and proved scientifically and technologically as Object in an objective way. This erroneous opinion is unmindful of a word uttered long ago, a word which Aristotle penned (Metaphysics IV, 4, 1006a 6ff.):

εστι γαρ απαιδευσια το μη γιγνωσχειν
τινων δει ζητειν αποδειξιν χαι τινων ου οει-

"Thus it is lack of culture not to perceive with respect to what things it is necessary to seek proofs and with respect to what things it is not necessary."

Pursuant to the suggestions given above, the following can be said with respect to the *third* theme, viz., the decision about the extent to which the theme of the consultation presents a genuine problem:

On the basis of the reflections upon the *second* theme, the way of posing the problem for the consultation must come to expression less ambiguously. In a deliberately pointed formulation it must read: "The problem of a non-scientific, non-technological thinking and speaking in contemporary theology."

It is easy to notice from this appropriate transformation that the problem as posed is not a genuine problem insofar as it is oriented to a presupposition the nonsense of which is apparent to everyone. Theology is not a natural science.

But behind the stated problem lurks the positive task for theology, viz., to discuss, within its own bounds, the bounds of the Christian faith, and out of faith's very essence, what it has to think and what it has to speak. This task at the same time includes the question of whether theology can still be a science, since it is probably not able to be a science at all.

CHAPTER FOUR

THE PROBLEM OF NATURAL THEOLOGY*
by John Macquarrie

The story of the decline and fall of natural theology is too well known
to need any long telling. There was a time when most theologians and
many philosophers believed that it is possible to demonstrate by rational argument the existence and beneficence of God, and some other
matters of religious concern as well, such as the immortality of the soul.
The proofs might be *a priori*, as in the case of St. Anselm's famous
ontological argument, or *a posteriori*, as in the case of St. Thomas'
equally famous Five Ways; but in any case it was supposed that one
might begin from premises that would be accepted by any rational
person, and go on from there to demonstrate by strict argument that
the fundamental convictions of religion are true. Thus there was laid
the foundation of a rational or natural theology, on which might be
raised the superstructure of revealed theology. And clearly, revealed
theology did derive support from this foundation of natural theology;
for if it could indeed be demonstrated that there is a beneficent God
and that man has an eternal destiny, then it would become almost
inherently probably that this God would go on to bring to men a fuller,
saving knowledge of himself, as revealed theology claims that he has
done.

But along came modern philosophy, bringing with it the criticisms
of Hume and Kant and their successors. The traditional arguments
were shown to be defective at various points. It began to seem as if
man can have no certain knowledge of anything that transcends the
world of natural phenomena. The traditional natural theology melted
away under increasingly stringent philosophical criticism. A typical

*Used with permission from the *Pittsburg Perspective*, Vol. V, No. 4, Pittsburg, Pennsylvania,
December 1964. First given as a lecture at the Institute for Social and Religious Studies,
New York.

contemporary philosophical attitude to the question is well expressed by Bertrand Russell, who writes:

> Ever since Plato, most philosophers have considered it part of their business to produce "proofs" of immortality and of the existence of God. They have found fault with the proofs of their predecessors—St. Thomas rejected St. Anselm's proofs, and Kant rejected Descartes'—but they have supplied new ones of their own. In order to make their proofs seem valid, they have had to falsify logic, to make mathematics mystical, and to pretend that deep-seated prejudices were heaven-sent intuitions.[1]

Russell rejects all this, and so too do a great many contemporary philosophers. Many theologians also have become convinced of the futility of natural theology, and they are left with revealed theology suspended somewhat perilously in mid-air, as it were, with its ancient support pulled out from beneath it.

There are, of course, still philosophical theologians who are prepared to fight a rearguard action on the natural theology front, and sometimes to fight it very brilliantly. One thinks, for instance, of F. R. Tennant's attempted rehabilitation of the teleological argument in his *Philosophical Theology;* or of Austin Farrer's restatement of the cosmological argument in *Finite and Infinite;* or of Pierre Teilhard de Chardin's persuasive endeavor in *The Phenomenon of Man* to argue from the empirical facts of terrestrial evolution to theistic conclusions. These restatements are not to be lightly dismissed, and they succeed in avoiding some at least of the weaknesses that had been exposed in earlier formulations. Yet these new statements of the arguments are still beset by the basic logical difficulty of arguing from empirical data to trans-empirical conclusions. Their authors are themselves prepared to concede that they do not claim for these arguments the cogency that was supposed to belong to the traditional proofs, but at most a measure of probability. A great many people, while prepared to acknowledge the ingenuity of some of the contemporary restatements, are not convinced that at bottom this ingenuity can really overcome the deepseated sickness of natural theology. So in spite of all efforts to rejuvenate it, it continues to languish.

There is, of course, another school of theology which frankly allies itself with anti-metaphysical philosophy in rejecting all natural theology as a mistaken endeavor. This school welcomes the downfall of natural theology and happily occupies itself with the revealed theology that has been left, so to speak, suspended midway between heaven and earth. One may recall Hume's jibe that so long as the philosopher is saying things that lend support to religious faith, the theologian will make him his ally; but as soon as he begins to say things that go against faith, the theologian suddenly remembers that the perverted "wisdom of this world" is only a snare and a delusion, and imcomparable with that heavenly wisdom to which he himself claims access through a divine revelation. This heavenly wisdom, we are told, needs no confirmation from the puny efforts of the philosopher or apologist; and more than that, it could not get support from such a source since it is quite incommensurable with any merely human wisdom.

The school which I have in mind is, of course, that of Karl Barth and his followers. One may recall Barth's early debate with Brunner, in which he angrily rejected the possibility of any natural theology, even the very meager kind which Brunner was prepared to allow. Whatever other changes may have taken place in Barth's thinking over the years, he has been consistent in this matter. There is no way from man to God, no way by which the human mind can rise to the knowledge of divine truth. This is not only because, as the anti-metaphysical philosophers would also say, man is essentially limited in his powers of knowing; it is also because of his fallen condition, which, it is alleged, has so perverted his intellect that any thought of God at which he might arrive could be nothing other than an idolatrous projection of his own reprobate mind. So the knowledge of God is found in revelation alone—and for Barth this means one specific revelation, the Christian biblical revelation.

Barth's insistence on revelation is surely well taken, and more will be said about revelation in the sequel. One might sympathize too with his sturdy defense of theological autonomy. But he goes to extremes in claiming that the knowledge of God is an isolated and even an arbitrary matter, given only in a specific revelation that is discontinuous with all that we can know through either common sense of philosophy. This encapsulation of the knowledge of God may be one way of rendering it invulnerable against the encroachments of secular philosophy, but it gives a security that is too dearly purchased and that is in addition a false security. It is in some ways reminiscent of the procedure of the ostrich which is said to hide its head in the sand. If a belief in God is worth holding, it cannot be an arbitrary matter, but must stand in continuity with all our beliefs and be compatible with them. There is sound common sense in the remark of a Scottish theologian of a generation ago, W. P. Paterson:

> It is not natural, and it may even be thought a psychological anomaly, that the same mind should be able to oscillate between the doubts of the sceptical philosopher and the childlike trustfulness of the humble believer.[2]

Paterson did not mean that there can be no alternation between faith and doubt, for this would obviously be false. What he did have in mind was the position represented by the Ritschlians in his day and by the Barthians in ours that were it not for the Christian revelation we would have no grounds for believing in God. Paterson rightly calls this position an "anomaly," which is a more forthright and accurate description of it than our contemporary jargon which talks euphemistically of "paradox." It is significant that one can think of a number of more or less prominent persons who have tried to combine a sceptical positivistic outlook in philosophy with a Barthian type of faith in an absolute, unique divine revelation, and who sooner or later have found intolerable the tension of this double-think (for I cannot describe it otherwise) and have passed into open atheism.

So we are in something of a dilemma. Little success seems to have been achieved by those who have sought to revive the fortunes of traditional natural theology, but even less attractive is the alternative presented by the Barthians of abandoning natural theology altogether and contenting ourselves with a revelation that is as odd as a rock in the sky. The challenge that confronts us in this situation is to construct a new natural theology—one which may be so new that it would be better to drop the old expression "natural theology" and call it perhaps simply "philosophical theology." I am firmly convinced that something of this kind is very much needed, and that we have been gravely misled by the tendency in recent times to evade the problems of philosophical theology and to talk as if biblical theology and biblical categories were all that is required. "There is a great deal of talk," writes H. E. Root, "about biblical categories, as though to claim their existence made it unnecessary to ask whether they were adequate for whatever it is they are supposed to express."[3] This quotation comes from an essay with the significant title "Beginning All Over Again," in which he shows that the sickness of natural theology is not just an academic concern but one of the factors that has contributed to making theology so utterly remote from and irrelevant to the secularized intelligence of our time.

The first step towards any reconstruction of natural theology—if we may for the present continue to use the expression—would be to get a clear idea of what its basic function is. At first glance, it might seem easy to state this function. Surely it is obvious that the basic function of natural theology is to demonstrate the reality of those matters about which the theologian speaks, that is to say, its business is to prove the existence of God, the immortality of the soul, and whatever else may be thought to be required as a presupposition of revealed theology.

But if this is indeed the basic function of natural theology, then we seem to be driven back to the position where we have to reject it. And this rejection will rest, in turn, not only on the criticism of the traditional arguments by modern philosophy but even more importantly on weighty theological reasons. There are several of these.

For one thing, contemporary theologians are perhaps more acutely aware than their predecessors of the radical finitude of human existence. It belongs to the very essence of such an existence that it must be lived in ambiguity and risk. Some philosophers have talked about the "thrownness" of human existence, by which they mean that man finds himself thrown into a world which he sees only from within and from the limited standpoint which he occupies. He has to decide about his life without having certitude about whence he comes or whither he goes and without having prevision of where the policies that he adopts will lead. Faith, or it may be unfaith, is a fundamental characteristic of what it means to exist as a human being. To demand the security of proof, of demonstrable answers to the ultimate questions of life, is to reject the essential finitude of our existence, indeed to reject our humanity and to demand that we should be not men but perhaps angels or gods. This is not to deny that to the best of our ability we must exercise our minds upon these problems, so that whatever faith we hold will be a reasonable faith, not in the sense of one that can be rationally demonstrated (in which case it would no longer be a faith), but in the sense of one that has been tested in the light of all the other knowledge and experience we have at our disposal. But we would never attain to anything like the certainty of logical demonstration. As Bishop Butler well said, "Probability is the guide of life."

For another thing, contemporary theologians very properly doubt whether God could possibly be the subject of a deductive argument. The traditional proofs, or at least the *a posteriori* ones, endeavor to proceed from the existence of one entity to that of another. But can we really think of God in this way? Whatever may be meant by talking of the "existence of God," the expression must have a very different logical status from what is meant when we talk, say, of the "existence" of a subatomic particle which might have to be postulated to account for some physical phenomenon or other.

It may be the case, however, that the obvious answer to the question about the basic function of natural theology is not the correct answer at all. Like so many answers that are claimed to be obvious or self-evident, this one may simply appear obvious because of long established assumptions which break down as soon as we examine them. Perhaps the basic function of natural theology is something quite different from offering a proof, and that it is due only to the operation of certain historical and cultural factors in the Western world that our traditional natural theology has in fact been formulated in terms of a logical demonstration.

Here we may notice that a number of contemporary writers have tried to introduce a new look into the traditional natural theology. Their approach is quite different from that of the thinkers mentioned earlier who sought to restate the arguments in a form that would escape the more damaging philosophical criticisms. The men whom we now have in mind have tried to let us see the traditional arguments in a different light, so that they are read no longer as logical demonstrations, but as having a different function. H. H. Price, for instance, maintains that the proofs of God's existence are not deductive arguments from premises that would be accepted by all rational men, but function rather as "analyses or clarifications of propositions which religious persons antecedently believe."[4] Perhaps the word "propositions" comes unfortunately here, but at any rate the general tenor of this remark is important. The proofs, it is being suggested, are not really proofs but are rather like that reflective and critical examination of our faith which was already mentioned in connection with the idea of a reasonable faith. Various interpretations can be put upon John Wisdom's parable

of the garden in his essay "Gods,"[5] but the suggestion there also seems
to be that the tracing of rival patterns by the theist and the atheist is
not something that starts cold, as it were, from a neutral observation
of the data, but rather each man is looking for features of the world
that would be relevant to the conviction that he already holds, although
whatever he finds will never be conclusive and the total picture will
remain ambiguous.

Of interest too are the remarks of the Catholic theologian, Karl
Adam. He insists that natural theology "is specifically different from
any profane inquiry, as for instance an investigation into the habits of
insects." By "specifically different," we must suppose that he means
that there is a difference in the logic of the two inquiries. This, I think,
comes out clearly in Adam's further remarks, which I quote in summary fashion:

> The conditional, finite imperfect character of our being gives the religious
> inquiry this specific character. The fact that there is an Absolute is not the
> laborious product of speculative philosophy, but rather the mediate conse-
> quence of a dispassionate consideration of my being. I do not stand on the
> same level with the Absolute, and so my mental attitude towards this Absolute
> must have a moral and religious character, that is to say, it must be char-
> acterized by humility, reverence, purity and love. When the inquiry is not
> based on this moral foundation, when a man enters upon it in full autonomy
> and with purely profane instincts, as though it were a purely indifferent ques-
> tion and one which did not concern man's vital interests, or even as though
> he were judge and God a suspected defendant, then he is sadly misconceiving
> the very basis of his being, and in a wholly inadmissible fashion making him-
> self absolute.[6]

No more than in the case of the other writers cited need we commit
ourselves to everything that Adam says here, but he is surely right in
pointing to the specific difference of natural theology from argument
concerning empirical matters of fact, and in finding this *differentia* in
what he calls the "moral foundation" of the inquiry in the very being
of man himself.

Of course, someone may object that those who are trying to give
the traditional natural theology a new look and to read it in a different
way from that in which we usually take it are simply making the best
of a bad job and trying to retrieve something from the wreckage. This
is doubtful for it could be argued that the words "reason" and "rational" had a much wider connection in the Middle Ages than they possess
today, and that only from the time of Descartes has there arisen the
modern and relatively narrow conception of rationalism, taking as its
model or paradigm mathematical reasoning. But however St. Thomas
and other thinkers of an earlier period thought of these matters, there
is no question that to modern minds the proofs can hardly be read as
anything but proofs or attempted proofs of the same order as proofs
concerning matters of empirical fact, and this must be counted another
weakness in them, for it now seems that they may really be saying one
thing while misleadingly appearing to say another thing.

Has this discussion brought us any nearer to finding an answer to our question about the basic function of natural theology? I think it has. It first of all confirms us in our rejection of the obvious answer to the question, namely, that the business of natural theology is to demonstrate the truth of the presuppositions of revealed theology. But beyond that, it points to a positive role for natural theology. This may be a more modest role than that of supplying a demonstration, but it is none the less a vital one, and one more truly in accord both with our understanding of man as a being who must live in risk and ambiguity, and with our understanding of God as not just another entity who somehow stands alongside the entities that we know within the world. This positive role which, I believe, has always been the basic function of natural theology, even when this function was obscured, is that of providing a solid link between the convictions that belong to religion, and the convictions that we derive from other sources. Or we might express the same idea in terms that would be more fashionable in contemporary philosophy by saying that the function of natural theology is to explore the connections between ordinary language and religious language. Those who have intempertately rejected all natural theology because they thought of it in terms of offering a proof have missed its basic function, and so they find themselves in the curious position of clinging to a revelation that has been set adrift from everything else. In this connection, we can see the truth in Root's claim that the decline of natural theology has been one factor contributing to the increasing irrelevance of all theology in the eyes of the world.

In one respect, the new type of natural theology visualized here would be more fundamental than the old type; for it would go behind the traditional proofs to the prior conviction of the reality of God which, it would seem, everyone who has ever attempted to prove God already had. Its approach, however, would be by way of description rather than by ways of demonstration, phenomenological rather than deductive. The aim would be to elucidate the kind of situations out of which the fundamental religious convictions arise. This procedure would involve the abolition of the traditional distinction between truths of reason and truths of revelation. It may well be the case that Barth is right in holding that all knowledge of God is revealed, that is to say, that in any experience in which man believes himself to attain such knowledge, the initiative is from the side of the divine. Where Barth is wrong is in trying to restrict this to one revelation or series of revelations. The aim of a natural theology in the new style would be to explore the conditions of a revelatory situation in general, on the assumption that there may be many such revelations. Perhaps the expression "general revelation" is unfortunate, since obviously every revelation has its own particular character, but the aim of natural theology would be to show that openness to the intimations of the divine is characteristic of human existence as such. It could not, of course, prove that any revelatory experience is valid, and the attempt to do so would be a lapse back into the old style of natural theology and a departure from the descriptive method. But a careful description of the revelatory situation makes clear what conditions would have to be fulfilled for this experience to be a valid one, and so makes it clear how probable or improbable we might think the claims of such an experience are.

The motivation of the new style natural theology would be much the same as that of the old. This motivation is twofold. On the one hand, for the man who already holds a religious conviction, its reflective and critical procedures lead in the direction of a reasonable faith, in the sense already explained, a faith that is firmly integrated with all the other convictions that the man may hold. Such reasonable faith contrasts with faith in a free-floating revelation, for this latter kind of faith lacks and may indeed despise the links which the other has with so-called "secular" knowledge; and lacking these, the faith that relies on a pure revelation may easily pass into mere superstition. On the other hand, there is also the apologetic motive, the interpretation of faith to the man who is without it. This, as it seems to me, can be better done by a descriptive type of natural theology than it was ever done by the old demonstrative type. It is doubtful if many people were ever brought to a religious faith by the traditional proofs of God's existence. Even if these proofs were taken as valid, they point to something much less than the God of religious faith. But the descriptive approach demands a kind of participation in a way that a purely intellectual argument does not, and could be the means of lighting up for the person to whom it is addressed the revelatory situation.

The starting-point for the new-style natural theology must be man himself—the experience of existing as a human being in the world which all of us have at first hand. Natural theology will describe the structure of this existence: its finitude, its responsibility, its frustrations, anxieties, discontents, its quest for wholeness and liberation. It is in terms of such universal experiences that the revelatory situation must be described and its claims discussed. It is in terms of this universal experience, too, that there can be brought into focus the contrast between the religious and the non-religious attitudes to life. The old style natural theology at least appeared to point up this contrast in terms of what one believed about supersensible entities or what might be our fate after death. The new style will show that the contrast has to do with our life here and now.

This new-style theology must be expressed in an entirely secular language. It must rigorously exclude from its descriptions specifically religious words such as "sin," "faith," "redemption," and even the word "God." Since its function is to provide a bridgehead from ordinary experience and ordinary language into the meaning of religion, it obviously cannot use religious words until it has provided a framework within which the meanings of these words may be indicated. To this end, it must explore the concepts and vocabulary of contemporary philosophy in search of descriptions in secular terms of those features of human existence in which religion and *a fortiori* theology have their roots. And if religion is indeed something that has to do with the center of life, then it should not be too difficult to find the required words. Even so theological an idea as revelation has its parallel in Heidegger's conception of "primordial thinking." Only in the last chapter of our natural theology can the specifically religious words be introduced, and only then because we have in terms of universally accessible experiences set up a framework within which these words can find a place and within which they can function meaningfully.

I have presented only a bare outline of how I conceive that a natural theology might be constructed, and its detailed working out would be a more difficult matter. That it is possible in principle, I do not doubt. My main endeavor, however, has been to show the necessity and the urgency of reconstruction in this field. Let me end with a quotation from John E. Smith's Dudleian Lecture on "The Permanent Truth in the Idea of Natural Religion":

> A religious tradition which seeks to insulate itself from all connection with man's general experience and knowledge on the supposition that God is not to be measured by the wisdom of this world, not only shows impiety toward the divine creation but also runs the risk of losing its very life. The history of religion is filled with examples of causes lost because their proponents believed it possible to preserve their ancient wisdom from all contaminating contact with insights derived from general experience and secular knowledge. A rational religion cannot afford to make that mistake.[7]

FOOTNOTES

1. *A History of Western Philosophy*, p. 863.
2. *The Nature of Religion*, p. 6.
3. *Soundings*, ed. A. R. Vidler, p. 12.
4. *Some Aspects of the Conflict Between Science and Religion*, p. 18.
5. *Philosophy and Psychoanalysis*, pp. 149-68.
6. *The Spirit of Catholicism*, p. 54.
7. *The Harvard Theological Review*, LIV/1, p. 19.

PART TWO:

THE HUMANIST
PERSPECTIVE

INTRODUCTION

Although there is almost always a great deal of diversity amongst the thinkers who make up any school of thought or ideological perspective, in the case of humanism this is especially true. Those who write from the humanistic perspective draw upon an exceptionally large variety of sources for their inspiration and direction, and thus they have fewer themes in common. Moreover, humanistic writers are to be found within a great number of different disciplines, all writing for differenct purposes, thereby making the pinpointing of common emphases all the more difficult. In spite of these difficulties, an effort must be made to sketch out some broad themes which could be said to characterize many, if not most, thinkers writing from within a humanistic perspective. Three main themes will be discussed, the first having to do with focus and the second and third having to do with methodology.

Like existentialism, humanism can be said to concern itself primarily with the priority of values in human existence. More specifically, humanist thinkers seek to extol and cultivate those creative and beneficent characteristics which distinguish mankind from all other forms of earth life. Drawing upon the insights and vitality of the Greco-Roman world, humanism "came of age" at the opening of the modern era, during the Renaissance and Enlightenment periods. Since that time it has received its greatest impetus for growth from the rise of modern science. Its chief concern has become the application of logical methodology and scientific knowledge to the task of developing a truly wise view of life and a truly beneficent society.

Some humanists focus their attention on man's ethical existence, and this gives them much in common with existentialists. Perhaps the one factor which distinguishes them from existentialists is their concern for rationality. Humanists tend to be far more concerned with being "reasonable" than are existentialists. Often, though not always, they are more optimistic than existentialists, as well. Some humanists, on the other hand, focus their attention on what might be termed an onto-logical approach to human existence. While not ignoring ethical questions, these writers would maintain that what is needed is a total worldview within which man's place can be ascertained more effectively. For this reason, some humanists have much in common with certain traditional metaphysicians.

Nearly all humanistic thinkers are of the opinion that their way of viewing the human situation is superior to that which has been advocated by traditional, organized religion. In one way or another, humanists see religion as the embodiment of mankind's higher aspirations. There is a basic difference, however, between those who think that religion ought to be *replaced* by humanism and those who argue that religion ought simply to be *reduced* to humanism. The former might be called "militant humanism" while the latter might be called "mitigated humanism." The difference is primarily one of methodology.

Militant humanists argue that while religious genius often expresses humanistic values, it is almost invariably imprisoned within the structures of orthodox dogma and conservative social ethics, which ultimately do more to harm personality and society than they do to help it. It is maintained that history abounds with evidence to the effect that religion has always been the enemy of human progress, whether in the field of education, social reform, or science. The obvious conclusion which is said to follow from this evidence is that religion needs to be replaced by a humanistic worldview which progressively seeks human welfare. This form of humanism also often argues that religious beliefs are almost exclusively superstitious and irrational. Much effort is expended arguing against the traditional beliefs of organized religion in an attempt to free mankind from such retrogressive beliefs. A classical example of a militant humanist from an age other than our own is Karl Marx, who provides a good motto for this branch of humanism: "religion is the opiate of the people."

The mitigated humanist, on the other hand, takes a somewhat different tack. He argues that although traditional and organized religion has often stood in the way of human advancement, for the most part it represents man's highest aspirations and has often made a significant contribution to social achievement. What is needed is not the abolition of religion, but its reformation. Whereas militant humanism regards religion as an enemy, mitigated humanism regards it as a misguided ally. It is instructive to note, however, that both brands of humanism tend to define themselves in contrast to religion, especially theistic religion.

Given this understanding of the relation between humanism and religion, the mitigated humanists set about to show, by means of philosophical and psycho-socio analysis, that religion actually reduces to humanism in the long run. There is here an awareness that aspirations and dreams of mankind will always express themselves in ways which are concrete and corporate, thus tending to become superstitious and binding rather than liberating and ennobling. Because of this inevitability, it is useless to attempt to irradicate religion. What must be done, it is argued, is to maintain constant vigilance with respect to religious beliefs and practices, by way of pointing out their humanistic values and reforming their dehumanizing limitations. One extreme example of mitigated humanism, taken again from another century, is the work of Auguste Comte, the father of positivistic philosophy and modern sociology. Comte actually sought to set up a humanistic religion in which the latter term was, in fact, reduced to the former term. Man's desire to worship was focused on his own "better" self—his own dreams and aspirations.

The selections which now follow exhibit most of the themes and brands of humanism discussed above. Moreover, at least one or two of them express themes which would justify placing them in another category altogether. Nonetheless, all of the writers included have exerted a profound influence upon contemporary philosophical and religious thought, and thus deserve to be studied for their own sake. In addition, however, they all deserve to be studied because they represent a perspective on the relation between philosophy and religion which is increasingly popular in our day.

It could, of course, be argued that Albert Camus' essay belongs in the existentialist section of this book. At the same time, as a reading of the essay will make clear, Camus' brand of existentialism is highly personal, ethical, and anti-metaphysical in the traditional sense. Moreover, his over-all position, as reflected in his novels, is that of humanism. Eric Fromm's interpretation of religion is as well known as it is provocative, and in the selections reprinted here his distinction between "authoritarian" and "humanistic" religion is central. The theme that religion is in reality an expression of man's aspirations is clearly expressed. The more rationalistic approach to humanism is presented in Bertrand Russell's "Why I Am Not a Christian," although the ethical thrust can hardly be said to be lacking. In sum, Russell finds traditional religion—and especially Christianity—an offense to both reason and moral sensitivity. He is clearly a "militant" humanist. Sidney Hook, on the other hand, provides an excellent and sympathetic, if "mitigated," analysis of the thought of existentialist and humanist thinkers alike in his "The Quest for 'Being'." Hook endeavors to sift out what he takes to be the real value of such a quest from its confusing and unproductive aspects.

CHAPTER FIVE

METAPHYSICAL REBELLION*

by Albert Camus

Metaphysical rebellion is the means by which a man protests against his condition and against the whole of creation. It is metaphysical because it disputes the ends of man and of creation. The slave protests against the condition of his state of slavery; the metaphysical rebel protests against the human condition in general. The rebel slave affirms that there is something in him which will not tolerate the manner in which his master treats him; the metaphysical rebel declares that he is frustrated by the universe. For both of them it is not only a problem of pure and simple negation. In fact in both cases we find an assessment of values in the name of which the rebel refuses to accept the condition in which he finds himself.

The slave who opposes his master is not concerned, let us note, with repudiating his master as a human being. He is repudiating him as master. He denies his right to deny him, as a slave, by making excessive demands. The master fails to the extent that he does not respond to a demand that he ignores. If men cannot refer to common values, which they all separately recognize, then man is incomprehensible to man. The rebel demands that these values should be clearly recognized as part of himself because he knows or suspects that, without them, crime and disorder would reign in the world. An act of rebellion seems to him like a demand for clarity and unity. The most elementary rebellion, paradoxically, expresses an aspiration to order.

This description can be applied, word for word, to the metaphysical rebel. He attacks a shattered world to make it whole. He confronts the injustice at large in the world with his own principles of justice. Thus all he originally wants is to resolve this contradiction and establish a reign

*Used with permission from *The Rebel*, translated by Anthony Bower, A. A. Knopf, Inc., New York, New York, 1954.

of justice, if he can, or of injustice if he is driven to the end of his tether. Meanwhile he denounces the contradiction. Metaphysical rebellion is the justified claim of a desire for unity against the suffering of life and death—in that it protests against the incompleteness of human life, expressed by death, and its dispersion, expressed by evil. If a mass death sentence defines man's condition then rebellion, in one sense, is its contemporary. When he refuses to recognize his mortality, the rebel simultaneously refuses to recognize the power that makes him live in this condition. The metaphysical rebel is, therefore, certainly not an atheist, as one might think him, but inevitably he is a blasphemer. He simply blasphemes, primarily in the name of order, by denouncing God as the origin of death and as the supreme disillusionment.

Let us return to the rebel slave to clear up this point. By protesting, he established the existence of the master against whom he rebelled. But, at the same time, he demonstrated that his master's power was dependent on his own subordination and he affirmed his own power: the power of continually questioning the superiority of his master. In this regard master and slave are in the same boat; the temporary sway of the former is as relative as the latter's submission.

At the moment of rebellion, the two forces assert themselves alternately, until the time comes for them to attempt to destroy each other and one or other temporarily disappears.

In the same way, if the metaphysical rebel ranges himself against a power whose existence he simultaneously affirms, he only admits the existence of this power at the very instant when he calls it into question. And then he draws this superior power into the same humiliating adventure as himself—the power being equally as ineffectual as our condition. He subjects it to the power of our refusal, bends it to the unbending part of human nature, forcibly integrates it into an existence which we render absurd and finally drags it from its refuge outside time and involves it in history—very far from the eternal stability that it can only find in the unanimous consent of all men. Thus rebellion affirms that, on this level, any superior being is contradictory if nothing else.

And so the history of metaphysical revolt cannot be confused with that of atheism. From one angle, it is even identified with the contemporary history of religious sentiment. The rebel defies more than he denies. Originally, at least, he does not deny God, he simply talks to Him as an equal. But it is not a polite dialogue. It is a polemic animated by the desire to conquer. The slave starts by begging for justice and ends by wanting to wear a crown. He too wants to dominate. His insurrection against his condition is transformed into an unlimited campaign against the heavens for the purpose of capturing a king who will first be dethroned and finally condemned to death. Human rebellion ends in metaphysical revolution. It progresses from appearances to facts, from dilettantism to revolutionary commitment. When the throne of God is overthrown, the rebel realizes that it is now his own responsibility to create the justice, order and unity that he sought in vain within his own condition and, in this way, to justify the fall of God. Then begins the desperate effort to create, at the price of sin if necessary, the dominion of man. This cannot come about without appalling consequences of which we are only, so far, aware of a few. But these consequences are in no way due to rebellion itself or, at least, they only occur to the extent that rebellion forgets its original purpose, tires of the tension caused by its positive and negative attitude and finally abandons itself to complete negation or total submission. Metaphysical insurrection in its primary stages offers us the same positive content as the slave's rebellion. Our task is to examine what becomes of this positive content of rebellion in the actions that it entails and to point out the path where the rebel is led by his fidelity or infidelity to the origins of his revolt.

THE SONS OF CAIN

Metaphysical revolt, in the proper sense, does not appear in any coherent form in the history of ideas until the end of the eighteenth century: modern times begin with the crash of falling ramparts. But, from this moment on, its consequences develop uninterruptedly and it is no exaggeration to say that they have shaped the history of our times. Historically speaking, the first coherent offensive is Sade's, who musters, into one vast war machine, the arguments of the free-thinkers up to Voltaire and Father Meslier. Naturally, his is also the most extreme negation of all. From rebellion, Sade can only deduce an absolute negative. Twenty-seven years in prison do not, in fact, produce a very conciliatory form of intelligence. Such a lengthy confinement makes a man either a weakling or a killer—or sometimes both. If the mind is strong enough to construct, in a prison cell, a moral philosophy which is not one of submission, it will generally be one of domination. Every ethic conceived in solitude implies the exercise of power. In this respect Sade is the archetype, for in so far as society treated him atrociously he responded in an atrocious fashion. The writer, despite a few happy phrases and the unconsidered praises of contemporary critics, is secondary. He is admired to-day, with so much ingenuity, for reasons which have nothing to do with literature.

He is exalted as the philosopher in chains and the first theoretician of absolute rebellion. He might well have been. In prison, dreams have no limits and reality is no curb. Intelligence in chains loses in lucidity what it gains in intensity. The only logic known to Sade was the logic of his feelings. He did not create a philosophy, he pursued a monstrous dream of revenge. Only the dream turned out to be prophetic. His desperate claim to freedom led Sade into the kingdom of servitude; his inordinate thirst for a form of life he could never attain was assuaged in the successive frenzies of a dream of universal destruction. In this way, at least, Sade is our contemporary. Let us follow the steps of his successive negations.

A Man of Letters

Is Sade an atheist? He says so, we believe, before he goes to prison in his *Dialogue between a Priest and a Dying Man;* and from then on we are staggered by his passion for sacrilege. One of his cruellest characters, Saint-Fond, does not in any sense deny God. He is content to develop a gnostic theory of a wicked demiurge and to draw the suitable conclusions from it. Saint-Fond, we remark, is not Sade. Of course not. A character is never the writer who created him. However, there are occasions when a writer is all his characters simultaneously. Now, all Sade's atheists admit the non-existence of God, on principle, for the obvious reason that His existence would imply that He was indifferent, wicked or cruel. Sade's greatest work ends with a demonstration of the stupidity and spite of the divinity. The innocent Justine runs through the storm and Noirceul, the criminal, swears to be converted if her life is spared by the divine anger (the celestial thunderbolt). Justine is struck by lightning. Noirceul triumphs and human sin continues to be man's answer to divine sin. And so there is a libertine wager in answer to the Pascalian wager.

The idea of God that Sade conceives for himself is, thus, of a criminal divinity who oppresses and denies mankind. That murder is a divine attribute is quite apparent from the history of religions. Why, then, should men be virtuous? Sade's first step as a prisoner is to jump to the most extreme conclusions. If God kills and repudiates mankind there is nothing to stop one repudiating and killing one's fellow-men. This angry challenge in no way resembles the tranquil negation which is still to be found in the *Dialogue* of 1782. The man who exclaims: 'I have nothing, I am nothing' and who concludes 'No, no, virtue and vice are indistinguishable in the tomb' is neither happy nor tranquil. The conception of God is the only thing, according to him, 'for which man cannot be forgiven.' The word 'forgiven' sounds strange in the mouth of this expert in torture. But it is himself whom he cannot forgive for a conception that his desperate view of the world, and his condition as a prisoner, completely refute. A double rebellion—against the order of things and against himself—is the guiding principle of Sade's reasoning. As this double revolt is self-contradictory except in the agitated mind of a victim, his reasoning is always either ambiguous or legitimate according to whether it is judged in the light of logic or in an effort to be compassionate.

He repudiates man and his morality, because God repudiates them both. But he repudiates God even though He has served as his accomplice and guarantor up to now. For what reason? Because of the strongest instinct to be found in someone who is condemned by his hatred for mankind to live behind prison walls: the sexual instinct. What is this instinct? On the one hand, it is the ultimate expression of nature and, on the other, the blind force which demands the total subjection of human beings, even at the price of their destruction.

Sade denies God in the name of nature (the ideological conceptions of his time presented it in mechanistic form) and makes nature a power bent on destruction. For him, nature is sex; his logic leads him to a lawless universe where the only master is the inordinate energy of desire. This is his impassioned kingdom, where he finds his finest means of expression: 'What are all the creatures of the earth in comparison to a single one of our desires!' The long processes of reasoning by which Sade's heroes demonstrate that nature has need of crime, that it must destroy in order to create and that thus we help it to create from the moment that we embark on self-destruction, are only aimed at creating an absolute liberty for Sade, the prisoner, who is too unjustly repressed not to long for the explosion that will blow everything sky high. In this, he goes against his times: the freedom that he demands is not one of principles but of instincts.

Sade dreamed, no doubt, of a universal republic, whose scheme he reveals through his wise reformer, Zamé. He shows us, by this means, that one of the aims of rebellion is the liberation of the entire world—in so far as rebellion is less and less willing to recognize limits as its demands become more pressing. But everything about him contradicts this pious dream. He is no friend of humanity, he hates philanthropists. The equality of which he sometimes speaks is a mathematical concept: the equivalence of the objects that comprise the human race, the abject equality of the victims. What drives him on, what makes him want to dominate everything, his real accomplishment, is hatred. Sade's republic is not founded on liberty but on libertinism. 'Justice,' this peculiar democrat writes, 'has no real existence. She is the divinity of all the passions.'

Nothing is more revealing, in this respect, than the famous lampoon, read by Dolmance in the *Philosophie du Boudoir* and which has the curious title: *People of France, one more effort if you want to be republican!* Pierre Klossowski is right in attaching so much importance to it, for this lampoon demonstrates to the revolutionaries that their republic is founded on the murder of the King—who was King by divine right—and that by guillotining God on January 21, 1793, they deprived themselves, forever, of the right to proscribe crime or to censure wicked instincts. The monarchy supported the conception of a God who, in conjunction with itself, created all laws. As for the Republic, it stood alone and morality was supposed to exist without benefit of the Commandments. However, it is doubtful if Sade, as Klossowski would have it, was profoundly convinced that this was a sacrilege and that an almost religious horror led him to the conclusions that he expresses. It is much more likely that he had already come to these conclusions and that afterwards he perceived the correct arguments to justify the absolute licence of morals that he wanted to impose on the government of his time. Logic founded on passions reverses the traditional sequence of reasoning and places the conclusion before the premises. To be convinced of this we only have to appreciate the admirable sequence of sophisms by which Sade, in this passage, justifies calumny, theft and murder and demands that they be tolerated in the New World.

However, it is then that his thoughts are most penetrating. He rejects, with exceptional perspicacity for his times, the presumptuous alliance of freedom with virture. Freedom, particularly when it is a prisoner's dream, cannot endure limitations. It must embrace crime or it is no longer freedom. On this essential point, Sade never varies. This man who never preached anything but contradictions only achieves coherence—and of a most complete kind—when he talks of capital punishment. An addict of refined ways of execution, a theoretician of sexual crime, he was never able to tolerate legal crime. 'My imprisonment, with the guillotine under my very eyes, was far more horrible to me than all the Bastilles imaginable.' From this feeling of horror he drew the strength to be moderate, publicly, during the terror, and to intervene generously on behalf of his mother-in-law, despite the fact that she had had him imprisoned. A few years later, Nodier summed up, without knowing it perhaps, the position obstinately defended by Sade: 'To kill a man in a paroxysm of passion is understandable. To have him killed by someone else after serious meditation and on the pretext of a duty honourably discharged is incomprehensible.' Here we find the germ of an idea which will be further developed by Sade: he who kills must pay in kind. Sade is more moral, we see, than our contemporaries.

But his hatred for the death penalty is, at first, no more than a hatred for the men who are sufficiently convinced of their own virture to dare to inflict capital punishment, when they themselves are criminals. You cannot simultaneously choose crime for yourself and punishment for others. You must open the prison gates or give an impossible proof of your own innocence. From the moment you accept murder, even if only once, you must allow it universally. The criminal who acts according to nature cannot, without prevarication, range himself on the side of the law. 'One more effort if you want to be republicans' means: 'Accept the freedom of crime, the only reasonable step, and enter forever into a state of insurrection as you enter into a state of grace.' Thus total submission to evil leads to an appalling penitence which cannot fail to horrify the Republic of enlightenment and natural goodness. By a significant coincidence, the manuscript of *One Hundred and Twenty Days of Sodom* was burned during the first riot of the Republic which could hardly fail to denounce Sade's heretical theories of liberty and to throw so compromising a supporter into prison once more. By doing so it gave him the regrettable opportunity of developing his rebellious logic still further.

The universal republic could be a dream for Sade, but never a temptation. In politics, his real position is cynicism. In his *Society of The Friends of Crime*, he declares himself ostensibly in favour of government and its laws which he, meanwhile, has every intention of violating.

It is the same impulse which drives the lowest criminals to vote for the conservative candidate. The republic of crime cannot, for the moment at least, be universal. It must pretend to obey the law. However, in a world that knows no other rule but murder, beneath a criminal heaven, and in the name of a criminal nature, Sade, in reality, obeys no other law but that of inexhaustible desire. But to desire without limit comes to accepting being desired without limit. Licence to destroy supposes that you yourself can be destroyed. Thus you must struggle and dominate. The law of this world is nothing but the law of strength; its driving force the will to power.

The advocate of crime really only respects two kinds of power: one, which he finds in his own class, founded on the accident of birth, and the other by which, through sheer villainy, an underdog raises himself to the level of the libertines of noble birth whom Sade makes his heroes. This powerful little group of initiates know that they have all the rights. Anyone who doubts, even for a second, in his formidable privileges, is immediately driven from the flock, and once more becomes a victim. Thus a sort of aristocratic morality is created where a little group of men and women entrench themselves above a caste of slaves because they withhold the secret of a strange knowledge. The only problem, for them, consists in organizing themselves for the complete exercise of their rights which have the terrifying scope of desire.

They cannot hope to dominate the entire universe until the law of crime has been accepted by the universe. Sade never even believed that his own nation could be capable of the additional effort which would make it 'republican.' But if crime and desire are not the law of the entire universe, if they do not reign at least over a specified territory, they are no longer unifying principles, but ferments of conflict. They are no longer the law and man returns to chaos and confusion. Thus it is necessary to create, from all these fragments, a world which coincides exactly with the new law. The need for unity, which Creation never satisfies, is fulfilled, at all costs, in a microcosm. The law of force never has the patience to await complete control of the world. It must fix the boundaries, without delay, of the territory where it holds sway, even if it means surrounding it with barbed wire and observation towers.

For Sade, the law of force implies barred gates, castles with seven-foot walls from which it is impossible to escape, and where a society founded on desire and crime functions unimpeded, according to an implacable system. Unbridled rebellion, insistence on complete liberty, lead to the subjection of the majority. Man's emancipation is fulfilled, for Sade, in these strongholds of debauchery where a kind of bureaucracy of vice rules over the life and death of the men and women who have entered, forever, the hell of their desires. His works abound with descriptions of these privileged places where feudal libertines, to demonstrate to their assembled victims their absolute impotence and servitude, always resume the Duc de Blangis' speech to the common people of the *One Hundred and Twenty Days of Sodom:* 'You are already dead to the world.'

Sade, likewise, occupied the tower of Freedom, but in the Bastille. Absolute rebellion took refuge with him in a sordid fortress from which none, neither persecuted nor persecutors, could ever escape. To establish his liberty, he had to create absolute necessity. Unlimited liberty of desire implies the negation of others and the suppression of pity. The heart, that 'weak spot of the intellect,' must be exterminated: the locked room and the system will take its place. The system, which plays a role of capital importance in Sade's fabulous castles, sanctifies a universe of mistrust. It helps to anticipate everything so that no unexpected tenderness or pity occurs to upset the plans for complete enjoyment. It is a curious kind of pleasure, no doubt, which obeys the commandment 'We shall rise every morning at ten o'clock . . . !' But enjoyment must be prevented from degenerating into attachment, it must be put in parentheses and tempered. Objects of enjoyment must also never be allowed to appear as persons. If a man is an 'absolutely material species of plant,' he can only be treated as an object and as an object for experiment. In Sade's fortress republic, there are only machines and mechanics. The system, which dictates the method of employing the machines, puts everything in its right place. His infamous convents have their rule—significantly copied from that of religious communities. Thus the libertine indulges in public confession. But the process is changed: 'If his conduct is pure, he is censured.'

Sade, as was the custom of his period, constructed ideal societies. But, contrary to the custom of his period, he codifies the natural wickedness of mankind. He meticulously constructs a citadel of force and hatred—pioneer that he is—even to the point of calculating mathematically the freedom he succeeded in destroying. He sums up his philosophy with an unemotional accounting of crimes: 'Massacred before the first of March: 10. After the first of March: 20. To come: 16. Total: 46.' A pioneer, no doubt, but a limited one, as we can see.

If that were all, Sade would not be worthy of the interest that attaches to all misunderstood pioneers. But once the drawbridge is up, life in the castle must go on. No matter how meticulous the system, it cannot foresee every eventuality. It can destroy, but it cannot create. The masters of these tortured communities do not find the satisfaction that they covet. Sade often evokes the 'charming habit of crime.' Nothing here, however, seems very charming—more like the fury of a man in chains. The point is to enjoy oneself, and the maximum of enjoyment coincides with the maximum of destruction. To possess what one is going to kill, to copulate with suffering—those are the moments of freedom towards which the entire organization of Sade's castles is oriented. But from the moment when sexual crime destroys the object of desire, it also destroys desire which exists only at the precise moment of destruction. Then another object must be brought under subjection and killed, and then another, and so on to an infinity of all possible objects. Thus occurs the depressing and dense accumulation of erotic and criminal scenes in Sade's novels, which leaves the reader with a paradoxical memory of a hideous chastity.

What part, in this universe, could pleasure play or the exquisite joy of acquiescent and accomplice bodies? In it we find an impossible quest for escape from despair—a quest which finishes, nevertheless, in a desperate race from servitude to servitude and from prison to prison. If only nature is real and if, in nature, only desire and destruction are legitimate, then, in that all humanity does not suffice to assuage the thirst for blood, the path of destruction must lead to universal annihilation. We must become, according to Sade's formula, nature's executioner. But even that position is not achieved too easily. When the accounts are closed, when all the victims are massacred, the executioners are left face to face in the deserted castle. Something is still missing. The tortured bodies return, in their elements, to nature and will be born again. Even murder cannot be fully consummated: 'Murder only deprives the victim of his first life: a means must be found of depriving him of his second . . .' Sade contemplates an attempt against nature: 'I abhor nature . . . I would like to upset its plans, to thwart its progress, to halt the stars in their courses, to overturn the floating spheres of space, to destroy what serves nature and to succour all that harms it; in a word, to insult it in all its works, and I cannot succeed in doing so.' It is in vain that he dreams of a technician who can pulverize the universe: he knows that, in the dust of the spheres, life will continue. The attempt against creation is doomed to failure. It is impossible to destroy everything, there is always a remainder. 'I cannot succeed in doing so . . .' the icy and implacable universe suddenly relents at the appalling melancholy by which Sade, in the end and quite unwillingly, always moves us. 'When crimes of passion no longer measure up to our intensity, we could, perhaps, attack the sun, deprive the universe of it, or use it to set fire to the world—those would be real crimes . . .' Crimes, yes, but not the definitive crime. It is necessary to go farther; the executioners eye each other with suspicion.

They are alone, and one law alone governs them—the law of power. Since they accepted it when they were masters they cannot reject it if it turns against them. All power tends to be unique and solitary. One must kill again and again: the masters will destroy each other in their turn. Sade accepts this consequence and does not flinch. A curious kind of stoicism derived from vice sheds a little light in the dark places of his rebellious soul. He will not try to live again in the world of affection and compromise. The drawbridge will not be lowered and he will accept personal annihilation. The unbridled force of his rejection, at its extremity, achieves an unconditional consent which is not without nobility. The master consents to be the slave in his turn and even, perhaps, wishes to be. 'The scaffold would be for me the throne of voluptuousness.'

Thus the greatest degree of destruction coincides with the greatest degree of affirmation. The masters throw themselves on one another and

Sade's work, dedicated to the glory of libertinism, ends by being 'strewn with corpses of libertines struck down at the height of their powers.' The most powerful, the one who will survive, is the solitary, the unique, whose glorification Sade has undertaken—in other words himself. At last he reigns supreme, master and God. But at the moment of his greatest victory, the dream vanishes. The Unique turns back towards the prisoner whose unbounded imagination gave birth to him and they become one. In fact he is alone, imprisoned in a blood-stained Bastille, entirely constructed around a still unsatisfied, and henceforth undirected, desire for pleasure. He has only triumphed in a dream and these ten volumes crammed with philosophy and atrocities recapitulate an unhappy spiritual experience, an illusory advance from the final no to the absolute yes, an acquiescence in death at last, which transfigures the assassination of everything and everyone into a collective suicide.

Sade was executed in effigy; he, too, only killed in his imagination. Prometheus ends his days as Onan. Sade is still a prisoner when he dies, but this time in a lunatic asylum, acting plays on an improvised stage with other lunatics. A derisory equivalent of the satisfaction that the order of the world failed to give him was provided for him by dreams and by creative activity. The writer, of course, has no need to refuse himself anything. For him, at least, boundaries disappear and desire can be allowed free reign. In this respect, Sade is the perfect man of letters. He created a fable in order to give himself the illusion of existing. He put 'the moral crime which is committed by writing' above everything else. His incontestable merit lies in having immediately demonstrated, with the unhappy perspicacity of accumulated rage, the extreme consequences of a rebel's logic—at least when it forgets its true origins. These consequences are an hermetic totalitarianism, universal crime, an aristocracy of cynicism and the desire for an apocalypse. They will be found again many years after his death. But having tasted them, he was caught, it seems, on the horns of his own dilemma and he could only escape the dilemma in literature. Strangely enough, it is Sade who sets rebellion on the path of literature down which it will be led still farther by romanticism. He himself is one of those writers of whom he says 'their corruption is so dangerous, so active, that they have no other aim in printing their monstrous works but to extend beyond their own lives the sum-total of their crimes; they can commit no more, but their accursed writings will lead others to do so, and this comforting thought which they carry with them to the tomb consoles them for the obligation which death imposes on them of renouncing this life.' Thus his rebellious writings bear witness to his desire for survival. Even if the immortality he longs for is the immortality of Cain, at least he longs for it, and despite himself bears witness to what is most true in metaphysical rebellion.

Moreover, even his followers compel us to do him homage. His heirs are not all writers. Of course he suffered and died to stimulate imagination in the right circles and in literary cafes. But that is not all.

Sade's success in our day is explained by the dream that he had in common with contemporary thought: the demand for total freedom and dehumanization coldly planned by the intelligence. The reduction of man to an object of experiment, the rule which specifies the relation between the will to power and man as an object, the sealed laboratory which is the scene of this monstrous experiment, are lessons which the theoreticians of power will learn again when they have to organize the age of slavery.

Two centuries ahead of time and on a reduced scale, Sade extolled totalitarian societies in the name of unbridled freedom—which, in reality, rebellion does not desire. With him really begin the history and the tragedy of our times. He only believed that a society founded on the freedom of crime must coincide with freedom of morals, as though servitude had its limits. Our times have only gone as far as to blend, in a curious manner, his dream of a universal republic and his technique of degradation. At last, what he hated most, legal murder, has availed itself of the discoveries that he wanted to put to the service of impulsive murder. Crime, which he wanted to be the exotic and delicious fruit of unbridled vice, is no more, to-day, than the dismal habit of a police-controlled morality. Such are the surprises of literature.

The Dandy's Rebellion

Even after Sade's time, men of letters still continue to dominate the scene. Romanticism, with its satanic rebellion, serves only for adventures of the imagination. Like Sade, romanticism is separated from earlier forms of rebellion by its perference for evil and for the individual. By putting emphasis on its powers of defiance and refusal, rebellion, at this stage, forgets its positive content. Since God claims all that is good in man, it is necessary to deride what is good and choose what is evil. Hatred of death and of injustice will lead, therefore, if not to the exercise at least to the vindication of evil and murder.

The struggle between Satan and death in *Paradise Lost,* the favourite poem of the romantics, symbolizes this drama; all the more profoundly in that death (and, of course, sin) is the child of Satan. In order to combat evil, the rebel renounces good, because he considers himself innocent, and once again gives birth to evil. The romantic hero first of all brings about the profound and, so to speak, religious blending of good and evil.[1] This type of hero is 'fatal' because fate confuses good and evil without man being able to defend himself. Fate does not allow evaluations. It replaces them by the statement that 'It is so'—which excuses everything, with the exception of the Creator who alone is responsible for this scandalous state of affairs. The romantic hero is also 'fatal' because, to the extent that he increases in power and genius, the power of evil increases in him. Every manifestation of power, every excess is thus covered by this 'It is so.' That the artist, particularly the poet, should be demoniac, is a very ancient idea which is formulated, provocatively, in the work of the romantics. At this period, there is even a demoniac imperialism whose aim is to annex everything, even the orthodox genius. 'What made Milton write with constraint,' Blake observes, 'when he spoke of angels and of God, and with audacity when he spoke of demons and of hell, is that he was a real poet and on the side of the demons, without knowing it.' The poet, the genius, man himself in his most exalted image, therefore cry out simultaneously with Satan: 'So farewell hope, and with hope farewell fear, farewell remorse . . . Evil, be thou my good.' It is the cry of outraged innocence.

The romantic hero, therefore, considers himself compelled to do evil by his nostalgia for impracticable good. Satan rises against his creator because the latter employed force to subjugate him. 'Whom reason hath equal'd,' says Milton's Satan, 'force hath made above his equals.' Divine violence is thus explicitly condemned. The rebel flees from this aggressive and unworthy God, 'Farthest from him is best,' and reigns over all the forces hostile to the divine order. The Prince of Darkness has only chosen this path because good is a notion defined and utilized by God for unjust purposes. Even innocence irritates the Rebel in so far as it implies being duped. This 'dark spirit of evil who is enraged by innocence' creates a human injustice parallel to divine injustice. Since violence is at the root of all creation, deliberate violence shall be its answer. An excess of despair adds to the causes of despair and brings rebellion to that state of contemptible debility which follows the long experience of injustice and where the distinction between good and evil finally disappears. Vigny's Satan can

> . . . no longer find in good or evil any pleasure
>   nor of the sorrow that he causes take the measure.

This gives a definition of nihilism and authorizes murder.

Murder, in fact, is on the way to becoming attractive. It is enough to compare the Lucifer of the renaissance painters with the Satan of the romantics. An adolescent 'young, sad, charming' (Vigny) replaces the horned beast. 'Beautiful, with a beauty unknown on this earth' (Lermontov), solitary and powerful, unhappy and scornful, he is off-hand even in oppression. But his excuse is sorrow. 'Who here,' says Milton's Satan, 'will envy whom the highest place . . . condemns to greatest share of endless pain.' So many injustices suffered, a sorrow so unrelieved, justify every excess. The rebel can therefore allow himself certain advantages. Murder, of course, is not recommended for its own sake. But it is implicit in the value—supreme for the romantic— attached to frenzy. Frenzy is the reverse of boredom: Lorenzaccio dreams of Han of Iceland. Exquisite sensibilities evoke the elementary furies of the beast. The Byronic hero, incapable of love, or only capable of an impossible love, suffers endlessly. He is solitary, languid, his condition exhausts him. If he wants to feel alive, it must be in the terrible exaltation of a brief and destructive action. To love someone whom you will never see again is to love like a flame and to cry out for self-annihilation into the bargain. One lives only in and for the moment, in order to achieve

> the brief and vivid union
> of a tempestuous heart united to the tempest.
>
> (Lermontov.)

The threat of mortality which hangs over us sterilizes everything. Only the cry of anguish can bring us to life; exaltation takes the place of truth. To this extent, the apocalypse becomes an absolute value in which everything is confounded—love and death, conscience and culpability. In a topsy-turvy universe no other life exists but that of the abyss where, according to Alfred Le Poittevin, human beings come 'trembling with rage and exulting in their crimes' to curse the Creator. The intoxication of frenzy and, ultimately, crime reveal, in a moment, the whole meaning of a life. Without exactly advocating crime, the romantics insist on paying homage to a basic system of revenge which they illustrate with the conventional images of the outlaw, the criminal with the heart of gold, and the kind brigand. Their works are bathed in blood and shrouded in mystery. The soul is delivered, at minimum expenditure, of its most hideous desires—desires which will later be assuaged in extermination camps. Of course these works are also a challenge to the society of the times. But romanticism, at the source of its inspiration, is chiefly concerned with defying moral and divine law. That is why its most original creation is not primarily the revolutionary, but logically enough the dandy.

Logically, because this obstinate persistence in satanism can only be justified by the endless affirmation of injustice and, to a certain extent, by its consolidation. Pain, at this stage, is only acceptable on condition that it is incurable. The rebel chooses the metaphysic of 'expecting the worst,' which is expressed in the literature of damnation from which we have not yet escaped. 'I was conscious of my power and I was conscious of my chains' (Petrus Borel). But these chains are valuable objects. Without them it would be necessary to prove, or to exercise, this power which, after all, one is not very sure of having. It is only too easy to end up by becoming a government employee in Algiers, and Prometheus, like the above-mentioned Borel, will devote the rest of his days to closing the cabarets and reforming colonial morals. All the same, every poet to be received into the fold must be damned. Charles Lassailly, the same one who planned a philosophic novel *Robespierre and Jesus Christ*, never went to bed without uttering several fervent blasphemies to give himself courage. Rebellion puts on mourning and exhibits itself for public admiration. Much more than the cult of the individual, romanticism inaugurates the cult of the 'character.' It is at this point that it is logical. Hoping no longer for the rule or unity of God, determined to take up arms against an antagonistic destiny, anxious to preserve everything of which the living are still capable in a world dedicated to death, romantic rebellion looked for a solution in the attitude it assumed. The attitude brought together, in aesthetic unity, all mankind who were in the hands of fate and destroyed by divine violence. The human being who is condemned to death is, at least, magnificent, before he disappears, and his magnificence is his justification. It is an established fact, the only one that can be thrown in the petrified face of the God of Hate. The impassive rebel does not flinch before the eyes of God. 'Nothing,' says Milton, 'will change this determined mind, this high disdain born of an offended conscience.' Everything is drawn or rushes towards the void, but even though man is humiliated, he is obstinate and at least preserves his pride. A baroque romantic, discovered by Raymond Queneau, claims that the aim of all intellectual life is to become God. This genuine romantic is a little ahead of his time. The aim, at that time, was only to equal God and remain on His level. He is not destroyed, but by incessant effort He is never submitted to. Dandyism is a degraded form of asceticism.

The dandy creates his own unity by aesthetic means. But it is an aesthetic of singularity and of negation. 'To live and die before a mirror': that, according to Baudelaire, was the dandy's slogan ... It is a coherent slogan, at any rate. The dandy is, by occupation, always in opposition. He can only exist by defiance. Up till now, man derived his coherence from his Creator. But from the moment that he consecrates his rupture with Him, he finds himself delivered over to the fleeting moment, to the passing days and to wasted sensibility. Therefore he must take himself in hand. The dandy rallies his forces and creates a unity for himself by the very violence of his refusal. Disoriented, like all people without a rule of life, he is coherent as a character. But a character implies a public; the dandy can only play a part by setting himself up in opposition. He can only be sure of his own existence by finding it in the expression of others' faces. Other people are his mirror. A mirror that quickly becomes obscured, it is true, since human capacity for attention is limited. It must be ceaselessly stimulated, spurred on by provocation. The dandy is, therefore, always compelled to astonish. Singularity is his vocation, excess his way to perfection. Perpetually incomplete, always on the margin of things, he compels others to create him, while denying their values. He plays at life because he is unable to live it. He plays at it until he dies, except for the moments when he is alone and without a mirror. For the dandy, to be alone is not to exist. The romantics only talked so grandly about solitude because it was their real horror, the one thing they could not bear. Their rebellion thrusts its roots deep, but from the Abbé Prevost's *Cleveland* up to the time of the Dadaists—including the frenetics of 1830 and Baudelaire and the decadents of 1880—more than a century of rebellion was completely satiated by the audacities of 'eccentricity.' If they all were able to talk of unhappiness it is because they despaired of ever being able to conquer it, except in futile comedies, and because they instinctively felt that it remained their sole excuse and their real claim to nobility.

That is why the heritage of romanticism was not claimed by Victor Hugo, peer of the realm, but by Baudelaire and Lacenaire, poets of crime. 'Everything in this world exudes crime,' says Baudelaire, 'the newspaper, the walls and the face of man.' Nevertheless crime, which is the law of nature, singularly fails to wear a distinguished air. Lacenaire, the first of the gentleman criminals, exploits it effectively; Baudelaire displays less tenacity but is a genius. He creates the garden of evil where crime only figures as one of the rarer species. Terror itself becomes an exquisite sensation and a collector's item. 'Not only would I be happy to be a victim, but I would not even hate being an executioner in order to *feel* the revolution from both sides.' Even Baudelaire's conformity has the odour of crime. If he chose Maistre as his master, it is to the extent that this conservative goes as far as he can and centres his doctrine on death and on the executioner. 'The real saint,' Baudelaire pretends to think, 'is someone who flogs and kills people for their own good.' His argument will be heard. A race of real saints is beginning to spread over the earth for the purpose of confirming these curious conclusions about rebellion. But Baudelaire, despite his satanic arsenal, his taste for Sade, his blasphemies, remains too much of a theologian to be a real rebel. His real drama, which made him the greatest poet of his time, was something else. Baudelaire can only be cited here to the extent that he was the most profound theoretician of dandyism and gave definite form to one of the conclusions of romantic rebellion.

Romanticism demonstrates, in fact, that rebellion is part and parcel of dandyism: one of its objectives is outward appearances. In its conventional forms, dandyism admits a nostalgia for ethics. It is only honour degraded as a point of honour. But at the same time it inaugurates an aesthetic which is still valid in our world, an aesthetic of solitary creators, who are obstinate rivals of a God they condemn. From romanticism onward, the artist's task will not only be to create a world, or to exalt beauty for its own sake, but also to define an attitude. Thus the artist becomes a model and offers himself as an example: art is his ethic. With him begins the age of the directors of conscience. When the dandies fail to commit suicide or do not go mad, they make a career and pursue prosperity. Even when, like Vigny, they exclaim that they are going to keep quiet, their silence is piercing.

But at the very heart of romanticism, the sterility of this attitude becomes apparent to a few rebels who provide a transitional type between the eccentrics and our revolutionary adventurers. Between the days of the eighteenth-century eccentric and the 'adventurers' of the twentieth century, Byron and Shelley are already fighting, however ostentatiously, for freedom.

THE REJECTION OF SALVATION

If the romantic rebel exalts evil and the individual, he does not do so on behalf of mankind, but merely on his own behalf. Dandyism, of whatever kind, is always dandyism in relation to God. The individual, in so far as he is created being, can oppose himself only to the Creator. He has need of God with whom he carries on a kind of baleful intrigue. Armand Hoog rightly says that, despite the Nietzschean atmosphere of such works, God is not yet dead in them. The damnation, so clamorously demanded, is only a clever trick played on God. But with Dostoievski the account of rebellion goes a step farther. Ivan Karamazov sides with mankind and stresses human innocence. He affirms that the death sentence which hangs over them is unjust. Far from making a plea for evil, his first impulse, at least, is to plead for justice which he ranks above divinity. He does not absolutely deny the existence of God. He refutes Him in the name of a moral value. The romantic rebel's ambition was to talk to God as man to man. Here evil was the answer to evil, pride the answer to cruelty. Vigny's ideal, for example, is to answer silence with silence. Obviously, the point is to raise oneself to the level of God, and that is already blasphemy. But there is no thought of disputing the power or position of the deity. The blasphemy is reverent, since every blasphemy is, ultimately, a participation in holiness.

With Ivan, however, the tone changes. God is put on trial, in His turn. If evil is essential to divine creation, then creation is unacceptable. Ivan will no longer have recourse to this mysterious God, but to a higher principle, namely justice. He launches the essential undertaking of rebellion, which is that of replacing the reign of grace by the reign of justice. Simultaneously, he begins the attack on Christianity. The romantic rebels broke with God for being the fountainhead of hate. Ivan explicitly rejects mystery and, consequently, God as the fountainhead of love. Only love can make us consent to the injustice done to Martha, to the exploitation of workers, and, to go a step farther, to the death of innocent children.

'If the suffering of children,' says Ivan, 'serves to complete the sum of suffering necessary for the acquisition of truth, I affirm from now onwards that truth is not worth such a price.' Ivan rejects the profound relationship, introduced by Christianity, between suffering and truth. Ivan's most profound utterance, the one which opens the deepest chasms beneath the rebel's feet, if his *even if:* 'I would persist in my indignation, even if I were wrong.' Which means that even if God existed, even if the mystery cloaked a truth, even if Zosime were right, Ivan would not admit that truth should be paid for by evil, suffering, and the death of innocents. Ivan incarnates the refusal of salvation. Faith leads to immortal life, but faith presumes the acceptance of the mystery and of evil and resignation to injustice. The man who is prevented by the suffering of children from accepting faith will certainly not accept eternal life. Under these conditions, even if eternal life existed, Ivan would refuse it. He rejects this bargain. He would only accept grace unconditionally and that is why he makes his own conditions. Rebellion wants all or nothing. 'All the knowledge in the world is not worth a child's tears.' Ivan does not say that there is no truth. He says that if truth does exist it can only be unacceptable. Why? Because it is unjust. The struggle between truth and justice is brought into the open for the first time—and it will never end. Ivan, by nature a solitary and therefore a moralist, will satisfy himself with a kind of metaphysical Don Quixotism. But a few decades more and a huge political conspiracy will attempt to prove that justice is truth.

In addition, Ivan is the incarnation of the refusal to be the only one saved. He throws in his lot with the damned, and for their sake rejects eternity. If he had faith, he could, in fact, be saved but others would be damned and suffering would continue. There is no possible salvation for the man who feels real compassion. Ivan will continue to put God in the wrong by doubly rejecting faith as he would reject injustice and privilege. One step more and from *All or Nothing* we arrive at *All or No one*.

This extreme determination, and the attitude that it implies, would have sufficed for the romantics. But Ivan[1] even though he also gives way to dandyism, really lives his problems, torn between the negative and the affirmative. From this moment onwards, he accepts the consequences. If he rejects immortality, what remains for him? Life in its most elementary form. When the meaning of life has been suppressed, there still remains life. 'I live,' says Ivan, 'in spite of logic.' And again: 'If I no longer had any faith in life, if I doubted a woman I loved, or the universal order of things, if I were persuaded, on the contrary, that everything was only an infernal and accursed chaos—even then, I would want to live.' Ivan will live, then, and will love as well 'without knowing why.' But to live is also to act. To act in the name of what? If there is no immortality, then there is neither reward nor punishment. 'I believe that there is no virtue without immortality.' And also: 'I only know that suffering exists, that no one is guilty, that everything is connected, that everything passes and equals out.' But if there is no virtue, there is no law: 'All is permitted.'

With this 'all is permitted' the history of contemporary nihilism really begins. Romantic rebellion did not go so far. It was content with saying, in short, that everything was not permitted but that, through insolence, it allowed itself to do what was forbidden. On the other hand, with the Karamazovs the logic of indignation turned rebellion against itself and confronted it with a desperate contradiction. The essential difference is that the romantics allowed themselves to be complacent, while Ivan compelled himself to do evil so as to be coherent. He would not allow himself to be good. Nihilism is not only despair and negation, but above all the desire to despair and to negate. The very man who so violently took the part of innocence, who trembled at the suffering of a child, who wanted to see 'with his own eyes' the lamb lie down with the lion, the victim embrace his murderer, from the moment that he rejects divine coherence and tries to discover his own rule of life, recognizes the legitimacy of murder. Ivan rebels against a murderous God; but from the moment that he begins to consider the reasons for his rebellion, he deduces the law of murder. If all is permitted, he can kill his father or at least allow him to be killed. Long reflection on our condition as people sentenced to death only leads to the justification of crime. Ivan simultaneously hates the death penalty (describing an execution, he says ferociously: 'His head fell, in the name of divine grace') and condones crime, in principle. Every indulgence is allowed the murderer, none is allowed the executioner. This contradiction, which Sade swallowed with ease, chokes Ivan Karamazov.

He pretends to reason as though immortality did not, in fact, exist, while he only goes so far as to say that he would refuse it if it did exist. In order to protest against evil and death, he deliberately chooses to say that virtue exists no more than does immortality and to allow his father to be killed. He consciously accepts his dilemma; to be virtuous and illogical, or logical and criminal. His double, the devil, is right when he whispers: 'You are going to commit a virtuous act and yet you do not believe in virtue, that is what angers and torments you.' The question which Ivan finally poses, the question which constitutes the real progress achieved by Dostoievski in the history of rebellion, is the only one we are interested in here: can one live and hold one's ground in a permanent state of rebellion?

Ivan allows us to guess his answer: one can only live in a permanent state of rebellion by pursuing it to the bitter end. What is the bitter end of metaphysical rebellion? Metaphysical revolution. The master of the world, after his legitimacy has been contested, must be overthrown. Man must occupy his place. 'As God and immortality do not exist, the new man is permitted to become god.' But what does becoming god mean? To recognize any other law but one's own. Without it being necessary to develop the intervening arguments, we can see that to become God is to accept crime (a favourite idea of Dostoievski's intellectuals). Ivan's personal problem is then to know if he can be faithful to his logic and if, on the grounds of an indignant protest at innocent suffering, he can accept the murder of his father with the indifference of a man-god. We know his solution: Ivan allows his father to be killed. Too profound to be satisfied with appearances, too sensitive to perform the deed himself, he is content to allow it to be done. But he goes mad. The man who could not understand how one could love one's neighbour, cannot understand, either, how one can kill him. Caught between unjustifiable conceptions of virtue and unacceptable crime, consumed with pity and incapable of love, a solitary deprived of the benefits of cynicism, this man of supreme intelligence is killed by contradiction. 'My mind is of this world,' he said, 'what good is it to try to understand what is not?' But he only lived for what is not of this world, and his proud search for the absolute is precisely what removed him from the world of which he loved no part.

The fact that Ivan was defeated does not obviate the fact that once the problem is posed, the consequence must follow: rebellion has started on the path of action. This has already been demonstrated by Dostoievski, with prophetic intensity, in his legend of the Grand Inquisitor. Ivan, finally, does not separate the creator from his creation. 'It is not God whom I reject,' he says, 'it is creation.' In other words it is God the father, inseparable from what He has created. His plot to usurp the throne, therefore, remains completely moral. He does not want to re-form anything in creation. But creation being what it is, he claims the right to free himself of it morally and to free all the rest of mankind with him. On the other hand, from the moment that the spirit of rebel-lion, having accepted the concept of 'all is permitted' and 'everyone or no one,' aims at reconstructing creation in order to assert the sovereignty and divinity of man—from the moment that metaphysical rebellion extends itself from ethics to politics—a new undertaking, of incalculable import, begins, which is also born, we must note, of the same nihilism. Dostoievski, the prophet of the new religion, had fore-seen and announced it: 'If Aliosha had come to the conclusion that neither God nor immortality existed, he would have immediately be-come an atheist and a socialist. For socialism is not only a question of the working classes, it is, above all, in its contemporary incarnation, a question of atheism, a question of the tower of Babel which is con-structed without God's help, not to reach the heavens, but to bring the heavens down to earth.'

After that Aliosha can in fact treat Ivan with compassion as a 'real greenhorn.' The latter only made an attempt at self-domination and failed. Others will appear who are more serious-minded and who, on the basis of the same despairing nihilism, are going to demand to rule the world. These are the Grand Inquisitors who imprison Christ and come to tell Him that His is not the right method, that universal hap-piness cannot be achieved by the immediate freedom of choosing be-tween good and evil, but by the domination and unification of the world. The first step is to conquer and rule. The kingdom of heaven will, in fact, appear on earth, but it will be ruled over by men—a mere handful to begin with who will be the Caesars, the ones who were the first to understand—and later, with time, by all men. The unity of all creation will be achieved by every possible means, since everything is permitted. The Grand Inquisitor is old and tired, for the knowledge he possesses is bitter. He knows that men are lazy rather than cowardly and that they prefer peace and death to the liberty of discerning between good and evil. He has pity, a cold pity, for the silent prisoner whom history endlessly deceives. He urges him to speak, to recognize his misdeeds and, in one sense, to approve the undertaking of the Inquisitors and of the Caesars. But the prisoner does not speak. The enterprise will continue, therefore, without him: he will be killed. Legitimacy will come at the end of time when the kingdom of men is assured. 'The affair has only just begun, it is far from being termi-nated, and the world has many other things to suffer, but we shall achieve our aim, we shall be Caesar, and meanwhile we shall dream of universal happiness.'

Long before that, the prisoner will have been executed: the Grand Inquisitors reign alone, listening to 'the profound spirit, the spirit of destruction and death.' The Grand Inquisitors proudly refuse freedom and the bread of heaven and offer the bread of this earth without freedom. 'Come down from the cross and we shall believe in you,' their police agents already cry on Golgotha. But He does not come down and, even, at the most tortured moment of His agony, he protests to God at having been abandoned. There are thus no other proofs but faith and the mystery that the rebels reject and the Grand Inquisitors scoff at. Everything is permitted and centuries of crime are prepared in that cataclysmic moment. From Paul to Stalin, the popes who have chosen Caesar have prepared the way for Caesars who quickly learn to despise popes. The unity of the world which was not achieved with God will, nevertheless, be attempted without Him.

But we have not yet reached that point. For the moment, Ivan only offers us the tortured face of the rebel plunged in the abyss, incapable of action, torn between the idea of his own innocence and his desire to kill. He hates the death penalty because it is the image of the human condition, and, at the same time, he is drawn to crime. For having taken the side of mankind, solitude is his lot. With him the rebellion of reason ends in madness.

ABSOLUTE AFFIRMATION

When man submits God to moral judgment, he kills Him in his own heart. And then what is the basis of morality? God is denied in the name of justice but can the idea of justice be understood without the idea of God? Have we not arrived at absurdity? It is absurdity that Nietzsche meets face to face. The better to avoid it, he pushes it to extremities: morality is the final aspect of God which must be destroyed before the period of reconstruction begins. Then God no longer exists and no longer guarantees our existence; man, in order to exist, must decide to act.

'We deny God, we deny the responsibility of God, it is only thus that we will deliver the world.' With Nietzsche, nihilism seems to become prophetic. But we can draw no conclusions from Nietzsche, except the base and mediocre cruelty that he hated with all his strength, unless we give first place in his work—well ahead of the prophet—to the diagnostician. The provisional, methodical, strategic character of his thought cannot be doubted for a moment. With him, nihilism becomes conscious for the first time. Diagnosticians have this in common with prophets—they think and operate in terms of the future. Nietzsche never thought except in terms of an apocalypse to come, not in order to extol it, for he guessed the sordid and calculating aspect that this apocalypse would finally assume, but in order to avoid it and to transform it into a renaissance. He recognized nihilism for what it was and examined it like a clinical fact.

He said of himself that he was the first complete nihilist of Europe.

Not by choice, but by condition, and because he was too great to refuse the heritage of his time. He diagnosed in himself, and in others, the inability to believe and the disappearance of the primitive foundation of all faith—namely the belief in life. The 'Can one live as a rebel?' became with him 'Can one live, believing in nothing?' His reply is in the affirmative. Yes, if one creates a system out of absence of faith, if one accepts the final consequences of nihilism, and if, on emerging into the desert and putting one's confidence in what is going to come, one feels, with the same primitive instinct, both pain and joy.

Instead of systematic doubt, he practised systematic negation, the determined destruction of everything that still hides nihilism from itself, of the idols which camouflage God's death. 'To raise a new sanctuary, a sanctuary must be destroyed, that is the law.' According to Nietzsche, he who wants to be a creator of good and of evil, must first of all destroy all values. 'Thus the supreme evil becomes part of the supreme good, but the supreme good is creative.' He wrote, in his own manner, the *Discours de la Méthode* of his period, without the freedom and exactitude of the seventeenth-century French he admired so much, but with the mad lucidity which characterizes the twentieth century which, according to him, is the century of rebellion.

Nietzsche's first step is to accept what he knows. Atheism for him goes without saying and is 'constructive and radical.' Nietzsche's superior vocation, so he says, is to provoke a kind of crisis and a final decision about the problem of atheism. The world continues on its course at random and there is nothing final about it. Thus God is useless, since He wants nothing in particular. If He wanted something, and here we recognize the traditional formulation of the problem of evil, we would have to assume Him responsible for 'a sum-total of pain and inconsistency which would debase the entire value of being born.' We know that Nietzsche was publicly envious of Stendhal's formula: 'the only excuse for God is that he does not exist.' Deprived of the divine will, the world is equally deprived of unity and finality. That is why it is impossible to pass judgment on the world. Any attempt to apply a standard of values to the world leads finally to a slander on life. Judgments are based on what is, with reference to what should be— the kingdom of heaven, eternal concepts, or moral imperatives. But what should be does not exist: and this world cannot be judged in the name of nothing. 'The advantages of our times; nothing is true, everything is permitted.' These magnificent or ironic formulae, which are echoed by thousands of others, at any rate suffice to demonstrate that Nietzsche accepts the entire burden of nihilism and rebellion. In his somewhat puerile reflections on 'training and selection' he even formulated the extreme logic of nihilistic reasoning: 'Problem: by what means could we obtain an exact definition of nihilism in its most extreme and infectious aspect which would teach and practise, with a completely scientific awareness, voluntary death?'

But Nietzsche enlists values in the cause of nihilism which, traditionally, have been considered as restraints on nihilism—principally morality. Moral conduct, as explained by Socrates, or as recommended by Christianity, is in itself a sign of decadence. It wants to substitute the mere shadow of a man for a man of flesh and blood. It condemns the universe of passion and emotion in the name of an entirely imaginary world of harmony. If nihilism is the inability to believe, then its most serious symptom is not found in atheism, but in the inability to believe in what is, to see what is happening and to live life as it is offered. This infirmity is at the root of all idealism. Morality has no faith in the world. For Nietzsche, real morality cannot be separated from lucidity. He is severe on the 'calumniators of the world' because he discerns in the calumny a shameful taste for evasion. Traditional morality, for him, is only a special type of immorality. 'It is virtue,' he says, 'which has need of justification.' And again: 'It is for moral reasons that good will, one day, cease to be done.'

Nietzsche's philosophy, undoubtedly, revolves around the problem of rebellion. More precisely, it begins by being a rebellion. But we sense the change of position that Nietzsche makes. With him, rebellion begins at 'God is dead' which is assumed as an established fact; then rebellion hinges on everything that aims at falsely replacing the vanished deity and reflects dishonour on a world which undoubtedly has no direction but which remains the only proving-ground of the gods. Contrary to the opinion of certain of his Christian critics, Nietzsche did not form a project to kill God. He found Him dead in the soul of his contemporaries. He was the first to understand the immense importance of the event and to decide that this rebellion among men could not lead to a renaissance unless it were controlled and directed. Any other attitude towards it, whether it were regret or complacency, must lead to the apocalypse. Thus Nietzsche did not formulate a philosophy of rebellion, but constructed a philosophy on rebellion.

If he attacks Christianity in particular, it is only in so far as it represents morality. He always leaves intact the person of Jesus on the one hand, and on the other the cynical aspects of the Church. We know that he admired, from the point of view of the connoisseur, the Jesuits. 'Basically,' he writes, 'only the God of morality is rejected.' Christ, for Nietzsche as for Tolstoy, is not a rebel. The essence of His doctrine is summed up in total consent and in non-resistance to evil. Thou shalt not kill, even to prevent killing. The world must be accepted as it is, nothing must be added to its unhappiness, but you must consent to suffer personally from the evil it contains. The kingdom of heaven is within our immediate reach. Not faith but deeds—that, according to Nietzsche, is Christ's message. From then on, the history of Christianity is nothing but a long betrayal of this message. The New Testament is already corrupt, and from the time of Paul until the Councils subservience to faith has led to the obliteration of deeds.

What is the profoundly corrupt addition made by Christianity to the message of its Master? The idea of judgment, completely foreign to the teachings of Christ, and the correlative notions of punishment and reward. From this moment, human nature becomes the subject of history, and significant history expressed by the idea of human totality is born. From the Annunciation until the Last Judgment, humanity has no other task but to conform to the strictly moral ends of a narrative that has already been written. The only difference is that the characters, in the epilogue, separate themselves into the good and the bad. While Christ's sole judgment consists in saying that the sins of nature are unimportant, historical Christianity makes nature the sole source of sin. 'What does Christ deny? Everything that, at the moment, bears the name Christian.' Christianity believes that it is fighting against nihilism because it gives the world a sense of direction, while it is nihilist itself in so far as it prevents, in imposing an imaginary meaning on life, the discovery of its real meaning: 'Every Church is a stone rolled onto the tomb of the man-god; it tries to prevent the resurrection, by force.' Nietzsche's paradoxical but significant conclusion is that God has been killed by Christianity, in that Christianity has secularized the sacred. Here we must understand historical Christianity and 'its profound and contemptible duplicity.'

The same process of reasoning leads to Nietzsche's attitude towards socialism and all forms of humanitarianism. Socialism is only a degenerate form of Christianity. In reality, he preserves a belief in the finality of history which betrays life and nature, which substitutes ideal ends for real ends, and contributes to enervating both the will and the imagination. Socialism is nihilistic, in the henceforth precise sense which Nietzsche confers on the word. A nihilist is not someone who believes in nothing, but someone who does not believe in what he sees. In this sense, all forms of socialism are manifestations, degraded once again, of Christian decadence. For Christianity, reward and punishment imply the truth of history. But, by inescapable logic, all history ends by implying punishment and reward; and from this day on collective Messianism is born. Similarly, the equality of souls before God leads, now that God is dead, to equality pure and simple. There again, Nietzsche wages war against socialist doctrines in so far as they are moral doctrines. Nihilism, whether manifested in religion or in socialist preachings, is the logical conclusion of our so-called superior values. The free mind will destroy these values and denounce the illusions on which they are built, the bargaining that they imply, and the crime they commit in preventing the lucid intelligence from accomplishing its mission: of transforming passive nihilism into active nihilism.

In this world rid of God and of moral idols, man is now alone and without a master. No one has been less inclined than Nietzsche (and in this way he distinguishes himself from the romantics) to allow himself to believe that such freedom would be easy. This unbridled freedom put him among the ranks of those of whom he himself said that they suffered a new form of anguish and a new form of happiness. But, at the beginning, it is only anguish which makes him cry out: 'Alas, grant me madness . . . By being above the law, I am the most outcast of all outcasts.' He who cannot stand his ground above the law, must find another law or take refuge in madness. From the moment that man believes neither in God nor in immortal life, he becomes 'responsible for everything alive, for everything that, born of suffering, is condemned to suffer from life.' It is to himself, and to himself alone, that he returns in order to find law and order. Then the time of exile begins, the endless search for justification, the nostalgia without an aim, 'the most painful, the most heart-breaking question, that of the heart which asks itself: where can I feel at home?'

Because his mind was free, Nietzsche knew that freedom of the mind is not a comfort, but an achievement that one aspires to and obtains, at long last, after an exhausting struggle. He knew that there is a great risk in wanting to consider oneself above the law, of finding oneself beneath that law. That is why he understood that the mind only found its real emancipation in the acceptance of new obligations. If nothing is true, if the world is without order, then nothing is forbidden; to prohibit an action, there must, in fact, be a standard of values and an aim. But, at the same time, nothing is authorized; there must also be values and aims in order to choose another course of action. Absolute domination by the law does not represent liberty, but nor does absolute freedom of choice. Chaos is also a form of servitude. Freedom only exists in a world where what is possible is defined at the same time as what is not possible. Without law there is no freedom. If fate is not guided by superior values, if chance is king then there is nothing but the step in the dark and the appalling freedom of the blind. At the conclusion of the most complete liberation, Nietzsche therefore chooses the most complete subordination. 'If we do not make of God's death a great renunciation and a perpetual victory over ourselves, we shall have to pay for that omission.' In other words, with Nietzsche, rebellion ends in asceticism. A profounder logic replaces the 'if nothing is true, everything is permitted' of Karamazov by 'if nothing is true, nothing is permitted.' To deny that one single thing is forbidden in this world amounts to renouncing everything that is permitted. At the point where it is no longer possible to say what is black and what is white, the light is extinguished and freedom becomes a voluntary prison.

It can be said that Nietzsche rushes, with a kind of frightful joy, towards the impasse into which he methodically drives his nihilism. His avowed aim is to render the situation untenable to his contemporaries. His only hope seems to be to arrive at the extremity of contradiction. Then if man does not wish to perish in the coils that strangle him, he will have to cut them at a single blow, and create his own values. The death of God accomplishes nothing and can only be lived through in terms of preparing a resurrection. 'If we fail to find grandeur in God,' says Nietzsche, 'we find it nowhere; it must be denied or created.' To deny was the task of the world around him which he saw rushing towards suicide. To create was the superhuman task for which he was willing to die. He knew in fact that creation is only possible in the extremity of solitude and that man would only commit himself to this staggering task if, in the most extreme distress of mind, he must undertake it or perish. Nietzsche cries out to man that his only truth is the world—to which he must be faithful and on which he must live and find his salvation. But, at the same time, he teaches him that to live in a lawless world is impossible because to live implies, explicitly, the law. How can one live freely and without law? To this enigma, man must find an answer, on pain of death.

Nietzsche, at least, does not flinch. He answers and his answer is bold: Damocles never danced better than beneath the sword. One must accept the unacceptable and contend the untenable. From the moment that it is admitted that the world pursues no end, Nietzsche proposes to concede its innocence, to affirm that it accepts no judgment since it cannot be judged on any intention, and consequently to replace all judgments based on values by absolute assent, a complete and exalted allegiance to this world. Thus, from absolute despair will spring infinite joy, from blind servitude freedom without obligation. To be free is, precisely, to abolish ends. The innocence of the ceaseless change of things, as soon as one consents to it, represents the maximum liberty. The free mind willingly accepts what is necessary. Nietzsche's most intimate concept is that the necessity of phenomena, if it is absolute, does not imply any kind of restraint. Total acceptance of total necessity is his paradoxical definition of freedom. The question 'Free of what?' is thus replaced by 'Free for what?' Liberty coincides with heroism. It is the asceticism of the great man: 'the bow bent to the breaking-point.'

This magnificent consent, born of affluence and fullness of spirit, is the unreserved affirmation of human imperfection and suffering, of evil and murder, of all that is problematic and strange in our existence. It is born of an arrested wish to be what one is in a world which is what it is. 'To consider oneself a fatality, not to wish to be other than one is . . .' The Nietzschean experiment, which is part of the recognition of fatality, ends in a deification of fate. The more implacable destiny is, the more it becomes worthy of adoration. A moral God, pity and love are enemies of fate to the extent that they try to make amends for it. Nietzsche wants no redemption. The joy of self-realization is the joy of annihilation. But only the individual is annihilated. The movement of rebellion, in which man claimed his own self, disappears in the individual's absolute submission to self-realization. *Amor fati* replaces what was an *odium fati*. 'Every individual collaborates with the entire cosmos, whether we know it or not, whether we want it or not.' The individual is lost in the destiny of the species and the eternal movement of the spheres. 'Everyone who has existed is eternal, the sea throws him back upon the shore.'

Nietzsche then returns to the origins of thought—to the pre-Socratics. The latter suppressed ultimate causes so as to leave intact the eternal values of the principles they upheld. Only power without purpose, only Heraclitus's 'strife,' is eternal. Nietzsche's whole effort is directed towards demonstrating the existence of laws which govern future events and that there is an element of chance in the inevitable: 'A child is innocence and forgetfulness, a new beginning, a gamble, a wheel which spins automatically, a first step, the divine gift of consent.' The world is divine because the world is illogical. That is why art alone, by being equally illogical, is capable of grasping it. It is impossible to give a clear account of the world, but art can teach us to reproduce it—just as the world reproduces itself in the course of its eternal gyrations. The primordial sea indefatigably repeats the same words and casts up the same astonished beings on the same sea-shore. But at least he who consents to his own return and to the return of all things, who becomes an echo and an exalted echo, participates in the divinity of the world.

By this subterfuge, the divinity of man is finally introduced. The rebel, who at first denies God, finally aspires to replace him. But Nietzsche's message is that the rebel can only become God by entirely renouncing rebellion, even the type of rebellion that produces gods to chastise humanity. 'If there is a God, how can one tolerate not being God oneself?' There is, in fact, a god . . . namely the world. To participate in his divinity, all that is necessary is to consent. 'No longer to pray, but to give one's blessing,' and the earth will abound in men-gods. To say yes to the world, to reproduce it, is simultaneously to recreate the world and oneself, to become the great artist, the creator. Nietzsche's message is summed up in the word 'creation,' with the ambiguous meaning it has assumed. Nietzsche's sole admiration was for the egotism and austerity proper to all creators. The transmutation of values consists only in replacing critical values by creative values; by respect and admiration for what exists. Divinity without immortality defines the extent of the creator's freedom. Dionysos, the earth-god, shrieks eternally as he is torn limb from limb. But at the same time he represents the agonized beauty which is the result of suffering. Nietzsche thought that to accept this earth and Dionysos was to accept his own sufferings. And to accept everything, both suffering and the supreme contradiction simultaneously, was to be king. Nietzsche agreed to pay the price for his kingdom. Only the 'sad and suffering' world is true—the world is the only divinity. Like Empedocles who threw himself down Etna to find truth in the only place where it exists, namely in the bowels of the earth, Nietzsche proposed that man should allow himself to be engulfed in the cosmos in order to rediscover his eternal divinity and to become Dionysos himself. The *Will to Power* ends, like Pascal's *Pensées* of which it so often reminds us, with a wager. Man does not yet obtain assurance but only the wish for assurance which is not at all the same thing. Nietzsche, too, hesitated on this brink: 'That is what is unforgivable in you. You have the authority and you refuse to sign.'

Yet, finally, he had to sign. But the name of Dionysos only immortal-
ized the notes to Ariadne which he wrote when he was mad.   *

In a certain sense, rebellion, with Nietzsche, ends again in the exaltation of evil. The difference is that evil is no longer a revenge. It is
accepted as one of the possible aspects of good and, with rather more
conviction, as part of destiny. Thus he considers it as something to be
avoided and also as a sort of remedy. In Nietzsche's mind, the only
problem was to see that the human spirit bowed proudly to the inevitable. We know, however, his posterity and the kind of politics that
were to be authorized by the man who claimed to be the last anti-
political German. He dreamed of tyrants who were artists. But tyranny
comes more naturally than art to mediocre men. 'Rather Cesare Borgia
than Parsifal,' he exclaimed. He begat both Caesar and Borgia, but
devoid of the distinction of feeling which he attributed to the great
men of the Renaissance. As a result of his insistence that the individual
should bow before the eternity of the species and should submerge himself in the great cycle of time, race has been turned into a special aspect
of the species and the individual has been made to bow before this
sordid god. The life of which he spoke with such fear and trembling
has been degraded to a sort of biology for domestic use. Finally a race
of vulgar overlords, with a blundering desire for power, adopted, in his
name, the 'anti-semitic deformity' on which he never ceased to pour
scorn.

He believed in courage combined with intelligence, and that was
what he called strength. Courage has been turned against intelligence
in his name; and the virtues that were really his have thus been transformed into their opposite . . . blind violence. He confused freedom and
solitude, as do all proud spirits. His 'profound solitude at midday and
at midnight' was nevertheless lost in the mechanized hordes which
finally inundated Europe. Advocate of classic taste, of irony, of frugal
defiance, aristocrat who had the courage to say that aristocracy consisted in practising virtue without asking for a reason and that a man
who had to have reasons for being honest was not to be trusted, addict
of integrity ('integrity that has become an instinct, a passion'), stub-
born supporter of the 'supreme equity of the supreme intelligence which
is the mortal enemy of fanaticism,' he was set up, thirty-three years
after his death, by his own countrymen as the master of lies and violence
and his ideas and attributes, made admirable by his sacrifice, have been
rendered detestable. In the history of intelligence, with the exception of
Marx, Nietzsche's adventure has no equivalent: we shall never finish
making reparation for the injustice done to him. Of course history
records other philosophies that have been misconstrued and betrayed.
But up to the time of Nietzsche and national socialism, it was quite
without parallel that a process of thought—brilliantly illuminated by
the nobility and by the sufferings of an exceptional mind—should have
been demonstrated to the eyes of the world by a parade of lies and by
the hideous accumulation of corpses from concentration camps. The

doctrine of the superman led to the methodical creation of sub-men —
a fact that doubtless should be denounced but which also demands interpretation. If the final result of the great movement of rebellion in
the nineteenth and twentieth centuries was to be this ruthless bondage
then surely rebellion should be rejected and Nietzsche's desperate cry
to his contemporaries taken up: 'My conscience and yours are no longer
the same conscience.'

We must first of all realize that we can never confuse Nietzsche with
Rosenberg. We must be the advocates for the defence of Nietzsche.
He himself has said so, denouncing in advance his bastard progeny,
'he who has liberated his mind still has to purify himself.' But the question is to find out if the liberation of the mind, as he conceived it, does
not preclude purification. The idea that comes to a head with Nietzsche,
and that supports him, has its laws and its logic which, perhaps, explain the bloody travesty of his philosophy. Is there nothing in his
work which can be used in support of definitive murder? Cannot the
killers, provided that they deny the spirit for the letter (and even what
still remains of the spirit in the letter), find their pretext in Nietzsche?
The answer must be yes. From the moment that the methodical aspect
of Nietzschean thought is neglected (and it is not certain that he himself always observed it) his rebellious logic recognizes no limits.

We also remark that it is not in the Nietzschean refusal to worship
idols that murder finds its justification, but in the passionate cohesion
which crowns Nietzsche's work. To say yes to everything supposes that
one says yes to murder. Moreover, it expresses two ways of consenting
to murder. If the slave says yes to everything, he consents to the existence of a master and to his own sufferings; Jesus teaches non-resistance.
If the master says yes to everything, he consents to slavery and to the
suffering of others; and the result is the tyrant and the glorification of
murder. 'Is it not laughable that we believe in a sacred, infrangible law,
thou shalt not lie, thou shalt not kill, in an existence characterized by
perpetual lying and perpetual murder?' Actually metaphysical rebellion,
in its initial stages, was only a protest against the lie and the crime of
existence. The Nietzschean affirmative, forgetful of the original negative, disavows rebellion at the same time that it disavows the ethic
which refuses to accept the world as it is. Nietzsche prayed for a Roman
Caesar with the soul of Christ. To his mind, this was to say yes to both
slave and master. But, in the last analysis, to say yes to both was to
give one's blessing to the stronger of the two, namely the master. Caesar
must inevitably renounce the domination of the mind in order to rule
in the realm of fact. 'How can one make the best of crime?' asks
Nietzsche, a good professor faithful to his system. Caesar must answer:
by multiplying it. 'When the ends are great,' Nietzsche wrote to his own
detriment, 'humanity employs other standards and no longer judges
crime as such even if it resorts to the most frightful means.' He died
in 1900, at the beginning of the century in which that statement was
to become fatal. It was in vain that he exclaimed in his hour of lucidity,

'It is easy to talk about all sorts of immoral acts; but would one have the courage to carry them through? For example, I could not bear to break my word or to kill; I should languish, and eventually I should die as a result—that would be my fate.' From the moment that assent was given to the totality of human experience, the way was open to others who, far from languishing, would gather strength from lies and murder. Nietzsche's responsibility lies in having legitimized, for worthy reasons of method—and even if only for an instant—the right to dishonour of which Dostoievski had already said that if one offered it to people one could always be sure of seeing them rushing at it. But his involuntary responsibility goes still further.

Nietzsche is exactly what he recognized himself as being: the most acute manifestation of nihilism's conscience. The decisive step that he compelled rebellion to take consists in making it jump from the negation of the ideal to the secularization of the ideal. Since the salvation of man is not achieved in God, it must be achieved on earth. Since the world has no direction, man, from the moment that he accepts this, must give it one which will lead eventually to a superior type of humanity. Nietzsche laid claim to the direction of the future of the human race. 'The task of governing the world is going to fall to our lot.' And elsewhere: 'The time is approaching when we shall have to struggle for the domination of the world, and this struggle will be fought in the name of philosophical principles.' In these words he predicted the twentieth century. But if he was able to predict it, it was because he was warned by the interior logic of nihilism and knew that one of its aims was ascendancy; and thus he prepared the way for this ascendancy.

There is freedom for man without God, as Nietzsche imagined him, in other words for the solitary man. There is freedom at midday when the wheel of the world stops spinning and man accepts things as they are. But *what is* becomes *what will be* and the ceaseless change of things must be accepted. The light finally grows dim, the axis of the day declines. Then history begins again and freedom must be sought in history; history must be accepted. Nietzschism—the theory of individual will to power—was condemned to support the universal will to power. Nietzschism was nothing without world domination. Nietzsche undoubtedly hated free-thinkers and humanitarians. He took the words 'freedom of thought' in their most extreme sense: the divinity of the individual mind. But he could not stop the free-thinkers partaking of the same historical fact as himself—the death of God—nor could he prevent the consequences being the same. Nietzsche saw clearly that humanitarianism was only a form of Christianity deprived of superior justification which preserved final causes while rejecting the first cause. But he failed to perceive that the doctrines of social emancipation must, by an inevitable logic of nihilism, lead to what he himself had dreamed of: superhumanity.

Philosophy secularizes the ideal. But tyrants appear who soon secularize the philosophies which give them their rights. Nietzsche had

already predicted this development in discussing Hegel whose origi-
nality, according to him, consisted in inventing a pantheism in which
evil, error and suffering could no longer serve as arguments against
the divinity. 'But the State, and the powers that be, immediately made
use of this grandiose initiative.' However, he himself had conceived of
a system in which crime could no longer serve as an argument against
anything and in which the only value resided in the divinity of man.
This grandiose initiative also had to be put to use. National socialism
in this respect was only a transitory heir, only the speculative and rabid
outcome of nihilism. In all other respects those who, in correcting
Nietzsche with the help of Marx, will choose to assent only to history
and no longer to all of creation will be perfectly logical. The rebel
whom Nietzsche set on his knees before the cosmos will, from now
on, kneel before history. What is surprising about that? Nietzsche, at
least in his theory of superhumanity, and Marx, before him, with his
classless society, both replace the Beyond by the Later On. In that way,
Nietzsche betrayed the Greeks and the teachings of Jesus who, according to him, replaced the Beyond by the Immediate. Marx like Nietzsche
thought in strategic terms and like Nietzsche hated formal virtue. Their
two rebellions, both of which finish similarly in adhesion to a certain
aspect of reality, end by merging into Marxism-Leninism and being in-
carnated in that caste, already mentioned by Nietzsche, which would
'replace the priest, the teacher, the doctor.' The fundamental difference
is that Nietzsche, in awaiting the superman, proposed to assent to what
exists and Marx to what is to come. For Marx nature is to be sub-
jugated in order to obey history, for Nietzsche nature is to be obeyed
in order to subjugate history. It is the difference between the Christian
and the Greek. Nietzsche at least foresaw what was going to happen:
'Modern socialism tends to create a form of secular Jesuitism, to make
instruments of all men,' and again: What we desire is well-being . . . As
a result we march towards a spiritual slavery such as has never been
seen . . . Intellectual Caesarism hovers over every activity of the business
man and of the philosophers.' Placed in the crucible of Nietzschean
philosophy, rebellion, in the folly of freedom, ends in biological or
historical Caesarism. The absolute negative had driven Stirner to defy
crime simultaneously with the individual. But the absolute affirmative
leads to universalizing murder and mankind simultaneously. Marxism-
Leninism has really accepted the burden of Nietzsche's free-will by
means of ignoring several Nietzschean virtures. The great rebel thus
creates with his own hands, and for his own imprisonment, the implacable reign of necessity. Once he had escaped from God's prison, his first
care was to construct the prison of history and of reason, thus putting
the finishing touch to the camouflage and consecration of that nihilism
whose conquest he claimed.

NIHILISM AND HISTORY

One hundred and fifty years of metaphysical revolt and of nihilism
have witnessed the persistent reappearance, under different guises, of

the same ravaged countenance: the face of human protest. All of them, decrying the human condition and its creator, have affirmed the solitude of man and the nonexistence of any kind of morality. But at the same time they have all tried to construct a purely terrestrial kingdom where their chosen principles will hold sway. As rivals of the Creator, they have inescapably been led to the point of reconstructing creation according to their own concepts. Those who rejected, for the world they had just created, all other principles but desire and power, have been driven to suicide or madness and have predicted the apocalypse. As for the rest, who wanted to create their own principles, they have chosen pomp and ceremony, the world of appearances, murder and destruction. But Sade and the romantics, Karamazov or Nietzsche only entered the world of death because they wanted to discover the true life. So that by a process of inversion, it is the desperate appeal for order that rings through this insane universe. Their conclusions have only proved disastrous or destructive to freedom from the moment that they laid aside the burden of rebellion, fled the tension that it implies and chose the comfort of tyranny or of servitude.

Human insurrection, in its exalted and tragic forms, is only, and can only be, a prolonged protest against death, a violent accusation against the universal death penalty. In every case that we have come across, the protest is always directed at everything in creation which is dissonant, opaque or promises the solution of continuity. Essentially, then, we are dealing with a perpetual demand for unity. The rejection of death, the desire for immortality and for clarity, are the main springs of all these extravagances, whether sublime or puerile. Is it only a cowardly and personal refusal to die? No, since many of these rebels have paid the ultimate price in order to live up to their own demands. The rebel does not ask for life, but for reasons for living. He rejects the consequences implied by death. If nothing lasts, then nothing is justified: anything that dies has no meaning. To fight against death amounts to claiming that life has a meaning, to fighting for order and for unity.

The protest against evil which is at the very core of metaphysical revolt is significant in this regard. It is not the suffering of a child which is repugnant in itself, but the fact that the suffering is not justified. After all, pain, exile, confinement are sometimes accepted when dictated by good sense or by the doctor. In the eyes of the rebel, what is missing from the misery of the world, as well as from its moments of happiness, is some principle by which they can be explained. The insurrection against evil is, above all, a demand for unity. The rebel obstinately confronts a world condemned to death and the fatal obscurity of the human condition with his demand for life and absolute clarity. He is seeking, without knowing it, a moral philosophy or a religion. Rebellion is a form of asceticism, though it is blind. Therefore, if the rebel blasphemes it is in the hope of finding a new god. He staggers under the shock of the first and most profound of all religious experiences, but it is a disenchanted religious experience. It is not rebellion itself which is noble, but its aims, even though its achievements are at times ignoble. At least we must know how to recognize the ignoble ends it achieves. Each time that it defies the total rejection, the absolute negation of what exists, it destroys. Each time that it blindly accepts what exists and gives voice to absolute assent, it destroys again. Hatred of the creator can turn to hatred of creation or to exclusive and defiant love of what exists. But in both cases it ends in murder and loses the right to be called rebellion. One can be a nihilist in two ways, in both cases by having an intemperate recourse to absolutes. Apparently there are rebels who want to die and those who want to cause death. But they are identical, consumed with desire for the true life, frustrated by their desire and therefore preferring generalized injustice to mutilated justice. At this point of indignation, reason becomes madness. If it is true that the instinctive rebellion of the human heart advances gradually through the centuries towards its most complete realization, it has also grown, as we have seen, in blind audacity to the inordinate extent of deciding to answer universal murder by metaphysical assassination.

The *even if*, which we have already recognized as marking the most important moment of metaphysical revolt, is in any case fulfilled only in absolute destruction. It is not the nobility of rebellion which illuminates the world to-day, but nihilism. And it is the consequences of nihilism which we must retrace, without losing sight of the truth innate in its origins. Even if God existed, Ivan would never surrender to Him in the face of the injustice done to man. But a longer contemplation of this injustice, a more bitter approach, transformed the 'even if you exist' into 'you do not deserve to exist,' therefore 'you do not exist.' The victims have found in their own innocence the justification for the final crime. Convinced of their condemnation and without hope of immortality they decided to murder God. If it is false to say that, from that day, began the tragedy of contemporary man, it is not true, either, to say that it ended there. On the contrary, this attempt indicates the highest point in a drama that began with the end of the ancient world and of which the last words have not yet been spoken. From this moment, man decides to exclude himself from grace and to live by his own means. Progress, from the time of Sade up to the present, has consisted of gradually enlarging the enclosure where, according to his own rules, man without God brutally wields power. In defiance of the divinity, the frontiers of this stronghold have been extended to the point of making the entire universe into a fortress erected against the fallen and exiled deity. Man, at the culmination of his rebellion, incarcerated himself; from Sade's lurid castle to the concentration camps, man's greatest liberty consisted only of building the prison of his crimes. But the state of siege gradually spreads, the claim for freedom must embrace all mankind. Then the only kingdom which is opposed to the kingdom of grace must be founded, namely the kingdom of justice, and the human community must be reunited on the debris of the fallen City of

God. To kill God and to build a Church is the constant and contradictory purpose of rebellion. Absolute liberty finally becomes a prison of absolute duties, a collective asceticism, a story to be brought to an end. The nineteenth century which is the century of rebellion thus merges into the twentieth, the century of justice and ethics, the century of violent self-recrimination. Chamfort, the moralist of rebellion, had already provided the formula: 'One must be just before being generous, as one must have bread before having cake.' Thus, the ethic of luxury will be renounced in favour of the bitter morality of the empire builder.

We must now embark on the subject of this convulsive effort to control the world and to introduce a universal rule. We have arrived at the moment when rebellion, rejecting every aspect of servitude, attempts to annex all creation. At each of its setbacks, we have already seen formulated the political solution, the solution of conquest. Henceforth, with the introduction of moral nihilism, it will retain, of all its other acquisitions, only the will to power. In principle, the rebel only wanted to conquer his own self and to maintain it in the face of God. But he forgets his beginnings and, by the law of spiritual imperialism, he sets out in search of world conquest by way of an infinitely multiplied series of murders. He drove God from His heaven, but with the spirit of metaphysical rebellion openly joining forces with revolutionary movements, the irrational claim for freedom is paradoxically going to adopt reason as a weapon, as the only means of conquest which appears to it entirely human. With the death of God, mankind remains: and by this we mean the history which we must understand and shape. Nihilism, which smothers the creative force in the very core of rebellion, only adds that one can shape it with all the means at one's disposal. Man, on an earth which he knows is henceforth solitary, is going to add, to irrational crimes, the crimes of reason that are bent on the domination of man. To the 'I rebel, therefore we exist,' he adds, with prodigious plans in mind which even include the death of rebellion: 'And we are alone.'

FOOTNOTES

1. A dominant theme in William Blake, for example.
1. It is worth noting that Ivan is, in a certain way, Dostoievski, who is more at his ease in this role than in the role of Aliosha.

CHAPTER SIX

PSYCHOANALYSIS AND RELIGION*
by Erich Fromm

It would far transcend the scope of this chapter to attempt a review of all types of religion. Even to discuss only those types which are relevant from the psychological standpoint cannot be undertaken here. I shall therefore deal with only one distinction, but one which in my opinion is the most important, and which cuts across nontheistic and theistic religions: that between *authoritarian* and *humanistic* religions.

What is the principle of authoritarian religion? The definition of religion given in the *Oxford Dictionary*, while attempting to define religion as such, is a rather accurate definition of authoritarian religion. It reads: "[Religion is] recognition on the part of man of some higher unseen power as having control of his destiny, and as being entitled to obedience, reverence, and worship."

Here the emphasis is on the recognition that man is controlled by a higher power outside of himself. But this alone does not constitute authoritarian religion. What makes it so is the idea that this power, because of the control it exercises, is *entitled* to "obedience, reverence and worship." I italicize the word "entitled" because it shows that the reason for worship, obedience, and reverence lies not in the moral qualities of the deity, not in love or justice, but in the fact that it has control, that is, has power over man. Furthermore it shows that the higher power has a right to force man to worship him and that lack of reverence and obedience constitutes sin.

The essential element in authoritarian religion and in the authoritarian religious experience is the surrender to a power transcending man. The main virtue of this type of religion is obedience, its cardinal sin is disobedience. Just as the deity is conceived as omnipotent or omniscient,

*Used with permission from *Psychoanalysis and Religion*, Yale University Press, New Haven, Connecticut, 1950.

man is conceived as being powerless and insignificant. Only as he can gain grace or help from the deity by complete surrender can he feel strength. Submission to a powerful authority is one of the avenues by which man escapes from his feeling of aloneness and limitation. In the act of surrender he loses his independence and integrity as an individual but he gains the feeling of being protected by an awe-inspiring power of which, as it were, he becomes a part.

In Calvin's theology we find a vivid picture of authoritarian, theistic thinking. "For I do not call it humility," says Calvin, "if you suppose that we have anything left. . . . We cannot think of ourselves as we ought to think without utterly despising everything that may be supposed an excellence in us. This humility is unfeigned submission of mind overwhelmed with a weighty sense of its own misery and poverty; for such is the uniform description of it in the word of God."[1]

The experience which Calvin describes here, that of despising everything in oneself, of the submission of the mind overwhelmed by its own poverty, is the very essence of all authoritarian religions whether they are couched in secular or in theological language.[2] In authoritarian religion God is a symbol of power and force, He is supreme because He has supreme power, and man in juxtaposition is utterly powerless.

Authoritarian secular religion follows the same principle. Here the Fuhrer or the beloved "Father of His People" or the State or the Race or the Socialist Fatherland becomes the object of worship; the life of the individual becomes insignificant and man's worth consists in the very denial of his worth and strength. Frequently authoritarian religion postulates an ideal which is so abstract and so distant that is has hardly any connection with the real life of real people. To such ideals as "life after death" or "the future of mankind" the life and happiness of persons living here and now may be sacrificed; the alleged ends justify every means and become symbols in the names of which religious or secular "elites" control the lives of their fellow men.

Humanistic religion, on the contrary, is centered around man and his strength. Man must develop his power of reason in order to understand himself, his relationship to his fellow men and his position in the universe. He must recognize the truth, both with regard to his limitations and his potentialities. He must develop his powers of love for others as well as for himself and experience the solidarity of all living beings. He must have principles and norms to guide him in this aim. Religious experience in this kind of religion is the experience of oneness with the All, based on one's relatedness to the world as it is grasped with thought and with love. Man's aim in humanistic religion is to achieve the greatest strength, not the greatest powerlessness; virtue is self-realization, not obedience. Faith is certainty of conviction based on one's experience of thought and feeling, not assent to propositions on credit of the proposer. The prevailing mood is that of joy, while the prevailing mood in authoritarian religion is that of sorrow and of guilt.

Inasmuch as humanistic religions are theistic, God is a symbol of *man's own powers* which he tries to realize in his life, and is not a symbol of force and domination, having *power over man*.

Illustrations of humanistic religions are early Buddhism, Taoism, the teachings of Isaiah, Jesus, Socrates, Spinoza, certain trends in the Jewish and Christian religions (particularly mysticism), the religion of Reason of the French Revolution. It is evident from these that the distinction between authoritarian and humanistic religion cuts across the distinction between theistic and nontheistic, and between religions in the narrow sense of the word and philosophical systems of religious character. What matters in all such systems is not the thought system as such but the human attitude underlying their doctrines.

One of the best examples of humanistic religions is early Buddhism. The Buddha is a great teacher, he is the "awakened one" who recognizes the truth about human existence. He does not speak in the name of a supernatural power but in the name of reason. He calls upon every man to make use of his own reason and to see the truth which he was only the first to find. Once man takes the first step in seeing the truth, he must apply his efforts to live in such a way that he develops his powers of reason and of love for all human creatures. Only to the degree to which he succeeds in this can he free himself from the bondage of irrational passions. While man must recognize his limitations according to Buddhistic teaching, he must also become aware of the powers in himself. The concept of Nirvana as the state of mind the fully awakened one can achieve is not one of man's helplessness and submission but on the contrary one of the development of the highest powers man possesses. . . .

Zen-Buddhism, a later sect within Buddhism, is expressive of an even more radical anti-authoritarian attitude. Zen proposes that no knowledge is of any value unless it grows out of ourselves; no authority, no teacher can really teach us anything except to arouse doubts in us; words and thought systems are dangerous because they easily turn into authorities whom we worship. Life itself must be grasped and experienced as it flows, and in this lies virtue . . .

Another illustration of a humanistic religious system is to be found in Spinoza's religious thinking. While his language is that of medieval theology, his concept of God has no trace of authoritarianism. God could not have created the world different from what it is. He cannot change anything; in fact, God is identical with the totality of the universe. Man must see his own limitations and recognize that he is dependent on the totality of forces outside himself over which he has no control. Yet his are the powers of love and of reason. He can develop them and attain an optimum of freedom and of inner strength.

The distinction between authoritarian and humanistic religion not only cuts across various religions, it can exist within the same religion. Our own religious tradition is one of the best illustrations of this point. Since it is of fundamental importance to understand fully the distinction between authoritarian and humanistic religion I shall illustrate it further from a source with which every reader is more or less familiar, the Old Testament.

The beginning of the Old Testament[3] is written in the spirit of authoritarian religion. The picture of God is that of the absolute ruler of a patriarchal clan, who has created man at his pleasure and can destroy him at will. He has forbidden him to eat from the tree of knowledge of good and evil and has threatened him with death if he transgresses this order. But the serpent, "more clever than any animal," tells Eve, "Ye shall not surely die: For God doth know that in the day ye eat thereof, then your eyes shall be opened, and ye shall be as gods, knowing good and evil."[4] God proves the serpent to be right. When Adam and Eve have transgressed he punished them by proclaiming enmity between man and nature, between man and the soil and animals, and between men and women. But man is not to die. However, "the man has become as one of us, to know good and evil: and now, lest he put forth his hand, and take also of the tree of life, and eat, and live for ever,"[5] God expels Adam and Eve from the garden of Eden and puts an angel with a flaming sword at the east "to keep the way of the tree of life."

The text makes very clear what man's sin is: it is rebellion against God's command: it is disobedience and not any inherent sinfulness in the act of eating from the tree of knowledge. On the contrary, further religious development has made the knowledge of good and evil the cardinal virtue to which man may aspire. The text also makes it plain what God's motive is: it is concern with his own superior role, the jealous fear of man's claim to become his equal.

A decisive turning point in the relationship between God and man is to be seen in the story of the Flood. When God saw "that the wickedness of man was great on the earth . . . it repented the Lord that he had made man and the earth, and it grieved him at his heart. And the Lord said, I will destroy man whom I have created from the face of the earth; both man, and beast, and the creeping thing, and the fowls of the air; for it repenteth me that I have made them."[6]

There is no question here but that God has the right to destroy his own creatures; he has created them and they are his property. The text defines their wickedness as "violence," but the decision to destroy not only man but animals and plants as well shows that we are not dealing here with a sentence commensurate with some specific crime but with God's angry regret over his own action which did not turn out well. "But Noah found grace in the eyes of the Lord," and he, together with his family and a representative of each animal species, is saved from the Flood. Thus far the destruction of man and the salvation of Noah are arbitrary acts of God. He could do as he pleased, as can any powerful tribal chief. But after the Flood the relationship between God and man changes fundamentally. A covenant is concluded between God and man in which God promises that "Neither shall all flesh be cut off any more by the waters of a flood; neither shall there any more be a flood

to destroy the earth."[7] God obligates himself never to destroy all
life on earth, and man is bound to the first and most fundamental command of the Bible, not to kill: "At the hand of every man's brother
will I require the life of man."[8] From this point on the relationship between God and man undergoes a profound change. God is no longer an
absolute ruler who can act at his pleasure but is bound by a constitution to which both he and man must adhere; he is bound by a principle
which he cannot violate, the principle of respect for life. God can pun-
ish man if he violates this principle, but man can also challenge God if
he is guilty of its violation.

The new relationship between God and man appears clearly in Abraham's plea for Sodom and Gomorrah. When God considers destroying
the cities because of their wickedness, Abraham criticizes God for violating his own principles. "That be far from thee to do after this manner, to slay the righteous with the wicked: and that the righteous
should be as the wicked, that be far from thee. Shall not the Judge of
all the earth do right?"[9]

The difference between the story of the Fall and this argument is
great indeed. There man is forbidden to know good and evil and his
position toward God is that of submission—or sinful disobedience.
Here man uses his knowledge of good and evil, criticizes God in the
name of justice, and God has to yield.

Even this brief analysis of the authoritarian element in the biblical
story shows that at the root of the Judaeo-Christian religion both principles, the authoritarian and the humanistic, are present. In the development of Judaism as well as of Christianity both principles have been
preserved and their respective preponderance marks different trends in
the two religions.

The following story from the Talmud expresses the unauthoritarian,
humanistic side of Judaism as we find it in the first centuries of the
Christian era.

A number of other famous rabbinical scholars disagreed with Rabbi
Eliezar's views in regard to a point of ritual law. "Rabbi Eliezar said to
them: 'If the law is as I think it is then this tree shall let us know.'
Whereupon the tree jumped from its place a hundred yards (others
say four hundred yards). His colleagues said to him. 'One does not
prove anything from a tree.' He said, 'If I am right then this brook shall
let us know.' Whereupon the brook ran upstream. His colleagues said
to him, 'One does not prove anything from a brook.' He continued and
said, 'If the law is as I think then the walls of the house will tell.' Whereupon the walls began to fall. But Rabbi Joshua shouted at the walls
and said, 'Fi scholars argue a point of law, what business have you to
fall?' So the walls fell no further out of respect for Rabbi Joshua but
out of respect for Rabbi Eliezar did not straighten up. And that is the
way they still are. Rabbi Eliezar took up the argument again and said,
'If the law is as I think, they shall tell us from heaven.' Whereupon a
voice from heaven said, 'What have you against Rabbi Eliezar, because

the law is as he says.' Whereupon Rabbi Joshua got up and said, 'It is written in the Bible: The law is not in heaven. What does this mean? According to Rabbi Jirmijahu it means since the Torah has been given on Mount Sinai we no longer pay attention to voices from heaven because it is written: You make your decision according to the majority opinion.' It then happened that Rabbi Nathan [one of the participants in the discussion] met the Prophet Elijah [who had taken a stroll on earth] and he asked the Prophet, 'What did God himself say when we had this discussion?' The Prophet answered, 'God smiled and said, My children have won, my children have won.'" [10]

This story is hardly in need of comment. It emphasizes the autonomy of man's reason with which even the supernatural voices from heaven cannot interfere. God smiles, man has done what God wanted him to do, he has become his own master, capable and resolved to make his decisions by himself according to rational, democratic methods. . . .

That early Christianity is humanistic and not authoritarian is evident from the spirit and text of all Jesus' teachings. Jesus' precept that "the kingdom of God is within you" is the simple and clear expression of non-authoritarian thinking. But only a few hundred years later, after Christianity had ceased to be the religion of the poor and humble peasants, artisans, and slaves (the *Am baarez*) and had become the religion of those ruling the Roman Empire, the authoritarian trend in Christianity became dominant. Even so, the conflict between the authoritarian and humanistic principles in Christianity never ceased. It was the conflict between Augustine and Pelagius, between the Catholic Church and the many "heretic" groups and between various sects within Protestantism. The humanistic, democratic element was never subdued in Christian or in Jewish history, and this element found one of its most potent expressions in the mystic thinking within both religions. The mystics have been deeply imbued with the experience of man's strength, his likeness to God, and with the idea that God needs man as much as man needs God; they have understood the sentence that man is created in the image of God to mean the fundamental identity of God and man. Not fear and submission but love and the assertion of one's own powers are the basis of mystical experience. *God is not a symbol of power over man but of man's own powers.*

Thus far we have dealt with the distinctive features of authoritarian and humanistic religions mainly in descriptive terms. But the psychoanalyst must proceed from the description of attitudes to the analysis of their dynamics, and it is here that he can contribute to our discussion from an area not accessible to other fields of inquiry. The full understanding of an attitude requires an appreciation of those conscious and, in particular, unconscious processes occurring in the individual which provide the necessity for and the conditions of its development.

While in humanistic religion God is the image of man's higher self, a symbol of what man potentially is or ought to become, in authoritarian religion God becomes the sole possessor of what was originally man's: of his reason and his love. The more perfect God becomes, the more imperfect becomes man. He *projects* the best he has onto God and thus impoverishes himself. Now God has all love, all wisdom, all justice—and man is deprived of these qualities, he is empty and poor. He had begun with the feeling of smallness, but he now has become completely powerless and without strength; all his powers have been projected onto God. This mechanism of projection is the very same which can be observed in interpersonal relationships of a masochistic, submissive character, where one person is awed by another and attributes his own powers and aspirations to the other person. It is the same mechanism that makes people endow the leaders of even the most inhuman systems with qualities of superwisdom and kindness.[11]

When man has thus projected his own most valuable powers onto God, what of his relationship to his own powers? They have become separated from him and in this process he has become *alienated* from himself. Everything he has is now God's and nothing is left in him. *His only access to himself is through God.* In worshipping God he tries to get in touch with that part of himself which he has lost through projection. After having given God all he has, he begs God to return to him some of what originally was his own. But having lost his own he is completely at God's mercy. He necessarily feels like a "sinner" since he has deprived himself of everything that is good, and it is only through God's mercy or grace that he can regain that which alone makes him human. And in order to persuade God to give him some of his love, he must prove to him how utterly deprived he is of love; in order to persuade God to guide him by his superior wisdom he must prove to him how deprived he is of wisdom when he is left to himself.

But this alienation from his own powers not only makes man feel slavishly dependent on God, it makes him bad too. He becomes a man without faith in his fellow men or in himself, without the experience of his own love, of his own power of reason. As a result the separation between the "holy" and the "secular" occurs. In his wordly activities man acts without love, in that sector of his life which is reserved to religion he feels himself to be a sinner (which he actually is, since to live without love is to live in sin) and tries to recover some of his lost humanity by being in touch with God. Simultaneously, he tries to win forgiveness by emphasizing his own helplessness and worthlessness. Thus the attempt to obtain forgiveness results in the activation of the very attitude from which his sins stem. He is caught in a painful dilemma. The more he praises God, the emptier he becomes. The emptier he becomes, the more sinful he feels. The more sinful he feels, the more he praises his God—and the less able is he to regain himself.

Analysis of religion must not stop at uncovering those psychological processes within man which underly his religious experience; it must proceed to discover the conditions which make for the development of authoritarian and humanistic character structures, respectively, from

which different kinds of religious experience stem. Such a sociopsycho-
logical analysis goes far beyond the context of these chapters. However,
the principal point can be made briefly. What people think and feel is
rooted in their character and their character is molded by the total con-
figuration of their practice of life—more precisely, by the socio-economic
and political structure of their society. In societies ruled by a powerful
minority which holds the masses in subjection, the individual will be so
imbued with fear, so incapable of feeling strong or independent, that
his religious experience will be authoritarian. Whether he worships a
punishing, awesome God or a similarly conceived leader makes little difference. On the other hand, where the individual feels free and responsible for his own fate, or among minorities striving for freedom and
independence, humanistic religious experience develops. The history of
religion gives ample evidence of this correlation between social structure
and kinds of religious experience. Early Christianity was a religion of
the poor and downtrodden; the history of religious sects fighting against
authoritarian political pressure shows the same principle again and again.
Judaism, in which a strong anti-authoritarian tradition could grow up
because secular authority never had much of a chance to govern and to
build up a legend of its wisdom, therefore developed the humanistic
aspect of religion to a remarkable degree. Whenever, on the other hand,
religion allied itself with secular power, the religion had by necessity to
become authoritarian. The real fall of man is his alienation from himself, his submission to power, his turning against himself even though
under the guise of his worship of God.

From the spirit of authoritarian religion stem two fallacies of reasoning which have been used again and again as arguments for theistic
religion. One argument runs as follows: How can you criticize the emphasis on dependence on a power transcending man; is not man dependent on forces outside himself which he cannot understand, much less
control?

Indeed, man is dependent; he remains subject to death, age, illness,
and even if he were to control nature and to make it wholly serviceable
to him, he and his earth remain tiny specks in the universe. But it is one
thing to recognize one's dependence and limitations, and it is something
entirely different to indulge in this dependence, to worship the forces on
which one depends. To understand realistically and soberly how limited
our power is is an essential part of wisdom and of maturity; to worship
it is masochistic and self-destructive. The one is humility, the other
self-humiliation.

We can study the difference between the realistic recognition of our
limitations and the indulgence in the experience of submission and powerlessness in the clinical examination of masochistic character traits. We
find people who have a tendency to incur sickness, accidents, humiliating
situations, who belittle and weaken themselves. They believe that they
get into such situations against their will and intention, but a study of
their unconscious motives shows that actually they are driven by one of

the most irrational tendencies to be found in man, namely, by an unconscious desire to be weak and powerless; they tend to shift the center
of their life to powers over which they feel no control, thus escaping
from freedom and from personal responsibility. We find furthermore
that this masochistic tendency is usually accompanied by its very opposite, the tendency to rule and to dominate others, and that the masochistic and the dominating tendencies form the two sides of the authoritarian
character structure.[12] Such masochistic tendencies are not always unconscious. We find them overtly in the sexual masochistic perversion
where the fulfillment of the wish to be hurt or humiliated is the condition
for sexual excitement and satisfaction. We find it also in the relationship
to the leader and the state in all authoritarian secular religions. Here the
explicit aim is to give up one's own will and to experience submission
under the leader or the state as profoundly rewarding.

Another fallacy of theological thinking is closely related to the one
concerning dependence. I mean here the argument that there must be
a power or being outside of man because we find that man has an ineradicable longing to relate himself to something beyond himself. Indeed,
any sane human being has a need to relate himself to others; a person
who has lost that capacity completely is insane. No wonder that man
has created figures outside of himself to which he relates himself, which
he loves and cherishes because they are not subject to the vacillations
and inconsistencies of human objects. That God is a symboof man's
need to love is simple enough to understand. But does it follow from the
existence and intensity of this human need that there exists an outer being who corresponds to this need? Obviously that follows as little as our
strongest desire to love someone proves that there is a person with whom
we are in love. All it proves is our need and perhaps our capacity . . . .

The underlying theme of the preceding chapters is the conviction that
the problem of religion is not the problem of God but the problem of
man; religious formulations and religious symbols are attempts to give
expression to certain kinds of human experience. What matters is the
nature of these experiences. The symbol system is only the cue from
which we can infer the underlying human reality. Unfortunately the discussion centered around religion since the days of the Enlightenment has
been largely concerned with the affirmation or negation of a belief in
God rather than with the affirmation or negation of certain human attitudes. "Do you believe in the existence of God?" has been made the
crucial question of religionists and the denial of God has been the position chosen by those fighting the church. It is easy to see that many
who profess the belief in God are in their human attitude idol worshipers
or men without faith, while some of the most ardent "atheists," devot-
ing their lives to the betterment of mankind, to deeds of brotherliness
and love, have exhibited faith and a profoundly religious attitude. Centering the religious discussion on the acceptance or denial of the symbol
God blocks the understanding of the religious problem as a human prob-

lem and prevents the development of that human attitude which can be called religious in a humanistic sense.

Many attempts have been made to retain the symbol God but to give it a meaning different from the one which it has in the monotheistic tradition. One of the outstanding illustrations is Spinoza's theology. Using strictly theological language he gives a definition of God which amounts to saying there is no God in the sense of the Judaeo-Christian tradition. He was still so close to the spiritual atmosphere in which the symbol God seemed indispensable that he was not aware of the fact that he was negating the existence of God in the terms of his new definition.

In the writings of a number of theologians and philosophers in the nineteenth century and at present one can detect similar attempts to retain the word God but to give it a meaning fundamentally different from that which it had for the Prophets of the Bible or for the Christian and Jewish theologians of the Middle Ages. There need be no quarrel with those who retain the symbol God although it is questionable whether it is not a forced attempt to retain a symbol whose significance is essentially historical. However this may be, one thing is certain. The real conflict is not between belief in God and "atheism" but between a humanistic, religious attitude and an attitude which is equivalent to idolatry regardless of how this attitude is expressed—or disguised—in conscious thought.

FOOTNOTES

1. Johannes Calvin, *Institutes of the Christian Religion* (Presbyterian Board of Christian Education, 1928), p. 681.

2. See Erich Fromm, *Escape from Freedom* (Farrar & Rinehart, 1941), pp. 141 ff. This attitude toward authority is described there in detail.

3. The historical fact that the beginning of the Bible may not be its oldest part does not need to be considered here since we use the text as an illustration of two principles and not to establish a historical sequence.

4. Genesis 3:4-5.

5. *Ibid.* 3:22.

6. *Ibid.* 6:5 ff.

7. *Ibid.* 9:11.

8. *Ibid.* 9:5.

9. *Ibid.* 18:25.

10. Talmud, Baba Meziah, 59, b. (My translation.)

11. Cf. the discussion about symbiotic relationship in *Escape from Freedom*, pp. 158 ff.

12. See *Escape from Freedom*, pp. 141 ff.

CHAPTER SEVEN

WHY I AM NOT A CHRISTIAN*
by Bertrand Russell

This lecture was delivered on March 6, 1927, at Battersea Town Hall under the auspices of the South London Branch of the National Secular Society.

As your Chairman has told you, the subject about which I am going to speak to you tonight is "Why I Am Not a Christian." Perhaps it would be as well, first of all, to try to make out what one means by the word *Christian*. It is used these days in a very loose sense by a great many people. Some people mean no more by it than a person who attempts to live a good life. In that sense I suppose there would be Christians in all sects and creeds; but I do not think that that is the proper sense of the word, if only because it would imply that all the people who are not Christians—all the Buddhists, Confucians, Mohammedans, and so on —are not trying to live a good life. I do not mean by a Christian any person who tries to live decently according to his lights. I think that you must have a certain amount of definite belief before you have a right to call yourself a Christian. The word does not have quite such a full-blooded meaning now as it had in the times of St. Augustine and St. Thomas Aquinas. In those days, if a man said that he was a Christian it was known what he meant. You accepted a whole collection of creeds which were set out with great precision, and every single syllable of those creeds you believed with the whole strength of your convictions.

*Used with permission from *Why I Am Not A Christian*, Simon and Schuster, New York, New York, 1957.

What Is a Christian?

Nowadays it is not quite that. We have to be a little more vague in our meaning of Christianity. I think, however, that there are two different items which are quite essential to anybody calling himself a Christian. The first is one of a dogmatic nature—namely, that you must believe in God and immortality. If you do not believe in those two things, I do not think that you can properly call yourself a Christian. Then, further than that, as the name implies, you must have some kind of belief about Christ. The Mohammedans, for instance, also believe in God and in immortality, and yet they would not call themselves Christians. I think you must have at the very lowest the belief that Christ was, if not divine, at least the best and wisest of men. If you are not going to believe that much about Christ, I do not think you have any right to call yourself a Christian. Of course, there is another sense, which you find in *Whitaker's Almanack* and in geography books, where the population of the world is said to be divided into Christians, Mohammedans, Buddhists, fetish worshipers, and so on; and in that sense we are all Christians. The geography books count us all in, but that is a purely geographical sense, which I suppose we can ignore. Therefore I take it that when I tell you why I am not a Christian I have to tell you two different things: first, why I do not believe in God and in immortality; and, secondly, why I do not think that Christ was the best and wisest of men, although I grant him a very high degree of moral goodness.

But for the successful efforts of unbelievers in the past, I could not take so elastic a definition of Christianity as that. As I said before, in olden days it had a much more full-blooded sense. For instance, it included the belief in hell. Belief in eternal hell-fire was an essential item of Christian belief until pretty recent times. In this country, as you know, it ceased to be an essential item because of a decision of the Privy Council, and from that decision the Archbishop of Canterbury and the Archbishop of York dissented; but in this country our religion is settled by Act of Parliament, and therefore the Privy Council was able to override their Graces and hell was no longer necessary to a Christian. Consequently I shall not insist that a Christian must believe in hell.

The Existence of God

To come to this question of the existence of God: it is a large and serious question, and if I were to attempt to deal with it in any adequate manner I should have to keep you here until Kingdom Come, so that you will have to excuse me if I deal with it in a somewhat summary fashion. You know, of course, that the Catholic Church has laid it down as a dogma that the existence of God can be proved by the unaided reason. That is a somewhat curious dogma, but it is one of their dogmas. They had to introduce it because at one time the free-thinkers adopted the habit of saying that there were such and such arguments which mere reason might urge against the existence of God, but of course they knew as a matter of faith that God did exist. The arguments and the reasons were set out at great length, and the Catholic Church felt that they must stop it. Therefore they laid it down that the existence of God can be proved by the unaided reason and they had to set up what they considered were arguments to prove it. There are, of course, a number of them, but I shall take only a few.

The First-cause Argument

Perhaps the simplest and easiest to understand is the argument of the First Cause. (It is maintained that everything we see in this world has a cause, and as you go back in the chain of causes further and further you must come to a First Cause, and to that First Cause you give the name of God.) That argument, I suppose, does not carry very much weight nowadays, because, in the first place, cause is not quite what it used to be. The philosophers and the men of science have not got going on cause, and it has not anything like the vitality it used to have; but, apart from that, you can see that the argument that there must be a First Cause is one that cannot have any validity. I may say that when I was a young man and was debating these questions very seriously in my mind, I for a long time accepted the argument of the First Cause, until one day, at the age of eighteen, I read John Stuart Mill's Autobiography, and I there found this sentence: "My father taught me that the question 'Who made me?' cannot be answered, since it immediately suggests the further question 'Who made God?'" That very simple sentence showed me, as I still think, the fallacy in the argument of the First Cause. If everything must have a cause, then God must have a cause. If there can be anything without a cause, it may just as well be the world as God, so that there cannot be any validity in that argument. It is exactly of the same nature as the Hindu's view, that the world rested upon an elephant and the elephant rested upon a tortoise; and when they said, "How about the tortoise?" the Indian said, "Suppose we change the subject." The argument is really no better than that. There is no reason why the world could not have come into being without a cause; nor, on the other hand, is there any reason why it should not have always existed. There is no reason to suppose that the world had a bginning at all. The idea that things must have a beginning is really due to the poverty of our imagination. Therefore, perhaps, I need not waste any more time upon the argument about the First Cause.

The Natural-law Argument

Then there is a very common argument from natural law. That was a favorite argument all through the eighteenth century, especially under the influence of Sir Isaac Newton and his cosmogony. People observed the planets going around the sun according to the law of gravitation, and they thought that God had given a behest to these planets to move in that particular fashion, and that was why they did so.

That was, of course, a convenient and simple explanation that saved them the trouble of looking any further for explanations of the law of gravitation. Nowadays we explain the law of gravitation in a somewhat complicated fashion that Einstein has introduced. I do not propose to give you a lecture on the law of gravitation, as interpreted by Einstein, because that again would take some time; at any rate, you no longer have the sort of natural law that you had in the Newtonian system, where, for some reason that nobody could understand, nature behaved in a uniform fashion. We now find that a great many things we thought were natural laws are really human conventions. You know that even in the remotest depths of stellar space there are still three feet to a yard. That is, no doubt, a very remarkable fact, but you would hardly call it a law of nature. And a great many things that have been regarded as laws of nature are of that kind. On the other hand, where you can get down to any knowledge of what atoms actually do, you will find they are much less subject to law than people thought, and that the laws at which you arrive are statistical averages of just the sort that would emerge from chance. There is, as we all know, a law that if you throw dice you will get double sixes only about once in thirty-six times, and we do not regard that as evidence that the fall of the dice is regulated by design; on the contrary, if the double sixes came every time we should think that there was design. The laws of nature are of that sort as regards a great many of them. They are statistical averages such as would emerge from the laws of chance; and that makes this whole business of natural law much less impressive than it formerly was. Quite apart from that, which represents the momentary state of science that may change tomorrow, the whole idea that natural laws imply a lawgiver is due to a confusion between natural and human laws. Human laws are behests commanding you to behave a certain way, in which way you may choose to behave, or you may choose not to behave; but natural laws are a description of how things do in fact behave, and being a mere description of what they in fact do, you cannot argue that there must be somebody who told them to do that, because even supposing that there were, you are then faced with the question "Why did God issue just those natural laws and no others?" If you say that he did it simply from his own good pleasure, and without any reason, you then find that there is something which is not subject to law, and so your train of natural law is interrupted. If you say, as more orthodox theologians do, that in all the laws which God issues he had a reason for giving those laws rather than others—the reason, of course, being to create the best universe, although you would never think it to look at it—if there were a reason for the laws which God gave, then God himself was subject to law, and therefore you do not get any advantage by introducing God as an intermediary. You have really a law outside and anterior to the divine edicts, and God does not serve your purpose, because he is not the ultimate lawgiver. In short, this whole argument about natural law no longer has anything like the strength that it used to have. I am traveling on in time in my review of the arguments. The arguments that are used for the existence of God change their character as time goes on. They were at first hard intellectual arguments embodying certain quite definite fallacies. As we come to modern times they become less respectable intellectually and more and more affected by a kind of moralizing vagueness.

The Argument from Design

The next step in this process brings us to the argument from design. You all know the argument from design: everything in the world is made just so that we can manage to live in the world, and if the world was ever so little different, we could not manage to live in it. That is the argument from design. It sometimes takes a rather curious form; for instance, it is argued that rabbits have white tails in order to be easy to shoot. I do not know how rabbits would view that application. It is an easy argument to parody. You all know Voltaire's remark, that obviously the nose was designed to be such as to fit spectacles. That sort of parody has turned out to be not nearly so wide of the mark as it might have seemed in the eighteenth century, because since the time of Darwin we understand much better why living creatures are adapted to their environment. It is not that their environment was made to be suitable to them but that they grew to be suitable to it, and that is the basis of adaptation. There is no evidence of design about it.

When you come to look into this argument from design, it is a most astonishing thing that people can believe that this world, with all the things that are in it, with all its defects, should be the best that omnipotence and omniscience have been able to produce in millions of years. I really cannot believe it. Do you think that, if you were granted omnipotence and omniscience and millions of years in which to perfect your world, you could produce nothing better than the Ku Klux Klan or the Fascists? Moreover, if you accept the ordinary laws of science, you have to suppose that human life and life in general on this planet will die out in due course: it is a stage in the decay of the solar system; at a certain stage of decay you get the sort of conditions of temperature and so forth which are suitable to protoplasm, and there is life for a short time in the life of the whole solar system. You see in the moon the sort of thing to which the earth is tending—something dead, cold, and lifeless.

I am told that that sort of view is depressing, and people will sometimes tell you that if they believed that, they would not be able to go on living. Do not believe it; it is all nonsense. Nobody really worries much about what is going to happen millions of years hence. Even if they think they are worrying much about that, they are really deceiving themselves. They are worried about something much more mundane, or it may merely be a bad digestion; but nobody is really seriously rendered unhappy by the thought of something that is going to happen to this world millions and millions of years hence. Therefore, although it is of course a gloomy view to suppose that life will die out—at least I suppose we may say so, although sometimes when I contemplate the things that people do with their lives I think it is almost a consolation —it is not such as to render life miserable. It merely makes you turn your attention to other things.

The Moral Arguments for Deity

Now we reach one stage further in what I shall call the intellectual descent that the Theists have made in their argumentations, and we come to what are called the moral arguments for the existence of God. You all know, of course, that there used to be in the old days three intellectual arguments for the existence of God, all of which were disposed of by Immanuel Kant in the *Critique of Pure Reason;* but no sooner had he disposed of those arguments than he invented a new one, a moral argument, and that quite convinced him. He was like many people: in intellectual matters he was skeptical, but in moral matters he believed implicitly in the maxims that the had imbibed at his mother's knee. That illustrates what the psychoanalysts so much emphasize—the immensely stronger hold upon us that our very early associations have than those of later times.

Kant, as I say, invented a new moral argument for the existence of God, and that in varying forms was extremely popular during the nineteenth century. It has all sorts of forms. One form is to say that there would be no right or wrong unless God existed. I am not for the moment concerned with whether there is a difference between right and wrong, or whether there is not: that is another question. The point I am concerned with is that, if you are quite sure there is a difference between right and wrong, you are then in this situation: Is that difference due to God's fiat or is it not? If it is due to God's fiat, then for God himself there is no difference between right and wrong, and it is no longer a significant statement to say that God is good. If you are going to say, as theologians do, that God is good, you must then say that right and wrong have some meaning which is independent of God's fiat, because God's fiats are good and not bad independently of the mere fact that he made them. If you are going to say that, you will then have to say that it is not only through God that right and wrong came into being, but that they are in their essence logically anterior to God. You could, of course, if you liked, say that there was a superior deity who gave orders to the God who made this world, or could take up the line that some of the gnostics took up—a line which I often thought was a very plausible one—that as a matter of fact this world that we know was made by the devil at a moment when God was not looking. There is a good deal to be said for that, and I am not concerned to refute it.

The Argument for the Remedying of Injustice

Then there is another very curious form of moral argument, which is this: they say that the existence of God is required in order to bring justice into the world. In the part of this universe that we know there is great injustice, and often the good suffer, and often the wicked prosper, and one hardly knows which of those is the more annoying; but if you are going to have justice in the universe as a whole you have to suppose a future life to redress the balance of life here on earth. So they say that there must be a God, and there must be heaven and hell in order that in the long run there may be justice. That is a very curious argument. If you looked at the matter from a scientific point of view, you would say, "After all, I know only this world. I do not know about the rest of the universe, but so far as one can argue at all on probabilities one would say that probably this world is a fair sample, and if there is injustice here the odds are that there is injustice elsewhere also." Supposing you got a crate of oranges that you opened, and you found all the top layer of oranges bad, you would not argue, "The underneath ones must be good, so. as to redress the balance." You would say, "Probably the whole lot is a bad consignment;" and that is really what a scientific person would argue about the universe. He would say, "Here we find in this world a great deal of injustice, and so far as that goes that is a reason for supposing that justice does not rule in the world; and therefore so far as it goes it affords a moral argument against deity and not in favor of one." Of course I know that the sort of intellectual arguments that I have been talking to you about are not what really moves people. What really moves people to believe in God is not any intellectual argument at all. Most people believe in God because they have been taught from early infancy to do it, and that is the main reason.

Then I think that the next most powerful reason is the wish for safety, a sort of feeling that there is a big brother who will look after you. That plays a very profound part in influencing people's desire for a belief in God.

The Character of Christ

I now want to say a few words upon a topic which I often think is not quite sufficiently dealt with by Rationalists, and that is the question whether Christ was the best and the wisest of men. It is generally taken for granted that we should all agree that that was so. I do not myself. I think that there are a good many points upon which I agree with Christ a great deal more than the professing Christians do. I do not know that I could go with Him all the way, but I could go with Him much further than most professing Christians can. You will remember that he said, "Resist not evil: but whosoever shall smite thee on thy right cheek, turn to him the other also." That is not a new precept or a new principle. It was used by Lao-tse and Buddha some 500 or 600 years before Christ, but it is not a principle which as a matter of fact Christians accept. I have no doubt that the present Prime Minister,° for instance, is a most sincere Christian, but I should not advise any of

°Stanley Baldwin

you to go and smite him on one cheek. I think you might find that he thought this text was intended in a figurative sense.

Then there is another point which I consider excellent. You will remember that Christ said, "Judge not lest ye be judged." That principle I do not think you would find was popular in the law courts of Christian countries. I have known in my time quite a number of judges who were very earnest Christians, and none of them felt that they were acting contrary to Christian principles in what they did. Then Christ says, "Give to him that asketh of thee, and from him that would borrow of thee turn not thou away." That is a very good principle. Your Chairman has reminded you that we are not here to talk politics, but I cannot help observing that the last general election was fought on the question of how desirable it was to turn away from him that would borrow of thee, so that one must assume that the Liberals and Conservatives of this country are composed of people who do not agree with the teaching of Christ, because they certainly did very emphatically turn away on that occasion.

Then there is one other maxim of Christ which I think has a great deal in it, but I do not find that it is very popular among some of our Christian friends. He says, "If thou wilt be perfect, go and sell that which thou hast, and give to the poor." That is a very excellent maxim, but, as I say, it is not much practiced. All these, I think, are good maxims, although they are a little difficult to live up to. I do not profess to live up to them myself; but then, after all, it is not quite the same thing as for a Christian.

Defects in Christ's Teaching

Having granted the excellence of these maxims, I come to certain points in which I do not believe that one can grant either the superlative wisdom or the superlative goodness of Christ as depicted in the Gospels; and here I may say that one is not concerned with the historical question. Historically it is quite doubtful whether Christ ever existed at all, and if He did we do not know anything about Him, so that I am not concerned with the historical question, which is a very difficult one, I am concerned with Christ as He appears in the Gospels, taking the Gospel narrative as it stands, and there one does find some things that do not seem to be very wise. For one thing, He certainly thought that His second coming would occur in clouds of glory before the death of all the people who were living at that time. There are a great many texts that prove that. He says, for instance, "Ye shall not have gone over the cities of Israel till the Son of Man be come." Then He says, "There are some standing here which shall not taste death till the Son of Man comes into His kingdom;" and there are a lot of places where it is quite clear that He believed that His second coming would happen during the lifetime of many then living. That was the belief of His earlier followers, and it was the basis of a good deal of His moral teaching. When He said, "Take no thought for the morrow," and things of that sort, it was very largely because He thought that the second coming was going to be very soon, and that all ordinary mundane affairs did not count. I have, as a matter of fact, known some Christians who did believe that the second coming was imminent. I know a parson who frightened his congregation terribly by telling them that the second coming was very imminent indeed, but they were much consoled when they found that he was planting trees in his garden. The early Christians did really believe it, and they did abstain from such things as planting trees in their gardens, because they did accept from Christ the belief that the second coming was imminent. In that respect, clearly He was not so wise as some other people have been, and He was certainly not superlatively wise.

The Moral Problem

Then you come to moral questions. There is one very serious defect to my mind in Christ's moral character, and that is that He believed in hell. I do not myself feel that any person who is really profoundly humane can believe in everlasting punishment. Christ certainly as depicted in the Gospels did believe in everlasting punishment, and one does find repeatedly a vindictive fury against those people who would not listen to His preaching—an attitude which is not uncommon with preachers, but which does somewhat detract from superlative excellence. You do not, for instance find that attitude in Socrates. You find him quite bland and urbane toward the people who would not listen to him; and it is, to my mind, far more worthy of a sage to take that line than to take the line of indignation. You probably all remember the sort of things that Socrates was saying when he was dying, and the sort of things that he generally did say to people who did not agree with him.

You will find that in the Gospels Christ said, "Ye serpents, ye generation of vipers, how can ye escape the damnation of hell." That was said to people who did not like His preaching. It is not really to my mind quite the best tone, and there are a great many of these things about hell. There is, of course, the familiar text about the sin against the Holy Ghost: "Whosoever speaketh against the Holy Ghost it shall not be forgiven him neither in this World nor in the world to come." That text has caused an unspeakable amount of misery in the world, for all sorts of people have imagined that they have committed the sin against the Holy Ghost, and thought that it would not be forgiven them either in this world or in the world to come. I really do not think that a person with a proper degree of kindliness in his nature would have put fears and terrors of that sort into the world.

Then Christ says, "The Son of Man shall send forth His angels, and they shall gather out of His kingdom all things that offend, and them which do iniquity, and shall cast them into a furnace of fire; there shall be wailing and gnashing of teeth;" and He goes on about the wailing and gnashing of teeth. It comes in one verse after another, and it is quite manifest to the reader that there is a certain pleasure in contemplating wailing and gnashing of teeth, or else it would not occur so often. Then you all, of course, remember about the sheep and the goats; how at the second coming He is going to divide the sheep from the goats, and He is going to say to the goats, "Depart from me, ye cursed, into everlasting fire." He continues, "And these shall go away into everlasting fire." Then He says again, "If thy hand offend thee, cut if off; it is better for thee to enter into life maimed, than having two hands to go into hell, into the fire that never shall be quenched; where the worm dieth not and the fire is not quenched." He repeats that again and again also. I must say that I think all this doctrine, that hell-fire is a punishment for sin, is a doctrine of cruelty. It is a doctrine that put cruelty into the world and gave the world generations of cruel torture; and the Christ of the Gospels, if you could take Him as His chroniclers represent Him, would certainly have to be considered partly responsible for that.

There are other things of less importance. There is the instance of the Gadarene swine, where it certainly was not very kind to the pigs to put the devils into them and make them rush down the hill to the sea. You must remember that He was omnipotent, and He could have made the devils simply go away; but He chose to send them into the pigs. Then there is the curious story of the fig tree, which always rather puzzled me. You remember what happened about the fig tree. "He was hungry; and seeing a fig tree afar off having leaves, He came if haply He might find anything thereon; and when He came to it He found nothing but leaves, for the time of figs was not yet. And Jesus answered and said unto it: 'No man eat fruit of thee hereafter for ever' . . . and Peter . . . saith unto Him: 'Master, behold the fig tree which thou cursedst is withered away.'" This is a very curious story, because it was not the right time of year for figs, and you really could not blame the tree. I cannot myself feel that either in the matter of wisdom or in the matter of virtue Christ stands quite as high as some other people known to history. I think I should put Buddha and Socrates above Him in those respects.

The Emotional Factor

As I said before, I do not think that the real reason why people accept religion has anything to do with argumentation. They accept religion on emotional grounds. One is often told that it is a very wrong thing to attack religion, because religion makes men virtuous. So I am told; I have not noticed it. You know, of course, the parody of that argument in Samuel Butler's book, *Erewhon Revisited*. You will remember that in *Erewhon* there is a certain Higgs who arrives in a remote country, and after spending some time there he escapes from that country in a balloon. Twenty years later he comes back to that country and finds a new religion in which he is worshiped under the name of the "Sun Child," and it is said that he ascended into heaven. He finds that the Feast of the Ascension is about to be celebrated, and he hears Professors Hanky and Panky say to each other that they never set eyes on the man Kiggs, and they hope they never will; but they are the high priests of the religion of the Sun Child. He is very indignant, and he comes up to them, and he says, "I am going to expose all this humbug and tell the people of Erewhon that it was only I, the man Higgs, and I went up in a balloon." He was told, "You must not do that, because all the morals of this country are bound round this myth, and if they once know that you did not ascend into heaven they will all become wicked"; and so he is persuaded of that and he goes quietly away.

That is the idea—that we should all be wicked if we did not hold to the Christian religion. It seems to me that the people who have held to it have been for the most part extremely wicked. You find this curious fact, that the more intense has been the religion of any period and the more profound has been the dogmatic belief, the greater has been the cruelty and the worse has been the state of affairs. In the so-called ages of faith, when men really did believe the Christian religion in all its completeness, there was the Inquisition, with its tortures; there were millions of unfortunate women burned as witches; and there was every kind of cruelty practiced upon all sorts of people in the name of religion.

You find as you look around the world that every single bit of progress in humane feeling, every improvement in the criminal law, every step toward the diminution of war, every step toward better treatment of the colored races, or every mitigation of slavery, every moral progress that there has been in the world, has been consistently opposed by the organized churches of the world. I say quite deliberately that the Christian religion, as organized in its churches, has been and still is the principal enemy of moral progress in the world.

How the Churches Have Retarded Progress

You may think that I am going too far when I say that that is still so. I do not think that I am. Take one fact. You will bear with me if I mention it. It is not a pleasant fact, but the churches compel one to mention facts that are not pleasant. Supposing that in this world that we live in today an inexperienced girl is married to a syphilitic man; in that case the Catholic Church says, "This is an indissoluble sacrament. You must endure celibacy or stay together. And if you stay together, you must not use birth control to prevent the birth of syphilitic children." Nobody whose natural sympathies have not been warped by dogma, or whose moral nature was not absolutely dead to all sense of suffering, could maintain that it is right and proper that that state of things should continue.

That is only an example. There are a great many ways in which, at the present moment, the church, by its insistence upon what it chooses to call morality, inflicts upon all sorts of people undeserved and unnecessary suffering. And of course, as we know, it is in its major part an opponent still of progress and of improvement in all the ways that diminish suffering in the world, because it has chosen to label as morality a certain narrow set of rules of conduct which have nothing to do with human happiness; and when you say that this or that ought to be done because it would make for human happiness, they think that has nothing to do with the matter at all. "What has human happiness to do with morals? The object of morals is not to make people happy."

Fear, the Foundation of Religion

Religion is based, I think, primarily and mainly upon fear. It is partly the terror of the unknown and partly, as I have said, the wish to feel that you have a kind of elder brother who will stand by you in all your troubles and disputes. Fear is the basis of the whole thing—fear of the mysterious, fear of defeat, fear of death. Fear is the parent of cruelty, and therefore it is no wonder if cruelty and religion have gone hand in hand. It is because fear is at the basis of those two things. In this world we can now begin a little to understand things, and a little to master them by help of science, which has forced its way step by step against the Christian religion, against the churches, and against the opposition of all the old precepts. Science can help us to get over this craven fear in which mankind has lived for so many generations. Science can teach us, and I think our own hearts can teach us, no longer to look around for imaginary supports, no longer to invent allies in the sky, but rather to look to our own efforts here below to make this world a fit place to live in, instead of the sort of place that the churches in all these centuries have made it.

What We Must Do

We want to stand upon our own feet and look fair and square at the world—its good facts, its bad facts, its beauties, and its ugliness; see the world as it is and be not afraid of it. Conquer the world by intelligence and not merely by being slavishly subdued by the terror that comes from it. The whole conception of God is a conception derived from the ancient Oriental despotisms. It is a conception quite unworthy of free men. When you hear people in church debasing themselves and saying that they are miserable sinners, and all the rest of it, it seems contemptible and not worthy of self-respecting human beings. We ought to stand up and look the world frankly in the face. We ought to make the best we can of the world, and if it is not so good as we wish, after all it will still be better than what these others have made of it in all these ages. A good world needs knowledge, kindliness, and courage; it does not need a regretful hankering after the past or a fettering of the free intelligence by the words uttered long ago by ignorant men. It needs a fearless outlook and a free intelligence. It needs hope for the future, not looking back all the time toward a past that is dead, which we trust will be far surpassed by the future that our intelligence can create.

CHAPTER EIGHT

THE QUEST FOR "BEING" *1
by Sidney Hook

I

During the last few years there has been a revival of the belief in the cognitive legitimacy of metaphysics and ontology. The positivist ban on expressions once called metaphysical or ontological has been lifted by some of the high priests of positivism themselves. Even in quarters where until recently only the austerities of symbolic logic were practiced, there is talk about ontological reference, ontological factors and entities. A good deal of. this is very innocent. The context of the term in the writings of some current logicians seems to indicate that the term "ontological" stands for the existential, or for the objective reference of statements, or the designation of a symbol.

I characterize this usage of the term as innocent because all it seems to do is to call attention to the fact, and, in some situations, to the controlling importance, of subject-matter. Physics, chemistry, sociology have an "ontological" character because their equations or laws describe something or point beyond themselves. Indeed, according to some writers the term "ontological" refers to the content of any communication about anything. This, of course, would mean that the only indisputable parts of ontology are the sciences themselves, because no one doubts that the physics of particles or the chemistry of colloids or the ecology of plants or the biology of mammals has a much more definite content than traditional ontology. Hence when Quine says, "Ontological statements follow immediately from all manner of casual statements of commonplace fact,"2 I cannot see in this anything more than an admission that ontology is a collection of supererogative truisms, some might say verbalisms.

*Used with permission from *The Journal of Philosophy*, Vol. 50, New York, New York, 1953.

There is another ontological aspect of the world which turns out to be nothing more than the recognition that from the character of a specific instrument in a determinate situation we can infer something about the character of the subject-matter or material on which we use the instrument. Thus one writer says: "Given an iron bar to cut, and a choice between a penknife and a hacksaw as instruments, it will require no great mechanical genius to discover that the hacksaw is much more convenient and suitable. From our knowledge of the instruments, and their different degrees of inadequacy here, we can surely draw the 'ontological' conclusion that the bar is *hard* rather than soft."[3] If this is a piece of ontological knowledge, then the fact that the size of a man's shoe is a good index of the size of his unbunioned foot, is also a piece of ontological knowledge—perfectly trivial and perfectly useless. Before we use the hacksaw we already know that the iron is hard, and don't have to infer that fact from the successful use of the hacksaw in cutting the bar; and that we have feet is not an ontological discovery made consequent upon our being shod.

No, the revival of ontology involves more ambitious claims. Its validity as a systematic discipline rests upon the contention that it gives us a knowledge about something or everything which is not communicated by any particular science or all of the sciences. It either tells us something that we didn't know before or makes us aware in some distinctive way of what in some sense we have already known.

The oldest as well as the most recent ontological claim is that the truths ontology gives us are about Being—about Being *as such*. Yet despite the enormous literature which has been written about Being, it is extremely difficult to find anything clear or intelligible in writings which contain that expression. The reasons are obvious. In ordinary discourse every significant word has an intelligible opposite. Being, however, as an all-inclusive category does not seem to possess an intelligible opposite. Not-Being is not the opposite of Being, because when it is taken as equivalent in meaning to Nothing, and Nothing is interpreted as a substantival entity, then Nothing is a Something (indeed, so concrete that some writers speak of it as an "abyss," others as "Death") and hence possesses Being, too. So that whatever is true of Being as such is true of Nothing, and whatever is true of Nothing is true of Something which has Being. If, on the other hand, non-Being means "falsity" and not a substantival entity, then we are dealing with a property of assertions; its opposite is "truth;" and we can banish the term "Being" from the vocabulary of philosophy.

However "Nothing" be considered, it is a derivative notion from something, related to an act, real or imagined, of negation. Bergson many years ago, in his striking analysis of "the idea of nothing," wrote: "If suppressing a thing consists in replacing it by another, if thinking the absence of one thing is only possible by the more or less explicit representation of the presence of some other thing, if, in short, annihilation signifies before anything else substitution, the idea of an 'annihila-

tion of everything' is as absurd as that of a square circle."[4] Precisely
for this reason the question originally asked by Schelling and repeated
in our time by Heidegger: "Why is there something: why is there
not nothing?" is devoid of sense except as a sign of emotional anxiety.

The same considerations apply to Tillich's "shock of non-being or
being not." He, too, asks: what kind of being must we attribute to non-
being? Aware that, to make ordinary sense, we should translate this
into what meaning can we attribute to the word or expression "non-
being," he rejects the reformulation as an ontological evasion. Any
theory, he asserts, according to which negation is a *logical* judgment
must be "rooted in an ontological structure."[5]

The only evidence that Tillich gives for this assertion is that there
are *expectations* in the world which are sometimes unfulfilled or disappointed. "Thus disappointed, expectation creates the distinction between
being and non-being."[6] Expectation, however, is an attitude possible
only to man. Where there is no man, there is no expectation, and therefore no non-being. Expectation, and therefore non-being, are purely
psychological categories. We should therefore expect Tillich to admit
that he is not dealing with a substantial force or power when he refers
to "non-being," but with a capacity limited to one species in a "sea of
being." Instead, he forgets that he has just told us that human expectation has "created" non-being and maintains that man "*participates* not
only in being but in non-being." But one cannot participate in a distinction which one creates unless one, of course, is everywhere, unless
one's self with one's power of expectation is always present everywhere.
And this is the implication of Tillich's further statement that "there can
be no world unless there is a dialectical participation of non-being in
being."[7]

One can doubt any particular judgment or assertion but one cannot
doubt all possible judgments or assertions because significant doubt
always rests upon something we accept. The logic is exactly the same
with denial. We may dialectically relate non-being to a specific being
but not to everything: non-being cannot be regarded as coeval with being.

Nor is the outcome any different if we define Being as the realm of
all possibles and consider the actual as the class of realized possibles.
For what on this view is the ontological status of the impossible? If by
the impossible we mean only the self-contradictory, then the possible
can only mean the self-consistent, and we are dealing merely with logical
notions, not ontological entities or traits. And if, by the impossible, we
mean only what violates scientific law or fact, we are dealing with an
unrealizable possibility after all, and the impossible becomes a species
of the possible, and we are back into the same semantic morass as we
were with the concept of Being.

It seems apparent that only by logical legerdemain can we start from
a conception of Being as such or pure Being, and end up with meanings or categories that are quite distinct from the *as-suchness* or *purity*
of Being. It is notorious that the Hegelian logic comes a cropper on its

very first triad. Its attempt to derive Becoming, and then Determinate
Being, from Pure Being is even more hopeless than the attempt to deduce, from the notion of God, the existence of the world—which is the
real secret of Hegel's ontology. Nor is the Thomistic ontology in a better logical position with respect to Being. Notice the way in which "the
good" and "the true" are identified with Being as transcendental notions equally applicable to each other. "Being" and "the good" (or
"valuable") cannot be identified with each other without making nonsense of the view that evils and disvalues are to be found in the world.
No matter what one's ontology, to deny existence of being to the many
evils of the world is so gratuitously arbitrary that any conception of
being from which it is a conclusion cannot be taken seriously. This conclusion cannot be avoided by the scholastic distinction according to
which although "ontological evil must be identical with nonbeing or
nothingness,"[8] yet it is logically distinct from the latter. For from this
it persumably follows that evil is not mere negation but privation, or
absence of a good, and is called a defect or deficiency of being only because by *definition* being and good are identical. I say by definition because if this view has any empirical content, then the tiniest twinge of
pain is enough to refute it. For if anything is positive in the world, if
anything proclaims itself with a scream or shout, it is pain. To regard
pleasure or happiness as the absence of pain is mistaken but credible.
To regard pain merely as the absence or privation of the good, no
matter in what we find the good—whether pleasure, happiness, the
beatific vision,—is both mistaken and incredible.

Why is it that the term "Being" generates by illogical fission so
many other characteristics in treatises on ontology—whether Thomistic,
Hegelian, or existentialist? Because it has been surreptitiously endowed
with the properties of Mind. This property makes not a category of
classical ontology but of *Tiefenpsychologie*. This is especially true for
Heidegger, the fount of almost all existentialist thinking today. Heidegger asserts that every metaphysical question concerns itself with every
other, so that *au fond* there is only one metaphysical question. He also
asserts that when a question is raised in metaphysics "the questioner
as such is by his very questioning involved in the question."[9] Metaphysics,
then, can never tell us anything about the world independent of its relation to us, of what could be true of Being if there were no human beings (or would be if there were no human beings). Its concern is quite
different from that of science. The sciences, says Heidegger, "allow the
object itself the first and last word," but "no matter where and however
deeply science investigates what-is it will never find Being."[10] Why? Because "Being is not an existing quality of what-is, nor, unlike what-is,
can Being be conceived and established objectively."

What is Heidegger trying to say? He is trying to say that Being is
a product of a Creative Act of an anonymous undifferentiated Ego
(although he does not use this term) in a process in which a substantial
Nothing is presupposed. It is a pagan and Teutonic rendering of the

theological myth of the creation out of nothing, which turns out to be really the mythical process of the self-realization of Mind.

No matter how inquiry is conceived, negation is a process of denying, distinguishing, and contrasting judgments or statements. The term "Nothing" has a meaning because in a given situation certain negations may be validly made, but it does not designate an entity. (It is a syncategorematic expression.) Heidegger asserts, however, that in denying there is such a thing as nothing we are already admitting not only that it is a meaningful term but that it is an entity of sorts. This is an even more fantastic inference than the claim that the assertion that round squares do not exist implies that round squares actually exist, otherwise how could we significantly deny them—a kind of argument which seems to me to have been laid to rest by Russell's theory of descriptions. But independently of the character of Heidegger's argument, he makes it unmistakably clear that for him "Nothing [*Das Nichts*] is the source of negation, not the other way about."[11] The nature of his *Nichts* is as positive as any concrete *Etwas* because it has definite powers. These powers are psychological. Notice the terms from which rational negation is supposed to be derived. "More abysmal than the mere propriety of rational negation is the harshness of *opposition* and the violence of *loathing*. More responsible the pain of *refusal* and the *mercilessness* of an interdict. More oppressive the bitterness of *renunciation*"[12] (my italics).

Opposition, loathing, refusal, mercilessness, renunciation—these are some of the modes in which *Das Nichts* appears. This is neither logic nor classic ontology but an ontologized, pseudo-psychological projection of the aggressions of a self-hating and other-hating Ego. It is not surprising that Heidegger says of Reason, Logic, or Common Sense that it "has no sovereignty in the field of inquiry into Nothing and Being." His work is an invitation to apply not logical analysis to his argument but psychoanalysis to his position. But as philosophers we cannot accept an invitation in these terms.

A less subjective conception of Being than Heidegger's is found in Nicolai Hartmann, who properly points out that Heidegger is concerned not with the nature of Being but with the "meaning of Being," i.e., not with the *Seienden als Seienden* but with the *Sinn von Sein*.[13] Hartmann's own conception of ontology, although less mystical than Heidegger's, is no more satisfactory. For him common-sense knowledge and scientific knowledge are both ontological because they exhibit an *initial* naive realism towards things as the objects of knowledge. But in this sense the basic ontological structure of "being" can hardly be considered as given in the same way. It requires a pretty sophisticated vision, physical or mental, to grasp the Being of this table over and above what we find in our naive perception of it as a common-sense thing or in our understanding of it as a scientific object.

The real difficulty is that Hartmann does not establish that there is anything corresponding to "Being" despite his use of the term on almost every page of his *Zur Grundlegung der Ontologie.* To be sure he says that Being is indefinable and not graspable (*begreifbar*); but since this is true in a sense of many other terms, like matter, consciousness, color, or sound, it is not a sufficient characterization. But the more important point is that for these *other* fundamental terms, although formal definitions cannot be offered, we can state the rules or linguistic conventions which guide our usage of them under certain conditions. We cannot do so for Being.

The scholastics were perfectly aware of the difficulty and sought to settle it by asserting that Being is neither a univocal term nor an equivocal term but is predicable of the different modes of Being *by analogy of proportion.* The analogy of proportionality is a technical and very interesting doctrine which calls attention to the familiar linguistic fact that many terms in discourse do not have a univocal meaning and yet cannot be said to be ambiguous. In such cases the context provides a principle of specification so that while we are aware that the shades of meaning in two uses of an expression or utterance are different, nonetheless the meanings are sufficiently similar to make the use of the expression or utterance appropriate. For example, if I say the sea is angry, I am using a metaphor. If challenged, I can say what I want to say without using that word or any synonym. Now, someone pokes a stick at a lion when he is feeding. The lion bares his fangs, roars, and leaps. I say, "The lion is angry." In saying the lion is "angry" I am convinced that it is an apropriate expression, and yet I am not convinced that it means the same thing as when I say of the game warden who comes running that "he is angry," and of the sea that "it is angry," although both expressions are properly used. The rules or conventions which determine the usage of the term "angry" for men, animals, and seas are not the same. This is even true when only feelings or emotions are involved. The mystics and poets tell us that "just as the hart pants for water, so the soul pants for God." The term "pant" has not the same meaning, but certainly there is no ordinary equivocation here, because instead of being confused or puzzled by the sentence, we find it more or less illuminating. And so it is argued that when we speak of God's feeling of wrath, although God is not a Creature, and although he cannot be said to feel angry like men and lions, nonetheless there is a greater appropriateness in referring to his *wrath*, in certain situations in which he presumably reveals himself, than in referring to his *mercy*. And so it is declared that all of God's properties are proportionally, analogically predicated of him—from which one consequence is the rejection of negative theology.

Now even if the doctrine of analogy of proportionality were sound, it cannot be applied to Being. And this, for two reasons. When I say God is a father to man somewhat in the same way as man is father to his family, I have at least a reasonably clear idea of what it means for a man to be a father, and I extend this notion to God where, although it cannot be literally true of him, it still applies with a greater appropriateness than some other notion like "nephew." We pray to "Our Father in Heaven," but no one would be likely to pray to "Our nephew in Heaven." Now, to predicate Being of some particular mode of Being, whether physical, mental, or logical, whether divine, earthly, or satanic, I must have at least as correspondingly a clear idea of Being as I had of anger or mercy *before* I attributed it to the Deity. But this is precisely what I do *not* have; this is just what I am seeking to make clear to myself. How, then, can I extend it by an analogy of proportionality from other modes of Being? By this procedure the obscure can only become obscurer. Secondly, we are told that "Being is affirmed of the finite [being] by its dependence on infinite being,"[14] that infinite being is the ground or cause of finite being, so that the primary analogue for the proportion is not the Being of finite Being but the Being of Infinite Being. But the fogginess of the term Being does not disappear when it is lifted from the dimension of the Finite to the Infinite.

Let us recapitulate as simply as possible some of the obvious distinctions we recognize in ordinary language and common-sense discourse which make the alleged category of "being" a non-cognitive as well as non-communicative, and therefore perfectly dispensable, term in discourse.

Being is not identical with spatio-temporal existence since there are many things of which we speak, like plans, meanings, memories, dimensions, that cannot be called spatio-temporal existences; nor are they treated as such.

Being is not identical with the imaginable, for there are many things in the world which are unimaginable.

Being is not identical with the intellectually conceivable or intelligible, for, as we have already seen, this means subject to the law of contradiction. Being would be synonymous with consistency which is not a category of ontology at all—but of logic or discourse. As I understand the sense in which C. I. Lewis uses the term "Being," it is like the expression "either A or not A," possessing zero connotation and universal comprehension in that it is applicable to anything mentionable or discoursed about.[15]

Finally, Being cannot be exhaustively characterized as that which is independent of presence, or relation, to the knowing mind in any or all of its participial modes, knowing, hoping, imagining, believing, etc. For if this is what is meant by Being—why, we would have to deny it to pains and aches and feelings and dreams which are certainly dependent upon presence or relation to "consciousness" or "mind," no matter how these terms are interpreted, in a way different from the presence or relation of sticks and stones to consciousness.

Before we abandon any further quest for an account of Being which makes sense, let us look at yet one other attempt by a distinguished theologian whose ontology has been widely acclaimed. I refer to Professor Paul Tillich.

For Tillich, philosophy and theology may be distinguished but not separated, for "whatever the relation of God, world and man may be, it lies in the frame of being."[16] Tillich takes being so seriously that he quotes with approval Heidegger's dictum as a definition of man, "Man is that being who asks what being is," a statement whose cognitive import does not differ from the nonontological statement that man is the only animal which possesses speech, and therefore asks questions. At the outset it seems as if in his ontology Tillich seeks to escape from the subjectivistic strain in Heidegger. Ontology concerns itself with *Being*, "as it *is*," while philosophical theology deals with Being "as it is *for us*," i.e., "what concerns us ultimately, inescapably, unconditionally." This brave differentiation collapses almost at once because, like Heidegger, Tillich takes human existence as paradigmatic of the structure of all Being—so that he is capable of writing: "a self is not a thing that may or may not exist: it is an original phenomenon which logically precedes all questions of existence."[17] This seems to me so patently false, if "logical" means logical not psychological, that I should regard it as much as a *reductio ad absurdum* of a philosophical position as I would solipsism, from which it really does not differ, since the self embraces not only the ego but the non-ego as in romantic post-Kantian idealism.

Now the great limitation of using the technique of the *reductio ad absurdum* in philosophical argument is that there is no absurdity, as Morris Cohen used to say, to which a philosopher will not resort to defend another absurdity. So instead of showing to what Tillich's views lead, I shall ask some simple questions about his starting point, the answers to which I have not been able to find either in his writings or in those of his commentators.

Tillich writes: "What is Being itself? What is that which is not a special being or group of beings, not something concrete or something abstract, but rather something which is always thought implicitly, and sometimes explicitly, if something is said to *be*?"[18] In another place, he writes: "Ontology asks: what does it mean that something is and is not *not*? Which [What?] characteristics does everything show that participates in Being?" I found no answers to these questions in Tillich's writings. He asks them and passes on to something else. The reason, it seems to me, that he doesn't answer these questions is that, as his very language shows, he has been misled by the *form* that a significant question has when it is asked about terms that have intelligible opposites, and uses the same *form* with words that have no opposites, and fails to see that when this is done he has not asked a significant question. It is an illustration of the by now familiar story and mistake of assuming that because two sentences have the same grammatical form, they have the same logical form.

Perhaps another way of saying the same thing is that Tillich is using the term Being as if it were an essence or universal, and his employment of the word "participates" suggests that he is treating it as a Platonic essence or universal.

I am going to rewrite the first of the above quotations from Tillich, substituting a term for Being which has an intelligible opposite and which can be treated as a genuine universal.

"What is triangularity itself? What is that which is not a special triangle in a group of triangles, not a concrete triangle or an abstract triangle, but rather what we always think explicitly, if something is said to *be* triangular?"

The answer is a definition of triangularity, not a triangle, or even an image of a triangle. It is a geometrical relation, that can be represented in many different ways, of a plane figure enclosed by three straight lines. That is what we explicitly or implicitly mean if something is said to be triangular. If I substitute the term "humanity" for Being in the above passage, it still makes sense, for I would then be asking for a definition of a predicate "human" which is shared by a number of individuals. Tillich, too, as the passage above shows, is asking for a definition of a predicate, but he is assuming that being (or existence) is a predicate. Now it seems to me that if Kant established anything, he showed that existence is not a predicate, or attribute, or property like triangular or human. By turning his back on Kant at this point (which has nothing to do with Kant's epistemology), Tillich is basing not only his ontology but his theology as well on a demonstrable logical mistake. There is no characteristic, to answer Tillich's question, which everything shows that participates in Being. An electron, a table, a mirage, a pain, a stone, an idea, $\sqrt{-1}$, a power, a dream, a memory, an army, a geological stratum, an after-image, a mirror image, the prime number between 1001 and 1011, a corporation, a dynasty, a mode of production—have nothing in common except that they are objects of discourse, or can be thought about. And "being mentionable" or "being thought about" is not a characteristic or property which belongs to anything in the way that triangular or human does.[19]

II

What, then, shall we conclude about Being? After all it is a word in the English language as well as in all other Indo-European languages. But the presence of a word does not require that we build an ontology to explain it any more than the use of the word "God" requires a theology, or an actual god, to explain it or than the word "infinite" entails the presence of an actual infinite.

I do not believe that the word "being" has the same meaning, even analogically, in all the contexts in which it appears. In the expression "He's being funny," the word "being" does not mean the same as it does when the poet apostrophizes a "glorious being" or when we say "he's being one of the boys" or when Heidegger says man is a being who asks what being is. The question is, however, whether the word "being" has *any* meaning in a philosophical context, and by a philosophical context I mean any activity which inquires into the logic and the *procedures* by which knowledge is built up and described.

In this kind of context, the word "being" seems to function sometimes as an "infinity or zero word," an expression Dewey borrows from
a metaphysical mariner by the name of Klyce who having read the
Encyclopedia Britannica from cover to cover published a book called
Universe, to which Dewey wrote an introduction.[20]

In this introduction Dewey makes the point that "in actual use
names call attention to features of a situation; that they are tools for
directing perception or experimental observations." But the situation
itself is always taken for granted. It cannot be exhaustively described,
so that at any point there is something grasped but unsaid, something
given over and beyond what is taken. It is understood implicitly as the
background without which what we say would make no sense. When
we come across a man talking to himself or when we hear an insane
man talk, even if we understand his separate words, or an isolated
sentence, we say he is not making sense. All discourse, every gesture,
every vehicle of communication, in addition to an explicit implication,
has an implicit implication (presupposition) of a background or situation or context, call it what you will, which is ineffable. "It is necessary to have a word," says Dewey, "which reminds us that whatever we
explicitly state has this implicit, unstateable, implication."

There is an entire class of "words," according to Dewey, which have
no definite meaning, and which are distinguished from "terms" which
have, and which function as reminders of the presence of something
always referred to, of that which we are discoursing about. In this class
of words are the expressions "everything," "existence" "the world,"
"Universe," "the non-mathematical infinite," and "*Being*." At least
one of their uses in sentences is not to designate or stand for any
identifiable trait but to remind us of *what* we are talking about but
which at that moment cannot itself be said.

Dewey's own analysis indicates that we don't need these particular
words and that the background of knowledge can be suggested by
the use of other words in the statements we make. His distinction between the cognitively explicit and the qualitatively implicit blossoms
out later into the distinction between knowing and having and in his
doctrine of the situation as always presupposed by inquiry and yet not
statable in inquiry. "The situation," Dewey says, "cannot present itself
as an element in a proposition any more than a universe of discourse
can appear as a member of discourse within that universe."[21]

This sentence makes the same point without the use of any "infinity
or zero" words. And it is a point relevant to an inquiry about the nature
of knowing, to an analysis of what it means for anything to be known,
rather than an analysis of what it means for anything to be.

Dewey never claimed to have an ontology and in his *Logic* defends
the view that logical forms need no ontological underpinning. He
does claim to have a metaphysics. But he wrote in his ninetieth year
that "nothing can be farther from the facts of the case" than "that I
use the word *metaphysical* in the sense it bears in the classic tradition

based on Aristotle."[22] He vowed at that time (as if he had all of eternity before him) "never to use the words [*metaphysics* and *metaphysical*] again in connection with any aspect of any part of my own position."[23]

When he did use the word "metaphysics," Dewey meant by it the description "of the generic traits of the natural world" or of existence. In contradistinction, the specific traits of the world are the subject-matter of the sciences.

Now I shall argue later that when Dewey spoke of metaphysics as the description of the generic traits of existence, he had in mind those pervasive traits of existence-as-experienced which were relevant to the formulation of ideals of human conduct or the charting of the paths of human wisdom. But he has not always been interpreted as meaning this, and his actual words are sometimes puzzling. Undoubtedly there are places where Dewey does seem to suggest that there is a subject-matter, viz., generic traits of all existence, which lends itself to empirical study by the same methods which the sciences use.

This is the notion I want now to examine. There are certain initial difficulties in understanding what is meant by the view that metaphysics is a science of existence (or being) as such whose task is the description of the generic traits exhibited by every field of knowledge and everything within it. For, as the view is sometimes formulated, some key ambiguities strike the eye.

(1) One writer tells us that

> If metaphysics be a sound analysis of being *qua* being, it could have the same relation to geology or astronomy or physiology that physics or chemistry have to each other, or chemistry and biology. Whenever scientists other than metaphysicians use such terms as cause or law or contingency, they ought to be using them in the same sense in which metaphysicians define them.[24]

We are not informed which metaphysician's definitions the scientist is to use—Hegel's, Aristotle's, or Whitehead's (or Hume's). One would have thought such information necessary in view of the tiresome habit metaphysicians have of contradicting each other—but let that pass for a moment. More important is the fact that the relationship between metaphysics and geology (or any other special science) will be one thing if it is like the present relationship between physics and chemistry, and something else again if it is like the *present* relationship between chemistry (or physics) and biology.

(a) As I understand it the present relationship between physics and chemistry is such that laws in both sciences are explained in terms of the same set of theoretical assumptions and basic terms, and these are the assumptions and terms of physics, so that chemistry roughly speaking consists of that branch of physics which studies certain special types of phenomenon. If metaphysics were related to geology as physics to chemistry, we should expect either that some propositions of geology should be derivable from propositions of metaphysics, or that they should be explicable in metaphysical terms. Now let us take any specific geological proposition, e.g., the principle of "posthumous movement" in structural geology which asserts that the earth's crust is more likely to crumple along a fold and particular direction in places where previous crumplings have occurred than in other places. Suppose that we deny this principle or that it turns out to be false. What possible difference would it make to any metaphysical theory? What generic trait of existence would thereby be denied? The answer, it seems to me, is "none whatsoever." The relation, then, between metaphysics and geology, whatever it is, cannot be like the relation between physics and chemistry, for if certain chemical phenomena accompanying the electrolytic dissociation of liquids and metals uniformly failed to occur, certain modifications in physical theory would be called for.

(b) The present relation between chemistry and biology is something different from that between physics and chemistry because not only are we unable at present to reduce laws of biology (say genetics) to those of chemistry but there are certain terms used in biology which cannot be defined by reduction to chemical terms at present. But no true biological statement is incompatible with any of the statements accepted as true in physics and chemistry. If this is the type of relationship which exists between metaphysics and geology (or any other science), then what is being said is that metaphysically true propositions are necessary conditions for the truths of geological propositions, and that the metaphysician has veto power over the findings of the scientist in the event that they do not square with metaphysical truth. What is ontologically false cannot be scientifically true. (Some philosophers actually said this about the theory of relativity and about certain results in atomic physics.)

But there are two difficulties here. (i) If this is the relation between metaphysics and geology (science), it is not sufficient to distinguish it from the relation between logic and geology (science). For logic, too, exercises veto power over what may be believed in science. It doesn't decree what the scientist must find but insists that what he says must be at least internally self-consistent. (And this is perhaps all the philosophic critics of quantum theory and relativity were protesting —not the discoveries but the needlessly paradoxical ways of formulating the discoveries.) (ii) Few metaphysicians, and none of those who define it as the study of generic traits, have the courage of their imperial claims. For sooner or later everyone of them admits that the relation between metaphysics and geology is not asymmetrical, as they boldly claimed at first, but symmetrical. The very same writer from who we quoted above goes on to say: "Whenever [scientists] reach formulations which show discrepancy with the principles of metaphysics, they either need the correction metaphysics can give or can furnish the correction metaphysics needs."[25] When they contradict each other, metaphysicians may correct the geologists or geologists may correct the metaphysicians! It now appears that they are as much a part of one discipline, after all, as physicists and chemists, and we come back to the first type of relation. But if what we have said is valid, then whether it is asserted that the first relationship between metaphysics and geology holds or that the second relation holds, both assertions are false.

(2) There is still another interpretation offered of metaphysics conceived as a science interested in the accurate descriptions of the generic traits which existence everywhere and always has. According to this view, what metaphysics does is to analyze the *meanings* of fundamental or generic terms. "Careful formulation of the principle of causality," we are told, "is legitimate metaphysics."[26] Not only is the analysis of the meaning of cause and effect part of metaphysics but also "the sense" in which events are said to be determined or contingent, the relation between necessity and chance, and "the nature of 'law' and its relation to the particular events which are said to 'obey' law."[27] If this is metaphysical analysis, how does it differ from logical analysis of basic concepts or the analysis of the language of science? Hume offered a careful formulation of the principle of causality in order to show that no metaphysical assumptions were involved in its consistent use. If the logical empiricists have been really prosecuting metaphysics in their prolonged discussion of "the nature of 'law' and its relation to the particular events which are said to 'obey' the law," why have they been accused of "persecuting" metaphysics?

If metaphysics consists in the analysis of the *meaning* of "causality" or any other category used to describe or explain events, how can we at the same time claim that "its conclusions will be probabilities with which we approach the future"?[28] Only statements of fact can be probable. Metaphysical statements on this view are presumably statements of empirical, generical fact. But an analysis of a concept is adequate or inadequate, clear or obscure. We may say of an attempted analysis that it is probable that it will be an adequate analysis. But we cannot say that the analysis is probable. And if we say, as does Professor Randall, that the conclusions of the metaphysician are not only probable but corrigible, we are obviously denying that metaphysics has anything to do with the logical analysis of concepts.[29]

(3) Do those who talk about empirical metaphysics really believe what they seem to say? Professor Randall writes:

> Metaphysics, in the light of its long history, is a rather specific scientific inquiry, with a definite field and subject-matter of its own, a science that like any other is cumulative and progressive, which has in fact in our own generation made remarkable progress. It is the science of existence as existence.[30]

I hesitate to take issue with such a distinguished historian of philosophy as Professor Randall but I venture to suggest that if the history of philosophy throws any light on the subject it establishes precisely the opposite of what Professor Randall writes, that far from being cumulative in its results, metaphysics is in a worse state of confusion and disagreement than in many periods of the past, and that far from having made remarkable progress in our generation, metaphysics has received such blows that metaphysicians spend an inordinate amount of their time trying to prove that they are not necessarily talking non-sense.

But the more important point I want to urge here is that just as there is no such thing as "Being," i.e., it is a word that neither designates nor refers to anything observable or discriminable in the world, and has neither a substantive nor attributive character, so there is no such thing as a generic or pervasive trait of existence as Professor Randall describes it. Metaphysics, he says, "analyzes the generic traits manifested by existences of any kind, the characters sure to turn up in any universe of disc ˙ʳse—those traits exhibited in any 'ουσια' or subject-matter whatever, the fundamental and pervasive distinctions in terms of which any subject-matter may be understood, as they are found within any subject matter."[31]

Very well, we ask him to name one such trait. Is time a category of metaphysics? It is not a generic trait of mathematics. It never turns up as a character in the universe of discourse of mathematics, or of logic either. Take space. It is not a generic trait of consciousness. The consciousness of space does not imply that there is a space of consciousness. Causality. It is completely irrelevant to that generic subject-matter known as the theory of numbers. Chance. Are all subject-matters characterized by "chance"? Depending upon how we define the term, the question is silly or the answer to it is indeterminate. The same is true of the scope of "law" or "necessity." Those traits which we identify as "life," "mind," "consciousness," "matter," "energy," are *not* manifested by existences of every kind, they do *not* turn up in every universe of discourse. I cannot call the roll of all the categories or alleged generic traits, but in almost every case it is obvious that none of them are generic traits as Randall defines them, that some subject-matter can be found in which either it is false to say they apply or it makes no sense even to ask whether they apply or not.

There are some apparent exceptions to this, e.g., individuality. Is individuality a generic trait of all subject-matters and an attribute of all universes of discourse? Before we can answer we must ask what it means for anything to be an individual or have individuality. And if we do so, I believe it can be shown that we are dealing with a cluster of different meanings of the same word and that the reason the word "individual" can be meaningfully used in statements that describe certain traits and properties of every universe of discourse is *not* that there exists a generic or pervasive trait, but that as we go from one universe of discourse to another, the rules of usage which determine whether the word is being employed correctly in its apropriate universe of discourse, as well as the psychological and sociological reasons for the development of those rules, vary. The term "individual" (like the term "unity") has the same systematic ambiguity as the term "exists." Thus the considerations which make it correct to speak of an individual atom because it is differentiated in space-time from another atom, vary from the reasons which make it correct for me to speak of an individual form or figure because it is unique, or of an individual number because of its position in a series, or of an individual shade of color of a certain hue and intensity because of its specificity. Have all these meanings, or the rules which determine their different, albeit proper, uses, something in common? I do not see that they have. The most I should be willing to say is that all the problems to which the answer consists in offering definitions, or descriptions, of individuality in any universe of discourse are problems which involve the question of when we are satisfied that we mean the same thing, person, event or class of things, persons, or events. In short, it is only for purposes of communication or identification that we ask the question: In what does its or his individuality consist?

The same analysis can be made of continuity, which is a polar term of individuality. It does not characterize all subject-matters in the same sense. Continuity sometimes means the presence of organization, sometimes quantitative variation, or qualitative variation, sometimes the structure of the mathematical continuum, sometimes evolutionary development, sometimes merely similarity. Where the meaning of the term is reasonably clear and definite it does not hold of all subject-matters; where it seems to be applicable to all subject-matters, we have in reality a cluster of different meanings, only some of which stand in familial relationships to each other.

This tendency to assume that a common term in different contexts means the same thing is the source of much confusion not only in philosophical writing but in the special sciences as well; e.g., terms like "field," "energy," "inertia," are carried over, and used not as helpful metaphors but as if they had some invariant significance. By the same argument by which one reaches the conclusion that "continuity" and "individuality" are generic traits, a metaphysician can establish that "inertia" is a metaphysical trait. After all, we can meaningfully employ statements which describe the inertia of a physical thing; the inertia of a system; the inertia of habits, mind, intelligence; the inertia of style, law, or society. Does this justify me in saying that it turns up in every universe of discourse? If the answer is that despite their variations in meaning each usage of "inertia" fixes our attention on a specific mode of a generic trait itself described by the expression "resistance manifested by anything under discussion to a force which would change the state or position or direction of its motion," this will still not give us anything which satisfies the conditions of a genuine generic trait, for terms like "resistance" and "force" and "motion" are just as ambiguous in these several contexts as the expression "inertia" itself.

That there is something anomalous here is suggested by the fact that some generic traits of subject-matter are discovered apparently by pure dialectical inference or definition by those who speak of empirical metaphysics. For example, Professor Randall tells us that "for the empirical metaphysician, his method is no different from the ordinary experimental methods of observation and tested generalization employed in any

existential science, and his conclusions share in the probable and corrigible character of the findings of all experimental science."[32] This does
not, however, seem to be an accurate description of the way in which he
actually brings some traits to light, e.g., the metaphysical trait of intelligibility or knowability. Thus Professor Randall tells us that "knowability or intelligibility is a trait of every object of inquiry, of every
subject-matter," and if we ask: Why? he continues: "else it could not be
inquired into or made known."[33] If this statement is true, it certainly has
not been established by familiar experimental methods of observation
but only as a consequence of some unproven postulate or of a definition
of what it means to be inquired into. How can we know—and as empirical metaphysicians to boot!—that *every* subject-matter, a term used
by Professor Randall interchangeably with existence, is such that it
must lend itself to inquiry, that it *can* be inquired into? Only, it seems
to me, by adopting a procedure different from the one that professor
Randall thinks he is using.

This procedure is suggested by Professor Woodbridge. Professor
Woodbridge was convinced that intelligibility is a metaphysical trait but
he reached such a conclusion because he believed that although scientific
knowledge and metaphysical knowledge are not opposed they are still
widely different. "Science," he says, "asks for the laws of existence and
discovers them by experiment. Metaphysics asks for the nature of reality
and discovers it by definition."[34] If, however, we refuse to settle the generic traits of existence by definitions of the real, then I should say that
it is a discoverable fact that not all actions, not all subject-matters, are
intelligible, that we sometimes use statements properly which contain
the expression "unintelligible," and that there is a fairly clear sense in
which we can say of the hermit found dead in the desert or of a drown-
ing man that *whether* he thought of his family just before he died and
what he thought is practically unknowable.

III

Does it follow from all this that the term "ontological" cannot be
consistently and correctly used or that there are no ontological statements of which truth or falsity may be predicated? I am not arguing for
such a drastic conclusion. I do not believe that there is any consistent
usage for the term "ontological." I therefore wish to propose that we
call "ontological" those statements or propositions which we believe to
be cognitively valid, or which assert something that is true or false, and
yet which are not found in any particular science, whether of physics,
psychology, or sociology, but which are obviously taken for granted by
the sciences. For example, here are some propositions of this character:
There are many colors in the world; Colors have no smell or sound; It
is possible to perceive two things at the same time; There are many
kinds of processes in the world; Some processes are evolutionary; Thinking creatures inhibit the earth.

Note with reference to the last two sentences that I am not saying that evolution and thinking are generic traits of existence but only that the world is such that evolutionary and thinking processes are exhibited or discovered in it. These facts are ontological only because no science owns them. (I do not even have to say that "the world is such that . . . ," because I am not talking about the whole of the world but only of a particular state of affairs or succession of events denoted by the phrase "evolutionary process.")

It seems to me that there is an indeterminate number of truths of this kind which nobody bothers to make explicit or to analyze unless such truths are denied or appear to be denied. The analysis we make turns out to be a more careful and explicit description of what we already know and the grounds on which we say we know it, without committing us to any specific theory as to how what we know was learned. To the extent that they are about the furniture of heaven and earth in the same sense as astronomical, physical, and biological statements are about that furniture, they may sometimes describe certain massive facts of existence and human experience and constitute a primitive or pre-scientific physics and/or psychology.

What I propose, then, to call ontological statements about the world might loosely be called common-sense statements about the world which all scientists, if not all sciences, take for granted (I say all scientists rather than all sciences because these common-sense truths are not all relevant to all the sciences; e.g., that tears are usually a sign of grief rather than of joy is not relevant to physics). Recognition of their truth provides the fundamental tests of normal perception and sanity of behavior.

Pre-scientific or primitive physics and psychology do not give us statements about being *qua* being, or about the generic traits of existence. For they always fall short of the fully generic, they always leave something out. As I interpret Dewey's position on the nature of the subject-matter of metaphysical inquiry (his language is not always consistent), this, is his view, too. He is not so much interested in the traits that are truly generic but in those that are *irreducible*, whether generic or not. And he is interested in our giving intellectual recognition to the irreducible traits of the world in order to rule out the legitimacy of inquiries into "first causes" or "ultimate creation," in order to deny that "potentiality" is a causal principle of explanation or a causal immanent force, and above all in order to oppose reductionism of the materialistic and idealistic varieties. He believes it is possible to analyze a situation without reducing quality to quantity, without abolishing the pluralities of the given, without denying the objectivity of relations, and particularly of time and evolution. "Specifically diverse existences, interaction, change," Dewey tells us, are generic and irreducible traits, but these three traits turn out to be the irreducible traits "of the subject-matter of inquiry in the natural sciences,"[35] which certainly is not coextensive with all subject-matters. If there are any doubts about this, his remarks about evolution should settle them. "Evolution," he tells us, "appears to be just one of the irreducible traits of the world," which constitute the subject-matter of metaphysics. Obviously it cannot be generic in Professor Randall's meaning because not all changes are evolutionary.

It seems to me that the first, if not the last, thing Dewey is trying to say about ontology in this sense is that "the attempt to give an account of any occurrence involves the genuine and irreducible existence of the thing dealt with." It is a negative counsel of methodological wisdom: don't call you subject-matter into question as a conclusion of your inquiry into it. The investigation of the causes and consequences of any phenomenon is not sound if it denies in the end the phenomenal data which pose the problem, and the existential data which are truly presupposed by, or given with, the phenomenal data. Ontology is then a collection of an indeterminately large number of commonplaces or truisms—e.g., the world is such that this, that, or something else is found in it, which has these, those, or some other characteristics— truisms which have a certain use and point when they are counterposed to absurdities. There will always be a need for such truisms to the extent that philosophers—and others—keep on uttering absurdities.

There is another class of ontological statements or rather another character that they may have in addition to stocking our arsenals of sanity. Why, we may ask, do philosophers select some features about the world for special attention rather than others out of the infinite range of fact? And I wish to suggest that they do so because of their belief that these features have especial relevance to the career of human life on earth. Truths about them constitute what may be called philosophical anthropology. Philosophical anthropology is what Dewey calls metaphysics in *Experience and Nature*. Its subject-matter is not Being *qua* Being but those features of the world which constitute, to use Dewey's words, "a ground map of the province of criticism."

It is relevance to the life and death of man and to the whole gamut of his experience which is the key to the set of traits Dewey or any other ontologist selects for analysis and description. When Morris Cohen charges that Dewey's metaphysics is anthropocentric, echoing Santayana's criticism that Dewey emphasizes the foreground of experience, Dewey replies to both that every metaphysics which is not a pretentious rival to or substitute for science or religion is inescapably anthropocentric and has its own foreground. Metaphysics in this sense gives us the kind of knowledge which, to indulge a fancy, a Platonic soul would like to have, after it has drunk of the waters of Lethe, and before it descends, in answer to the questions: What kind of a world am I going to live in? What is the life of man like on earth? The answers to these questions may be vague but they are significant. And it is arguable that to the extent that good literature as a vehicle of communication has a cognitive content what it says can be expressed as answers to such questions. In answering these questions we don't seek scientific detail nor do we read the *Encyclopedia Britannica*. We are content with descriptions of life and existence in the large in which the human predicament, or the life of man, is taken *not* as analogue of the nature of nature, as in the myths of existentialism, but as a reflection, and outgrowth, of certain traits of nature, in which the human spirit, although not constitutive or pervasive in nature, is just as much a part, just as much at home, just as natural, as any other aspect or expression of nature.

The traits to which Dewey pays the greatest attention show that a standard of selection is at work. Individuality and constant relations; contingency and need; movement and arrest; the stable and precarious. These are not the categories of science but of the cosmic theatre of human destiny. Of all of them one can say what Dewey says of one of them: "Barely to note and register that contingency is a trait of natural events has nothing to do with wisdom. To note, however, contingency in connection with a concrete situation of life is that fear of the Lord which is at least the beginning of wisdom. The detection and definition of nature's end is in itself barren. But the undergoing that actually goes on in the light of this discovery brings one close to supreme issues: life and death" *(Experience and Nature, p. 413)*.

This is not romantic existentialism but scientifically grounded *Lebensphilosophie*. No verbal bars or taboo will prevent people from discussing questions such as these. The only legitimate goal in this connection is to ask that the questions first make sense, and then to find out whether the answers make good sense.

FOOTNOTES

1. The first section of this paper has been adapted from a contribution, "The Quest for 'Being,'" submitted to the XIth International Congress of Philosophy, 1953, and printed in its Proceedings, Vol. XIV, pp. 17-25.

2. Willard V. Quine, "On What There Is," *Review of Metaphysics*, Vol. II, No. 5 (Sept. 1948), p. 29.

3. Irving M. Copi, "Philosophy and Language," *Review of Metaphysics*, Vol. IV, No. 3 (March 1951), p. 435.

4. Bergson, *Creative Evolution*, Authorized Translation by Arthur Mitchell (New York, H. Holt, 1911), p. 283.

5. Paul Tillich, *Systematic Theology*, Vol. I (Univ. of Chicago Press, 1951), p. 187.

6. *Ibid.*, p. 187.

7. *Ibid.*, p. 189.

8. P. Coffey, *Ontology* (New York, Peter Smith, 1938), p. 182.

9. Martin Heidegger, *Existence and Being* (Chicago, H. Regnery, 1949), p. 355.

10. *Ibid.*, p. 384.

11. *Ibid.*, p. 372.

12. *Ibid.*, p. 373.

13. Nicolai Hartmann, *Zur Grundlegung der Ontologie*, p. 43.

14. Coffey, *Ontology*, p. 38.

15. C. I. Lewis, *An Analysis of Knowledge and Valuation* (La Salle, Ill., Open Court, 1946), p. 48.

16. Paul Tillich, *The Protestant Era* (Univ. of Chicago Press, 1948), p. 86.

17. *Systematic Theology*, Vol. I, p. 169.

18. *Ibid.*, p. 163.

19. The distinction Tillich makes between being and existence is irrelevant to the point at issue. For him God "is being-itself beyond essence and existence," so that God cannot be a specific thing or self (*Systematic Theology*, I, p. 205). But, as we have seen, "being" is inconsistently treated as a predicate in the same way as any essence. And since being is more than the merely logically possible, according to Tillich, but is also necessary, it not only is but necessarily is, so that despite his denial, Being is endowed with a certain kind of existence—that which cannot not be. Tillich conceals this from himself by speaking of Being as the absolutely unconditioned. But as Kant wrote in his critique of the ontological argument: "To use the word *unconditioned*, in order to get rid of all the conditions which the understanding requires, when wishing to conceive something as necessary, does not render it clear to us in the least whether, after that, we are still thinking anything or perhaps nothing, by the concept of unconditionally necessary" (*Critique of Pure Reason*, tr. by Max Müller, 2d ed., p. 478). This seems quite apt as a commentary on Tillich's procedure.

20. Scudder Klyce, *Universe* (Winchester, Mass., 1921), pp. iii ff.

21. Dewey, *Philosophy and Civilization* (New York: Minton, Balch 1931), p. 198.

22. Dewey, "Experience and Existence: A Comment," *Philosophy and Phenomenological Research*, Vol. IX (June 1949), p. 712.

23. *Ibid.*, p. 713.

24. Sterling P. Lamprecht, "Metaphysics: Its Function, Consequences, and Criteria," this *Journal*, Vol. XLIII (July 18, 1946), pp. 400-401.

25. *Ibid.*, p. 401.

26. *Ibid.*, p. 399.

27. *Ibid.*, p. 396.

28. *Ibid.*, p. 396.

29. John Herman Randall, Jr., "Metaphysics: Its Function, Consequences, and Criteria," this *Journal*, Vol XLIII (July 18, 1946), p. 408: "For the empirical metaphysician, his method is no different from the ordinary experimental methods of observation and tested generalization employed in any existential science, and his conclusions share in the probable and corrigible character of the findings of all experimental science." I am assuming that Professor Randall is not using "corrigible" in the sense in which it is applicable to geometrical proof.

30. *Ibid.*, p. 403.

31. *Ibid.*, p. 404.

32. *Ibid.*, p. 408.

33. *Ibid.*, p. 409.

34. F. J. E. Woodbridge, *Nature and Mind* (New York, Columbia University Press, 1937), pp. 40-41.

35. Dewey, "The Subject-Matter of Metaphysical Inquiry," this *Journal*, Vol. XII (June 24, 1915), p. 340.

PART THREE:

THE
PROCESS
PERSPECTIVE

INTRODUCTION

One of the fastest growing influences on the contemporary theological scene is the movement under discussion in this section. Process theology takes its cue from process philosophy, and together they form a perspective which must be reckoned with for some time to come. The history of this perspective can be traced as far back as Heraclitus, but its maturity must be said to date from middle of the last century when the work of Darwin effected a profound influence upon the philosophical world as well as upon the biological world. Two philosophers who caught the "evolutionary spirit" were Henri Bergson and Alfred North Whitehead.

Bergson argued against traditional metaphysics because it was far too static and monolithic to do justice to the ebb and flow of human experience. He maintained that the basic character of reality is revealed in its process nature, in its continual struggle to supercede itself. He labeled this character the "elan vital," and saw in it the foundation for a sound view of human freedom and moral growth. Bergson viewed reality as controlled by a dynamic force, not by static principles. Whitehead sought to overcome the deadening influence of the Newtonian view of reality as a closed, mechanical, materialistic system. He argued that this view focused too exclusively on objects and their location in space to do justice to the complex and flexible nature of reality. For Whitehead, the best way of viewing reality is in terms of the events, or "actual occasions," of experience. These events are a function of the relationships and interactions amongst various kinds of entities, such as objects and persons. It is these occasions which are the most real factors in human experience, and not the objects which make them up. In a word, for Whitehead, reality is one constant process.

Although there most certainly are other motifs in the thought of Bergson and Whitehead, it is their common emphasis on the growth and flexibility of experience and reality which serves as the foundation for what is here termed the process perspective. It should be clear at the outset that this point of view stands one step closer to traditional metaphysics than do either the existentialist or the humanistic perspectives. Here the emphasis is not so much on human values as it is upon coming to an understanding of the basic structure of reality. At the same time, it should also be noted that process philosophy stands opposed to traditional metaphysics because of the latter's tendency toward static, closed and object-centered systems. Another thing which distinguishes this perspective from the existentialist and humanistic is its employment of a somewhat rationalistic methodology. Traditional, speculative and logical processes are used as a means of arriving at conclusions. On the other hand, the process perspective makes far too frequent use of scientific developments to please either existentialists or traditional metaphysicians. Humanists, by and large, would not object to this procedure.

One of the primary reasons that a process approach to philosophy and theology has become increasingly popular is that it is in harmony with the character of the times, especially in America. To begin with, the rapid expansion of scientific and technological knowledge has greatly increased the pace of contemporary life. This increased pace tends to increase the need for a model of reality which focuses on changing events rather than on eternal objects and/or principles. The same can be said concerning the effects of the vastly increased mobility which characterizes modern existence. People who are constantly on the move find that a process perspective appeals to them far more than the classical perspective. Perhaps the change in the contemporary "way of being world" which most obviously contributes to the appeal of the process perspective is that which has taken place in communications. The message of our time is that the nature of our existence has been radically altered by the nature of our media. Marshal McLuhan is at least partly right when he argues that the shift from printed media to electronic media has a tendency to bring about a corresponding shift from a sequential, relatively static form of existence to one characterized by simultaneous awareness and processional involvement. It can be argued that this new form of existence necessitates a new perspective, namely that of process, with which to view experience and reality.

Another contemporary development which lends support to a process-centered worldview is the revolution that has taken place in the natural sciences. Beginning with Darwin's evolutionary ideas on down to the DNA molecule and recent work in genetics, the biological sciences have increasingly called attention to the dynamic, developing character of all life forms. In physics the results of Einstein's theories and sub-atomic research have raised serious difficulties for such standard concepts as "space," "matter," "time," and "cause." Clearly, a process perspective is in much greater harmony with these recent developments than is a more classical, Idealist perspective.

Finally, something ought to be said about the implications of the process perspective for the contemporary understanding of the concept of God. Space will only permit the introduction of two aspects of such implications. With respect to the character of God, it has been customary to conceive of Him as eternal and immutable, or in Aristotle's terms as an "unmoved mover." Even though there has always been an effort on the part of theologians to overcome the tendency to draw the conclusion from this conception of God that He is static in character, this effort has not been altogether successful. The orthodox concept of God still must be said to emphasize transcendence more than it does immanence. Needless to say, the application of the process perspective to this issue will necessitate some rather radical changes. Those writing from within this perspective seek to emphasize the actual involvement of God in the life process itself. With respect to the question of the nature of God, here again the application of the process perspective will render a number of far reaching changes necessary. The orthodox con-

ception of God has consistently maintained that His nature is fully
perfected and actualized in every way. Many process thinkers have
found it necessary to abandon this conception of God in favor of one
which allows for a growing, self-actualizing God. One question which
must be borne in mind is whether such an abandonment necessarily
involves a changing God, or only a changing conception of God.

These and other issues are brought to the fore in the following essays. Although there are other writers in this field, the ones included in
this section are both influential and representative. Moreover, these
particular essays focus attention on the nature of the relationship between philosophy and religion as seen from within the process perspective.

Although the "death of God" movement as a whole does not reflect a process perspective, certain aspects of Thomas J. J. Altizer's
thought are predicated upon such a perspective. This is especially true
of those aspects which are derived from the influence of Hegel, many
of which find expression in his essay reprinted in this section. It is, of
course, true that a dialectical process is not altogether the same as an
evolutionary one, but Altizer's position does represent a process approach to the relation of philosophy of religion. Charles Hartshorne is
famous primarily because of his expositions of Whitehead's thought
and his defense of the ontological argument for God's existence. In
his essay in this section, however, he focuses these concerns in terms of
the question of attributing qualities to God. His process emphasis
manifests itself more in the content of this essay than in its methodology.
John B. Cobb, Jr. has also sought to apply the insights of Whitehead
to theology, and his essay addresses itself to the implications of such
an application. Cobb sees this application as a revival of "natural,"
or rational, theology. Schubert A. Ogden's "Theology and Objectivity"
differs from Cobb's essay by virtue of being a detailed consideration
of a specific problem rather than a programmatic foray. Ogden's process
prespective is more apparent in his methodology than in the particular
content of his thought. As the nationalities of these authors indicate, the
process perspective is an American phenomenon.

CHAPTER NINE

THE SACRED AND THE PROFANE: A DIALECTICAL UNDERSTANDING OF CHRISTIANITY*

by Thomas J. J. Altizer

The contemporary student of religion is living at a time when not only the reality but also the very meaning of religion threatens to disappear. Innumerable Christian theologians insist, however naively, that Christianity is not a religion, and humanistic scholars seem unable to employ a meaning of religion that can give direction and purpose to their own work. All of us in some sense must share the fruits of a Faustian dissolution of faith, even when our own labors of Sisyphus have seemingly carried us beyond the Western world. We inevitably think and speak under the impact of a peculiarly Western form of absolute world-affirmation.

Students of religion know that the primal forms of religious discourse are by one means or another dialectical, and thus they must inevitably exist in tension with the dominant modes of contemporary thought and experience. All dialectical thinking directs itself to the negation of the Given, of that which happens to appear or to be at hand. In all the various expressions of its multiple forms, dialectical thinking must set itself against the autonomy of that which appears before it, seizing upon the immediate being which is manifest about it as the initial spring-board to its own movement of negation. A dialectical movement is, of course, never a movement of simple or sheer negation. Being neither a Gnostic escape from the world nor a romantic flight from history, dialectical thinking moves by means of a negation

*Used with permission from *Radical Theology and the Death of God*, The Bobbs-Merrill Company, Inc., Indianapolis, Indiana, 1966.

that is simultaneously affirmation. The Given is negated only to be affirmed in a transfigured form. Dialectical thinking thinks both to and from what the Western rational mind knows as "contradiction." It appears when a seemingly unbridgeable chasm arises between the True or the Real and the immediately Given, and it culminates in a *coincidentia oppositorum,* a final coming together of those opposites whose initial opposition or contradiction occasioned its own creation. Consequently, dialectical thinking is inseparable from the Given which it must oppose; and it can only appear in conjunction with the manifestation of a Given which itself contains the seeds of its own negation.

Hegel, who identified philosophy with dialectical thinking, also believed that philosophy is identical with religion insofar as both must negate the Given: "For religion equally with philosophy refuses to recognize in finitude a veritable being, or something ultimate and absolute, or non-posited, uncreated, and eternal" (*Logic,* Vol. I, Bk. I, Ch. 3). All expressions of religion must in some sense share such a movement of negation, for religion must necessarily direct itself against a selfhood, a history, or a cosmos that exists immediately and autonomously as its own creation or ground. So it is that critical definitions of religion in all their variety show that the sacred and the religious life is the *opposite* of the profane and the secular life. Just as the prophet calls upon his hearer to turn away from his immediate existence in the world, the mystic envisions an eternal Now that dissolves the time of duration. Furthermore, and as the work of Mircea Eliade has so fully demonstrated, mythical and ritual patterns the world over are intended to effect a negation of concrete time and space leading to a repetition of the primordial Beginning or to a passage to the "Center" of the world. Yet a primordial Beginning and a sacred "Center" are meaningful only insofar as a chasm lies between the sacred and the profane. A profane worldliness is not simply the mask or the veil of the sacred. Only the religious vision can know the world as *maya* or "Old Aeon." Profane worldiness is rather a positive and even absolute defiance or reversal of a sacred existence. In contrast, an existence embodying or pointing to the sacred is the dialectical opposite of existence in the profane. Seen in this perspective, religion itself can only appear or arise in conjunction with a rupture between the sacred and the profane, a rupture testifying to the alienation of immediate existence from a sacred or transcendent ground. Christianity has named this rupture the "Fall," and no religion has so profoundly emphasized the gulf between the sacred and the profane as Christianity. All religions, however, in one way or another witness to the loss of innocence or paradise, just as all religions proclaim or celebrate a way *to* the sacred *from* the profane.

If religion arises as a positive response to the appearance of the world or human existence in a fallen form, then one might expect the movement of religion to revolve about the repetition or re-presentation *(anamnesis)* of a primordial paradise. Conceived in this sense, the idea of an original or primordial paradise is bound to no particular symbolic form, and it could just as readily lend itself to apocalyptic symbols of the End when these are apprehended under the form of a final repetition of a primordial Beginning. It is a striking fact that images of paradise throughout the history of religions bear the marks of a dialectical negation or reversal. Paradise appears in the religious consciousness as a dialectical inversion of the *here* and *now* of profane experience, whether symbolized in a spatial form as celestial transcendence or in a temporal form as the Beginning or the End. An unfallen Beginning can express itself in symbolic form only to the extent that it is known as the opposite of a fallen present. But whether by way of myth and ritual, or through interior meditation or prophetic faith, religion seeks to annul all opposition between the sacred and the profane, thereby seeking a renewal of paradise in the present moment. Both the mystic, who directs himself to the negation or the emptying of consciousness, and the prophet, who calls for a total reversal of all worldly conditions, have chosen a path of abolishing the profane. Yet the sacred that becomes manifest through a negation of the profane must be a primordial Reality, an original paradise that has been hidden or lost by the advent of the profane, and thus a paradise that can be actualized by an unveiling or a reversal of the present. As Proust so aptly remarked, the only true paradise is always the paradise we have lost.

Religion is a quest for the primordial Beginning, a backward movement to an original paradise or a sacred "Center." With its goal of arriving at the primordial Totality, it follows a path of involution, a path that inverts or reverses the evolution of history and the cosmos out of an original Unity, thereby annulling those antinomies which have created an alienated and estranged existence. At first glance it would seem that those higher expressions of religion which proclaim the triumphant realization of the Kingdom of God, or the sole reality of Brahman-Atman, or the blissful totality of grace of Nirvana, do not fall under such a conception of religion since they transcend a tension or opposition between the sacred and the profane. Rather than conceding that the higher expressions of religion transcend the form and the imagery of religion itself, it would be wiser to note that such expressions of religion are fulfillments of a universal religious goal. When faith celebrates the final victory of the Kingdom of God, or contemplation becomes totally absorbed in Brahman-Atman or Purusha, or *satori* releases the all-pervading reality of Sunyata or Tao, the profane reality has been totally abolished or annulled. If a Zen practitioner were to say that nothing happens in *satori*, or that truly and actually there is no fallenness, no guilt, no alienation, and no estrangement, then we could only reply that from the point of view of the profane consciousness he has succeeded in abolishing the very memory of the profane. Moreover, if a Zennist were to persist in his denial and to assert that Nirvana is Samsara and Samsara is Nirvana—or that there is no difference whatsoever between the sacred and the profane—we would be forced to respond that his language is only meaningful in the context of the complete dissolution of the profane consciousness. A Buddhism that identifies Nirvana and Samsara can do so only on the basis of a discovery that all existing reality is empty or void (*sunya*) of reality itself, and this discovery is inseparable from an absolute and final negation of a profane reality. This negation annuls the opposition between the sacred and the profane by abolishing both the reality and the memory of the profane opposite itself. On the other hand, if a Christian were to insist that Christianity affirms both the reality and the goodness of the creation, he should simply be informed that originally Christianity was an apocalyptic faith looking forward to the end of the world as the cataclysmic destruction of the "Old Aeon" or old creation, and such an apocalyptic negation of the world is inseparable from a total affirmation of the Kingdom of God. A faith that could look forward to God's becoming all in all could rejoice in the imminent collapse of the reality of the world, thereby celebrating an End that is a repetition of a primordial Beginning. An End that abolishes the creation repeats or re-presents the Beginning that existed *prior* to the creation. Again, a total epiphany of the sacred occurs only by means of a total abolition of the profane.

The forms of Oriental mysticism and Biblical eschatology coincide insofar as they must culminate in an absolute negation of the Given. Only a mystical dissolution or an apocalyptic reversal of the reality of the profane can make possible a final or a total manifestation of the sacred. Even the language by which we speak of the higher expressions of religion is inevitably dialectical. We speak of a mystical *dis*solution or an apocalyptic *re*versal, thereby testifying to the negative movement of religion. Of course, this negation is dialectical. This means that here negation and reversal are grounded in affirmation; time and space are negated in their profane or fallen form only to be regenerated or resurrected in their sacred or primordial form. Underlying all forms of religion is a dialectical movement of repetition; the negation of the immediately Given is but the hither or apparent side of the repetition of the primordial or eternally Given. Negation and repetition are but two sides of the same movement, two manifestations of a single dialectical process, whose meaning or appearance varies solely in accordance with the intention from which it is viewed. From the perspective of the immediately or apparently Given, religion is a movement of negation. Yet so likewise from the perspective of faith or vision, religion is a movement of repetition or regeneration. Its seeming negation of the profane is at bottom an epiphany or renewal of an original and primordial sacred. A dialectical negation of time and space culminates in a regeneration of Eternity—a renewal or repetition of a primordial Totality—and therefore an absolute negation of the profane is equivalent to a total affirmation of the sacred. Accordingly, the higher expressions of religion are consummations of the religious movement itself—"Old Aeon" passes into "New Aeon," Samsara is identical with Nirvana. The *coincidentia oppositorum* is a universal religious symbol, a symbol unveiling both the goal and the ground of religion.

All too naturally we employ a Latin phrase in speaking of the "coincidence of the opposites," for it is not too clear if we are speaking of a coincidence, a harmony, a unity, or an identity of the opposites, and with this ambiguity the meaning of the opposites themselves is obscured. When the negative movement of religion is understood as being a *reversal* of the profane, there is a clear implication that religion acts by way of a backward movement or *return*, with the inevitable corollary that the sacred is an original or primordial Reality. Certainly the higher Oriental symbols of the sacred point to an eternal, an inactive, or a quiescent Totality, and a Totality that only truly appears through the disappearance or inactivity of all motion and process. Moreover, it is the very *dis*appearance or *in*activity that repeats or resurrects an original Totality. Here, repetition and resurrection are expressions of a cosmic and universal process of regeneration. Such a process of regeneration, however, is in no way to be identified, with a process in space and time. On the contrary, a fully mystical regeneration annuls or dissolves both spatial location and temporal duration; hence, the Oriental mystic invariably speaks of a timeless Eternity, a Nothing, or a Void. Whether by way of the *wu wei* or inaction of Taoism and Zen, or the Yogic discipline of emptying the contents of consciousness, or the purposeless action of the *Bhagavad Gita,* the way of Oriental religions is a way *backwards.* A primordial Totality can be reached only by a reversal of the movements of consciousness and history, and this reversal of the profane is equivalent to an epiphany or renewal of an original sacred. Yet a reversal in this sense can only mean that a profane time and space cease to exist in their own form and movement. Or, rather, a repetition of a primordial sacred reveals the sacred identity of the profane. A mystical regeneration inverts the concrete expressions of time and space, leading to the resurrection of a primordial Totality. A Totality, however, comprehends all reality whatsoever, and a sacred Totality must annul the possibility of profane existence. A *coincidentia oppositorum* in this sense must identify the opposites by abolishing their opposition, an abolition effected by an absolute negation of the profane. *Coincidentia* here must finally mean a non-dialectical "identity," for it is an identity that only appears with the disappearance of the opposites. A mystical epiphany of the primordial Totality dissolves the opposition between the sacred and the profane by annulling the fallen reality of space and time. Space and time then become manifest in their primordial or eternal form, and such an original Totality is free of the polar or dialectical meaning of either the sacred or the profane. Thus the *coincidentia oppositorum* in Oriental mysticism is an identity of the opposites. The profane reality ceases to move or disappears, thereby becoming identical with the sacred, and the sacred now ceases to exist in opposition to the profane.

May we say that the goal and ground of Biblical eschatology is a *coincidentia oppositorum* that likewise identifies the sacred and the profane? Does the prophetic faith of the Bible revolve about a return

(or "turning," *metanoia*) to a primordial Beginning? Or does it culminate in an apocalyptic End which is a final repetition of the Beginning?
If so, it would seem to follow that an eschatological faith must seek to
abolish the opposites either by collapsing the profane into the sacred or
by annihilating the form and movement of the profane. Yet such a
formulation does violence both to an eschatological faith's engagement
with the world and to the New Testament and Christian meaning of
Incarnation. Ever since its establishment in the second century, Christian theology has either chosen the language of a purely rational and
non-dialectical thinking, or it has repudiated all thinking that is directed
to the meaning of its Biblical foundation. In either case, Christian
theology has refused a thinking that incorporates the primal forms of
Biblical faith, just as it has turned aside from any attempt to think
through to its own ultimate implications. Consequently, Christian theology has never sought to unveil the meaning of an apocalyptic *coincidentia oppositorum*. It need not surprise us that such a form of theology has always been uncertain about its religious ground. While
frequently claiming that the soul is naturally Christian, or dogmatically
if uncritically insisting that Christianity is the fulfillment of the world's
religions, Christian theology has nevertheless condemned "idolatry"
and opposed all paganism (*i.e.*, non-Biblical religion). The contemporary
theologian is even embarked upon a quest for a "religionless" Christianity. Kierkegaard—who conceived of paganism as an immediate
relationship to God—already sensed that the Christian faith is grounded
in a negation of religion. Unfortunately, neither Kierkegaard nor his
twentieth-century followers succeeded in creating a fully dialectical
theology. Never being able to break from their Lutheran roots, they
have clung to a non-dialectical dualism, and have employed dialectical
thinking only to attack the profane expressions of faith. Inevitably such
a dialectical theology falls back upon a dogmatic and non-dialectical
form of faith or belief, thereby foreclosing the possibility of reaching a
coincidentia oppositorum. But if Christian theology has the legitimate
goal of unravelling the meaning of a "religionless" Christianity, it must
take far more seriously than ever before the relationship between
Christianity and religion, and this must mean that it is now called to a
full encounter with the higher expressions of religion.

Earlier we remarked that Christianity emphasizes the Fall more
radically than any other form of religion. The Fall is an actual and real
event; the world and human existence are judged to be actually and
truly estranged from their original divine ground, and consequently the
process of redemption must occur in the arena of concrete time and
space. The Fall is never an ultimately real event in Oriental religion.
Thus for Shankara it can only be through a great cosmic ignorance or
maya that God and the world can be known as moving and existing out
of the depths of Brahman-Atman; and for Nagarjuna, Nirvana is non-
ceasing and unachieved, because there has been no initial Fall, and
there is no need for a re-transformation. When the profane is under-

stood as the opposite of the sacred in a wholly negative sense, then the movement of religion must be conceived as an eternal repetition of an unfallen sacred, and the profane reality must be judged to be an illusory mask or veil of the sacred. Only an acceptance or an affirmation of the fallen *reality* of the profane can make possible a faith that encounters the concrete actuality of the world, and moves *forward* through alienation and estrangement to an eschatological End that transcends a primordial Beginning. Just as Christianity is the only religion to have abandoned an original paradise, so Christianity alone among the world's religions affirms the ultimate reality of the Fall, and opens itself to the actual processes of time and space as the arena of redemption. Owen Barfield's distinction between an "original" and a "final" participation —in his fascinating and deeply illuminating book, *Saving the Appearances*—does much to unveil the uniqueness of the Christian faith. Images of paradise invariably testify to a longing or a nostalgia for an original paradise, *i.e.*, for participation in an original cosmic Totality, a Totality present in a primordial time prior to the advent of the rupture between the sacred and the profane, a time when suffering, death, and alienation had not yet come into existence. Barfield identifies original participation as paganism, and insists that the Old Testament's condemnation of idolatry was a negation of original participation. From this point of view, only the loss of original participation or a primordial paradise can make possible a final participation, *i.e.*, an ultimate participation that is reached by moving *through* fallenness and death to a definitive and final reconciliation between the sacred and the profane.

Whether we conceive of religion as a quest for original participation, or as a repetition of an unfallen Beginning which abolishes the opposites by negating the reality of the profane, it is clear that Christianity cannot be judged in this sense to be a religion, or at the very least that the Christian faith is finally directed to a non-religious goal. Insofar as faith in its Christian expression moves through the factuality of estrangement and death, it can never accept a mere negation of the profane. Nor for that matter can a faith accepting the reality of the Fall seek an unfallen sacred or a primordial moment of time. Only an actual reversal of a fallen and profane *reality* can lead to a final participation that transcends a primordial Beginning. Such a reversal would be consistently and radically dialectical. It would occur by means of what Hegel terms "pure negativity" or the "negation of negation," and it would move through the reality of the profane to a final or eschatological sacred that reconciles the profane with itself. Despite the fact that Buddhist logic is grounded in negation, Th. Stcherbatsky, in his magisterial study of Buddhist logic, points out that Indian logic has never known the negation of negation. Only an acceptance of the reality of a negative or fallen reality can make possible a *coincidentia oppositorum* that is a coming together of the dual reality of the sacred and the profane. It is precisely this *coincidentia* of the opposing realms of the sacred and the profane that makes possible Christianity's celebration of the Incarnation as an actual and real event, an event that has occurred and does occur in concrete time and space, and an event effecting a real tranformation of the world. Faith, in this consistently dialectical sense, must oppose or negate a sacred that is an unmoving Eternity or a quiescent Totality. A sacred that annuls or transcends the reality of the profane can never become incarnate in a fallen form, and thus it could never affect or transform the given or immediate reality of a fallen world. Only a sacred that negates its own unfallen or primordial form can become incarnate in the reality of the profane. To the extent that faith or vision knows an eternal and unmoving sacred it can never know the reality of the Incarnation.

When religion is conceived as a dialectical movement that culminates in an abolition of the opposites, *i.e.*, as a return to an unfallen and primordial Beginning, then its movement may be understood by means of Kierkegaard's category of "recollection." Believing that recollection is the pagan life-view, a life-view affirming that all that is has been, Kierkegaard conceived of recollection as a backward repetition. From this point of view, all priestly or cultic religion, including its Biblical and Christian expressions, is a recollection or re-presentation *(anamnesis)* of a sacred history of the past. Mystical religion could then be understood as an interior movement of recollection, or as a translation into interior meditation of a cultic and mythical regeneration of history and the cosmos. In either case, religion is a backward movement to an archaic, or sacred, or a timeless past, *i.e.*, a past having only a negative relation to the concrete actuality of the present. But Kierkegaard opposed "repetition" to "recollection," attempting to define repetition as a transcendent or religious movement by virtue of the absurd, while noting that "eternity is the true repetition" *(Repetition,* p. xxii). Repetition, in this sense, must be conceived as a forward movement. Whereas the backward movement of recollection arises from the judgment that all that truly is has been, the movement of repetition embodies the present and actual becoming of an existence which has been. Nevertheless, repetition and recollection are the same movement, only in opposite directions; "for what is recollected has been, is repeated backwards, whereas repetition properly so called is recollected forwards" *(Ibid.,* p. 4). It cannot be said that Kierkegaard thought through the full meaning of his own category of repetition, but it is clear that he intended repetition to have a specifically or uniquely Christian meaning, and that it is the forward movement of Christianity which distinguishes it from its pagan or religious counterparts. Yet such a forward movement cannot culminate in an abolition of the opposites by returning to a primordial Beginning. Like its analogue in the prophetic faith of the Old Testament, it must be grounded in an eschatological End, and it can be consummated in that future End only by moving through a rebirth or renewal of *all* that existence which has been.

Therefore a renewal occurring through a specifically Christian movement of repetition could only culminate in a transformation of the opposites. The opposites cannot be simply annulled or negated, for then there would be neither a forward movement nor an eschatological End. It is precisely because the totality of existence is being renewed or transformed that the opposites cannot be abolished or dissolved. A pagan or religious "recollection" must, it is true, dissolve the opposition between the sacred and the profane, but recollection cannot move forward to eternity. Only a movement through the fallen reality of the opposites can issue in a genuinely New Creation or New Aeon. Conceived in this sense, an eschatological End cannot be a repetition of a primordial Beginning. If Christian repetition makes all things new, then it must abolish or negate a memory or recollection of an original participation, and thus it must negate the movement of negation in religion. With this negation of negation, an original sacred must itself be negated. By this radical negation every image and every expression of the religious movement of recollection must be transcended. Of course, the higher expressions of mysticism have always known a transcendence of images, but they transcend imagery by abolishing the profane consciousness, or by dissolving all that history lying between the present and the Beginning. As opposed to this backward movement of the religious expressions of mysticism, a Christian repetition must move forward beyond the death of a primordial or original sacred to an eschatological *coincidentia oppositorum* that reconciles and unites the sacred and the profane. Quite naturally Christian theology has turned aside from the problem of the meaning of such a movement of repetition, just as it has refused the task of thinking through to its own ground in an eschatological End. Insofar as Christian theology is bound to an eternal and primordial God, it cannot be open to a negation of original participation, nor can it accept the possibility of an End that transcends the Beginning. Nonetheless the most radical Christian seers—who are fully exemplified in their own respective ways by a Blake and a Hegel— have long insisted that it is the Christian God and the Christian religion which are the deepest obstacles to an eschatological, a consistently dialectical, or a total redemption.

The non-dialectical ground of historical Christianity has been unveiled simply by taking up the problem of the dialectical meaning of religion. For not only do the priestly and institutional forms of Christianity submit to the heteronomous authority of a series of events that are irrevocably past, but the thought of the Christian theologian himself has been closed to a truly dialectical meaning of the sacred. None of the schools of Christian theology has been able to accept a fully kenotic meaning of the Incarnation, despite the fact that such a meaning has again and again been declared to be the goal of Christian thinking. If the Incarnation is the descent of God into human flesh, *i.e.*, if Christ in being born in the likeness of men emptied himself of the form of God (Phil. 2:5-7), then a dialectical understanding of the Incarnation must go beyond the New Testament and recognize that a kenotic Christ cannot be known as an exalted Lord or cosmic Logos. Only a theology which abandons an original and primordial sacred, and opens itself to a forward moving process of repetition, can acknowledge that God has truly and actually become incarnate in concrete space and time. When the Incarnation is understood as a descent into the concrete, or as a movement from a primordial and unfallen sacred to an actually fallen profane, then it cannot be conceived as not affecting a supposedly eternal Godhead, or as being a static or unchanging extension of the God who is the transcendence of Being. Nor for that matter can an understanding of the Incarnation as a process of repetition allow the Incarnation to be confined to a once and for all event of the past. A theology which remains bound to the language and imagery of the New Testament must refuse the very thesis that the Incarnation is a forward movement or process. An authentically kenotic movement of "incarnation" must be a continual process of Spirit becoming flesh, of Eternity becoming time, or of the sacred becoming profane. Yet its forward movement is inseparable from a continual process of self-negation or self estrangement. Spirit can continue to become flesh only by negating its own past expressions. A Spirit that ceases to move or to negate itself is no longer an Incarnate Word. Christianity invariably becomes religious at precisely those points where it refuses to become incarnate.

Seen in this perspective, historical Christianity must be judged to be a discordant synthesis between a religious movement of recollection and an eschatological or non-religious movement of repetition. Religious Christianity parallels the non-Christian expressions of religion insofar as it is a recollection of an original or primordial sacred. Here is found a nostalgia for a lost paradise, a re-presentation of a sacred history of the past, and a belief in God as the "Unmoved Mover" who is the pure actuality (energeia) of Being. When the Christian God appears as the Wholly Other, the sovereign and transcendent Creator, he is manifest in his religious form as a primordial Deity, the El Shaddai of the Book of Job whose very sacrality annuls or negates the existence of the profane. So likewise a Christian faith that lets "God be God" is a submission to a primordial sacred, a recollection of the Beginning, and therefore it cannot respond to an Incarnation which is a movement of the sacred into the profane. Insofar as Christian theology has understood the Incarnate Word as an epiphany of the primordial Deity, it has set itself against the actual process of the Incarnation by understanding it as a backward movement to the Beginning rather than as a forward movement to the End. Only a Word that negates its ground in the primordial sacred can actually move into the fallen reality of the profane. To the extent that the Christian Word fails to negate its original form, it cannot be a forward moving process, not can it be a process of renewal, or a progressive descent into the concrete. Not only does a religious understanding of the Word reverse the forward movement of the Incarnation, but it encloses the Word in a static and lifeless form, thereby isolating its power and confining its role to one of passive quiescence. When the Word is understood as a dynamic movement of

Spirit into flesh, then it must be conceived as a process of reversing the original identity of Spirit, and, in contrast, of transforming the fallen reality of flesh. Consequently, a forward movement of repetition must culminate in an abolition of its original ground. The primordial God of the Beginning must die to make possible a union of Spirit with flesh.

"God is dead" are words that may only truly be spoken by the Christian, not by the religious Christian who is bound to an eternal and unmoving Word, but by the radical Christian who speaks in response to an Incarnate Word that empties itself of Spirit so as to appear and exist as flesh. A kenotic Word acts or moves by *reversing* the forms of flesh and Spirit. Moreover, a dialectical reversal in this sense cannot lead to an identification of the sacred with the profane or of the Spirit with flesh; Spirit must negate itself as Spirit before it can become manifest as flesh. When the world is affirmed as an actually fallen and profane reality, then it cannot be known as a mask or veil of the sacred, and the sacred and profane must exist in a state of opposition to each other insofar as each retains its original or primal reality. Such a state of opposition can only be effected by a dual movement of the opposites into their respective Others—Spirit empties itself of Spirit so as to become flesh, and flesh negates itself as flesh so as to become Spirit. True, a forward moving process of repetition culminates in a *coincidentia oppositorum.* Yet *coincidentia* now bears an eschatological meaning. Only at the End will flesh and Spirit become identical, and their identity will be established only when flesh has actually ceased to be flesh and Spirit has perished as Spirit. Thus there can be no question of a fully eschatological *coincidentia* being known as a recollection or an epiphany of a primordial Beginning. Both recollection and repetition culminate in a *coincidentia oppositorum,* but whereas recollection is a backward movement to the Beginning, repetition is a forward movement to the End.

Is Kierkegaard correct in identifying recollection and repetition as the same movement, in opposite directions? Or does a single dialectical movement assume a different meaning and reality in accordance with the direction in which it moves? Just as recollection revolves about an absolute negation of the profane, may one say that repetition revolves about an absolute negation of the sacred? Insofar as the religious movement of negation is dialectical, its negation of the profane is at bottom an affirmation of the sacred. Is it likewise true that a Christian or consistently eschatological negation of an original sacred must culminate in an affirmation of the radical profane? Here, it is true, there is a genuine and actual movement of the sacred into the profane. But does the actuality of this movement derive from the renewal or repetition of the profane? We have seen that a religious repetition of a primordial Beginning annuls or reverses the life and movement of the profane. Can one now say that the process of the Incarnation annuls and reverses an original quiescent Totality, thereby making possible a progressively forward movement and expression of the profane? Simply to raise these questions in the context of our time and situation is to recognize the possibility that the death of God—*i.e.*, the dissolution of all images and symbols of an original sacred, and the collapse of a sacred or transcendent realm underlying this dissolution—is a culminating expression of the forward movement of the Incarnation. When the sacred and the profane are understood as dialectical opposites whose mutual negation culminates in a transition or metamorphosis of each into its respective Other, then it must appear that a Christian and eschatological *coincidentia oppositorum* in this sense is finally a coming together or dialectical union of an original sacred and the radical profane. By a kenotic negation of its primordial reality, the sacred becomes incarnate in the profane. Yet this movement of the sacred into the profane is inseparable from a parallel movement of the profane into the sacred. Indeed, the very movement of repetition and renewal—precisely because it is an actual and concrete movement—testifies to the ever more fully dawning power of the reality of the profane. Consequently, a consistently Christian dialectical understanding of the sacred must finally look forward to the resurrection of the profane in a transfigured and thus finally sacred form.

CHAPTER TEN

THREE STRATA OF MEANING IN RELIGIOUS DISCOURSE*[1]

by Charles Hartshorne

"Primary words do not stand for things, but they intimate relations. . . . Men wish to regard a feeling (called feeling of dependence . . . more precisely, creaturely feeling) as the real element in the relation with God. . . . Yes; in pure relation you have felt yourself to be simply dependent . . . and simply free, too, . . . both creaturely and creative. . . . We take part in creation. . . .

The man who prays . . . knows that he has—in an incomprehensible way—an effect upon God, even though he obtains nothing from God. . . . And the man who makes sacrifices? I cannot despise him, this upright servant of former times, who believed that God yearned for the scent of his burnt-offering. In a foolish but powerful way he knew that we can and ought to give to God. This is known by him, too, who offers up his little will to God and meets Him in the grand will. 'Thy will be done,' he says, and says no more: but truth adds for him 'through me whom thou needest.' . . . Magic desires to obtain its effects without entering into relation. . . . But sacrifice and prayer are set 'before the Face,' in the consummation of the holy primary word that means mutual action: they speak of Thou, and then they hear." M. Buber, in *I and Thou*, trans. R. G. Smith, Pp. 3, 81, 83.

A common doctrine is that religious statements are not meant "literally," but "symbolically." Descriptions of God, for example, are held to use words in unusual ways whose meaning is not obvious from their ordinary use or meaning. I wish to argue that two kinds of predicates are applied to God, and while those of one kind are symbolic, those

*Used with permission from *The Logic of Perfection*, Open Court Publishing Co., La Salle, Illinois, 1961.

of the other are not. We need to distinguish between formal and mate-rial predications. To compare deity with a rock, a king, a shepherd, or a parent is a material description, that is, one in terms of a concrete species of entity, a particular part of the psycho-physical universe. Such predications are not literal, for God is not just another ruler, together with human kings, or another parent together with human parents.

But there is a radically different sort of predication concerning deity, in which no one part of the universe more than any other is involved in the comparison. Rather, in such predications, deity is compared to any concrete being you please other than Himself. This non-material mode is illustrated when one speaks of such negative properties of God as "non-corporeal," "non-temporal," "non-relative," and so on. Here no material difference between rock and man, or rock and sand, or one man and another, comes in, but only purely abstract and general philosophical categories, such as space, time, becoming, relation.

I wish now to emphasize my conviction that the formal predicates of deity are not exclusively negative, and accordingly, some positive properties of deity can be connoted by non-symbolic designations.[2] I have spent, and I hope not wasted, much of my life exploring the positive formal characterizations which seem compatible with the reli-gous meaning of the term "God." This religious meaning is well in-dicated by the phrase, "supremely worshipful." If one is conditioned by early training to react negatively to certain words, like relativity or con-tingency, then of course one cannot worship God and also call Him, in any respect, relative or contingent. But this negative evaluation of relativity and contingency seems to me a confusion. Is the relative or the contingent as such essentially bad or mediocre? On the contrary, all the beauty of the actual world seems to consist in its relationships and its contingencies. A "good" man is not, compared to a bad or inferior one, any less relative or contingent; but rather, he is more adequately related to other things and richer and more harmonious in his accidental qualities.

To be sure, it is not good to be too dependent upon, or relative to, any *one* aspect or part of the total environment, or too sensitive to merely momentary changes. But such excess of sensitivity consists in an imbalance between our response to some things and persons and our response to the remaining things and persons. The wise and strong respond to each stimulus for what it is worth, in comparison with other available stimuli; they do not fall on this man's neck and then turn coldly away from some other who has as much or more to offer, or whose claims for attention are quite as legitimate. Also, the wise person bal-ances the stimuli of the moment against the background of past stimuli and past decisions of his own, and against the ultimate ideals of life. Balanced appropriateness in one's relativity to other things or persons, not non-relativity, is the mark of wisdom and goodness. The non-rela-tive or merely inflexible person, who will not be influenced, who will not or cannot adjust to the actual situation sensitively and quickly, need not be especially admired. Yet according to many metaphysicians and theologians, from the Stoics and Philo down to out time, such inflexible persons ought, it seems, to be deeply revered.

There is another confusion we need to clear away. This is the failure to distinguish between relativity, or dependence, with respect to an individual's existence or personal identity and dependence merely with respect to the concrete state or experience of the individual, granted that "he" exists as that very individual. For instance, one does not depend for being, and for being oneself, upon any particular state of the weather, though one does depend upon it for some of the details of one's experiences, assuming that one goes out, or looks out of the window, or even hears a weather report. To depend for very existence, or individual identity, upon changeable factors is indeed a mark of mediocrity; and no being so characterized could properly be worshipped. A sufficiently radical change in the weather would destroy your personal existence or mine; and this is one mark of our not being truly worshipful. But in simple logic there are two ways, and not one way only, of conceiving independence with respect to existing-as-oneself.

The usual way, on which classical theism wagered everything, is to suppose the existentially independent to have no need to adjust to changes, to be indifferent or neutral to them all. But there is another way. This is to identify existential independence with an invincible power and will to achieve self-consistent adjustment to any changes whatever. We human beings adjust successfully to a wide range of diversities, but there comes a point beyond which we cannot achieve adjustment, and accordingly, we lose consciousness, or sanity, or life itself. Is there any rule of logic telling us that the mere idea of "adjustment" means the possibility of failure? By that principle, the mere idea of "existing" should imply the possibility of failing to exist, and then God could not exist unless contingently. Since nearly all theologians have held that God's very existence cannot be contingent, we face the question, is His necessary existence or absoluteness to be conceived as an infallible power to harmonize relativities in Himself, to respond coherently to diverse stimuli, or simply as the absence of relativity, of power to respond to other beings? This dilemma, I hold is between literal alternatives. No concrete difference among things is in question, only the categorial difference between the contingency of the proposition asserting your existence or mine (or an elephant's), and two categorially or formally opposite ways of interpreting the necessary truth of the proposition, "divinity exists" (or, if you prefer, is real). In either interpretation such necessary existential truth is as literally necessary as contingent existential truth is contingent. Nor is it merely negative; for necessary truth is definable as the common factor in all possible truths. All-pervasiveness with respect to the possible *is* necessity. And the very idea of God as creator implies that not only was this world so much as possible solely because of the creative power which produced it, but also "other worlds" were or are possible only in that the same power would have been, or would be, adequate for their production. The divine power is thus conceived as, by definition, all-pervasive with respect to possibility. To be possible is to be a possible-creature-of-the-creator. Accordingly, the creator, as such, is constituent in every possibility.

I am not saying (with some proponents of the Ontological Argument) that the divine existence must forthwith be conceded, since it is necessary; that would be going too fast; I am saying rather: *either* the divine existence must be conceded, *or* we must reject the conception of God as meaningless or absurd. For what it cannot connote is an unactualized potentiality of existence; since its very meaning is that all power or potency is derivative from divine power taken as real. This is both compatible with and implies the contingency of ordinary existence to which Anselm's critics so irrelevantly and monotonously point!

Are such general categories as "Existence" symbolic or literal? Philosophers certainly construe them in different ways, and thus their meaning is not to be made ostensively obvious in the same fashion as the meaning of "rock" or "king." But neither are such concepts, when applied to God, symbolic in the sense in which "divine shepherd" is symbolic. For "necessary existence" takes no account, in its meaning, of the difference between one non-divine thing and another. Rather the contrast, necessary-contingent, sets up a dichotomy between God and everything else. True enough, necessary existence is a different kind of existence from contingent existence—Anselm's great discovery, widely misunderstood—but can anyone understand "contingent existence" and not know what the contrasting term is? The two sides of such a contrast seem inseparable. It is quite different with true "symbols." The sense in which God is "ruler" is not categorially definable, even by negation, since "divine ruler" assumes the idea of God, and "superhuman ruler" is insufficient. "Ruler of all things" is more helpful, since here we do use the category of totality, but it still does not tell us what *kind* of rule can apply to all things. Necessary existence, however, is literally definable, for it must mean *either* non-capacity for contingent properties *or* (as I hold) an invincible capacity to achieve, a certainty of possessing, some contingent property expressing the identity of the being—regardless of what other beings exist or fail to exist. Here there is nothing material, and so nothing symbolic.

I should now like to point a moral. The denial that divine predicates can be both positive and literal (e.g., "common element of all possibilities," or "relative to all things") has derived from a misconception, not simply of God, but, implicitly, of the creatures. God must, it is thought, be non-relative, because relativity is bad, which implies that when we compare creatures as good rather than bad we compare them with respect to the number of things they escape being relative to. But this is contrary to what we really do in evaluating creatures. I believe that every basic error in theology similarly reflects a corresponding error in the conception of the creatures. If we have (unwittingly) a non-literal, i.e., vague, ambiguous, inconsistent, notion of creaturely "existence," "dependence," "relativity," or "better" and "worse," then we cannot arrive at positive literal ideas about the divine existence, independence, absoluteness, or goodness. But if we are literally correct about the creatures, perhaps we can be so about certain formal, positive attributes of deity.

If God is formally describable as ideally and infallibly relative, rather than as simply non-relative, then the contradictions to which many writers point, between the formal properties of God and the non-formal ones, do not obtain. He can be loving, in the sense of adequately sensitive to the needs of others, rather than (self-contradictorily) both responsive to their needs and wholly devoid of intrinsic relatedness to them. The dogmatic refusal to consider positive formal properties of God has saddled theology with the impossibility of making even decent symbolic sense out of such religious terms as love or purpose, all imply-ing relativity, without covertly abandoning the formal negations. Ad-mittedly, the divine sensitivity is not just one more case of sympathetic response to need; yet that which distinguishes it from the human form is not to be found in the direction of sheer insensitiveness, mere neutral-ity or non-relativity. Atoms are much less variously and richly sensitive, less relative, more "absolute," than men. Is not the divine sensitivity inconceivable to us because of the richness of the divine relationships to the creatures (not simply between persons of the Trinity!) and their balanced integration into one life, rather than because of complete poverty in such relatednesses? Again, is not God incomparably complex in His total reality, rather than incomparably "simple?"

Besides obviously formal and obviously material ideas about God we have descriptions whose classification depends partly upon one's philosophical beliefs. To say that God has awareness, feeling, memory, sympathy seems to be a material statement, for do not some rather than all creatures have these qualities? Yet, according to panpsychism, psy-chical concepts are categorial, universal in scope. However, even so they must be different from the purely formal concepts, for example, con-tingency, which has a single literal meaning applicable to all cases, the meaning of excluding some positive possibilities. But in what sense, for instance, is "feeling" of a frog the same thing as "feeling" of a man? Here there seem to be innumerable differences of degree, and of specific kind. Frog feeling is "analogous" to human feeling, rather than the same. Much more, then, is divine feeling merely analogous to creaturely feeling. I think here the old term "analogical" is best, rather than "symbolic." God is symbolically ruler, but analogically conscious and loving, and literally both absolute (or necessary) in existence and relative (or contingent) in actuality—that is, in the concrete modes of His exis-tence. True, His relativity is not the same in scope as ours, for He is relative to all things, and we are relative only to some. But the point is, that "all" and "some" have here their literal logical senses; whereas who can say literally how divine love differs qualitatively from ours?

Quantitatively, yes, for He loves all creatures, we love only some. But how does He love them? Here we have no literal grasp, for we cannot love anything as God loves each and every creature.

There is another way of showing that the analogical concepts differ from the literal, on the one hand, and the formal on the other. Contingency and relativity apply not only to individuals but to groups of individuals, and not only to concrete, but also to more or less abstract entities. Only the completely abstract is non-contingent or absolute, everything less abstract is contingent and relative; but in order to feel or remember, an entity must be quite concrete, as well as singular. Groups do not feel, except in so far as their members do, but whatever existence they have is contingent and relative, like that of their members. Similarly, abstract common qualities of specific groups do not feel; but they exist contingently. Thus, even assuming panpsychism, the most general psychical terms, though universally applicable to concrete singulars, and in this sense categorial, are not purely formal in the same sense as the other categorial terms. To apply them to things, one must know on what level of concreteness the things are.

And yet there is a strange sense in which the analogical concepts apply literally to deity, and analogically to creatures. We say that human beings "know" various things, but then we have to qualify by adding that this does not mean the possession of such evidence as to make mistakes impossible. What then does it mean? The entertaining of beliefs which by mere good luck happen to be correct? This is an odd meaning for "know." So we must mean that men have evidence, falling short of absolute proof, that certain beliefs are true. But how far short of conclusiveness can the evidence be, and still entitle the beliefs to be termed "knowledge"? We see that the term "know" in the human case turns out to have a rather indefinite meaning. In the divine case, the matter is simple: God, as infallible, has absolutely conclusive evidence concerning all truths, so that if knowledge is possession of perfect evidence as to the state of affairs, then God simply knows—period. No such plain definition will work for human knowledge. In this sense, it is the theistic use only of psychical conceptions which has literal meaning, a meaning from which all other meanings are derived by qualification, diminution, or negation. So, instead of the old "negative theology," one might propose a new "negative anthropology."

It is the same with love. If this means such things as appreciating the qualities of others, caring about their weal and woe, wishing them well, or what you will, then either one has to admit that in no case of human love is it simply true that one does these things, or one must leave their meaning extremely vague. A human being appreciates the qualities of this or that other person—except the qualities he does not appreciate, through some limitation of his own; he cares about the other's weal or woe, with similar exceptions; he wishes him well—except so far as (perhaps unconsciously) he has impulses to wish him harm, whether from envy, rivalry, fear, or what not. But God appreciates the qualities of all things—period. There is no envy, rivalry, fear. He wishes all creatures well—period. He cares about their weal and woe— there is no material qualification or negation. That God cares about "all" is purely formal, and positive. True, God "cannot" wish the weal of one while disregarding (as, to a greater or lesser extent we always do) the woe of others; for no woe is ever merely indifferent to God. (But this is a double negative—he cannot not regard—and so it is positive.) There may be those who think otherwise, who suppose that God can wish well to the sick child in such fashion as literally not to care about the woes of bacteria causing the sickness. But such persons, in my opinion, are thinking anthropomorphically about God who must always relate Himself to absolutely all creatures. This is often forgotten, but it is a formal requirement of the idea of deity.

It is obvious enough, but widely overlooked, that if we allocate to outselves divine properties, such as literal, simple knowing or loving, then in so far we have nothing left with which to characterize deity. Could this be part of the secret of the "negative theology?" We say, for example, that "memory" is unworthy to be attributed to deity, "forgetting" how infinitesimal is our remembering compared to our forgetting. To remember is "to be aware of the past"—who but God could literally be so? We are aware (with any degree of clarity) of but tiny scraps of the past, and these are constantly coming and going, into and out of our consciousness. God, however, is aware of the past, *simpliciter*. He remembers—period. No mere creature can do anything of the sort.

Again, we say that it is not enough for God to be everlasting, He must be simply devoid of becoming altogether. And one reason we think so is that we have blithely attributed everlastingness to ourselves, at least as a possibility, without really facing the question of whether or not such an absolute property as infinite duration is appropriate to creatures so limited in every other respect. And even those who do not regard themselves individually as immortal are likely, consciously or not, to take it for granted that at least our species is immortal, again without serious consideration of the reasonableness of this belief. We shall never see clearly what "God" means until we see how problematic if not absurd are all such ascriptions of infinity to ourselves. Man endures for a while; God endures.

There is an opposite way of so conceiving the creatures that God becomes inconceivable: that of denying to man, or some of the creatures, even a bare minimum of excellence under some category. Thus we may say that all human love is really pure selfishness, there is no such thing as love; and so the way is barred that should lead to the idea of divine love. Again if we say with Hume and his countless followers that there is no intrinsic connection between any state of experience and any other before or after it, or that causality is merely the fact that this follows that, then the idea of God causally affecting all things would merely mean that what goes on in the world happens to be what God thinks, or resolves, should go on. There is no rational way to God if we have denied even the inferior version of causal power which is all that, in the creatures, could represent the divine power. If, on the other hand, we exaggerate causal influence by making it mean absolute determination of effects, including volitions, then too we have deprived ourselves of any analogical basis for the idea of the creative power of God. We should have to put some cause behind the supreme volition and hold that this supercause absolutely determined the divine action, so that precisely this world had to be created. And then all evil must be good, since it proceeds necessarily from the divine perfection. The way to avoid this difficulty is to admit that action always has some leeway, in spite of causality, or because of the proper meaning of "cause." It is then consistent to ascribe supreme leeway or scope to the divine creativity.

In the foregoing discussion I am indebted to a lecture by Paul Tillich. But I think also that his own procedure illustrates how true it is that a correct view of the creatures and of the supreme creator-creature must develop together. Tillich denies that contingency and novelty can apply literally to God. Yet he rightly holds that God must be all-inclusive. If then the creatures are literally contingent, there must be divine constituents which are literally contingent. But in truth Tillich never reaches a clear notion of the root of contingency in creativity; he speaks sometimes quite like an Augustinian determinist. He never clearly envisages the issue between classical and neoclassical views, whether of God or of the creatures. And the idea of a God who responds lovingly to the world is lost in the indifferent absoluteness of "unconditioned" being. I think Whitehead's God is closer to Christianity than this.

If the position I have been taking is correct, the desire of the best men for clear knowledge about themselves cannot be satisfied without facilitating the attainment of what some of them do not consciously desire, clear knowledge about God. If it could be satisfied save on this condition, then atheism would be in a very strong position. But history is strewn with misconceptions of man serving as barriers to an intelligible conception of deity. The present scene is still strewn with them. Communism is one example; it is very shrewd in some respects in its anthropology, and very blind in other ways, and its blindness here is closely connected with its blindness concerning God. It tends to worship national power as a quasi-deity, confused more or less with party and Marxian dogma, and it cannot face honestly and with rational modesty the limitations of human nature which characterize the nation, the party, the dogma. If faces individual death bravely, but never mentions collective death. Yet what meaning would remain to the whole enterprise in that event? Its dialectical notion of cosmic history is a confused version of providence, as often remarked; its theory of historical determinism is a confused compromise between the dream of absolute cosmic regularity and the admission of human creativity. And so on. But all these mistakes in slightly different form are older than Marxism, and some of them are found in theological traditions also. We have pretty much all been at fault in confusing the issue of theism. History is still young. If we collectively survive the atomic phase, we may yet do far better.

In one respect communist theory is closer to true piety as I understand it than are the ideas of many well-meaning Christians. The communists do realize that ultimately the individual is contributory to what is beyond himself: that his fulfillment is in serving, for a time, an enduring Cause. The Cause is misconceived, but at least it is not Self. Unless we make haste and learn this lesson, a partial moral, and in a sense religious, superiority will continue to give the communists their dangerously great appeal. God cannot be "seen" steadily, and without confusion with self, by those of us who, however subtly and innocently, accept for ourselves roles which are proper to God—for instance the role of being finally recipient of values, rather than, finally, ourselves contributory to the treasury of achieved goods. To say to God, "I shall serve Thee forever—on condition that Thou serve me forever"! is that really so pious?

Individualism has a noble side and an ugly side. In our tradition the two sides have never been adequately distinguished. We are in great danger partly for that very reason. Individualism is right in holding that a person is not a mere means to a collectivity, for this has no realization of value save in its members; moreover, all creation of value is individual, and the uniqueness of each individual is his central value, his most basic contribution to the greater Cause. But it does not follow that he makes this contribution by enjoying infinite duration in some transcendental community. For in that case, he contributes forever and above all to himself. And then "enlightened self-interest" is given transcendental justification. Is it any wonder that sacrifice in the national safety seems hard to elicit just now? We have too much of the feeling, all things ought to serve Me. Ought they? They ought to serve the Supreme, who serves each and all to be sure, but in their time and place. He, however, is to be served evermore. Or, He is to be served.

The individual is demeaned if he serves only a collectivity, which is not even a definite consciousness, and does not begin to know him in his concreteness. But he is not degraded if by promoting the welfare of the collectivity he serves God, who is conscious and knows us all. To clear the way to the idea of God we need to get rid of all rivals to Him as the ultimate recipient of the fruits of our labors. In our brief time, of course, we do receive such fruits, the privileges of living for the highest and sanest of all ideals; but God receives the fruits both in our time and everlastingly. This is His privilege. How can this be understood if we have put ourselves in His place?

It is also unlikely that we shall effectively "see God" if we refuse to make any effort to look upon our neighbors as we look upon ourselves, that is, in terms of needs, capacities, thoughts, and feelings. The crass materialism which many of us betray by evaluating other people, not in terms of what they feel, think, and do, but almost exclusively in terms of some external marks of color, bones, hair, sex, wealth, or the physical location of some of their ancestors, is hardly calculated to make the divine perspective upon the world intelligible. We have scarcely begun to see the infinite implications of loving the other "as oneself." In some ways the Buddhists have seen this more clearly than Christians.

It comes to this: the inaccessibility of God to the rational mind upon which atheists and many theologians so nearly agree is correlative to the inaccessibility of our own natures, hidden beneath self-serving illusions about them. Piety may be more than modesty concerning our human estate, but it can scarcely be less than that. Have we not tried to make it less, in our very theologies and philosophies? The question at least deserves scrutiny.

But so does the correlative question: do we honor deity by denying to ourselves and the creatures generally even the most modest analogon to the divine attributes—for instance, some genuine, however humble, capacity of creation, some little leap beyond the causally inevitable, or some little simulacrum of the divine participation in the lives of all, some slight measure of sympathy or love? If God is all in all, in some sense everything, we must be something of this everything, not bare nothing. We have no divine attribute in its fullness or infinity, but yet we are not zero in comparison to any attribute.

An all too negative theology made God the great emptiness, and an all too negative anthropology made the creatures also empty. I suggest that nothing is only nothing, that the divine attributes are positive, and the creatures' qualities are between these and nothing.

FOOTNOTES

1. The first half of this essay appeared originally in *The Southern Philosopher*, III (1956).

2. An ingenious attempt to rescue the negative theology by modern linguistic interpretations is given by Ramsey, in the work already referred to (see footnote to p. 31). I think he is very kind to this tradition, and I hope he is prepared to be as kind or kinder to the neoclassical technique, even though it is a less conspicuous strand through the centuries. See *Religious Language*, Ch. 2.

CHAPTER ELEVEN

THE THEOLOGICAL TASK *

by John B. Cobb, Jr.

1. CHRISTIAN NATURAL THEOLOGY

In *Living Options in Protestant Theology*, I argued that there is need for a Christian natural theology and that the philosophy of Whitehead provides the best possibility for such a theology. Critics quite reasonably complained that I did not develop such a theology in that book or even provide adequate clues as to what shape it would have. This book is my attempt to fulfill the obligation I imposed on myself by making that proposal. It intends to be a Whiteheadian Christian natural theology. This expression needs clarification.

By theology in the broadest sense I mean any coherent statement about matters of ultimate concern that recognizes that the perspective by which it is governed is received from a community of faith.[1] For example, a Christian may speak coherently of Jesus Christ and his meaning for human existence, recognizing that for his perception of ultimate importance in the Christ event he is indebted to the Christian church. In this case, his speech is theological. If, on the other hand, he speaks of the historic figure of Jesus without even implicit reference to Jesus' decisive importance for mankind, his speech is not theological. Also, if he claims for statements about Jesus' ultimate significance a self-evidence or demonstration in no way dependent upon participation in the community of faith, he would not intend his statements to be theological in the sense of my definition.

Most theological formulations take as their starting point statements that have been sanctioned by the community in which the theologian's perspective has been nurtured, statements such as creeds, confessions, scriptures, or the fully articulated systems of past theologians. But ac-

*Used with permission from A *Christian Natural Theology*, The Westminster Press, Philadelphia, Pennsylvania, and W. L. Jenkins, 1965.

cording to my definition of theology, this starting point in earlier verbal formulations is not required. One's work is theology even if one ignores all earlier statements and begins only with the way things appear to him from that perspective which he acknowledges as given to him in some community of shared life and conviction.

Definitions are not true and false but more or less useful. Hence, I shall try to justify this way of defining theology as being helpful in understanding what actually goes on under the name of theology. First, it distinguishes theology from the attempt to study religion objectively — from the point of view of some philosophy, some branch of science such as psychology or sociology, or simply as a historical phenomenon. There are those who wish to erase this distinction and to identify theology with, or as inclusive of, all study of religion.[2] However, the normal use of the term points away from this extension. The psychologist who studies religious experience, perhaps quite unsympathetically, does not think of himself as a theologian. Those who do think of themselves as theologians, on the other hand, do not concern themselves primarily with discussing religion. For the most part they talk about God, man, history, nature, culture, origins, morality, and destiny. The beliefs of the community that has nurtured them may be called religious beliefs, but for the most part they are not beliefs *about* religion.

Second, my definition suggests that theology cannot be distinguished by its subject matter from all other ways of thinking. It is so distinguished from many of them because it limits itself to questions of importance for man's meaningful existence, but it can claim no monopoly on such topics. Philosophers also discuss them as do psychologists and artists. The line of distinction here is very vague, for theology may extend itself into questions of less and less obviously critical importance for man's existence. This may be the result of more or less idle curiosity on the part of the theologian, of the conviction that his authorities are also normative with regard to such matters, or of the belief that all truth is so interconnected that he must concern himself with everything. However, almost everyone agrees that a classification of plants is less "theological" than a discussion of man's true end, even if the plant classification is based more directly on Biblical texts than is the discussion of human destiny. Furthermore, the work of the theologian can be distinguished from that of some philosophers only to the degree that the theologian acknowledges, and the philosopher resists, dependence on any particular community of ultimate concern for his perspective. Since the theologian may, in fact, be quite independent and original, and since the philosopher may in fact recognize that some of his ideas arose from a culture deeply influenced by a particular community of faith, no sharp demarcation is possible. We can only speak in some instances of the more or less theological or philosophical character of some man's thought. But this may not be a fault of the definition, since it seems to correspond to common practice and to help clarify that practice. Philosophical theology, as theology that makes extensive and explicit use of philosophical categories, merges by imperceptible degrees into a philosophy that denies dependence upon any community of faith as the source of its insights.

Third, my definition makes no reference to God. This is terminologically strange, since "theology" means reasoning about God. But we must be cautious about understanding words in terms of their roots. "Theology" as doctrine of God still exists as a branch of philosophy with this original meaning, such that one may quite properly speak of Aristotle's "theology." Likewise "theology" as doctrine of God exists as a branch of theology as I have defined it. As long as the two meanings are clearly distinguished, the term can and should be used in both senses. The branches of thought and inquiry they designate are overlapping. There can be, and is, extensive discussion of the question as to whether or not God exists that is not theological in the sense of my definition, and there is a great deal of theological work in the sense of my definition that does not treat of God.

One important advantage of defining theology as I have done, rather than as reasoning about God, is that it makes possible the recognition of the close parallel between the efforts to articulate Christian faith and similar efforts in such movements as Buddhism. In some forms of Buddhism there is with respect to God only the doctrine of his nonexistence. Thought in the Buddhist community focuses upon man and his possibilities for salvation or illumination. According to my definition, there need be no hesitancy in speaking of Buddhist theology as the thought arising out of the Buddhist community.

A more questionable feature of my definition is that it makes no reference to the holy or sacred. The communities out of which has arisen what we normally call theology are communities in which the power of the sacred is alive. This is just as true of Buddhist atheism as of Christian theism. The reason for omitting all reference to this element is that many leading Christian thinkers today deny that Christianity essentially has anything to do with the sacred. Christianity, they tell us, is not a religion. The correlation of God's act in Christ with Christian faith is absolutely unique and not to be compared with religious experience. Some of these theologians, and others as well, believe that Christian theology is most relevantly compared with doctrines about the meaning of life that are usually called secular, such as communism, fascism, romantic naturalism, and rationalistic humanism. Christianity is held to be worthy of adherence because of its superior illumination of the questions also treated by these movements, which do not think of themselves as religious or as having to do with the sacred. To define theology as having to do with the sacred, or as expressive of a perspective formed in a community that has apprehended the sacred, would be to rule out much of the work being done by men today who regard themselves, and are generally regarded, as theologians.

The price paid for this breadth of definition is that the term "theology" must then be extended beyond the limits of its most common application. This extension is already widely occurring for just this reason, so such extension is not an eccentricity; nevertheless, it reflects only the recent history of the use of the term. According to this definition we must speak also of communist, fascist, naturalist, and humanist theologies. However, a major qualification is preserved in this respect. If the Communist insists that his doctrine is purely scientific, that his view of history is a function of purely objective rational inquiry unaffected by the community of which he is a part, then his work is not theology but bad science. Others who are not persuaded that the Communist thinker in question is really so free from the influence of his community may of course insist that his thought is covertly theological. But I have defined theology in terms of the *recognition* of indebtedness to a community of faith, and this element may be lacking. Other Communists, more honest than this, may recognize their work as theological in the sense of the definition. Naturalists and humanists, on the other hand, may find that the community that mediates and supports their perspective is extremely diffuse. They may claim, more reasonably than most Communists, that they have come to their convictions relatively independently and have only then found some support in a wider community. To whatever extent this is the case, their thought is less theological by my definition. Again, we must recognize that we are dealing with a question of degree and not with a clear either/or.

A final feature of the definition is that it excludes from theology the work of the originator of a community. Of course, it may be his theological reflection as a member of an earlier community that has led to the new insight or religious experience. But insofar as there is real discontinuity, insofar as the apprehension of the holy is direct and not mediated by the community, or insofar as the understanding of the human situation is the result of radically independent reflection, we have to do with a prophet, a seer, or a philosopher, rather than with a theologian. Again, the distinction may be a matter of degree. Many of the originators of communities have understood themselves as recovering authentic traditions from the past rather than as initiating something new. To that degree their thinking is theological. But the *radically* originative element is not. The greatest religious geniuses have *not* been theologians!

Once again let me emphasize that other definitions are perfectly legitimate. They will draw the lines of inclusion and exclusion differently. One may approve or disapprove theology in any one of its meanings. It is better not to begin with an assumption either that theology is good or that it is bad, and then to arrange a definition that supports this contention. One may identify theology with dogmatism in the sense of blind appeal to authority and refusal to be honest about the facts. In such a case he may and should despise it. But then he should also be willing to learn that most of the men who have been thought of as theologians have not done the kind of work implied in his definition. He must be willing to try to find some other term by which he will refer to those whom others call theologians. Or one may identify theology as speaking in obedience to the Word of God. But then he must recognize that only those who believe that there is a "Word of God" can believe that there is a theology. To those on the outside, the great majority of the human race, what he calls theology will appear at best the confession of the faith of one community among others. He will also require some other term to describe what is done in other communities where the "Word of God" is not obeyed.

The definition of theology here employed is relatively neutral on the question of its virtue or evil. Those who believe that the only fruitful thinking is that which attempts strenuously to clear the slate of all received opinion and to attain to methods that can be approved and accepted by men of all cultures, will disapprove of the continuance of a mode of thought that recognizes its dependence upon the particularities of one community. On the other hand, those who believe that there are questions of greatest importance for human existence that are not amenable to the kind of inquiry we associate with the natural sciences, will be more sympathetic toward theology.

My own view is that theology as here defined has peculiar possibilities for combining importance and honesty. Practitioners of disciplines that pride themselves on their objectivity and neutrality sometimes make pronouncements on matters of ultimate human concern, but when they do so they invariably introduce assumptions not warranted by their purely empirical or purely rational methods. Usually there is a lack of reflective awareness of these assumptions and their sources. The theologian, on the other hand, confesses the special character of the perspective he shares and is therefore more likely to be critically reflective about his assumptions and about the kind of justification he can claim for them. If in the effort to avoid all unprovable assumptions one limits his sphere of reflection to narrower and narrower areas, one fails to deal relevantly with the issues of greatest importance for mankind, leaving them to be settled by appeals to the emotions. The theologian insists that critical reflection must be brought to bear in these areas as well as in the rigorously factual ones.

In the light of my definition of theology, we can now consider what *natural* theology may be. Some definitions of natural theology put it altogether outside the scope of theology as I have defined it. This would be highly confusing, since I intend my definition of theology to be inclusive. However, we should consider such a definition briefly. Natural theology is often identified with that of theological importance which can be known independently of all that is special to a particular community. In other words, natural theology, from this point of view, is all that can be known relative to matters of ultimate human concern by reason alone, conceiving reason in this case as a universal human power. This definition is, of course, possible, and it has substantial continuity with traditional usage. It is largely in this sense that Protestant theologians have rejected natural theology. A consideration of the reasons for this rejection will be instructive.

In principle, natural theology has been rejected on the ground that it is arrogant and self-deceptive. It is argued that reason alone is not able to arrive at any truth about such ultimate questions. When it pretends to do so it covertly introduces elements that are by no means a part of man's universal rational equipment. Every conviction on matters of ultimate concern is determined by factors peculiar to an historically-formed community or to the private experience of some individual. Since no doctrine of theological importance can claim the sanction of universal, neutral, objective, impartial reason, what is called natural theology can only be the expression of one faith or another. If Christian thinkers accept the authority of a natural theology, they are accepting something alien and necessarily opposed to their own truth, which is given them in the Christian community.

The last point leads to a consideration of the substantive or material reason for the rejection of natural theology. The philosophical doctrines traditionally accepted by the church on the basis of the authority of philosophical reason have, in fact, been in serious tension with the ways of thinking about God that grew out of the Old and New Testaments and the liturgy of the church. The philosophers' God was impassible and immutable whereas the Biblical God was deeply involved with his creation and even with its suffering. Brilliant attempts at synthesis have been made, but the tensions remain.

My·view is that it is unfortunate that natural theology has been identified substantively with particular philosophic doctrines. There is no principle inherent in reason that demands that philosophy will always conclude that God is impassible and immutable and hence, unaffected by and uninvolved in the affairs of human history. Philosophers may reach quite different conclusions, some of which do not introduce these particular tensions into the relation between philosophy and Christian theology.[3] The modern theological discussion of natural theology has been seriously clouded by the failure to distinguish the formal question from the substantive one.

On the formal question, however, I agree with the rejection of natural theology as defined above. The individual philosopher may certainly attempt to set aside the influence of his community and his own special experiences and to think with total objectivity in obedience to the evidence available to all men. This is a legitimate and worthy endeavor. But the student of the history of philosophy cannot regard it as a successful one. It is notorious that the ineradicable ideas left in Descartes's mind after he had doubted everything were products of the philosophical and theological work, or more broadly of the cultural matrix, that had formed his mind. There is nothing shameful in this. Descartes's work was exceedingly fruitful. Nevertheless, no one today can regard it as the product of a perfectly neutral and universal human rationality. If one should agree with him, he should recognize that he does so decisively because his fundamental experience corresponds to that of Descartes. He cannot reasonably hope that all equally reflective men will come to Descartes's conclusions.

To put the matter in another way, it is generally recognized today that philosophy has a history. For many centuries each philosopher was able to suppose that his own work climaxed philosophy and reached final indubitable truth. But such an attitude today would appear naive if the great questions of traditional philosophy are being discussed. Insofar as philosophers now attempt to reach final conclusions, they characteristically abandon the traditional questions of philosophy and limit themselves to much more specialized ones. In phenomenology, symbolic logic, and the analysis of the meaning of language, attempts are still being made to reach determinate conclusions not subject to further revision. These attempts are highly problematic, and in any case questions of ultimate concern cannot be treated in this way. If natural theology means the product of an unhistorical reason, we must reply that there is no such thing.

However, responsible thinking about questions of ultimate human importance continues to go on outside the community of faith. Furthermore, many of the members of the community of faith who engage in such thinking consciously or unconsciously turn away from the convictions nurtured in them by the community while they pursue this thinking. It is extremely unfortunate that the partly legitimate rejection of natural theology has led much of Protestant theology to fail to come effectively to grips with this kind of responsible thinking. Some theologians have idealized a purity of theological work that would make it unaffected by this general human reflection on the human situation. They have attempted so to define theology that nothing that can be known outside the community is relevant to its truth or falsehood, adequacy or inadequacy. I am convinced that this approach has failed.[4]

In almost all cases, the theologian continues to make assumptions or affirmations that are legitimately subject to investigation from other points of view. For example, he assumes that history and nature can be clearly distinguished, or that man can meaningfully be spoken of as free. He may insist that he knows these things on the basis of revelation, but he must then recognize that he is claiming, on the basis of revelation, the right to make affirmations that can be disputed by responsibly reflective persons. If he denies that science can speak on these matters, he thereby involves himself in a particular understanding of science that, in its turn, is subject to discussion in contexts other than theology. He must either become more and more unreasonably dogmatic, affirming that on all these questions he has answers given him by his tradition that are not subject to further adjudication, or else he must finally acknowledge that his theological work does rest upon presuppositions that are subject to evaluation in the context of general reflection. In the latter case he must acknowledge the role of something like natural theology in his work. I believe that this is indispensable if integrity is to be maintained and esotericism is to be avoided.

The problem, then, is how the theologian should reach his conclusions on those broader questions of general reflection presupposed in his work.

The hostility toward natural theology has led to a widespread refusal to take this question with full seriousness. Theologians are likely to accept rather uncritically some idea or principle that appears to them established in the secular world. For example, a theologian may assume that modern knowledge leads us to conceive the universe as a nexus of cause and effect such that total determinism prevails in nature. Conversely, he may seize the scientific principle of indeterminacy as justifying the doctrine of human freedom. Or he may point to the dominant mood of contemporary philosophy as justifying a complete disregard of traditional philosophy. My contention is that most of this is highly irresponsible. What the theologian thus chooses functions for him as a natural theology, but it is rarely subjected to the close scrutiny that such a theology should receive. It suffers from all the evils of the natural theologies of the past and lacks most of their virtues. It is just as much a product of a special point of view, but it is less thoroughly criticized. In many cases it is profoundly alien to the historic Christian faith, and yet it is accepted as unexceptionably authoritative.

If there were a consensus of responsible reflection, then the adoption of that consensus as the vehicle for expression of Christian faith might be necessary. But there is no such consensus that can be taken over and adopted by the Christian theologian. Hence, if natural theology is necessary the theologian has two choices. He may create his own, or he may adopt and adapt some existing philosophy.

If the theologian undertakes to create a philosophy expressive of his fundamental Christian perspective, we may call his work Christian philosophy in the strict sense. There can be no objection in principle to this undertaking, but historically the greatest philosophical work of theologians has never been done in this way. Many philosophies have been Christian in the looser sense that their starting points have been deeply affected by the Christian vision of reality. But the conscious recognition of this dependence on a distinctively Christian perspective has been rare.

Practically and historically speaking, the great contributions to philosophy by theologians have been made in the modification of the philosophical material they have adopted. Augustine's work with Neoplatonic philosophy and Thomas' adaptation and development both of Aristotle and of Augustinian Neoplatonism are the great classical examples. Both Augustine and Thomas were superb philosophers, but neither undertook to produce a new Christian philosophy. They brought to the philosophies they adopted questions that had not occurred to the philosophers with comparable force. In the process of answering these questions, they rethought important aspects of the philosophies. In doing this they did strictly philosophical work, appealing for justification only to the norms of philosophy. But even in making their philosophical contributions they were conscious that the perspective that led them to press these questions arose from their Christian convictions. This source of the questions does not lessen the value of their work as philosophy, but it does mean that their philosophical work was a part of their work as theologians.

Theology is not to be distinguished from philosophy by a lesser concern for rigor of thought!

If, then, we are today to follow in their footsteps, our task will be to adopt and adapt a philosophy as they did. I suggest that in implementing this program the theologian should accept two criteria for the evaluation of available philosophies.

First, he should consider the intrinsic excellence of the structure of thought he proposes to adopt and adapt. The judgment of such excellence may be partly subjective, but it is not wholly so. Despite all the irrationalism of the modern world there remains the fact that consistency and coherence where they are possible, are to be preferred over inconsistency and incoherence. A theory that proposes to explain many things must also be judged as to its success in doing so. If a few broad principles can unify a vast body of data, the employment of many *ad hoc* principles is to be rejected. Criteria of this sort have almost universal practical assent, so that it is always necessary to give special reasons for their rejection. If a particular position that claims philosophical authority is markedly inferior by these criteria, there can be no justification for adopting it to serve as a natural theology.

Second, there is no reason for accepting as a natural theology a position hostile to Christian faith, if another position more congenial to faith is equally qualified according to the norms suggested above. The study of the history of thought suggests that there is a plurality of philosophical doctrines, each of which can attain a high degree of excellence by all the norms on which they agree in common. This does not mean that any of them are wholly beyond criticism, but it does mean that the finally decisive criticisms stem from a perception of the data to be treated in philosophy that is different from the perception underlying the philosophy criticized. Diverse visions of reality lead to diverse philosophies and are, in turn, strengthened by the excellence of the philosophies to which they give birth.

For example, there are persons to whom it is wholly self-evident that sense data are the ultimate givens in terms of which all thought develops and who are equally convinced that the only acceptable explanation of the way things happen follows mechanical models. These convictions will lead to a particular philosophical position. Against this position it is useless to argue that there are data that this philosophy does not illumine, and that mechanical models capable of explaining the processes of thought have not been devised. The philosopher in question does not agree that there are other data and assumes that the lack of adequate models is a function of continuing human ignorance.

The particular position I have described would be a caricature of any major philosophical thinker, but it does point to a type of mentality that is not rare in our culture. When I realize that the particular conclusions generated by the serious reflection that arises from such assumptions have only the authority of those assumptions, then I feel free to turn to another philosophy that includes among its data human persons and their interactions; for my perception of reality is such that these seem to me at least as real and ultimate as sense data and mechanical relations. I cannot prove the truth of my vision any more than the sensationalist can prove the truth of his, but this does not shake me in my conviction. I may well recognize that my way of seeing reality has been nurtured in the community of faith, but this provides no reason for accepting as my natural theology the conclusions derived from the sensationalist-mechanist vision. On the contrary, it provides excellent reasons for choosing the conclusions of a personalistic philosophy, always providing that as a philosophy, measured by the appropriate criteria of that discipline, it is of at least equal merit. Every natural theology reflects some fundamental perspective on the world. None is the pure result of neutral, objective reason. Every argument begins with premises, and the final premises cannot themselves be proved. They must be intuited. Not all men intuit the same premises. The quest for total consensus is an illusion, and indeed there is no reason to accept majority rule in such a matter if the majority does not share one's premises. Hence, a Christian theologian should select for his natural theology a philosophy that shares his fundamental premises, his fundamental vision of reality. That philosophy is his Christian natural theology, or rather that portion of that philosophy is his natural theology which deals most relevantly with the questions of theology. It would be confusing to include under the heading of natural theology all the technical aspects of philosophy, but, on the other hand, no sharp line can be drawn, and the coherence of the whole is of decisive importance for selection.

In the sense now explained, natural theology is the overlapping of two circles, the theological and the philosophical. Natural theology is a branch of theology because the theologian in appropriating it must recognize that his selection expresses his particular perspective formed in a community from which he speaks. On the other hand, it is also philosophy because it embodies thinking that has been done and judged in terms of philosophical norms.

There may seem to be some tension here. Philosophy is critical, imaginative, and comprehensive thinking that strives to free itself from the conditioning of particular traditions and communities, whereas a criterion for the selection of a philosophy by a theologian should be its sharing of a basic vision of reality. But there is no contradiction. The philosopher does not set out to show how the world appears from the perspective of a community of faith, and to some degree, he can free himself from such perspectives. Even if he is a Christian, for example, he can set aside all the particular beliefs about Jesus Christ, God, miracles, salvation, and eternal life that he recognizes as peculiar to that tradition. He can and should refuse to accept as relevant to his philosophical work, any data that do not appear to him to be generally accessible. He will begin with ordinary language, or the findings of science, or widespread experience of mankind, rather than with the special convictions of his community. This starting point will lead the philosopher to the consideration of many questions ordinarily not treated by Christian theology and to the omission of many questions usually treated by theology. It will also lead to the consideration of overlapping questions.

However, beyond this level of conviction, life in a community also produces a primary perspective, a basic way of understanding the nature of things, a fundamental vision of reality. It is at this level that the philosopher cannot escape his perspective.[5] He can, of course, reject a perspective that he may have at one time accepted, but he can do so only in favor of some other perspective. And it should be said that changing perspectives in this sense is not simply a voluntary matter. Conscious decisions may affect the process but they do not in themselves constitute it. The decision on the part of the Christian theologian as to where he should turn for his natural theology should involve the judgment as to whether the vision of reality underlying the philosophical system is compatible with that essentially involved in the Christian faith.

In this book, I am proposing a Christian natural theology based on the philosophy of Alfred North Whitehead. Whitehead's philosophy was, I believe, Christian, in the sense of being deeply affected in its starting point by the Christian vision of reality. To some extent he himself seems to have recognized this fact. Furthermore, Whitehead's most important philosophical work grew out of his Gifford Lectures, a lectureship in natural theology. Hence, the judgment that Whitehead's philosophy provides us with a suitable Christian natural theology is not altogether an alien imposition upon him. One might well simply select the relevant doctrines in his thought and treat them as the appropriate natural theology.

Nevertheless, I see the relation of the Christian theologian to Whitehead's philosophy as analogous to that of theologians of the past to the philosophies they have adopted from the Greeks. Whitehead's work is obviously already Christianized in a way Greek philosophy could not have been. Hence, it proves, I am convinced, more amenable to Christian use. Nevertheless, the questions in the foreground of concern for the Christian theologian were on the periphery of concern for Whitehead. Philosophy of science, epistemology, ontology, logic, and mathematics, along with broad humanistic concerns, dominated his thought. He never organized his work extensively around the doctrine of man or the doctrine of God. Hence, the theologian approaches Whitehead's work, asking questions the answers to which are not readily available. He must piece together fragments from here and there. Furthermore, at certain points, more crucial to the theologian than to Whitehead, the questions are simply unanswered or are answered in ways that do not seem philosophically satisfactory when attention is focused upon them.

For these reasons, the present book is a development of my own Christian natural theology rather than simply a summary of Whitehead's philosophy in its relevant aspects. It is *heavily* dependent on Whithead. Much of it is simply borrowed from him. But I have also entered into discussion with him as to how some of the doctrines might better be formulated.

It should be reemphasized that the work of Christian natural theology does not involve an unphilosophical imposition of conclusions on recalcitrant materials. At no point in previous discussion have I intended to replace philosophical argument by dogmatic assertion or to distort Whitehead so as to render him more amenable to Christian use. My attempt has been to make the philosophical doctrines conform more fully to the philosophical norms, especially to Whitehead's own norm of coherence. The role of my Christian point of view has been to focus attention upon certain questions. If indeed, beyond this it has dictated solutions that are philosophically inferior to available alternatives, I ask only to be corrected. A Christian natural theology must not be a hybrid of philosophy on Christian conviction. It must be philosophically responsible throughout. Where my philosophical work is poor it is to be judged simply as poor philosophy and not justified by my Christian convictions.

The choice of Whitehead as the philosopher on whom to base a Christian natural theology requires only brief comment. Obviously I have chosen him because I am persuaded by him. But I can speak more objectively. If there has been any great philosopher in the twentieth century who stands in the tradition of comprehensive syntheses of human knowledge, that philosopher is Whitehead. Beside him every other candidate seems specialized, and in my view, less profound. Although many have given up the effort to understand him, and others have rejected his whole enterprise, most of those who have worked through his philosophy with care recognize its excellence by all the standards normal for the evaluation of a philosophy.[6] I cannot prove that excellence here, yet I hope that even my presentation of fragments of his thought has evoked some sense of its coherence, adequacy, and power.

Whether I judge rightly as to the appropriateness of Whiteheadian thought for Christian use is for the reader to decide. Clearly there is no overwhelming consensus among Christians as to what the faith is. For this reason no unanimous agreement on the suitability of any natural theology is conceivable. Yet I believe that in Whitehead we have an excellent philosophy unusually free from the tensions with Christian faith characteristic of other philosophies that Christians have tried to employ.

2. RELATIVISM

In the preface and elsewhere in the book, I have indicated my conviction that a cosmology inspired by the natural sciences has played the dominant role in undermining Christian understanding of both God and man. I have developed at some length aspects of a Whiteheadian cosmology which, I believe, both does more justice to the natural sciences and creates a new possibility of Christian understanding of man, God, and religion. But there is another factor that has contributed to the decline of faith in modern times, which has not yet been seriously considered. This is the historical study of culture and thought. This study has led to the view that every kind of human activity and thought can only be understood as an expression of a particular situation, that all value and "truth" are culturally and historically conditioned, and that this means also that our attempts to find truth must be understood as nothing more than an expression of our conditioned situation.

In the foregoing discussion of Christian natural theology I expressed my own acquiescence in this relativistic understanding to a considerable degree. It is because no philosophy can be regarded as philosophically absolute that the Christian can and should choose among philosophies (so long as they are philosophically of equal merit) the one that shares his own vision of the fundamental nature of things. But if so, then are we not engaged in a fascinating and difficult game rather than in grounding our affirmations of faith? If we can pick and choose among philosophies according to our liking, what reason have we to suppose that the one we have chosen relates us to reality itself? Perhaps it only systematizes a dream that some of us share. The problem of relativism is fundamental to our spiritual situation and to our understanding of both theology and philosophy. Before bringing this book to a close, I want to confront this problem directly, and, though I cannot solve it, perhaps shed some light upon it as Whitehead helps us to see it.

Few philosophers have recognized as clearly as Whitehead did the relativity of their own philosophies.[7] Yet in Whitehead's vision the relativity of philosophies need not have so debilitating an effect as some views of the relativity of thought suggest. He understands the relativity of philosophies as closely analogous to the relativity of scientific theories.[8]

In the field of science the fundamental principles now applied are remote from the fundamental principles of the Newtonian scheme. Nevertheless, the Newtonian scheme is recognized as having a large measure of applicability. As long as we focus attention upon bodies of some magnitude and upon motion of moderate velocity, the laws of science developed by the Newtonians hold true. They have, therefore, real validity, and those who accepted them were not deceived. These laws did not cease to be true when science passed beyond them to the investigation of elements in the universe to which they do not apply. What happened was that heretofore unrecognized limits of their truth came to light. Certainly the Newtonian apprehension of nature was conditioned by history and culture, but it was also substantiated in its partial truth by centuries of patient thought and experimentation. That thought and experimentation are not discredited.

Whitehead believed that the situation in philosophy is similar. No philosophical position is simply false. Every serious philosophy illumines some significant range of human experience. But every philosophy also has its limits. It illumines some portion of experience at the cost of failure to account adequately for others.[9] Also, science and history keep providing new data of which philosophy must take account. The task of the philosopher in relation to the history of philosophy is not to refute his predecessors but to learn from them. What they have shown is there to be seen. A new philosophy must encompass it. Where there are apparent contradictions among philosophers, the goal must be to attain a wider vision within which the essential truth of each view can be displayed in its limited validity.[10]

There are, of course, sheer errors in the work of philosophers. These can and should be detected, but this has nothing to do with the problem of relativism. Indeed the possibility of showing errors presupposes a non-relativistic principle at work. And no philosophical position is built upon sheer error. The more serious problem arises at the point at which philosophers draw inferences based on the assumption that their systematic positions are essentially complete. These inferences will prove erroneous, because in the nature of the case no system of thought is final. All must await enlargement at the hands of the future.

If Whitehead is right, and surely he is not entirely wrong here, then we should employ a philosopher's work with proper caution. We should never regard it as some final, definitive expression of the human mind beyond which thought cannot progress. But we need not suppose that the entire validity of his work depends upon the chance correctness of some arbitrarily selected starting point. What the philosopher has seen is there to be seen or he would not have seen it. His description may be faulty, and what he has seen may have blinded him to other dimensions of reality. He may have drawn inferences from what he has seen that he would not have drawn if he had also seen other aspects of reality — perhaps those other aspects dominating the work of another philosophical school. But when all is said and done, we may trust philosophy to give us positive light on problems of importance.

Whitehead's excellence is impressive when judged by his own principle. Within the total corpus of his thought one can understand the truth of Plato, the truth of Aristotle, the truth of Descartes, the truth of Hume, the truth of Kant, the truth of Dewey, the truth of Bradley, and many others. From the broad perspective he grants us, we can grasp the aspects of reality that dominated the thought of each of these men, can see the limited correctness of the inferences they draw, and can note how the work of the others is needed to correct and supplement what each has done. Whitehead looks forward to a future when a still more comprehensive vision can be attained in which his own work will be seen as also fragmentary in its grasp of reality. We too may look forward to that time, but we should not expect it imminently. The work of great philosophers is rarely superseded rapidly. And Whitehead is a great philosopher.

Whitehead also recognized and insisted upon the relativity of values. There is not one good. In the primordial vision of God there is an appetition that all possible values be realized. No one pattern of excellence is finally preferred.[11]

But this does not mean that values are not worth achieving. It does indeed mean that our contemporary ideals are not absolute and that no pattern of mores, however fine, can be anything other than one among many. There is no natural law, if that would mean an eternal sanctioning of one such pattern. But there is an objectivity of value. There is real better and worse. There are criteria by which various achievements, even achievements in various cultures governed by diverse visions of excellence, can be judged. The relativity of values does not mean that values are not real.

On both of these points Whitehead has dealt with the problem of relativity seriously and has removed from it its nihilistic sting. There is no human attainment of final truth, but there are more and less adequate approximations. There is no human value that is eternally sanctioned for all times and places. But there are real excellences to be achieved in many ways, all eminently worth achieving. Can we rest with this solution to the problem of relativism?

On this point I, for one, am deeply torn. I find Whitehead's thought so powerfully persuasive, and I find it so comprehensively illuminating of the history of thought, that I am for the most part disposed to act and think of it as just what it claims to be—the most adequate approach to philosophic truth yet found. In these terms the fact that we know it is not final, that the future will supersede it by showing its limitations, is not disturbing. We must in any age act upon the truth that is given us.

But at the same time that I find Whitehead's thought so deeply satisfying, I realize that there are others, more intelligent and sensitive than myself, who see all things in some quite different perspective. Can I believe that they are simply wrong? From my Whiteheadian perspective I can usually understand why they adopt the view they hold, what factors in the whole of reality have so impressed themselves upon them that they allow their vision to be dominated by those factors. But is there not an ultimate and unjustified arrogance in supposing that my perspective can include theirs in a way that theirs cannot include mine? Must I not reckon more radically with the possibility of sheer error in my own vision?

Here I think we must come to terms with an aspect of the modern sensibility that we cannot transcend. Just because we humans can trancend ourselves, we can and must recognize the extreme finitude of all our experiences, all our judgments, all our thoughts. Every criterion we establish to evaluate our claims to truth must be recognized as itself involved in the finitude it strives to transcend. From this situation there is no escape. We must learn to live, to think, and to love in the context of this ultimate insecurity of uncertainty.

This may suggest to some theologians that the whole enterprise of natural theology is, after all that has been said, misguided. It seeks support for theology in a philosophy that cannot transcend relativity and uncertainty. These theologians may hold that Christian theology should remain faithful only to the Word of God that breaks through from the absolute into the relative. But there is no escape here. I can be no more sure of the truth of the claim that the absolute has shown itself than of the truth of the philosophical analysis. However certain the absolute may be in itself, it is mediated to me through channels that do not share that absoluteness. If the appeal is to some unmediated act of the absolute in the believer, there must still be trust beyond certainty that the act has truly occurred and been rightly interpreted. Faith does not free us from involvement in relativities any more than does philosophy.

Yet, in another sense, faith is the answer to the human dilemma of being forced to live in terms of a truth that one knows may not be true. Perhaps even here Whitehead can help us or at least we can sense in him a companion in our struggles.

One of the enduring problems of philosophy is that of the relation between appearance and reality. For our present purposes we may consider appearance to be the world given us in sense experience and reality to be those entities treated in the physical sciences that seem to be the agencies by which experience is aroused in us. Whitehead developed a penetrating analysis of this process that takes full account of physics and physiology and is effectively integrated into his account of human experience. But Whitehead's account left unsettled the kind of relation that might actually exist between the objects in the external world and the sense experience of them. Is there some meaningful sense in which the grass is really green, or does the conformity of our experience to that of the entities that we prehend go no farther than the occasions of experience in the eye? Certainly it would be strange to say that the light that mediates between the grass and the eye is also green. Yet man's instinctive belief that the outside world really possesses the qualities it arouses in him is so deep, that Whitehead is reluctant to regard this belief as wholly illusory. At this point philosophical analysis breaks down. It cannot assure us that the whole of our aesthetic experience is not fundamentally deceptive.

Whitehead's discussion of peace has already been treated twice in this volume, but it has not been exhausted. One element in particular remains. Ingredient in peace, for Whitehead, is an assurance that ultimately the vision of the world given in sense experience is true.[12] This is the assurance that reality does not ultimately deceive. It is an assurance that exceeds rational demonstration. It is faith.

In the context of the present discussion this faith must be that the necessity to live and act by a belief whose truth we cannot know is accompanied by an assurance that as we do so we are not wholly deceived. We will not pretend to a privileged apprehension of reality as a whole. We will not suppose that those who disagree with us are therefore wrong. We can only witness to the way that our best reflection leads us to perceive our world. But we can and must believe that in this witness also, somehow, the truth is served.

3. THE OTHER TASKS OF THEOLOGY

Insofar as the theologian appeals for the justification of his statements to the general experience of mankind, he is engaged in Christian natural theology. He may have gained his insight from special revelation, but he is asking that it be accepted on its own merit as illuminating the human situation. Much of the work that has been done, even by those who have most vehemently attacked natural theology, is Christian natural theology in this sense. But there is another dimension to the theologian's task. He must also witness directly to what is peculiar to his own community and to that revelation of truth by which it is constituted. At this point he is engaged in Christian theology proper.

There is no one way of carrying out this theological enterprise. Men equally responsible to their faith and to their community approach their task of Christian reflection in many different ways. Of these we will consider a few briefly, without any intention of disparaging still other approaches.

First, there is interpretation of the text. Especially in Protestantism the community has attributed a normativeness to the Bible that makes its exposition and proclamation central to the theological task. This point of view has been maintained with special effectiveness in those Continental European traditions which have provided the greatest intellectual leadership in the nineteenth and twentieth centuries. Here, especially in the contemporary scene, the theologian is not sharply distinguished from the Biblical scholar. Instead, they share the one task of understanding and making relevant the message found in the text. The Biblical scholar may focus more narrowly on the understanding, the theologian on the relevance, but even this division of labor is hardly maintained. In recent years it has often been the Biblical scholars rather than the systematic theologians who have done the most creative and influential theological work and who have been most effectively engaged with the question of relevance to the modern situation.

In this country this near identification of theology with interpretation of the text is sometimes confused with conservatism. It may, of course, be conservative in spirit and is so at least to the extent that it begins with the assumption that the Scriptures remain normative for the church. But the radicality with which the criticism of Scripture has been carried out in terms of modern historiographical methods, the intense concern to find within the Scripture that meaning and message which is of vital relevance in our situation, should warn us that the distinction of conservative and liberal is not relevant to the distinction between this approach to theology and others.

Second, the theologian may take as his approach to the proper task of theology, confession based on reflection on what has occurred and continues to take place in the community. This will involve him in considering the role of Scripture in the community and in employing Scripture as a source for determining the formative events of the community. Nevertheless, the role of Scripture and its interpretation is quite different in this confessional approach to theology from that discussed above. Here the community rather than the Bible is taken as the point of reference.

The first approach to theology discussed above is characteristic of the Reformation and the theological currents that have maintained closest continuity with it. Biblical study in the tradition of the Reformation is distinctively theological by virtue of its assumption that truth for man's existence is to be found in the text. A scholar who approached the Bible without any conviction of its existential importance might contribute to the discipline of Biblical scholarship and indirectly to theology, but he would not himself be engaged in the theological enterprise. Similarly in the confessional approach, only if the man who speaks of what has taken place and now takes place in the community does so as a believing participant, is his work theological.[13] An outsider might discuss the same topics, and the theologian might learn much from him. But the work of the outsider will be history or sociology and not theology.

The confessional theologian reflects upon the history that has formed the community of which he is a part and that has given him the meanings in terms of which he sees all of life. He confesses the redemptive and revelatory power of the key events in this history. He speaks of the meaning and nature of that faith by which the power of the events becomes effective in the believer. Again, he does not attempt to describe this faith as a psychologist might. He speaks of it in its living immediacy as a power effective in the community and shared by him. He explains how it seems to arise and how it affects the whole quality of life and action. He discusses the response that is appropriate to it and how it binds men together in fellowship. Beyond this there is the life and practice of the community. This too must be described from within in its peculiar meaning for its members. There are preaching and sacraments to be understood and interpreted in their relation to the revelatory events and the faith of the believer. There is the understanding of historical continuity and discontinuity to be worked out, the role and limits of innovation. There is the attempt to understand how God is peculiarly at work in all of this and how his present work is related to his work in the revelatory events.

In principle, confessional theology makes no affirmations with application beyond the community or subject to verification outside of it. But theology proper may take a third form which I will call, quite arbitrarily, "dogmatic" theology. The dogmatic theologian makes claims of truth which are relevant to all men whether or not they are within the community. He may speak of the human situation as such, and not just of the situation of the believer. Insofar as the theologian appeals to the general evidence available to those both within and without the community for the vindication of such affirmations, he is involved in Christian natural theology. But insofar as he makes affirmations about the universal human situation that are not warranted in general experience but only in the revelatory events by which the community lives, he is in my terms a dogmatic theologian. For example, the dogmatic theologian may affirm on the grounds of the resurrection of Jesus that all men will be resurrected, without supposing that there is other evidence for this truth or that objective proof is possible.

I suggest that in working out these approaches to theology proper, Whiteheadian categories will prove hardly less useful than in the formulation of a natural theology. The presence of God in Jesus Christ, the way in which the Christian is bound to him in faith, the nature of the new being in him, the sacraments, the present working of the Holy Spirit —all these are subject to clarification and illumination by the use of Whiteheadian concepts. That task still lies ahead of us.

But in our day the encounter of Christianity with the other great world religions renders questionable the continuing work of Christian theology in any of its forms. This encounter is not new, but as the world draws together politically, economically, and culturally, the divisiveness of organized religions all continuing to confess their several faiths, becomes increasingly intolerable to many. It is, of course, possible to continue business as usual. But the knowledge that there have been other great revelations by which communities have lived cannot simply be set aside. The work of the theologian must be set in a new key. The inner tension of Christianity, between its particularism and its universalism, expresses itself again in the responses to this situation.

One response is to attempt to distance ourselves from all the particular traditions and communities in order to be able to study each impartially and to accept only what is common to all. But what each shares with the others may be that which is least valuable rather than that which is best. The highest common denominator of all religions may prove to offer nothing by which man can find meaning in life. Hence, others insist that that procedure is impossible. They believe that it is from the perspective given by one community in which we are genuinely and committedly involved that we can learn most effectively from other communities. Believers from the several traditions can engage in a dialogue from which all can learn, although there can be no expectation of agreement or conversion. A third response is to give up what I have called Reformation and dogmatic theology and to limit theology proper to the confessional form. By claiming no special knowledge about man as man but only about the believer as believer, this confessional theology refuses to engage in controversy with other faiths. A fourth response is to deny that the several communities are on the same level at all. One community is claimed to be founded upon the one truth given uniquely to it. Hence theological reflection within that community is the only responsible way of articulating universal truth.

Can natural theology help us here? It cannot help in the sense once supposed when it was thought that human reason could reach conclusions on matters of theological importance that transcend all the relativities of religion and perspective. I have argued that the theologian must select a philosophy according to its compatibility with his fundamental vision as well as according to its philosophical excellence. He cannot then suppose that adherents of other faiths should simply accept his choice as a common basis for joint reflections.

Yet what is remarkable about Whitehead's extraordinarily comprehensive and original philosophy is that it has also many points of contact with the East. The emphasis on immanence, the rejection of any substance underlying the succession of experiences, the relation of man to nature, the primacy of aesthetic categories in the understanding of ethics, all have affinities to this or that Asiatic philosophy or religion. I have tried to suggest in the preceding chapter how several forms of religious experience more fully developed in the East than in the West can be understood in their genuineness in Whiteheadian categories. Hence, the judgment that finally Whitehead's philosophy favors the Judeo-Christian concern for persons and interpersonal relations, its monotheism, and its belief that there is meaning in the historical process, does not mean that Eastern thought is simply rejected. Indeed, it might be quite possible for a Buddhist to develop from Whitehead's philosophy a Buddhist natural theology almost as reasonably as I have developed a Christian one.[14] Whitehead certainly would not object.

Whether or not Whitehead might provide a natural theology common to East and West, he can offer great aid to the West in its task of re-thinking its faith in the light of the reality of the great religions of the East. What has made the encounter so often painful has been the sense that where the religions differ, if one is right, the others must be wrong. Ultimately, at some points, this may be so. But if we can learn to see the multiplicity of authentic types of religious experience, if we can see also the truth that is present in so many different ways of apprehending the nature of things, then we can begin by confronting the truth in each faith with the truth in others. At some points each tradition must learn to state its truth more carefully to avoid the falsehood that arises from ex-aggeration, or from insensitivity to the fragmentariness of every human apprehension. The points of conflict will recede as this is done. Each can believe the truth of the other without becoming less convinced of the truth of that which has been revealed to it.

I do not mean to suggest that we can solve our problems of religious diversity simply by adding together the beliefs of all faiths. I do mean to suggest that we can begin by assuming that what each claims to be true—claims with greatest confidence based on its primary revelation and surest intuitions—is true. The experiences it affirms do take place. The benefits it has found are real. But men cannot individually encom-pass all the multiplicity of religious experiences. If a man attempts to enrich his life with all the possible blessings, he will gain few indeed. Life requires a definiteness, a decision, a focus. The final question be-tween the religions of the world must be one of value. Granted the truth each apprehends, where ultimately can man's final need be met?

When that question is asked with utter honesty, none of the great re-ligious communities of our world can provide the answer. Each has iden-tified itself with doctrinal and cultural elements too specialized to speak to the condition of man as man. A greater purity and therefore a greater universality of relevance can be found in the great classical figures of the religious traditions. But among them also, relativity remains. The Bud-dha's vision of reality is not that of the Christ, and both differ profoundly from that of Socrates.

Nevertheless, it may be that all are not in the end on the same plane.

It may be that man's *final* need finds its answer only in one. What the Christian dare not claim for himself or for his church, he may yet claim for Jesus Christ, namely, that there the universal answer is to be found. The task of vindicating such a claim lies before us as Christians, both in the challenge of personal witness and in the demand for theological reflection.

FOOTNOTES

1 In this section I am following Tillich in using "faith" and "ultimate concern" interchangeably.

2 See, for example, John A. Hutchinson, *Language and Faith* (The Westminster Press, 1963), Ch. IX.

3 That this is so is fully established by the work of Hartshorne. See especially *The Divine Relativity*.

4 In *Living Options in Protestant Theology*, I have tried to show in each case how, whether recognized or not, theological positions depend systematically on affirmations that are not private to theology. I acknowledge the brilliance of Barth's near success in avoiding such dependence.

5 Whitehead saw the work of the creative philosopher in terms of the novelty of his perspective. The philosopher "has looked at the universe in a certain way, has seen phenomena under some fresh aspect; he is full of his vision and anxious to communicate it. His value to other men is in what he has seen" (*Dial 266*). Whitehead also recognized that the philosopher's vision is affected by the historic community in which he stands. "Modern European philosophy, which had its origins in Plato and Aristotle, after sixteen hundred years of Christianity reformulated its problems with increased attention to the importance of the individual subject of experience, conceived as an abiding entity with a transition of experiences." (*RM 140*).

6 As an exception, note Blyth, *Whitehead's Theory of Knowledge*. Blyth argues that there are fundamental inconsistencies in Whitehead's position. The difficulty arises chiefly from Whitehead's frequent unfortunate references to mutual prehensions. If taken literally, this terminology implies that contemporary occasions prehend each other, a doctrine explicitly repudiated by Whitehead. Sherburne's explanation of Whitehead's probable meaning handles most of Blyth's criticisms. (Sherburne, pp. 73-76.)

7 *ESP* 87.

8 *PR* 20-21.

9 *FR* 70-71.

10 *PR* 11-16.

11 This has been discussed above, p. 104.

12 *AI* 377 ff.

13 A borderline case is that of the man who enters empathetically into an alien perspective and imaginatively presents its convictions. I would say that in this sense a Buddhist can write a Christian theology.

14 Hartshorne has emphasized the affinities of Whitehead's philosophy with some forms of Buddhism, e.g., *The Logic of Perfection* (The Open Court Publishing Company), p. 273; Kline, p. 25.

CHAPTER TWELVE

THEOLOGY AND OBJECTIVITY *

by Schubert A. Ogden

A problem at the center of recent theological discussion is "The Problem of Nonobjectifying Thinking and Speaking in Contemporary Theology."[1] Although this formulation as such might suggest that the interest behind it is essentially historical, it is evident that the main concern of the discussion quite transcends any merely descriptive treatment of the problem. The real focus of interest is on the systematic or normative issue which this formulation expresses; and the purpose of the present essay is to help to clarify and perhaps even to resolve this issue.

This being so, it will hardly do to remain wholly within the frame of reference in which the issue as thus formulated arises. Questions are to a considerable extent already answers;[2] and when one's controlling purpose is to arrive at a normative judgment on an issue, his first order of business is always to take pains with how the question itself is to be formulated. Recognition of this seems to me nowhere more important than with respect to the assertion that theological thinking and speaking are, or (since the assertion is really normative) ought to be, nonobjectifying. If the previous discussion of this assertion has proved anything, it is that one must first of all unpack the word "nonobjectifying" to see just what kinds of goods it contains, what kinds of questions it is capable of expressing and, therefore, what kinds of answers it also partially determines.

I do not suppose this essay can provide all such clarification as may be necessary. Yet it can at least make a beginning; and I ask that what follows be considered primarily as an attempt to heighten our self-consciousness about the real issue under discussion. I shall analyze four related yet distinct meanings which the term "nonobjectifying" has disclosed

*Used with permission from *The Reality of God and Other Essays*, Harper & Row, New York, New York, 1965.

itself to have and in this way try to illumine some of the main alternatives for approaching and answering the principal question. At each stage, I will also seek to enter into discussion with these alternatives, pointing up some of the difficulties they entail and suggesting which of them, if any, indicate the direction in which an adequate answer is most likely to be found. Thus, although the burden of the essay will be analytic and, I hope, clarifying, I will also attempt to develop at least the outlines of a possible constructive position with respect to the underlying issue. To do less than this would seem to me to disappoint the expectation aroused by my title—even if to do more is impossible, given the present status of the discussion and the limitations of a single essay.

Before turning to the analysis, however, I must offer a provisional clarification of the phrase "theological thinking and speaking." Since it is just what is to be understood by this phrase that is the real underlying issue expressed by the original formulation, my own position on this issue can be made clear only by the whole of the subsequent argument. Yet this argument can hardly be either developed or understood unless we have a general idea of the question it is directed toward clarifying and, to some extent, answering. Accordingly, I propose the following preliminary definition of how "thinking" and "speaking" are to be taken when used in connection with the undertaking properly designated "theology." I assume, naturally, that the sense of the word "theology" appropriate here is not the generic sense with which we might properly use it in other contexts, but the specific sense explicity conveyed by the words "Christian theology."

On this assumption, *theological thinking and speaking are a more or less distinguishable type or level of thinking and speaking about God as apprehended through the witness of faith of Jesus Christ.* It will be noted that this definition leaves open exactly how one is to understand the relation of theology to other possible types or levels of thought and speech about God as known through Christ. This is done deliberately, since one of the purposes of the later discussion will be to clarify this relation. The thing to recognize now is simply that all theological thought and speech are thought and speech having the God of Jesus Christ as their object or referent, although it is not possible, on the view to be developed here, to convert this proposition.

But even this, it may be thought, is a "persuasive definition" that already begs too many of the questions needing clarification. Surely one must recognize that the Christian theologian properly thinks and speaks about all sorts of things other than God and that, if the language he uses is any indication, much of what he thinks and says, when considered out of its total context, is not strictly "about" anything whatever. The point of this objection is well taken, although it does not, I believe, affect the validity of the provisional definition. Even if one grants that Christian theologians do properly think and speak about matters other than God and that assertion of some kind is not the only use to which they put their language, it does not follow that these things account for their being theologians or that they could be such at all apart from the specific difference set forth in the definition. That God is somehow the object of all theological thinking and speaking need not mean—nay, perhaps, cannot mean—that he is the only such object; and one may hold that theological language, when taken in its total context, always functions somehow to assert something without claiming that this is the only function it serves. But far from obvious to me is that one could properly speak of "theology" at all without assuming the minimal meaning suggested by the word as used historically and also re-expressed in the proposed definition—namely, a thinking whose primary object is God as disclosed through the witness of Christian faith and a speaking which, whatever its other uses, intends to assert something meaningful about that same divine object.

This does not mean that some particular concept of God or its corresponding vocable is an essential element in theological thinking and speaking. According to the definition, thought and speech are determined as theological by their actual intentional object or referent, God himself, not by any concept of God or the term expressing it. Therefore, unlike certain verbally similar definitions, the tentative definition of theology given above is not persuasive or tendentious in the sense of covertly assuming some particular conception of God and arbitrarily restricting what may be counted as theological speech. Whether the term be "God" or "the transcendent" or "the unconditioned" or "being-itself," or any number of other terms that readily come to mind, it can very well function as an instance of theological speaking in the sense of the definition. And the same is true, *mutatis mutandis*, of the various conceptualities of which all such terms are the linguistic expressions. If any conceptuality serves in a certain way or at a certain level to conceive God as understood by Christian faith, then it is, on my terms, a theological conceptuality, and the thinking it makes possible is theological thinking.

There are no doubt many other questions that the provisional definition raises. But perhaps enough has been said to provide the essential preliminary clarification, and, in any event, it is necessary now to go on to the analysis itself. Some of the remaining questions will be answered as we proceed, and the definition should come to seem less arbitrary than it may now appear.

I

It may be assumed, I think, that the word "nonobjectifying," which appears in the original formulation of the problem, is the literal English equivalent of a German word formed from the infinitive *objektivieren*. This, then, should be sufficient indication of the general frame of reference presupposed by the formulation. Broadly speaking, one may say that the standpoint thereby revealed is that of the existentialist philosophy and theology which have been such determinative influences on the thought of our century and whose principal exponents are all more or less well known.

One of the hallmarks of such philosophy and theology is the claim that our cognitive encounter with reality is disclosed by careful analysis to have a basic twofold form.[3] On the one hand, there is our original internal awareness of our own existence in relation to the manifold reality encountering us, which awareness in some modification is the most distinctive feature of our being as men, as selves or persons. On the other hand, there is the quite different kind of perception somehow grounded in this original existential awareness. This is our derived external perception of reality distinct from our selves as the object of our ordinary sense experience. I cannot pause here to show how this characteristically existentialist analysis of our knowledge as both "existential" and "objectifying" is directly connected with the Kantian and neo-Kantian analyses that preceded it. But I believe it will be granted that just this analysis, in its context in a certain strand of post-Kantian philosophy, is the natural home of the word *objektivieren*, its various cognates, and their English equivalents. If so, then one may say that the notion of nonobjectifying thinking and speaking is to be understood, first of all, in relation to this account of our knowledge as, in one of its basic forms, an objectifying knowledge. Accordingly, the first form of the principal question is whether, given the understanding of nonobjectifying thinking and speaking suggested by this account, theology as provisionally defined is nonobjectifying.

So formulated, the question is not difficult to answer, and there is likely to be considerable agreement in answering it. It is widely recognized by contemporary Protestant theologians that theological thinking and speaking are, or ought to be, "nonobjectifying" in this first meaning of the word. This is certainly the case with those whom I have broadly spoken of as existentialist theologians; whether one thinks of Rudolf Bultmann or Paul Tillich or any of several others whose positions are essentially similar, the claim that theology is in this sense nonobjectifying is self-evident. But the same is true of a large number of other theologians whom one would hardly speak of as existentialist in their basic standpoints.

Thus, wherever theologians argue—as perhaps most Protestant theologians today do argue—that there is a difference in principle between the thinking and speaking of science and the thinking and speaking proper to theology, this same claim is, in effect, advanced. This becomes evident as soon as one recognizes that science generally, and the so-called "special sciences" individually, are but developments at a certain level of the objectifying knowledge that is one of the basic forms of our cognitive encounter with ourselves and the things around us. What the scientist thinks and speaks about is reality insofar as it can be made the object of particular external perceptions. Hence, to hold that the theologian's thinking and speaking differ in principle from those of the scientist is to hold in fact, if not in so many words, that theology is in this sense nonobjectifying. A common way of maintaining this in terms made current by the analytic philosophers of our English-speaking tradition is to deny that the meaning of theological assertions is of the same logical type as that of scientific statements. Whereas the test of the meaningfulness of a scientific hypothesis is that it should be capable, in principle, of falsification by external perception, the same test cannot be applied to the distinctive statements of theology, since they are logically different from scientific hypotheses and so incapable of this kind of falsification.

There are theologians, to be sure, who are unwilling to concede that theological thought and speech are nonobjectifying even in this first meaning of the word. Fearing lest this concession imply that theological language asserts nothing at all and thus has some wholly noncognitive use and meaning, they reject any sharp distinction between theology and science and hold that theological statements are, after all, in principle falsifiable. The serious difficulties of this position, however—especially of the device of "eschatological verification" by which some seek to defend it—are notorious, and I myself regard it as untenable.[4] The decisive objection to it is its implication that theological assertions about the being and nature of God are somehow about an actual or potential object of our ordinary sense perception. If such assertions are even "eschatologically" verifiable in the manner of scientific hypotheses, it is not clear to me why they should be considered properly theological assertions at all. Here I would recall Bultmann's insistence that the chief objection to a "mythological" representation of God is not that it comes into conflict with the essential procedure and claims of modern science, but that it seriously misrepresents God's transcendence as apprehended by Christian faith. By objectifying God in the sense of thinking and speaking of him under the same conditions as apply to the objects of our external perception, myth in effect denies God's qualitative difference from all things other than himself and thus fails to express its own intention in an appropriate way. The same would be true, Bultmann argues, of any representation of God in the terms and categories of modern science. Like myth, science can think and speak about reality only as the object of our sense perceptions, and so could represent God only by similarly misrepresenting the uniqueness of his reality as God. Consequently, the main reason for demythologizing and for seeking a theological conceptuality alternative to that of science as well as to that of myth is, as Bultmann says, "faith itself"—by which he means not only faith's character as a mode of existential self-understanding, but also faith's distinctive apprehension, precisely as such self-understanding, of the transcendent reality of God.[5]

Reference to demythologizing also enables me to introduce a certain refinement in the answer to the first form of the question. If, as I have argued, theological thinking and speaking ought by all means to be nonobjectifying in the first meaning of the word, this implies neither that all that has usually been regarded as such thinking and speaking conforms to this norm nor that failure to conform to it *eo ipso* disqualifies thought and speech from any theological relevance. Obviously much of what has been traditionally accepted as theology, to say nothing of the far larger corpus of the church's pretheological witness, is not nonobjectifying even in this first sense. True, if we consider the actual uses of traditional theological language, it becomes clear that, far more often than not, it served, and continues to serve, a rather different primary purpose from that of the language of modern science and of the ordinary objectifying thinking of which such science is the development. Even so, the view that theology should, at least to this extent, be nonobjectifying requires one to say that much which has hitherto passed for theology can no longer be so considered, except as an essentially inadequate approximation to the norm thereby expressed.

On the other hand, one need not conclude that such "theology" is without real theological significance, although one does have to give a revised account of what its significance is. So-called "theological" thinking and speaking that are in this first sense objectifying are related to theology proper not as thought and speech about God of the same type or at the same level, but as part of the pretheological thinking and speaking that I comprehend by the word "witness" and take to be the primary datum of the critical interpretation in which theology properly consists. This is also the view expressed by Bultmann when he stresses that the task of demythologizing is not to *eliminate* mythology, but to make the genuinely hermeneutical effort to *understand* it. In this view, objectifying thinking and speaking about God definitely have a place and, at their own level, maybe even an indispensable place. Yet this place is not that of an essential element in theology itself, but that of a certain level or stratum in the historically given witness to God, which it is the business of theology to understand and critically interpret.[6]

II

We move to the next stage of the analysis by observing that even some of the existentialist philosophers and theologians themselves hold the basic twofold account of our knowledge as either existential or objectifying (in the sense previously explained) to be inexhaustive. They recognize that, in addition to the awareness of ourselves and others through our self-understanding and the perception of reality as the object of our sense experience, there is a third form of knowledge that discloses itself in our being able to distinguish between the other two forms. The type of knowledge illustrated by a phenomenological analysis of our existence and of the basic types of cognition it makes possible is neither existential nor objectifying (again, in the sense previously clarified), but is a distinct type related to, yet different from, these other types. Thus Martin Heidegger, in *Sein und Zeit*, distinguishes between the "existential" (*existenziell*) understanding uniquely present in each individual existence as his own personal encounter with reality and the "existentialist" (*existenzial*) understanding exemplified in a descriptive analysis of the phenomenon of existence in general, such as constitutes the first step toward what he there calls "ontology."[7]

Interestingly, just this distinction opens the way to giving a second meaning to the word "objectifying." The introduction of this ambiguity is perhaps most obvious in Bultmann's use of the word; for him, objectifying thinking and speaking come to include not only modern science and the more basic level of thought and speech of which such science is the methodical development, but also the existentialist analysis that Heidegger takes to be the fundamental task of philosophy.[8] If one asks how this extension of meaning is possible, the most likely answer seems to be that, from the beginning, the objectifying thinking and speaking which have become fully developed in modern science are different from their existential counterparts not simply in one respect but in two. In the first place, they have to do not with our own existence, but with reality as distinct from ourselves. This, one may say, is their difference with respect to the object to which they are directed. But they also differ from existential thinking and speaking in being derived rather than original, peripheral rather than central, with respect to the real origin or center of human existence. Whereas existential thinking and speaking have to do quite directly with the gain or loss of our authentic existence as selves, our thought and speech about the objects of our external perception are only indirectly related to this paramount concern. Hence another familiar way of expressing this second difference between existential and objectifying knowledge is to represent the former as "concerned" or "involved," the latter as "disinterested" or "detached."[9]

However the second difference is expressed, it has to do not with the object of our knowledge, whether ourselves or reality as other than ourselves, but with what one may call the subjective form of our knowledge. In this respect, there is obviously something common between our external perception of objects, particularly in its developed form as science, and the kind of knowledge illustrated by an existentialist analysis such as Heidegger presents in *Sein und Zeit*. As contrasted with our existential self-understanding, such analysis is a reflective matter which has to do only indirectly with realizing our authentic existence and so is (relatively) disinterested instead of concerned, detached instead of involved.

Whatever the reason, Bultmann holds that existentialist understanding is also scientific with respect to its subjective form and must therefore be regarded as objectifying in character. But with this, the words "scientific" and "objectifying" take on new and slightly different meanings, which require a second and correspondingly different formulation of the question as to the character of theological thinking and speaking.

Other existentialists, to be sure, have denied that a scientific analysis of human existence is possible and have refused to accept this more extended meaning of the term "objectifying." Karl Jaspers, notably, has held that "the philosophy of existence would at once be lost were it again to believe that it knows [*wissen*] what man is,"[10] and he has insisted on the difference between Heidegger's existentialist analysis and his own "clarification of existence" (*Existenzerhellung*).[11] But, as I have argued elsewhere,[12] Bultmann's reply to Jaspers at this point seems conclusive. Whatever Jaspers' intention, he "cannot help explicating what he calls 'clarification of existence' in such a way that it becomes universally understandable, i.e., he must objectify it as doctrine."[13] Bultmann concludes, significantly, that so long as we recognize this to be true of Jaspers' clarification, it is a merely verbal issue whether we call it "existentialist analysis" or speak of it as "scientific." I should hope the preceding analysis has made clear the sense in which this issue is verbal and has also shown how it is to be resolved.

Much more significant for my main purpose, however, is Bultmann's contention in the same context that theology, too, is objectifying in this second sense.[14] If, with him, one includes under "objectifying" all thinking and speaking sharing in a reflective subjective form essentially like that of modern science, the claim that theology ought to be non-objectifying may well appear more problematic than it did at the first stage of the analysis. Indeed, this claim proves to be sufficiently problematic that the contrary position taken by Bultmann presents itself as a more adequate way of answering the principal question when posed in this second form. Since I have developed the reasons for this judgment rather fully in another essay,[15] I confine myself here to a brief summary of the essential points.

Even if one grants with Heinrich Ott that theology is "a movement of faith itself" and that there is, in consequence, a continuity between the existential understanding of faith and the more reflective levels of thinking and speaking represented by witness and theology,[16] still it is imperative that one be able to distinguish clearly between each of these different levels. Only so, as Ott himself recognizes,[17] can one escape the untenable consequences that the man of faith alone can either witness to faith or understand it theologically and that the witness or theologian is to be regarded *ipso facto* as a faithful man. Yet how is one to distinguish between faith, witness, and theology, except by seeing them as points along the continuum defined by the two poles of existential self-understanding and objectifying knowledge, in the second sense I have tried to clarify?

Faith as such is obviously the extreme contrast to objectifying knowledge in this meaning of the term, and this is true, even though as itself a type of understanding, faith is quite distinct from immediate feeling and somehow identical with the other points lying closer to the opposite end of the continuum. Insofar as it is conscious—and it is doubtful whether one can really speak of an "unconscious faith"—it is already explicit as some form of belief, although such belief represents the maximum of personal concern and involvement. As for witness, its character is well suggested by Alfred North Whitehead in a remarkable description of the sayings of Jesus in the Sermon on the Mount and the parables.

The reported sayings of Christ are not formularized thought. They are descriptions of direct insight. The ideas are in his mind as immediate pictures, and not as analyzed in terms of abstract concepts. He sees intuitively the relations between good men and bad men; his expressions are not cast into the form of an analysis of the goodness and badness of man. His sayings are actions and not adjustments of concepts. He speaks in the lowest abstractions that language is capable of, if it is to be language at all and not the fact itself.[18]

What Whitehead says here about Jesus' witness seems to me applicable, *mutatis mutandis,* to all witness whatever, which is to say, to spontaneous confession and preaching, prayer, and the more nonreflective forms of the church's teaching. In all these, too, speaking is ideally more a matter of action than of adjusting concepts, and the language naturally used tends to be only slightly less concrete than the reality to which it refers. There are, to be sure, differences between the various things I am comprehending under the word "witness." But common to them all is what I spoke of earlier as their pretheological character. They represent a type of thinking and speaking distinct from the more original existential understanding of faith, on the one hand, and the more derived reflection of theology proper, on the other. The latter's distinctive character, as Whitehead also suggests, is precisely its higher degree of generality as betrayed by its use of universal concepts and the greater abstractness of its language. Just when theology is true to its hermeneutical task of critically interpreting the church's witness in an appropriate and understandable conceptuality, it cannot but involve a more reflective and so more objectifying type of thinking and speaking than is represented either by the various forms of witness or by the still more existential phenomenon of faith itself.

Such, at any rate, is the conclusion I draw in the absence of any equally clear and convincing explanation of the distinctions one must make between faith itself and the witness and theology through which it is differently expressed. Although I fully concur in Ott's insistence that these distinctions are not absolute and that we must think of faith and theology as different levels of understanding somehow continuous with one another, I do not see how the difference between the levels can be adequately accounted for except by regarding theological thinking and speaking as objectifying in the sense he wishes to deny.

Before passing to the next stage of the analysis, I must consider another objection to the position that theology is necessarily objectifying in the second sense that has been distinguished. There are those who would take this position, or one rather like it, but only on condition that the object of theological thinking and speaking be understood differently from the understanding of it in my provisional definition. While faith, they argue, may indeed be made the object of the scientific or objectifying reflection which is theology, the same can hardly be said of God himself. God is always Subject and never object, and so theology can be held to have a scientific character only by restricting it to the critical interpretation of Christian faith or witness and denying that it is in any sense an objectifying thinking and speaking about the God to whom faith is directed.[19]

Some such view is widely enough represented on the contemporary theological scene that it might seem to require either that one radically revise the definition of theology with which we began or else reconsider the position at which we have now arrived, that theological thinking and speaking are in this second sense objectifying. I hold, however, that it is this conventional view itself which must be reconsidered and revised, since it is open to at least two decisive objections.

In the first place, it involves an obvious self-contradiction. The assertion that one may not think and speak about God in an objectifying way is itself an instance of such thinking and speaking—or, at any rate, can be defended as more than an empty assertion only by appealing to such. It is one thing to acknowledge God existentially as eminent Subject or Thou, but it is quite another to lay down the general principle that only by thus acknowledging him can one know him concretely as God. Clearly, such a principle or the general assertions about God from which it alone can be deduced cannot be anything but objectifying thinking and speaking directly about God himself. But, in the second place, this view begs the very question to which only objectifying thinking about God can provide the answer. As Charles Hartshorne has convincingly demonstrated, the hidden premise of the view is the ancient dogma of classical natural theology that God is so essentially "simple" that one cannot distinguish diverse aspects of his being, but must think of him either as wholly subject or as wholly object.[20] Since, however, this particular objectifying conception of God is only slightly more problematic with respect to its understandability than with respect to its appropriateness as a conception of the God of Jesus Christ, it provides an odd basis on which a Christian theologian should argue his case.

I conclude, therefore, notwithstanding the conventional wisdom on the issue, that theology may very well be objectifying in this second sense, even when thought of in terms of the provisional definition. If one understands the issue properly, there is as much reason for God to be the object of the objectifying thinking and speaking of theology as for him to be the eminent Subject whom I can know as *my* God here and now only in my own existential understanding of faith.[21]

III

The definition of theology we set out with is certain to seem questionable from still another standpoint, which is closely connected with a third meaning that the word "nonobjectifying" is sometimes taken to have. There are several philosophers of religion and theologians oriented to modern analytic philosophy who hold that any thinking or speaking that is nonobjectifying in the first sense of the word I distinguished is not only "nonscientific" (again, in the first sense of the word), but also "noncognitive."

The assumption these thinkers make is that the form of knowledge represented by modern science—or, more broadly, by the ordinary external perception of which science is the methodical refinement—is the only form of knowledge there is. True, they also allow for the purely analytic knowledge constituted by the tautological statements of mathematics and formal logic. But these statements, they claim, involve no knowledge in the sense of reference to "how things are," the possibility of such reference being restricted solely to the assertions of the various sciences and other assertions open in principle to the same kind of falsification. From this standpoint, to affirm, as I did earlier, that theological assertions are not subject to this kind of falsification is to concede that they are not really (i.e., logically) assertions at all, but linguistic expressions having some other noncognitive meaning or use. Since those who occupy this standpoint would also affirm this, they can only conclude that a definition of theological thinking and speaking such as I began by proposing is utterly problematic. Theological utterances, they argue, cannot really be "about" anything, much less about some divine object called "God." Rather, they can only have some function other than that of making assertions, and the values "true" and "false" simply have no application to them.

This general view has been worked out in different ways by a number of analytic philosophers making what has been called "the left-wing response" to the positivist challenge that all meaningful assertions must be falsifiable by external perception.[22] The familiar proposal of R. M. Hare that religious and theological utterances be taken as expressions of a *"blik"* or basic attitude toward the world has usually been understood as a particular development of such a view.[23] This is certainly how one must understand the equally well-known lecture of R. B. Braithwaite, *An Empiricist's View of the Nature of Religious Belief,*[24] which is perhaps the classic formulation of this viewpoint from the strictly philosophical side.

More recently, this view has been given forcible theological expression by Paul M. van Buren in his book, *The Secular Meaning of the Gospel.*[25] Following closely the interpretation of religious utterances set forth by Braithwaite and Hare, van Buren argues that the statements of the Christian gospel are in no sense to be taken cognitively as assertions about a divine reality, but are to be interpreted as expressions of a certain human stance or attitude which he calls a "historical perspective."[26] He recognizes, of course, that such a view entails a radical "reduction" of what have traditionally counted as theological statements.[27] But this by itself, as we have seen, in no way distinguishes his proposal from the position fairly widely shared by contemporary Protestant theologians. Once one grants that theological thinking and speaking cannot be objectifying in the sense for which modern science provides the paradigm, the extent of what can pass for theological statements is bound to be reduced—mythological statements, for instance, no longer qualifying as properly theological.

What *is* distinctive about van Buren's proposal, however, is that this necessary reduction of what can be counted as genuinely theological statements is, in its terms, also the delimiting of such statements to wholly noncognitive and, in that sense, nonobjective utterances. Putative assertions about the being or nature of the Christian God (to which van Buren does not wish to deny a place in the church's witness) must be critically interpreted by theology as really expressions of the attitude or perspective of the Christian man.[28] As such, they are indirectly related to certain meaningful assertions. Although in themselves they assert nothing at all, the statement that a certain person has the perspective they express is open to empirical falsification. Hence, insofar as theological utterances may be considered even indirectly to assert something, they assert nothing whatever about God, merely something about man and his conative perspective or posture. Indeed, van Buren argues, the relation between the church's traditional witness, with its statments about a transcendent God, and a properly critical theology is analogous to the relation between astrology and scientific astronomy or alchemy and modern chemistry.[29] This does not mean, to be sure, that the congruence between such a theology and our "empirical attitudes" as modern secular men is the only reason for demanding it. While van Buren insists that this congruence must indeed characterize any adequate contemporary theology, he also claims a far deeper justification for his apparently radical redefinition of theological thinking and speaking. The gospel itself, he holds, makes both possible and legitimate this reduction of theology to a merely "secular" content.[30]

The merit of van Buren's argument, as I see it, is to have brought to the point of genuine decision a central issue that has too long been left ambiguous and undecided in much recent Protestant theology. If his view is accepted, then, as I suggested above, the more traditional definition of theology with which this analysis began can only be abandoned. If, on the other hand, some such definition is still to be maintained, this can be done only by showing that it remains the most tenable alternative open to us even after the objections of van Buren and those who share his general view. Since I am confident this can be shown, and that, of the two alternatives, the revisionist position involves by far the greater difficulties, I must now try, in the remainder of the essay, to lay down the lines of an effective counter-argument.

I consider, first, van Buren's claim that his wholly nonobjective interpretation of the church's gospel is justified as both possible and legitimate by the character of that gospel itself. I submit that this claim is starkly paradoxical, in the sense that the primary use of language evident in Christian witness is, on this interpretation, explained away instead of theologically accounted for. Whatever else Christians have usually supposed themselves to be doing in witnessing to their faith, whether through personal confession, prayer, preaching, or teaching, they have most surely believed they were somehow responding cognitively to a divine reality radically different from themselves, in whose gracious initiative and approach alone their witness has its basis and object. They have also known that their response through these various forms was an expression of the existential understanding of faith and that the various assertions they supposed themselves to be making about this divine re-

ality were all bracketed, as it were, by the words "I believe," which so
characteristically open their creeds. Even when, in the ages of "orthodoxy," the content of their witness has been most consistently misunderstood as "right doctrine," there has remained at least some recognition
of its double reference to an existential decision that each individual
believer alone is required to make. But what Christians have hardly ever
recognized, I believe, is that their witness is *nothing but* this human decision, that it can be appropriately interpreted as making no reference
whatever to the objective reality of God, and that it asserts, if anything,
merely something about themselves and their own subjective attitude
toward life.

My point, in brief, is that van Buren's interpretation of the Christian
witness has but a one-sided relation to the actual uses of language evident in that witness and utterly fails to account for the most truly distinctive of these uses. Hence it seems to me that one can accept his
proposal not as a literal account of the meaning of Christian witness, but
only as (in a phrase I borrow from another analytic philosopher, Stephen
Toulmin) a "disguised comparison."[31] I hope we would all agree that
the language in which faith comes to expression is in important respects
like the language in which we otherwise express our attitudes or seek to
get others to share them. Yet, when this perfectly acceptable compar-
ative judgment is made as it is by van Buren, only under the disguise
that the language of witness simply *is* such expressive or imperative language, then we have no choice, I believe, but to reject it. We may fully
agree with him that the witness of faith evinces no use of language literally identical with the use distinctive of modern science. But we can
hardly join him in inferring from this that Christian witness is wholly
noncognitive in meaning, making no assertions whatever. Even logically
this conclusion can be made to follow only by assuming a further premise; and, if we respect all the uses of language the witness of faith evinces,
we will not find it easy to make this assumption. The most we can say is
that, while the language of witness is indeed not literally the same as
that of science, it is in important respects sufficiently *like* the language
of science that to deny it any assertive meaning whatever is seriously to
misunderstand it.

The reason van Buren can conclude more than this is that he makes
this further assumption. And here I would consider the second line of
argument by which he seeks to justify his proposal. He claims, as has
been noted, that no theology can be fully congruent with the empirical
commitments of the modern secular man unless it concedes that (apart
from mathematics and formal logic) the scope of thinking and speaking
as involving cognition is strictly coextensive with the thinking and speaking fully developed in modern science.[32] But this claim, too, in my
judgment, involves one rather obvious but nevertheless serious difficulty.
It is simply a fact that nothing which can claim to represent a "consensus" in contemporary philosophy—even in contemporary analytic philosophy!—can be fairly made to include the demand for such a conces-

sion.[33] A generation and more ago, no doubt, the situation did appear rather more as van Buren represents it. But, in recent years, this characteristic demand of the earlier logical positivists has been increasingly subjected to critical scrutiny, so that even among philosophers who are the sons of the positivists it has lost much of its erstwhile plausibility.

Thus an ordinary language philosopher like Toulmin, for instance, has presented a most impressive case against the philosopher who has "too narrow a view of the uses of reasoning" because "he assumes too readily that a mathematical or logical proof or a scientific verification can be the only kind of 'good reason' for any statement.[34] The words "I know" as we ordinarily use them, Toulmin argues, have an exceedingly broad scope, being properly used (although not with literally the same meaning in each case) in fields as different as science, ethics, aesthetics, and theology.[35] If some such view as Toulmin's has come to be more frequently expressed even by linguistic analysts, to recall the great number of modern philosophers who have never accepted the positivistic restriction of cognition is to have ample reason to question van Buren's reading of the contemporary philosophical consensus. It is one thing to claim that sentences having the logical form of scientific assertions must prove their cognitive status by reference to the principle of verification as conventionally interpreted. It is quite another thing to claim with the positivists that this principle determines the only kind of cognitive status there is. I hold that Bultmann is completely justified in regarding the former claim as something no responsible contemporary theology can fail to accept. But I also hold that van Buren's attempt to regard the latter claim in the same way is lacking in anything like the same justification. Modern man cannot so easily be made a positivist in his understanding of the scope of cognition.

My conclusion is that van Buren fails to show that his proposal to interpret theological thinking and speaking as wholly nonobjective is either possible or necessary and that one still has ample reason to stand by my original definition in spite of van Buren's counsel to abandon it. One may admit that an adequate contemporary defense of the understanding of theology which this definition formulates requires far more than many who subscribe to it have been either able or willing to offer. Of this I shall have more to say in the fourth section of the essay. But when this admission is set over against the difficulties entailed by van Buren's own proposal, its problems seem to me by far the less serious— although I realize that my confidence in the defensibility of the more traditional view is largely based on a different understanding of the present situation in philosophy from that shared by van Buren and many of my other theological colleagues.

It is significant, I think, that Bultmann, for all his insistence on the need for thoroughgoing existentialist interpretation, has stoutly resisted the kind of theological reduction that van Buren and others hold to be required. In replying to the charge of his critics that consistent demythologizing makes any direct objective reference to God and his action impossible, Bultmann has clarified his intention in the following terms: "If speaking about God's act is to be meaningful, *it must indeed be not simply a figurative or 'symbolic' kind of speaking* [i.e., simply a way of designating man's own subjective self-understanding], but must rather intend a divine act in the fully real and 'objective' sense."[36] That Bultmann sets the word "objective" here in quotation marks may prove that he has not yet found a fully adequate conceptuality in which to state his position—or even that he himself is finally reluctant to accept all that an adequate defense of this position demands. But I submit that the direction he here points is far closer to the direction in which a tenable answer to the question can be found than that pointed by the other main alternative. From him one may receive at least token support for the view that theology neither can nor must be nonobjectifying, if that means wholly noncognitive, and so lacking in all direct objective references to God and his gracious action.[37]

IV

Much more than this, however, I do not believe Bultmann is in a position to provide. True, he has attempted to show how his intention could be more adequately realized by sketching out a theory of analogy that complements or, as I should prefer to think, more fully explicates, his hermeneutical method of existentialist interpretation.[38] Yet this theory of analogy, while profoundly suggestive, and even essentially correct, is too fragmentary and undeveloped to secure Bultmann's intention against misunderstanding and to enable one who shares it to make a carefully reasoned defense of his case.[39]

Moreover, Bultmann so largely shares yet another characteristic assumption of his existentialist colleagues that it is doubtful whether he is even open to all one must take upon himself if he is to make such a defense. This is the assumption that, if theological thinking and speaking are nonobjectifying in the first sense I clarified, they must also be exempt from any kind of rational assessment or justification. Although, as we have seen, Bultmann resists the view that the statements of Christian witness and theology are wholly noncognitive, he also seems to reject the demand that these statements make good their claim to cognitive status by reference to some clearly specified criterion of meaning and truth.[40] Thus it is evident there is yet a fourth meaning that the notion of a nonobjectifying thinking and speaking may have. With Bultmann, one may also understand this notion to imply that, although theological utterances do somehow have a genuine cognitive meaning or use, they nevertheless cannot be referred to any generally applicable principle of verification, so that the issue of their truth or falsity cannot be rationally adjudicated. In consequence, still another form of the principal question is whether theological thinking and speaking are or should be "nonobjectifying" in this fourth (and, for this essay, final) meaning of the word.

It is already evident that the only answer I am able to give to this form of the question, too, is negative. This is because I fully accept the argument, not only of van Buren, but of virtually all contemporary analytic philosophers, that cognitive status may be claimed for statements only if one is prepared to support the claim by clearly specifying the principle in accordance with which the truth of the statements can be rationally determined. If we neither can nor need deny that theological statements intend to assert something true about the objective reality and action of God, then we neither can nor need deny that these statements are somehow susceptible of rational justification.

This answer is frequently taken to be problematic, I believe, because of certain conventional assumptions and confusions. Thus Bultmann himself, for instance, characteristically denies that theological assertions can in any way be rationally verified, because he tacitly assumes that the only meaning of verification is that illustrated by the deductive proofs of mathematics and logic or the inductive procedures of the special sciences and history. But this assumption clearly belongs to the narrow, positivistic view of the scope of cognition which we considered earlier and saw Bultmann rightly refusing to accept. If the class of meaningful assertions cannot be restricted solely to those of mathematics and the empirical sciences, then why should we suppose that the only kinds of rational argument are those employed in these particular disciplines? I conclude there is no good reason and that the temptation of all of us in our age to succumb to scientism and positivism is nowhere more clearly confirmed than in the case of theologians who assume otherwise. As Toulmin and other analytic philosophers have been trying to remind us, "the uses of argument" are actually many, and acceptance of the challenge that theological assertions also must be argued for does not require one to hold that the relevant kind of argument is that either of mathematics or of the special sciences.

Yet perhaps an even greater obstacle to such acceptance is the common confusion that faith itself must then be held to be directly verifiable or demonstrable. From standpoints for which the distinction between faith and theology is either denied or obscured, such confusion may be all one has the right to expect. But when this distinction is clearly made in some such way as I suggested earlier, it is hard to see why this issue need be confused. In any case, I should agree immediately that there is something profoundly mistaken in supposing that faith itself either must or could be directly verified. If faith is taken *stricto sensu* as existential self-understanding, then one may indeed speak of a justification *by* faith, but certainly not of a justification *of* faith. To speak of the latter is clearly a μεταβασις εις αλλο γενος since the level or our actual existence, which is the level of faith as such, is simply not the level at which the question of rational justification arises. Where it does properly arise is at the level of thought and speech through which the existential understanding of faith is theologically explicated—provided, of course, that such thought and speech are held to have some genuine cognitive import. If theological statements not only express faith, but also assert something about the divine reality in which faith understands itself to be based, the question of how they are to be rationally justified is an altogether appropriate question. To object to this on the ground that faith as such cannot be verified, which in itself is true enough, is to confuse an issue about which a theology oriented to the Reformation has little excuse to be unclear.

But such confusions and assumptions are hardly the only or the most important reasons why the position I am proposing is so rarely held today by Protestant theologians. A more basic reason is what can only be described as a profound skepticism about metaphysics, which both reinforces and is reinforced by a highly selective reading of philosophical developments in the modern period. If, as I have argued, the primary (although not the only) use of theological statements is to make what are in some sense meaningful assertions, the only kind of assertions they can logically make is metaphysical assertions. That is, they express assertions which at once have objective reference to "how things are" and yet are not empirically falsifiable as are the hypotheses of the special sciences. Such assertions cannot be thus falsifiable because their specific use or function is to represent not the variable details of our experience of reality, but its constant structure—that which *all* states of experience, regardless of their empirical contents, necessarily have in common. Thus, if a theological or metaphysical assertion is false, this is not because it fails in predicting what is disclosed by our particular external perceptions, but because it misrepresents the common structure of all of our experiences, of which we are originally aware internally, and thus is falsified by *any one* of them we choose to consider. Please notice, however, that I have not said theological assertions simply *are* metaphysical assertions. On the definition of theology given here, this could not be said, since theological statements have a necessary relation to specifically *Christian* faith in God that would not obtain in the case of metaphysics. My point, rather, is that the class to which theological statements, insofar as they express assertions, logically belong is the general class of metaphysical assertions and that, therefore, the kind of rational justification to which they are open is the kind generically appropriate to all assertions of this logical class.

Yet it is the deep doubt whether there either can or should be any such metaphysical justification that is one of the chief underlying conditions of much recent Protestant theology. It is widely held that the intensive critical work of Spinoza, Hume, and Kant, as well as others, has rendered untenable the *philosophia perennis* of "Christian philosophy" of the classical metaphysical tradition. Equally evident to most theologians is that the great idealistic systems of the nineteenth century are scarcely less problematic than the classical metaphysics their builders intended them to replace. The dominant movements in the philosophy of our own century, whether on the Continent or in the English-speaking countries, have been un- or even anti-metaphysical, and it is from them that most Protestant theologians have taken their orientation. Thus to "overcome metaphysics," either in Heidegger's way or in some

other, has come to be one of the most frequently expressed goals of the
Protestant theology of our time.

All but completely ignored by most theologians, however, is that
metaphysics itself has recently passed through one of the decisive transformations in its long history and is now showing every sign of having a
future as well as a past. I cannot detail this important development here,
beyond suggesting that as good a characterization of it as any is Hartshorne's, when he says that "Leibniz was its Newton," and "Whitehead
is its Einstein."[41] In Whitehead's thought especially, all the main
themes of the metaphysical tradition are given a neoclassical expression,
which seeks to incorporate the contributions of modern philosophy, while
also showing how its criticisms of classical metaphysics might possibly
be met and overcome.[42] Through Hartshorne and others, then, these
same neoclassical insights have been extensively developed and applied
to the traditional problems of "natural" or philosophical theology. Thus
Hartshorne, for instance, has given considerable attention to the logic of
metaphysical statements and has issued a clear challenge to the positivistic dogma that no assertion can both have objective reference and not
be empirically falsifiable.[43] More important, he has also worked out
in detail the neoclassical theory of analogy to which Bultmann's remarks
on the subject are at best a pointer, and he has made plain to all who
have eyes to see that the whole question of the theistic proofs has far
more than a merely historical interest.[44]

All this, of course, is strictly of a piece with a method of approach
and conception of God, as of being generally, that are in important respects radically different from the method and conception of classical
metaphysics. But just this points up the limitation of the wholesale de-
nunciations of metaphysics that are the stock in trade in certain theological quarters. The conventional view that one's only choices are either to
accept some traditional metaphysics or else reject metaphysics altogether
is the result of selective perception and is utterly misleading as to the
philosophical options which are presently available. I have not the slightest question that the metaphysics of Whitehead and Hartshorne may one
day be superseded, and I would dispute the claim that it is even now the
only place to which one needs to look for philosophical resources significant for the theological task. Yet I have equal confidence that no contemporary philosophy is nearly so well qualified to integrate the cumulative insights of the whole Western philosophical tradition, so as to do
justice to the legitimate motives both of classical metaphysics and of the
various forms of modern, critical philosophy. Unlike existentialism and
linguistic analysis, process philosophy is not simply a philosophical frag-
ment that purchases a greater depth of phenomenological insight or a
higher degree of conceptual precision at the price of abandoning philosophy's ancient quest for an integral secular wisdom. To the contrary,
it offers itself as a comprehensive philosophical outlook, which has something of the same dimensions as the "Christian philosophy" of our intellectual tradition and whose possible hermeneutical significance for the-

ology would seem to be at least correspondingly great.

Students of recent ecumenical developments have commented more than once on the challenge put to us as Protestants by Roman Catholic theology at just this point. As Jaroslav Pelikan formulates the question, "Can Protestantism provide its adherents with a world view which is as comprehensive and yet as Christian as the Thomistic? Or must Protestant thought choose between comprehensiveness and evangelical loyalty?"[45] To agree with Pelikan that Protestantism by its nature will always have room for a plurality of world views is neither to deny the need for a comprehensive philosophy nor to be willing to settle for fragmentary alternatives whose hermeneutical significance, however genuine, is nevertheless partial. But if an integral metaphysics in some form is a theological necessity—the only possible basis of a fully adequate hermeneutical principle and procedure—then, I ask, what metaphysics has more claim on one's attention as a Protestant theologian today than that represented by Whitehead and Hartshorne? It is simple to show— in fact, it has already been largely shown[46]—that the points at which these thinkers have revised classical metaphysics are the very points at which an evangelical understanding of Christian faith has found such metaphysics most seriously lacking. I am prepared to argue, therefore, that if any contemporary philosophy can be regarded historically as a "secularized" Protestant theology, it is far less likely to be the philosophy of Heidegger or existentialism generally than the philosophy of process in its most mature and fully developed forms.

In any case, I am quite certain that, apart from the resources that some such philosophy is in a position to provide, the claim of theological statements to cognitive status cannot be responsibly made or supported. If theological thinking and speaking have to do properly and primarily with the God who discloses himself in Jesus Christ, then they involve claims to truth that can be conceptually stated and justified solely in terms of an adequate metaphysics and philosophical theology. I wholly agree, therefore, that the challenge laid down by van Buren and others can be effectively met only by a theology that is frankly and fully metaphysical and thus is prepared to take responsibility for the meaning and truth of its assertions.

That I have not even tried to develop such a theology here is consistent with the critical, analytical emphasis of this whole undertaking. Yet I have at least sought to show how it might be developed by pointing to the philosophical resources that seem to me adequate to the task. I would be less content with this than I am if the resources to which I have pointed had been critically appropriated in the theological discussion or if this kind of a theology itself had already been seriously tried and found wanting. But, as it is, the resources have for the most part not even been discovered, much less discussed, and the theological approach I have proposed is so far from having been tested that there is time enough to see whether it cannot be worked out as a serious contemporary alternative.[47]

I have comprehended the argument of this essay under the title, "Theology and Objectivity," and I trust by now the reason for this will have become obvious. Although I agree, and even insist, that theological thinking and speaking are different in principle from what goes on in modern science, this point also seems to me to exhaust the claim that they ought properly to be nonobjectifying. For the rest, the important points are the old ones, long since made by the church's Fathers, Doctors, and Reformers: that theology is in its own way scientific; that its statements in their most proper part are assertions about God and his action; and that the justification of these assertions, so far as they are rationally justifiable at all, can only be a metaphysical justification. As I see it, the problem of nonobjectifying thinking and speaking in contemporary theology is that this threefold objectivity, which is of the very essence of the theological enterprise, will be obscured rather than clarified, abandoned rather than forthrightly affirmed.

FOOTNOTES

1. This was the theme of the Second Consultation on Hermeneutics convened by the Graduate School of Drew University, Madison, New Jersey, April 9-11, 1964. The present essay was originally offered as a contribution to that consultation.

2. See Felix Cohen, "What Is A Question?" *The Monist*, July, 1929, pp. 350-64 (cited by Susanne K. Langer, *Philosophy in a New Key: A study in the Symbolism of Reason, Rite, and Art*, New York: Penguin Books, 1948, p. 2).

3. A classically simple statement of this claim is Rudolf Bultmann's in "On the Problem of Demythologizing," *Journal of Religion*, April, 1962, pp. 96-102.

4. For a summary discussion of these difficulties, see William T. Blackstone, *The Problem of Religious Knowledge*, Englewood Cliffs, N. J.: Prentice-Hall, Inc., 1963, pp. 108-24.

5. H. W. Bartsch (ed.), *Kerygma und Mythos*, Vol. II, Hamburg: Herbert Reich-Evangelischer Verlag, 1952, p. 207 (English translation by R. H. Fuller in H. W. Bartsch [ed.], *Kerygma and Myth*, New York: Harper & Row, 2d ed., 1961, p. 210).

6. In Bultmann's terms, myth has the place of "symbol," "figure" (*Bild*), or "cipher." See, e.g., his *Jesus Christ and Mythology*, New York: Charles Scribner's Sons, 1958, pp. 67-70. Significantly, an almost identical view is expressed by Charles Hartshorne, who holds that religious "symbols" must be interpreted in terms of theological "analogies," which belong to a different "stratum" of "religious discourse" (*The Logic of Perfection and Other Essays in Neoclassical Metaphysics*, La Salle, Ill.: Open Court Publishing Co., 1962, pp. 133-47).

7. *Sein und Zeit*, Halle: Max Niemeyer Verlag, 1927, p. 12.

8. See *Kerygma und Mythos*, Vol. II, pp. 187, 189, where Bultmann refers to existentialist analysis as a "science that speaks of existence without objectifying it to worldly being" and as "a science that is nothing more than the clear and methodical explication of the understanding of existence given with existence itself." On the face of it, Bultmann here seems to deny that existentialist analysis is objectifying. Elsewhere, however, in his discussion with Karl Jaspers (see below), it becomes clear that this is not his intention; and the apparent contradiction is in fact resolvable if one gives due heed to the words "worldly being." What Bultmann here denies is not that existentialist analysis is objectifying, but that it is objectifying in the same sense as modern science.

9. See, e.g., Paul Tillich, *Systematic Theology*, Vol. II, Chicago: The University of Chicago Press, 1957, p. 26.

10. *Die geistige Situation der Zeit*, Berlin: Walter De Gruyter & Co., 1931, p. 146. In places, Jaspers indicates a willingness to speak of philosophy as in some sense "science" (*Wissenschaft*); see, e.g., *Über Bedingungen und Möglichkeiten eines neuen Humanismus*, Stuttgart: Philipp Reclam Jun., 1962, p. 14.

11. See H. W. Bartsch (ed.), *Kerygma und Mythos*, Vol. III, Hamburg: Herbert Reich-Evangelischer Verlag, 1954, pp. 14 ff. (English translation in Karl Jaspers and Rudolf Bultmann, *Myth and Christianity*, New York: The Noonday Press, 1958, pp. 7-11).

12. See James M. Robinson and John B. Cobb, Jr. (eds.), *The Later Heidegger and Theology*, New York: Harper & Row, 1963, p. 165.

13. *Kerygma und Mythos*, Vol. III, p. 54 (Eng. trans., pp. 64 f.). Here I correct my earlier translation by a more literal rendering of the original (see James M. Robinson and John B. Cobb, Jr. [eds.], *op. cit.*, p. 165).

14. *Kerygma und Mythos*, Vol. III, p. 58 (Eng. trans. p. 70).

15. See James M. Robinson and John B. Cobb, Jr. (eds.), *op. cit.*, pp. 159-73.

16. *Ibid.*, pp. 77-111; see also Ott's *Denken und Sein, Der Weg Martin Heideggers und der Weg der Theologie*, Zollikon-Zürich: Evangelischer Verlag, 1959, pp. 171-75, especially p. 174.

17. See James M. Robinson and John B. Cobb, Jr. (eds.), *op. cit.*, p. 92.

18. *Religion in the Making*, New York: The Macmillan Co., 1926, pp. 56 f.

19. See, e.g., Gustaf Aulén, *The Faith of the Christian Church*, trans. E. H. Wahlstrom, Philadelphia: Muhlenberg Press, 2d ed., 1960, p. 3.

20. See Charles Hartshorne, *op. cit.*, pp. 3 f.

21. See my essay in William L. Reese and Eugene Freeman (eds.), *Process and Divinity: The Hartshorne Festschrift*, La Salle, Ill.: Open Court Publishing Co., 1964, pp. 493-513.

22. See William T. Blackstone, *op. cit.*, pp. 73-107.

23. See Anthony Flew and Alasdair Macintyre (eds.), *New Essays in Philosophical Theology*, London: SCM Press Ltd., 1955, pp. 99-103.

24. Cambridge: Cambridge University Press, 1955.

25. New York: The Macmillan Co., 1963.

26. *Ibid.*, pp. 97, 135-45.

27. *Ibid.*, pp. 197 ff.

28. *Ibid.*, pp. 156, 157-92.

29. *Ibid.*, pp. 197 f.

30. *Ibid.*, pp. 199 f.

31. *An Examination of the Place of Reason in Ethics*, Cambridge: Cambridge University Press, 1950, pp. 190-93. Much the same idea is also expressed by P. H. Nowell-Smith's "Janus-principle," according to which "a given word cannot only do two or more jobs at once, but also is often, in the absence of counterevidence or express withdrawal, presumed to be doing two or more jobs at once" (*Ethics*, Harmondsworth: Penguin Books Ltd., 1954, p. 100).

32. At points, van Buren seems to want to qualify this claim by appealing to a "loose" meaning of "empirical" (*op. cit.*, p. 106) and to "a modified verification principle" (*ibid.*, p. 15). This is because he is forced to recognize that "words such as 'free,' 'love,' and 'discernment' are not empirically grounded in the same way as are 'undiluted,' 'gravitational attraction,' and 'sense data' " (*ibid.*, p. 171). Yet, so far as I can see, this in no way leads him to extend the scope of cognition beyond the limits allowed for by ordinary empirical falsification. If statements having to do with the field of the "personal" or the "ethical" have any meaning, then this is the meaning determinable, however indirectly, solely through the tests of external perception (see, e.g., what is said concerning the verification of "sense-content statements" generally and Peter's Easter confession in particular, *ibid.*, pp. 129 f.)

33. In general, van Buren's attempt to support his position by referring to "a rough consensus among contemporary analysts of the language of faith" (*ibid.*, p. 96) must be taken *cum grano salis*. I regard it as highly questionable, for example, whether Ian Ramsey can be made a *Bundesgenossen* of Hare and Braithwaite in the way van Buren seeks to do.

34. Stephen Toulmin, *op. cit.*, p. 46.

35. *Ibid.*, pp. 67-85, and especially *The Uses of Argument*, Cambridge: Cambridge University Press, 1958, *passim*.

36. *Kerygma und Mythos*, Vol. II, p. 196 (Eng. trans., p. 196).

37. Such support is also provided by John A. T. Robinson, who graciously but firmly rejects van Buren's attempt (*op. cit.*, p. 200, n. 5) to represent their two views as essentially the same (John A. T. Robinson and David L. Edwards [eds.], *The Honest to God Debate*, London: SCM Press Ltd., 1963, pp. 249-56). Robinson holds that theological statements "are not objective propositions about 'things in themselves'; but neither are they simply affirmations of my outlook or perspective on life. They are statements about the reality in which my life is grounded as I respond to that reality at the level of 'ultimate concern' (as opposed to proximate concern—the level at which scientific statements, etc., are true)" (*ibid.*, pp. 252 f.). Robinson's view is thus essentially the same as Bultmann's, though like Bultmann, he has not yet developed it with the necessary adequacy (see my essay, "Beyond Supernaturalism," *Religion in Life*, Winter, 1963-64, pp. 7-18).

38. See *Kerygma und Mythos*, Vol. II, pp. 196 f. (Eng. trans., pp. 196 f.); also *Jesus Christ and Mythology*, pp. 67-70.

39. See my *Christ Without Myth: A Study Based on the Theology of Rudolf Bultmann*, New York: Harper & Row, 1961, pp. 90 ff., 147; see also the essay referred to above in n. 21.

40. I say "seems" here because there are places that perhaps point to another interpretation. Bultmann has consistently opposed any merely authoritarian understanding of the decision of faith and, in this context, has been willing to speak of a "criterion for the truth" of Christian witness and theology (see *Glauben und Verstehen*, Vol. I, Tubingen: J. C. B. Mohr, 2d ed., 1954, p. 284; also *Kerygma und Mythos*, Vol. III, pp. 57 f. [Eng. trans., pp. 69 f.]). Furthermore, he at one point forthrightly rejects the relativistic conclusion of Dilthey and others by maintaining that the question of the true or legitimate *Weltanschauung* can and should be answered by reference to the "historicity of the human being" invoked as a criterion (*The Presence of Eternity: History and Eschatology*, New York: Harper & Brothers, 1957, pp. 148 f.). On the other hand, his most characteristic statements evidently entail a blanket denial that theological assertions are subject to rational justification (on this, see the evidence brought forward by Ronald W. Hepburn in Anthony Flew and Alasdair Macintyre [eds.], *op. cit.*, pp. 227-42). Thus, while it is tempting to argue, rather as I did above in n. 8, that Bultmann's intention in such statements is to exempt theological assertions, not from all rational tests, but only from those of the special sciences and history, the bulk of the evidence supports the contrary interpretation. Nevertheless, one may hold that at this point Bultmann is at cross-purposes with himself and fails fully to follow through with certain of his other basic intentions.

41. *Reality as Social Process: Studies in Metaphysics and Religion*, Glencoe, Ill.: The Free Press, 1953, p. 31.

42. See especially Ivor Leclerc, *Whitehead's Metaphysics: An Introductory Exposition*, London: George Allen & Unwin Ltd., 1958.

43. See his "Metaphysical Statements as Nonrestrictive and Existential," *Review of Metaphysics*, September, 1958, pp. 35-47; *The Logic of Perfection*, pp. 280-97; and his contribution to Ivor Leclerc (ed.), *The Relevance of Whitehead*, London: George Allen & Unwin Ltd., 1961, pp. 107-21. In the latter essay, Hartshorne formulates the criterion of metaphysical necessity or truth as "the absence of any positive meaning for the denial of a statement or—the same thing—the failure of the statement to exclude any positive state of affairs" (p. 111). Subsequently he explains that "although a statement which denies no contingent possibility also affirms no contingent possibility, yet it does not follow that it affirms nothing at all, and 'says nothing about the world.' The necessary is indeed compatible with any affirmation you please, but not with any negation you please. Rather it is exclusively positive. It affirms that about the world which would be real no matter what possibilities were actualized, and which therefore cannot be denied except by impossible formulae. If 'information' means a description of what distinguishes one state of affairs from other conceivable states, then necessary statements are not informative; but if 'information' includes reference to the factor which all possible positive states of existence have in common, then necessary statements are informative" (*ibid.*, pp. 112 f.). In terms of some such criterion, I suggest, one can also take responsibility for the proper assertions of Christian theology.

44. See *The Logic of Perfection*, pp. 28-117, 133-47; *Man's Vision of God and the Logic of Theism*, New York: Harper & Brothers, 1941, pp. 174-205, 251-341; and "The Idea of God—Literal or Analogical?" *Christian Scholar*, June, 1956, pp. 131-36.

45. *The Riddle of Roman Catholicism*, Nashville: Abingdon Press, 1959, p. 227.

46. See especially Hartshorne's discussion of "the two strands in historical theology" in *Man's Vision of God*, pp. 85-141.

47. Here I may refer to the criticisms directed to some of my earlier statements in the second part of Robert C. Coburn's article, "A Budget of Theological Puzzles," *Journal of Religion*, April, 1963, pp. 83-92. Coburn is no doubt justified, given his primary interests, in finding many of my statements about "the thing called 'God'" in *Christ Without Myth* "puzzling." And I quite agree that the constructive alternative I tried to outline there is peculiarly vulnerable at just the logical or philosophical points to which he gives attention. Nevertheless, I cannot regard his criticisms as a serious test of that alternative, since they proceed on the unexamined assumption that the only criterion of meaningful assertions is that which is relevant to scientific statements, thus failing to consider the one possibility that would, I think, make sense of what is said about God in that book, as well as explain its several clear indications of the philosophical ground on which I should want to stand. Coburn does seem to see that I should be content with none of the four replies he imagines my possibly making to his Flew-like demand that all assertions be falsifiable by external perception. But whence his confidence that these are the only possible replies? I can only think that Coburn, like van Buren and many others, is so under the spell of a certain logical dogma that he has still to discover the challenge put to it by analytic philosophers like Toulmin, as well as contemporary metaphysicians such as Hartshorne. On the other hand, I acknowledge that each of us must take responsibility for his own assertions and that I as a theologian cannot evade this responsibility by appealing to Hartshorne or Toulmin or any other philosopher. The value of Coburn's criticisms has been to underline the job that must be done, and I can only hope the present essay, as well as this volume as a whole, gives indication that I am at work on it.

PART FOUR:

THE
ANALYTIC
PERSPECTIVE

INTRODUCTION

Traditionally the relation between philosophy and religion has been one either of identity, as in the early Middle Ages, or of hostility, as in the Age of Reason. In the eighteenth and nineteenth centuries this hostility focused on the question of whether the claims of religion are true, and the task of the religious philosopher was to show how the assertions of religious language can indeed be true. Within the last thirty years the situation has been transformed by the rise of the philosophical movement known as "logical empiricism." This movement hurls a completely different challenge at those who make religious assertions. Religious language is no longer accused of being *false*, it is now accused of being *meaningless*.

At first religious thinkers were at a loss as to how to respond to such a challenge, except to ignore it. Within the last ten years, however, a sizable number of scholars, particularly in Britain, have attempted to meet the challenge. Much of the impetus for this response has come from the influence of Ludwig Wittgenstein's later philosophy, which is usually termed "ordinary language philosophy," or "linguistic analysis." Those who concern themselves with this approach to the relation between philosophy and religion can be said to write from within an analytic perspective. The focus of this perspective is upon the structure of language in general and the function of "God-talk" in particular. The key question pertains to the ways in which God-talk can be said to be meaningful.

The challenge that logical empiricism presents to those who use language religiously can be summarized in a variety of ways. The following syllogistic statement of this challenge serves to distinguish the various responses to it quite clearly, and so it is especially appropriate for the purposes of this introduction.

1. All cognitively meaningful language (i.e., language which is subject to being judged true or false) is either logical (i.e., based exclusively on definitions) or empirical (i.e., based on sensory experience) in nature;
2. No religious language is either logical or empirical in nature;
3. Therefore, no religious language is cognitively meaningful.

Among those thinkers who have not deemed religious language irrelevant as a result of the above argument, there are four main responses which have been developed. Some writers, by training and vocation usually more philosophical than theological, respond to the argument by accepting the truth of both premises and the conclusion, without concluding that religious language is irrelevant or nonsensical. They maintain that religious language is not cognitively meaningful, it is very significant from an emotional, ethical, or existential point of view. That is to say, once we get straight about the true nature of God-talk, the challenge of logical empiricism is no longer devastating, since it is misplaced. Though it may not be judged true or false, these thinkers maintain that religious language fulfills other functions altogether.

A second group of thinkers, by training and vocation usually more theological than philosophical, respond to the challenge by rejecting the major premise (1) The main contention of those taking this approach is that cognitive meaning cannot be confined to logical and/or empirical language alone. They maintain that religious knowledge, along with other forms of metaphysical knowledge involves a form of cognition that has a unique nature. Since such knowledge is embodied in religious language, the latter may be cognitively meaningful even though it is neither logical nor empirical in nature.

Another way of responding to the challenge of logical empiricism is to reject the minor premise (2) of the argument, and there are those who have so responded. The main drive of this approach is to be found in the attempt to relate religious language to experience and thereby to establish it as cognitively meaningful. The claim is that God-talk very often fulfills empirical functions and is, therefore, at those times cognitively meaningful. The main burden of such an approach is to specify the exact situations in which religious language can be said to be empirical.

Although each of the foregoing responses has enjoyed a certain amount of success, and has made a significant contribution to the analytic perspective, each has also had difficulty making its claims stick. The biggest problem for all of these thinkers has come from the fact that they have all sought to work out their response within the confines of the "rules" implicit within the logical empiricist approach to meaning. It would seem that a more creative and effective response might be developed by backing up far enough to raise some basic questions about the assumptions which underlie the logical empiricist challenge. Much of the responsibility for the construction of such a response has been shouldered by several of the authors whose essays comprise the following section.

One of the themes which unites those working on this approach is the attempt to broaden the concept of cognitive significance so as to give a more adequate account of how in fact language in general functions. There is a common conviction that the limits of cognitivity have been drawn too narrowly by logical empiricism. Special attention is given to exploring the logic of paradoxical and metaphorical discourse. More specifically, an effort is made to apply the insights of such exploration to talk about God. This application is paralleled by a concern to show the similarity between the use of models in scientific discourse and their use in theology.

The *modus operandi* of the analytic perspective is to examine actual uses of religious and theological language in their natural contexts. It is felt that far too many of those passing judgment on God-talk have been operating as "arm-chair" philosophers. To paraphrase Wittgenstein, from whom those working in this field draw their inspiration and insight, far too many thinkers have been *thinking* about how religious discourse must function without actually *looking* to see how it does, in fact, function. Consequently, the analytic perspective seeks to map the logic of God-talk within its own environment by way of coming to an understanding of its function and structure. Each of the following essays makes its contribution to this mapping.

Kai Nielsen's essay is aimed against those who seek to justify religious language as something wholly unique, based on faith alone, and beyond philosophical scrutiny. He argues that the insights of linguistic philosophy have shown such a tack to be illegitimate. He also contends that "God-talk" must be shown to be related to other forms of human discourse. John Wisdom, while not necessarily disagreeing with Nielsen's view insists that one must maintain a wide range of tolerance and healthy respect for seemingly "odd-talk" in general and religious talk in particular. He focuses on the function of metaphorical and paradoxical language, and also seeks to trace an example the type of reasoning which is often used to justify such talk. Wisdom may well be the most "Wittgenstinian" of all contemporary philosophers. Frederick Ferré takes a great deal of care in tracing out the parallels between the function of models in science and their function in theology. He suggests that such a study establishes the position that all "odd-talk" is not found in religious language, but forms an essential part of scientific language as well. Ian Ramsey, who has been called "the dean of analytic theologians" directs his attention more exclusively to the function of models in God-talk, and reflects a Wittgenstein motif, both in method and in content.

CHAPTER THIRTEEN

CAN FAITH VALIDATE GOD-TALK?[*]

by Kai Nielsen

THESIS: *Philosophical analysis provides fideism with a crucial problem. It seems that we can accept on faith only what we can understand. For if we cannot understand something, we cannot know what it is we are to accept on faith. Yet crucial religious assertions appear to be completely without truth value. But if they are, how then can we possibly accept them on faith? This essay examines some efforts to get around this barrier to an appeal to faith and concludes that fideism can only be a satisfactory apologetic stance if the factual intelligibility of key religious utterances has been established.*

To be a fideist is to believe that fundamental religious beliefs rest solely and completely on faith. Finite and sinful man cannot by the use of his unaided reason come to know God. Belief and unbelief are intellectually on a par, religious experience is unalterably ambiguous as to the reality of its object, and the existence of God can never be established by empirical investigation or philosophical demonstration. But the storms and stresses of our lives will drive us to faith. We must turn to God to overcome despair and the "threat of meaninglessness." Without God life can indeed be nothing more than a "tale told by an idiot." Faith will give our lives an anchor, will enable us to overcome that sickness unto death that goes with a loss of God, but with or without faith, we will only see through a glass darkly, for God remains an utter mystery and a thorough scandal to the intellect. Intellectually speaking, a belief in God is absurd; taken as a hypothesis it is at best fanciful. The believer, the "knight of

*Used with permission from *Theology Today*, Vol. 20, No. 2, July 1963. Reprinted in *New Theology No. 1*, The Macmillan Co., New York, New York, 1964.

faith," can only trust that he is not "whistling in the dark," is not believing something that is thoroughly illusory, when he accepts the God revealed in the Scriptures as an ultimate reality. Here, the quest for certainty or even for a guide that will give us "reasonable probabilities" is a quixotic quest. The believer must simply take the leap of faith without any intellectual assurance at all that he is leaping in the right direction. But this total risk is well worth it for without God man's life is without meaning.

Fideism has an ancient and respected lineage. One finds it in Tertullian, Pascal, Hamann, and Kierkegaard. In our time it finds expression in one way or another in the theologies of Barth, Brunner, Nygren, and the Niebuhrs. It is even a dominant motif in the writings of such a perceptive linguistic philosopher as Alastair MacIntyre.[1] But in characterizing fideism as I have, I have not been concerned to set forth a view which necessarily fits the exact views of any of these men. Kierkegaard, it seems to me, presents the purest case of such an orientation, but while I do not wish to do battle with straw men or tilt with windmills, I am not concerned here with the history of a movement. In the defenses of religion given by the men mentioned above, such fideistic approaches are dominant though other claims are made as well. I want here to take the core concepts of fideism—concepts that are frequently appealed to in theological discussion—and subject them to examination without attempting to prove that any theologian of note holds exactly the view I have characterized as fideism.[2]

I

Such fideistic approaches to religion have an obvious appeal. Natural theology, which has somewhat extravagantly been called "the Sick Man of Europe," can now be bypassed; the harassed man who is struggling to decide whether he can accept the claims of religion can ignore the ambiguities of metaphysics and the rarified atmosphere of philosophical analysis. Fideism provides him with a rationale for rejecting such claims as little intellectual games that are irrelevant to his quest for God.

It is true that we do not and cannot know whether there is a God, whether there is an omniscient and just Being who looks after us, as a perfect father would, or whether Jesus is God. If we feel this scepticism and if deep in our hearts the claim that Jesus is God remains—along with the other central claims of the Christian faith—a "shocking but relevant possibility," fideism will attract us.[3] Given that our need to believe is strong enough, it may incite our assent. By an act of faith we accept the absurd claims of Christianity not as mere possibilities but as actualities that will direct our lives and give fiber to our deepest hopes.

Yet the fact remains that for many philosophers of an analytical persuasion, it is just this initial claim that such alleged beliefs are *intelligible possibilities* that serves as the greatest stumbling block to religious belief. Christian and, more generally, theistic talk is indeed a part of the languages of the West. (There is, or course, no special Christian language.) If we can speak English we can and do learn to speak of God.

If we take religion as a kind of myth (albeit an important and moving myth), we will generally have no overwhelming difficulty in understanding religious talk in the way we understand and accept all myths. But while no Jew or Christian should deny that religious discourse has mythical elements, the Jewish and Christian tradition would insist that there is something more there, too. In some sense, divine existence is taken to be more than a human creation, a human ideal, no matter how worthy, projected onto the universe. But in trying to *say* what more is involved, all the trouble begins.

When the fideist says that this "more" is a possibility he will opt for with his whole heart and his whole mind, it is the very *meaning* of his claim that perplexes the contemporary philosophical analyst. How can we presuppose it and then act on it? If it is a possibility, what would it be like for it to be actualized? What would have to happen or not have to happen in order for "Jesus is God" or "There is a God" or "God governs the world" to be either true or false? While the nineteenth-century sceptic characteristically puzzled over whether there was sufficient evidence for "There is a God" to be true or even probable, the twentieth-century sceptic has come to be perplexed over the question of what it *means* even to affirm *or* deny the existence or love of God. This last question was seen to be logically prior to questions about the truth of religious beliefs.

Here's the rub for the fideist. Before we can intellibly say, as an atheist, "There is no God," or as a believer, either fideist or non-fideist, "There is a God" or, as an agnostic, "We do not have sufficient evidence to either affirm or deny there is a God," we must know what such sentences *mean*. But do we? Do we have any idea what it would be like for any of these utterances to be used to make true or false statements? Many philosophers, rightly or wrongly, have concluded that we do not. If they are right, these theistic utterances are then *factually* meaningless utterances, though they indeed have some emotive, ceremonial, or pseudofactual (ideological) meaning.[4]

These philosophical contentions themselves have been subject to fierce controversy among philosophers and theologians, but from this discussion it has become apparent that the logical status of certain crucial theistic utterances is extremely controversial. Some find the whole mode of theistic discourse in its essential respects meaningless or chaotic and, as a result, disapprove of religion; others argue that one can never justifiably say of a whole mode of discourse, a form of life, that it is meaningless or chaotic, and they may go on to conclude, as does the Oxford philosopher, I. M. Crombie, that "seen as a whole religion makes rough sense, though it does not make limpidity."[5] But for all parties, the central philosophical puzzle is about the very *meaning* of religious talk. The puzzle here is not only about various analyses of religious discourse but over whether central aspects of first-order religious talk are themselves intelligible.

It is tempting to suppose that fideism shows how the man, seriously involved with religion, can put such abstruse and baffling concerns aside as the twaddle of philosophers. Those who accept religion on faith, those who operate within "the circle of faith," need not bother about what "God" means. They clearly realize that they cannot understand what many of the central theistic claims mean. But this is just as it should be. After all, religion is a mystery. But God, in his majesty and grace, infuses religious utterances with meaning, though to man they remain meaningless. The man of faith does not and cannot understand them; he simply accepts God's word, though these words (as well as the very word "God") remain meaningless to him.

It can be plausibly argued that this fideist defense cannot be correct, for such remarks are without sense.[6] If the believer doesn't understand the utterances *at all*, he cannot accept or reject them, for he literally would not understand *what* he is accepting or rejecting. If they are meaningful *at all*, they must be intelligible to at least some men. If we do not understand what "God" means or what it would be like for "There is a God" to be true or false, to say we accept God on faith is like saying we accept Irglig on faith or "There is an Irglig" on faith. Before we can make the leap, before we can accept a claim on faith or refuse to accept it on faith, we must at least have some minimal understanding of *what* it is we are accepting or rejecting. *At this level*, faith cannot be a way to understanding. Faith cannot insure the meaningfulness of religious utterances; quite to the contrary, faith presupposes that the discourse in question is itself meaningful (intelligible). If we lack evidence for x, we may take x on faith, but we cannot by an act of faith step from what we do not understand to what we do understand. If I do not know what is meant by x, I cannot intelligibly say that I have faith in x, that I place my trust in x, or that I accept x on authority. I may say: "I have faith that segregation will come to an end in the South in the next five years" or "I have faith in the farm policies of Secretary Freeman." Here I mean that I trust Secretary Freeman or trust that his policies will work out for the best and trust that segregation will come to an end within five years. I trust that these things will take place but I have no evidence that they will take place or even that they are likely to take place. Yet I trust that they will. In the latter case, I might do this simply because I trust Freeman. As the fideist takes the Bible or the church as his authority in matters of religion, so I simply accept Freeman's statements as authoritative on questions of farm policy. But in the two non-religious cases, I know what it would be like for the authoritative statements to be true or false. The *meaning* of the statements taken on faith is perfectly clear. To understand their meaning we do not and cannot invoke faith. Faith has no role at all to play here. I *must* understand the *meaning* of a proposition before I can accept or fail to accept it on faith or on authority.

If we could reasonably assume that religious utterances were meaningful (intelligible), then the fideist's claim would be perfectly understandable, though it might still fail to be convincing. But this is just what we cannot assume, for it is just this that is at issue. Fideism only works when we know what the religious claims in question *mean* and simply lack evidence for their *truth*. For traditional fideists the appropriate question is not "What do they mean?" or "Are they intelligible?" but, granting they are intelligible, why should we accept them when we cannot establish their truth or even establish that they are probable. The fideists are trying to show us why we should believe, even though we haven't one iota of evidence for our beliefs. It is this last question that Pascal, Kierkegaard, and Barth wrestle with, while (in effect) assuming that there is no puzzle about the *meaning* of religious utterances.[7] But it is just this logically prior question that disturbs contemporary philosophers when they think about religion, and to this question it would seem that fideism is no answer at all nor is it a way around the problem. We are, whether we like it or not, left with the crucial question: Are religious utterances intelligible, can we meaningfully assert or deny there is a God? This logically prior question remains a question of first importance in an examination and defense of religion. Apologetics cannot reasonably skirt it. To ask someone to understand by faith is nonsense, though if he already understands what his phonemic sequences mean, then it may well be (in some contexts at least) perfectly reasonable to ask him to accept the truth of what they are used to assert on faith—that is, understanding their meaning, we may be asked to accept on faith that what is asserted by their use is true. We still may not find it reasonable to opt for anything for which we lack evidence, but like William James or Soren Kierkegaard we may so believe though we lack evidence for our beliefs. We may, out of our despair and infinite hope, come to believe in the absurd, take it on faith that there is a God and that for God all things are possible, and at the same time be fully aware of the intellectual scandal involved in such a belief. Here we can legitimately talk of what a man can bring himself to do or not to do. But we must *presuppose*, in all such reasoning, that theistic utterances are (in the appropriate sense) meaningful.

A man deeply involved in religion may indeed *not* wish to engage in the philosopher's abstruse talk about talk or (more accurately) talk about the *uses* of talk. "Leave that to the philosophers" is his feeling; "I live by faith and all such philosophical chatter is entirely irrelevant to my faith. I will not cry out, like John Osborne, that 'We're along in the universe, there's no God, . . . (and) somehow we've just got to make a go of it.' I will believe!"

The fideist can of course say this and he can say it from the anguish of his heart, but unless he is clear, genuinely clear, in his own mind that he understands what is meant by "God," then he is really, consciously or unconsciously, being evasive and obscurantist. Fideism does not seem to provide an "out" here, for as a matter of fact questions about the very intelligibility of religious discourse are hotly controversial. If we wish to be religious and still wish to be nonevasive about our religion, we must tackle these difficult philosophical questions of meaning; we cannot simply go the way of faith.

II

I wish now to consider if fideism can in some reasonable way overcome the challenge put to it in section one.

It might be argued, as J. N. Findlay has argued, that it is a mistake
to link "understanding x" or "knowing the meaning of x" too closely with
"the method of establishing x to be true or false."[8] Just such a close
linkage is implicit in my preceding argument. I have, in effect, argued
that to understand the meaning of x, where x is a sentence purportedly
used to state a fact, we must know what conceivably *could* count for the
truth or falsity of x. For x to have *factual* meaning, x must have truth
conditions. If we do not know what these truth conditions are, x is meaningless to us, and that God might know what they are does not make x
an intelligible bit of human discourse. It still remains a factually meaningless English expression.

Findlay claims this is a dogma that has created "gratuitous quandries
which have haunted thought in the past decades."[9] It would be nice
to know why this is so, but Findlay does not tell us; however, he does
assert what could be good news for the fideist, namely "that we may go
quite a long ways towards validating an assertion whose meaning we do
not understand *at all*."[10] (If we don't understand it *at all*, *what* is it
that we are validating? How could we possibly have the slightest notion
that it is *it* that we validated?) Findlay says that we do this "whenever
we pin our faith to an assertion that we do not understand, but which
has been made by some expert or reliable person."[11] This would fit
our fideistic interpretation of the religious use of language very well.

Yet there are plenty of difficulties in Findlay's account. Findlay goes
on to say that "true" has a standard use in which we "lend assent to assertions with whose precise content we are not for some reason conver-
sant."[12] We can know something to be true when we know little or
nothing of it. "Physicists," Findlay points out, "assert and make use of
many sentences to which they have not given a satisfactory sense." But
the cat is out of the bag with "a satisfactory sense" or "a precise content." In order for a sentence to serve as the vehicle for a *factual* assertion, we must be able to say what would count for the truth or falsity
of this putative assertion. It must have *that* much meaning and this is
not excluded in the physicist's case, even though the precise content or
the full elaboration of his sentence may not be clear.

But this will not cover Findlay's *first situation* where we do not understand the meaning of the utterance *at all*, for there we cannot understand what it is to which we are to lend our assent. If we do not have
any idea at all of what an utterance means, we literally cannot lend or
fail to lend assent to it for, after all, how could we identify what it is we
are lending our assent to? The physicist can say, "We don't understand
very well what we mean by 'x' but when this happens (and he specifies
some state of affairs) we would say 'x,' and if it does not occur we would
not say 'x.' " If the believer can say something similar about "There is

a God," then his utterance can be said to have a factual meaning, though we need not and ought not assert "There is a God" is identical in meaning with a sentence asserting that these test conditions obtain. If this is the case, then the religious utterance has an appropriate meaning. But where we do not understand the utterance *at all* we cannot even say what would make it true or false; and this being so, we can have no idea of what it would be like to validate it. If x is meaningless, x can be neither true nor false, validated nor invalidated, accepted nor rejected. A completely meaningless set of marks can never become the object of faith or of disbelief.

Findlay might argue that this is too harsh. It does not at all fit our linguistic practice. Consider again the analogy with physics. Many intelligent and reflective people understand little or nothing of physics. They don't understand what the physicist is talking about when he makes certain crucial statements that are a part of quantum mechanics. They don't understand his utterances at all. But they have seen our technological transformation—transformations beyond the dreams of the bold men of the Renaissance. And they have been *told* that there is a very important connection between some of these technological transformations and the (to them) mysterious statements that are a part of quantum theory. They see the fruits of science—how could they not see them?—and they trust the physicist; they trust that there is this intimate connection between his theories and these technological transformations, though they do not at all understand the physicist's statements when he states some of the key claims of quantum mechanics. They are meaningless gibberish to the non-physicist, but trusting the physicist (having faith in the physicist and in physics) they accept them humbly on faith (trust) though they do not understand their meaning. To them they remain empty formulae, but they have faith that these formulae do in reality mean something, that the physicist is asserting *something* (the layman knows not what) that is true. Such a layman has faith that such formulae are part of a coherent language game.

Why cannot the fideist, the knight of faith, do exactly the same thing? A language game of ancient lineage is being played here. The believer does not understand what is meant by certain crucial utterances that are a part of this language game, but by an act of faith, of trust in his religious authority, he accepts that what is being said is not without meaning—is part of a coherent language game. Such a fideist freely admits that such key religious utterances are gibberish to him, but he has faith that his religious authorities are saying *something* that is intelligible to them (but not to him), *something* that is important and true.

The first thing to be noted here is that by making such a claim the fideist has changed the conditions of the argument. He is no longer claiming that he has faith in meaningless propositions. His present argument in fact commits him to the claim that the propositions are meaningful. He is now only making the much less exciting claim that he can believe them even though they are meaningless to him and others like him. If the analogy with physics is close, there are certain religious figures—priests, theologians, some kind of holy men—who understand these key religious utterances. The fideist trusts them; they are his religious authorities, but, on the argument presently being made, the religious utterances are meaningful to the religious authorities in question, though they are not meaningful to the ordinary believer. Such a believer trusts the religious authority—*assuming*, as Danto so nicely puts it, that somebody knows what he is talking about.[13] The believer, as a fideist, may justifiably bypass the puzzling arguments about the very intelligibility of key theistic utterances but only on condition that his religious authority does not do so, for to argue as our fideist just has is to assume that his religious authority understands what the words and utterances mean. But philosophically significant fideists make no such claim. The purer and philosophically interesting and significant fideism that we are talking about claims that the religious authority, no matter how august, is in exactly the same boat as the plain believer. Such religious authorities have no key to the meaning of religious utterances. The propositions are not only meaningless to the uninitiate, they are meaningless to the theologian and holy man, too. These men too must accept such propositions purely on faith. They do not understand their meaning any more than the plain man does. They accept them simply on faith, as we all must, if we are to be genuinely religious. In this respect, the theologian or holy man is in a very different position from the physicist; and such religious men seem to be very much in the intellectual predicament described in section one. If this is so the plain man—attempting to adopt a fideistic approach to religion—cannot with justice turn to the theologian here. The analogy with science won't do.

Secondly, even forgetting the very crucial difficulty noted above, there is still trouble with the analogy, as my last remark in the above paragraph should have suggested. If a man knows nothing of physics, it is reasonable for him to accept what competent quantum physicists claim is so about quantum mechanics. The religiously perplexed layman may feel that the same thing holds for religion. There is no more point in everyone being his own theologian than everyone being his own physicist or doctor.[14] There are crucial differences in the cases—differences that destroy the point of the analogy. The theologian whom the believer relies on will claim (if he is a fideist) that he does not understand the key religious claims involved, since he, too, is a man and finite, sinful man cannot possibly understand such claims. Everyone (including the theologian) must accept such claims simply on faith without understanding their *meaning*. But once this admission is made, the analogy with physics has been destroyed and the points made in section one become apposite. How can anyone have faith, if no one can understand what it is we are to have faith in or what it is we are to accept solely on faith? When the theologians or holy men insist that they do not and cannot understand what they call their "articles of faith," how can we be expected to go on trusting them?

To this it may be replied, "Well, we just do. We mouth (utter) the words they tell us to mouth (utter), pray, go to communion, orient our life ethically in the way they tell us to, not understanding the superstructure they attach it to. (We utter the words in prayer, but they are words without meaning.) This gives our lives a meaning." Such a defense might continue in this manner: "There are a bunch of words that are part of our language. They can be used to make what some people would be willing to call statements. We do not understand them—no one does except God and appeal to him here would be viciously circular. Yet as the layman can accept something in physics that he does not understand at all, so we believers can accept something in religion that we do not understand at all. We trust that these key religious utterances are sometimes used to assert *something*, though we and no one else can say what they assert."

If the claim is made this weak, then even a Freudian or Marxian may claim that he can, in a sense, go along with it. Such utterances do typically assert something but, such a critic might aver, they can go the believer "one better" and say what that something is. Such God-sentences really refer to one's father, though the person who asserts them is actually confused about their reference. But the fideist will, of course, claim that when he says that these religious utterances assert something, though we do not understand them at all, he *means* that they assert some supernatural, spiritual, or transcendent something. But then he seems to be implicitly admitting he does understand them to a degree, and he is bringing in with "supernatural" and the like just the sort of word he claims is not understood at all and need not be understood. But it now seems that "supernatural," "spiritual," or "transcendent" must be understood if he is going to be able to claim, as he wants to, that his key religious utterances assert something that is distinct from what such a Freudian or Marxist materialist would be willing to assert. At this point the fideist may latch on to the first part of his argument alone. All he can justifiably say, he now concedes, is that believers mouth (utter) certain words (words that we humans do not understand) and act in a certain way. But this, he contends, is enough for belief.

If such a reply is made it seems to me that the fideist, if he is really willing to stick with this, cannot be dislodged by rational argument or shown, if he does nothing to adorn this position, that his position is senseless or unintelligible. It *may* be an irrational position, a position which no thoughtful man, once he had taken proper cognizance of the many thousands of conflicting religions and sects, would wish to embrace, but it is not an unintelligible position and I know of no purely logical or conceptual arguments that would defeat it.[15] But it is important to take note that if someone chooses to rest his argument here he cannot draw sustenance from the analogy with physics, for the physicist has no such need to appeal to faith or to do things in conjunction with accepting formulae whose meaning he does not *at all* understand. In the religious case we have nothing that is genuinely comparable to following the doc-

tor's orders, though we do not understand the rationale of what the doctor would have us do, or accepting on trust that the physicist knows what
he is talking about though we do not. With the fideist we have the claim
that *no* one understands what he is doing, no one understands the meaning of the religious utterances in question, but we are to accept them all
the same. But where this is so, it is not at all apparent that to believe
under such circumstances is a reasonable thing to do and we are left
with our original nagging problem—a problem posed most clearly by
modern linguistic analysis: what would it be like to accept on faith or
otherwise something as a factual proposition if we have *no idea* of what
would confirm or disconfirm it, if we have *no idea* of under what circumstances we would be prepared to say it was true or false? The fideist
claims that it is a *fact* that there is a God, that God created the world,
that God loves us and the like. But if we have no idea of what it would
be like for such statements to be either true or false, how can we meaningfully assert that they are statements of *fact*? And if we cannot meaningfully assert that statements asserting these claims are in reality statements of fact, how can we accept on faith that "There is a God," etc.
are facts? Can fideism non-evasively and justifiably avoid this problem?
I have just indicated one "out" that can be taken, but this "out" appears
to be evasive. There is one more, ostensibly non-evasive move that the
fideist might make. Let us now examine that.

      In attempting to avoid the difficulties mentioned in section one, a
fideist might state his position in the following way: " 'There is a God'
is true" *means*, where Jesus is the religious authority, "Jesus asserted
'There is a God.' " (If Jesus is not the religious authority, then whoever
or whatever is the religious authority should replace "Jesus" in the
above-mentioned sentence.) Let us designate as (A) " 'There is a God'
is true," and as (B) "Jesus asserted 'There is a God.' " A fideist might
argue that (B) is verifiable (testable) in principle. And that Jesus uttered,
or would have been prepared to utter, the Hebrew equivalent of "There
is a God" is indeed verifiable in principle. (B) is not a mysterious utterance. Its truth-value is plain enough. The fideist then stipulates either
that when he affirms (A) he means (B), or that when he affirms (A), (B) is
at least an essential part of what he intends. But since (B) is intelligible
(has a truth-value), then (A) is, to that degree, intelligible, too, and the
fideist hasn't fallen into the analyst's trap after all. It is true that he does
not understand what "There is a God" or "God loves us" *mean*. These
utterances are meaningless to him, but he does know *what* it is he places
his trust in—his faith is in something he does understand, namely, he understands that Jesus (or his religious authority) asserted that there is a
God or that God loves us.

      When we ask the fideist what he means when he says " 'There is a
God' is true," he can reply that he at least means this: "Jesus asserted
'There is a God' and because Jesus asserted it, it is true." If we ask,
"*What* did Jesus assert?" he will reply that Jesus asserted "There is a
God" and that we finite, sinful creatures no more understand "There

is a God" then we understand "There is an Irglig." However, we don't have to, for all we need to know is that if Jesus asserts something, we are to affirm that phonemic sequence. To the question, "What are you affirming?" we answer that we don't know; but whenever Jesus asserts something, we properly apply "true" to it. Since this is so, our statements expressive of our beliefs have truth-conditions and thus are intelligible, factual statements.

It is not true that they are compatible with anything and everything; we can say something about the conditions under which it would be appropriate to assert or deny them. Thus, though they are meaningless in one sense, they are meaningful in another, and a person can proclaim and adhere to them as his most basic commitments, the deepest articles of his faith. God Himself is unknowable—we don't even understand what "God" means—but Jesus is knowable and we take on faith his assertions about God to be true. In this way true faith may precede understanding.

This reply has at least one crucial defect. It claims Jesus asserted "p" where "p" is admittedly unintelligible to believer and non-believer alike, though supposedly intelligible to Jesus. But does it make sense to say "He asserted p" where "p" is unintelligible to us? We could say "He *uttered* p" or "He *wrote* p" but are we entitled to say he *asserted* p or *stated* p?[16] To assert something is to vouch for its truth. Now, how would it be possible for us to know that someone had asserted something except by seeing that he was willing to stick by it, give evidence for it if some moral considerations did not intervene, attempt to meet counterclaims and the like? In general, to know that he had *asserted* it, and not just *said* it, would be to know that he had behaved in certain distinctive ways. Consider this case. I say "The river is over its banks and we will have to move out to keep from being flooded." I say this but I make no effort to move out and I have no idea of how to take or direct you to a place where you could make observations of the river. To compound the confusion I keep on making the above utterance no matter what happens. Finally—after being pressed—I acknowledge that I didn't mean to claim that what I said was true but that I simply wanted to perplex you and to exercise my vocal chords. In such a situation you would *not* be entitled to say that I had asserted what I uttered but only that I had said it without meaning it. To assert something is to claim with honesty that it is true. Phonemic sequences or sentences cannot be true or false; only statements or assertions made through the use of sentences can be true or false. Before we can say that something is a *bona fide* assertion, as distinct from a sentence or a phonemic sequence, we must know what would count as evidence for the truth or falsity of what we are saying. But if we do not understand what p means we cannot understand what is would *mean* to say that p is true. Not understanding this, we cannot say what would count for the truth of p. Thus (B) ("Jesus *asserted* 'There is a God'") is unintelligible. But now we have also lost our footing for saying (A) is intelligible. Thus, our fideist has not by such a move been able to maneuver around the difficulty with fideism developed in section one.

It is not an adequate rebuttal to reply that it is enough to say "Jesus said 'There is a God,'" for "said" will either in this context bear the meaning of "asserts" or it will simply mean "uttered the sentence-token 'There is a God.'" If it means the latter it is indeed intelligible and would be just as intelligible if Jesus had said "Bright is the equation grief regains." But where "said" doesn't and couldn't do the job of "asserts" or "states," it is *not* correct to say that what Jesus said is *true* or *false*, and if that is so, then it does not make sense to say we will assert or deny what Jesus asserted or denied, for Jesus did not, and in this instance could not, assert or deny anything. For the same reasons, it makes no sense to say that Jesus's utterance is true or false, for an utterance or a sentence can't be true or false but only a statement, assertion, or a judgment can be true of false. Since in this instance he can't be asserting (or for that matter stating or judging) anything, he of course cannot be asserting (stating, judging) anything true or false. On this reading, (B) can't be an assertion—true or false—and since (A) has what meaning it has in virtue of (B), (A) cannot be an assertion either, and thus cannot be an object of our faith.

III

It is now time to sum up. Contemporary perplexity over religion typically arises from the conviction or anxiety that key religious utterances are in some appropriate sense meaningless. Fideism, I have argued, is no way around this problem. If we human beings have no understanding at all of what would or could count as an appropriate object of a religious attitude, we cannot understand what we are to take as the object of our religious trust, reverence, or faith. Such a "faith" is so blind, so objectless, that it is no faith at all. The best face we can put on the attempt to develop a fideism compatible with the admission that our key religious utterances are meaningless—utterly beyond all human understanding—comes down to the claim that "to believe solely on faith" consists in *nothing more* than repeating certain words we do not and cannot understand and carrying or attempting to carry out certain principles of action that we trust will give a deep, though not clearly definable, point to our lives. So limited, fideism is an intelligible theological stance, even in a world in which believers and non-believers alike acknowledge that God-talk or the crucial bits of God-talk are unintelligible. But it is natural to demand more of religious belief; and where more is demanded, fideism cannot justify bypassing the contention that the claims of religion are in reality no claims at all because key religious words and utterances are without intelligible factual content. If such a sceptical claim is justified, religious claims are illusory and fideism is no adequate defense of religion.

If the fideist finally grants us that we cannot have faith in or place our trust in what is meaningless and then goes on to say "But, of course,

'There is a God,' 'God loves us,' 'God created the heavens and the earth,' and the like, all do have meaning, for after all they have a *use* in our 'mother-tongue,' " he has shifted the argument. I have only been concerned here to argue that we cannot (with the qualification already mentioned) intelligibly maintain that we can have faith in meaningless propositions. If God-talk is meaningless or unintelligible, then fideism crumbles along with the other defenses of religious belief. If phonemic sequences like those mentioned above are understood as meaningful (true or false) assertions, then we can indeed believe they are *true, de fide.* Fideism would then be an intelligible though *perhaps* an irrational apologetic position. It seems to me, however, that we do not know the truth-conditions associated with "There is a God" and the like. In fact, we do not even know if they have truth-conditions. If this is so, then there seem to be no grounds for claiming that such religious utterances are used in such a way that they can count as assertions which we may take or fail to take on faith.[17] But this is a large subject that deserves attention on another occasion.

FOOTNOTES

1. See particularly his "The Logical Status of Religious Belief" in *Metaphysical Beliefs*, ed. S. Toulmin *et al.* (London: 1957) and his *Difficulties in Christian Belief* (London: 1957).

2. That such a view is not the straw man of an eager, all-too-eager, philosophical analyst, but a powerful tradition within Christian theology, is amply shown by Richard Popkin in his "Theological and Religious Scepticism," *The Christian Scholar*, vol. XXXIX (June, 1956), pp. 150-8 and in his "Kierkegaard and Scepticism," *Algemeen Nederlands Tijdschrift Voor Wijsbegeerte En Psychologie*, vol. 51 (No. 3), pp. 123-41.

3. Paul Holmer, "Philosophical Criticism and Christology," *The Journal of Religion*, vol. XXXIV (April, 1954), p. 90.

4. For an analysis that construes certain key religious utterances as ideological utterances, see my "On Speaking of God," *Theoria*, vol. XXVIII, Part 2 (1962), pp. 110-137.

5. I. M. Crombie, "Theology and Falsification," *New Essays in Philosophical Theology*, ed. by A. G. N. Flew (New York: 1955), p. 130.

6. See Bernard Williams' brilliant essay, "Tertullian's Paradox," *New Essays in Philosophical Theology*, ed. by A. G. N. Flew (New York: 1955), pp. 208-11.

7. They do not see or do not face the semantical puzzle, "What cognitive meaning could such utterances have if we *can* have no grounds at all for saying they are true?"

8. J. N. Findlay, "Some Reflections on Meaning," *The Indian Journal of Philosophy*, vol. I (August, 1959), pp. 15-16.

9. *Ibid.*, p. 16.

10. *Ibid.*, p. 15 (italics mine).

11. *Ibid.*

12. *Ibid.*

13. Arthur C. Danto, "Faith, Language and Religious Experience: A Dialogue," in *Religious Experience and Truth*, ed. by Sidney Hook (New York: 1961), p. 146.

14. If the "plain man" has read much theology or has run onto Walter Kaufmann's "Theology," he might, or at least he should, feel differently about this, though perhaps if he had done this he would not really be a "plain man." See Walter Kaufmann, "Theology," in *Self, Religion and Metaphysics*, ed. by Gerald E. Myers (New York: 1961), pp. 83-109.

15. I shall return on another occasion to the very strong claim that fideism in particular and theistic religion in general are irrational and therefore ought to be abandoned.

16. Some of the relevant distinctions between "saying," "asserting," and "stating" are nicely drawn by Isabel Hungerland in her "Contextual Implication," *Inquiry*, vol. 3 (Winter, 1960).

17. If arguments like those made by Ziff in his "About 'God'" are correct what I have said here would need modification. But it seems to me that Paul Edwards' arguments against Ziff's contentions are very strong if not decisive. See Paul Ziff, "About 'God,'" pp. 195-202 and Paul Edwards, "Some Notes on Anthropomorphic Theology," pp. 244-5, both in *Religious Experience and Truth*, ed. by Sidney Hook (New York: 1961).

CHAPTER FOURTEEN

THE LOGIC OF GOD*

by John Wisdom

THE MODES OF THOUGHT AND THE LOGIC OF GOD

I

I should like to say what I aim to do in these lectures and then do it. But there are difficulties about this. I have nothing to say—nothing except what everybody knows. People sometimes ask me what I do. Philosophy I say and I watch their faces very closely. 'Ah—they say—that's a very deep subject isn't it?' I don't like this at all. I don't like their tone. I don't like the change in their faces. Either they are frightfully solemn. Or they have to manage not to smile. And I don't like either. Now scientists don't have to feel like this. They tell us what we don't know until they tell us—how very fast germs in the blood breed and that this stuff will stop them, what will or at least what won't take the stain out of the carpet. Even if I were a historian it would be better. Maybe you don't want to know just how the Abbey at Bury St. Edmunds was run in the time of Abbot Samson, but at least you probably don't know and if only I did I could tell you. But as it is I haven't anything to say except what everybody knows already. And this instantly puts into my head a thought which I try not to but can't help but think namely 'Have I anything to say at all worth saying'—a question which I fear is by now in your mind even if it wasn't before I started. Fortunately this brings me to what I want to do. For I want to urge that one who has nothing to say except what everybody knows already may yet say something worth saying and I want to bring out a little how this happens. This is itself something which everybody knows so if I succeed I succeed twice over rather like one who proves that someone in this room is whispering by pointing

*Used with permission from *Paradox and Discovery*, Basil Blackwell-Publisher, Oxford, England, 1965.

to someone who is whispering and saying, in a whisper, 'He is whispering.' On the other hand even if I fail to demonstrate that what I claim is true it may still be true. Of course—for as everybody knows, one who says 'Someone is whispering' may be right although in attempting to support this statement he points to the wrong person. And everybody knows that a child *may* get the right answer to a sum although he has made at least one mistake in his calculations. Everybody knows this. But don't we sometimes become unduly confident that what a man says is false because his argument is invalid or his premisses false? And if we do then there are occasions on which it is worth saying to us 'A man may be right in what he says although his argument is invalid and/or his premisses false'—a thing which everybody knows.

Perhaps you now hope that satisfied with these antics I will say no more. But no. I am not satisfied. For I am not content to show that it is sometimes worth saying what everybody knows—that seems to me hardly worth saying. I want if I can to bring out a little of how, when, and why it is sometimes worth saying what everybody knows. I want to bring out the several ways of doing this and also how it is connected with informing people of what they do not know—Unlike philosophers, scientists need feel no embarrassment about accepting the salaries they are paid. Motor vans hurry with the late editions. And very properly. For we want to know what won. But how does anyone ever say to another anything worth saying when he doesn't know anything the other doesn't know?

And yet of course there are those who manage this. They say 'You look *lovely* in that hat' to people who know this already. But this instance isn't a very clear one. For those to whom such things are said sometimes know not merely that what is said is so but are also very well aware of how what is said is so. Imagine something different. Imagine someone is trying on a hat. She is studying the reflection in a mirror like a judge considering a case. There's a pause and then a friend says in tones too clear, 'My dear, it's the Taj Mahal.' Instantly the look of indecision leaves the face in the mirror. All along she has felt there was about the hat something that wouldn't quite do. Now she sees what it is. And all this happens in spite of the fact that the hat could be seen perfectly clearly and completely before the words 'The Taj Mahal' were uttered. And the words were not effective because they referred to something hidden like a mouse in a cupboard, like germs in the blood, like a wolf in sheep's clothing. To one about to buy false diamonds the expert friend murmurs 'Glass,' to one terrified by what he takes to be a snake the good host whispers 'Stuffed.' But that's different, that *is* to tell somebody something he doesn't know—that that snake won't bite, that cock won't fight. But to call a hat the Taj Mahal is not to inform someone that it has mice in it or will cost a fortune. It is more like saying to someone 'Snakes' of snakes in the grass but *not* concealed by the grass but still so well camouflaged that one can't see what's before one's eyes. Even this case is different from that of the hat and the woman. For in the case of the snakes the element of warning, the element of predictive warning, is still there mixed, intimately mixed, with the element of revealing what is already visible. This last element is there unmixed when someone says of a hat which is plainly and completely visible 'It's the Taj Mahal.' And there is another difference. There's nothing preposterous about calling a snake a snake, but to call a hat the Taj Mahal—well, it involves poetic licence.

At this point someone protests. In philosophy there's always someone who protests. And here he says, 'I don't know what you're making all this fuss about. In the first place a woman who says of a hat "It's the Taj Mahal" just means "It is like the Taj Mahal" or "It is in some respects like the Taj Mahal." By saying this she makes her friend feel that the hat is impossible. Well what of it? What has all this got to do with what you say is your main point, namely, that one person may show something to another without telling him anything he doesn't know? In this case nobody shows anybody anything—all that happens is that somebody is persuaded not to buy a hat. The hat you say was seen perfectly clearly from the first. Now it isn't seen any more clearly at the finish. The change is a change in feeling. It may be expressed in the words "I see now" or "It's impossible" but that is just an expression of a different attitude to the hat.

'And by the way may I ask what all this has got to do with philosophy? Here is mankind bewildered in a bewildering world. And what do you offer? Talk about talk about a hat.'

My answer is this: In the first place it isn't true that the words about the hat only influence the hearer's feelings to the hat. They alter her apprehension of the hat just as the word 'A hare' makes what did look like a clump of earth *look* like an animal, a hare in fact; just as the word 'A cobra,' may change the look of something in the corner by the bed. It is just because in these instances words change the apprehension of what is already before one that I refer to them.

Again it isn't true that the words 'It's the Taj Mahal' meant 'It is like the Taj Mahal.' This more sober phrase is an inadequate substitute. This reformulation is a failure. It's feebler than the original and yet it's still too strong. For the hat isn't like the Taj Mahal, it's much smaller and the shape is very different. And the still more sober substitute 'It is in some respects like the Taj Mahal' is still more inadequate. It's *much* too feeble. Everything is like everything in some respects—a man like a monkey, a monkey like a mongoose, a mongoose like a mouse, a mouse like a micro-organism, and a man after all is an organism too. Heaven forbid that we should say there are no contexts in which it is worth while to remark this sort of thing. But it is not what the woman in the hat shop remarked. What she said wasn't the literal truth like 'It's a cobra' said of what is, unfortunately, a cobra. But what she said revealed the truth. Speaking soberly what she said was false but then thank heaven we don't always speak soberly. Someone has said 'The best of life is but intoxication' and that goes for conversation. People sometimes speak wildly but if we tame their words what we get are words which are tame and very often words which don't do anything near what the wild ones did. If for 'It's the Taj Mahal' we put 'It is in some respects like the Taj Mahal' we get the sort of negligible stuff that so often results from trying to put poetry into prose, from submission to the muddled metaphysics which pretends that a metaphor is no more than an emotive flourish unless and until we happen to have the words and the wits to translate it into a set of similes.

'But,' says the protesting voice, 'what she said about the hat wasn't poetry.'

'All right, all right it wasn't poetry. And the bread in the upper room wasn't the body of Christ that later hung upon the Cross. Nor of course are there three incorruptibles and yet but one incorruptible, three persons yet one God. But sometimes one is less concerned with whether what one says is true, literally true, than one is to press past illusion to the apprehension of reality, its unity and its diversity.'

'Well let that pass,' says the sober voice, 'since it agitates you so much, let it pass. It all seems rather vague to me and I don't know what you mean about the judge and his judgements. Could anything be further from poetry, more sober? However let it pass, let it pass and come to my second point. What has this conversation about a hat got to do with philosophy, this rather bizarre conversation about a hat?'

My answer is this: Is conversation about the nature and reality of goodness and beauty philosophical, metaphysical conversation? Is conversation about the reality and ultimate nature of the soul philosophical, metaphysical conversation? Is conversation about the reality and ultimate nature of matter philosophical, metaphysical conversation? Is conversation about the reality and ultimate nature of philosophical, metaphysical discussion philosophical, metaphysical conversation? It is. Well, the conversation about the hat throws light on all that—and more immediately conversation about conversation about the hat is a bit of metaphysics and bears on other bits. It *is* a member of the family of metaphysical conversations and its character throws a light on the other members of that family; and the conversation about the hat itself is a member of the family of *Attempts to come at the truth* and its character throws light on the character of the other members of that vast family. The character of any one human being throws light on the characters of all the rest and they on it. For what is the character of a woman, of a man, of anything at all but the way she, he, it is like and unlike men, monkeys, microbes, the dust, the angels high in heaven, God on his throne—all that is and all that might have been.

'Hold on, hold on,' says the voice. 'This sounds rather like church. It's so obscure.'

This makes me want to mutter 'Thank heaven for the church.' It is often obscurantist. But sometimes in those lecture halls we endeavour to substitute for it the light seems a thought too bright and on the brilliant plains of intellectual orthodoxy we half remember something lost in Lyonesse or something that was never found. Still—I must answer that voice of protest, that voice which somehow in spite of its anticlerical bias is also the voice of honesty, order, law, conscience saying 'Let's get this clear. How can consideration of a conversation about a hat make metaphysics more manageable? Even if the conversation about the hat does a little illuminate the hat, isn't it a far cry to philosophy which professes to illuminate reality?'

II

At the end of the last discussion I was left facing the question: Why all this about a hat and the Taj Mahal? If you want to bring out the fact that we sometimes use words neither to give information as when we say 'That will be fifteen guineas' nor to express and evoke feeling as when we exclaim *'Fifteen* guineas!' but to give a greater apprehension of what is already before us then why don't you choose a better example? For instance why not take the case of an accountant who has before him the assets and liabilities of a firm and asks 'Are they solvent?' or a statistician who has before him the records of births and deaths for the last 50 years and asks 'Has the average man today a greater expectation of life than he had 20 years ago?' Here are questions which can be settled on the basis of facts already ascertained and which are yet definite questions which can be settled by an agreed, definite, mathematical, deductive procedure. Why choose as an example a statement so preposterous and loosely worded that the question 'Is it true?' is hardly a question at all ... It not only cannot be answered by collecting new data by observation but also cannot be answered by any definite deductive procedure.

My answer is: That is why I chose it. We all know and, what is more, we all recognize that there are questions which though they don't call for further investigation but only for reflection are yet perfectly respectable because the reflection they call for may be carried out in a definite demonstrative procedure which gives results Yes or No. My point is that this isn't the only sort of reflection and that the other sorts are not poor relations. Maybe they tend to have deplorable associates but they themselves we cannot afford to ignore. For they too take us toward a better apprehension of reality and also help us to understand better the character of all reflection including the more normal members of the family.

We do not deny that vague and queer things are said and that people make some show of considering them. We do not say that drama, novels, poetry, never show us anything of the truth. But we are apt to half-feel that what is said in poetry is always more a matter of fancy than of fact, that it is not within the scope of reason. I am urging that there is more of poetry in science and more of science in poetry than our philosophy permits us readily to grasp. 'There is within the flame of love a sort of wick or snuff that doth abate it' is not so far from 'There is within the central rail on the Inner Circle a sort of current that, etc.' 'There is between a rising tide and the rising moon a sort of bond that, etc.' Newton with his doctrine of gravitation gave us a so much greater apprehension of nature not so much because he told us what we would or would not see, like Pasteur or one who predicts what will be first past the post, but because he enabled us to see anew a thousand familiar incidents. To hint that when we are concerned with questions which are still unanswered even when we have left no stone unturned, no skid mark unmeasured, then thinking is no use, is to forget that when the facts are agreed upon we still must hear argument before we give judgement. To hint that, when argument cannot show that in the usual usage of language the correct answer is Yes or No it shows us nothing, is to forget that such argument is in such a case just as necessary and just as valuable for an apprehension of the case before us as it is in those cases when it happens that we can express that greater apprehension in a word—Guilty, Not Guilty, Mad, Not Mad, Negligent, Not Negligent, Cruel, Not Cruel. To hint that whenever, in our efforts to portray nature, we break the bonds of linguistic convention and say what is preposterous then counsel must throw up the case because we are no longer at the bar of reason— to say this is to denigrate the very modes of thought that we need most when most we need to think.

And yet, in one's efforts to think clearly it is easy to speak as if it were a waste of time to try to answer a question which hasn't an answer Yes or No, Right or Wrong, True or False. And when lately some people had the courage to say, 'A statement hasn't really a meaning unless it can be settled either by observation or by the sort of definite procedure by which questions of mathematics or logic are settled, otherwise it isn't a real, meaningful, worthwhile question but verbal, emotive, or nonsensical' then we welcomed this bold pronouncement because it seemed to say what we had long felt but not had the courage to say.

It is easy to see that this principle as it stands won't do. Consider the question 'Here are the records for births and deaths for the last fifty years. Does the average man live longer today than he did twenty years ago?' This is not itself a hypothetical, mathematical question. It is not the question '*If* the figures were as follows what *would* the answer be?' It is the question 'These being the figures what *is* the answer?' This is a question about what has actually happened.

However it is settled by a definite deductive procedure. So such a case leaves it open to us to reformulate our tempting principle as follows: A question is a real, meaningful question only if either it can be answered by observation or it can be answered by demonstration from premises which are either self-evident or obtained by describing what we have observed.

This unspoken formula frames I submit a prevalent, though often unspoken, habit of thought. We know the man who when we are vigorously discussing some point interposes with 'Look—we must define our terms, mustn't we?' He has been educated; he has been taught. His intentions are of the best. He is an ally against fluffy and futile talk. And yet so often by the time he has finished it seems somehow as if the questions he has answered aren't the ones we were interested in and worse still we seem to be unable to say what we were interested in. For example, suppose a man says to his wife, 'The children ought to clean their shoes be-

fore going to school.' 'Oh, don't be so fussy,' she says. 'I am not being
fussy,' he says, 'I'm merely concerned that the children should learn the
ordinary politeness of taking some care of their appearance and not arrive at school in a slovenly state.' '*Slovenly*,' she says but at this point
the good friend intervenes. He addresses himself to the wife, 'Look,'
he says with his pleasant smile, 'we must define our terms, mustn't we?'
One can't begin to answer a question until one has defined one's terms.'
'In that case one can't begin,' she says, 'for when one defines a word one
puts another in its place.' 'Yes,' he says, 'but you know I don't mean that
we ought to define *every* word we use. I mean we need to define the
vague ones.' 'By equally vague ones I suppose,' she says. 'No, no,' he
says, 'by more precise ones.' 'But,' she says, 'if what you put in place of
the vague is something not vague then the new words can't have the
same meaning as the old ones had.' 'I see what you mean,' he says, 'but
still, what is the use of arguing about a question which hasn't a definite
answer? One must know what one means.' 'Certainly one must know or
come to know what one means,' she says, 'but that doesn't mean that
there is no use in arguing about questions which haven't definite answers.
They are just the ones which are most interesting—those and the ones
which can't mean what they seem to mean, because they are so preposterous. For instance I said just now that Jack was fussy. We both knew
what I meant—I meant like an old hen. I daresay there is something to
be said for saying he is not fussy. But if so I want to have it said and I
want to have my say too. Now you say that we can't discuss this question until we have defined our terms. I suppose you mean the terms
"fussy" or "slovenly." But we were discussing it until you interposed.'
'Well,' he says, 'I interposed because it seemed to me that you were discussing a question which couldn't be answered. You said Jack was fussy,
he said he wasn't. But this wasn't a real dispute, it was a question of
words.'

She: It *wasn't* a question of words, it was a real question, a very
real question.

He: Well of course it was a question you and he had strong feelings
about. Or rather the word 'fussy' is an *emotive* word because it expresses
our feelings and when you said that Jack was fussy because he said the
children ought to clean their shoes before going to school, you expressed
how you felt about their doing this and about Jack—and when he said
he was not fussy he expressed his feelings about this and about you.
But there wasn't any real question between you.

She: What d'you mean, no *real* question?

He: Well, I mean 'Is Jack fussy?' isn't a question like 'Has Jack
diphtheria?' which can be settled by taking a swab from his throat. Nor
is it like 'Has he the money for the tickets? They cost 15/- and he
has 10/-, one shilling, three sixpences and half a crown. Now is that
15/-?' There is a procedure for settling such a question.

She: You are not now saying that we can't answer a question unless
we can define our terms. But what are you saying? Is it that questions

which can't be settled by observation nor by deduction aren't really
questions? But what do you mean 'aren't really questions'? Do you mean
that there is no definite procedure for answering them? But what d'you
call a definite procedure? Is legal procedure when cases are quoted in
order to show for example that in the case before the court there was
negligence or that there was not—is this a definite procedure? And does
it always lead to an answer? Whenever I get a glimpse of what you mean
it seems preposterous and it only doesn't seem preposterous when I don't
know what you mean. But I want to *come* to know what you mean. I
want to know what's at the back of your saying that questions which
seem to be real questions aren't really; I want to know what makes you
say it, what reasons you have, whether you are right or wrong or neither.
Or is this not a real question because it hasn't a definite answer so that
it is futile to discuss it?

'Well,' he says, 'I think you know what I mean. I mean that there are
lots of questions which seem as if they could be answered by observation
or deduction when they can't be really because they are matters of words
or matters of feeling.'

She: We all know that this sometimes happens. For instance one person might say that a certain food is in short supply and another that it
is not because the one means that people can't get as much of it as they
want to buy and the other means that there is no less of this food on the
market than usual. Or to take a more trivial but simpler instance: I remember I once said of two horses which had the same father that they
were half-brothers and someone else said that they were not and it turned
out that this was because he didn't call *horses* half-brothers unless they
had the same *mother*.

He: I don't mean just trivial instances like that. I mean that there are
questions which seem important to us and seem to call for much thought
because they seem difficult to answer when really they are difficult to
answer only because there is no way of answering them, so that they have
no answers. For instance take an old question which has very much concerned people—the question 'Did someone make the world?' 'Is there
Someone behind it all?' This seems as if it could be answered like 'Who
made this watch?' 'Who laid out this garden?' 'Is there a master mind
behind all these seemingly disconnected crimes?' But it can't be answered
in that way. It couldn't be. What I mean is this: when you are told that
there is someone, God, who brings the young lions their prey and feeds
the cattle upon a thousand hills, it is natural to think that if you watch,
perhaps in the hush at dawn or at sunset, you will see something to confirm this statement. You watch. What d'you see? Antelopes feeding perhaps, or zebras come down to drink. A lion springs—with wonderful acceleration it is true—but still his own acceleration. And if anything
saves that zebra it's the way be comes round on his hocks and gets going.
There are the stars and the flowers and the animals. But there's no one
to be seen. And no one to be heard. There's the wind and there's the
thunder but if you call there's no answer except the echo of your own

voice. It is natural to infer that those who told us that there is someone who looks after it all are wrong. But that is a mistake we are told. No such inference is legitimate they say, because God is invisible.

She: God is a spirit and cannot be seen nor heard. But the evidences of his existence lie in the order and arrangement of nature.

He: Ah. That is what is so often said. But it suggests that in nature there are evidences of God as there are in a watch the evidences of a maker, in a cathedral, the evidences of an architect, in a garden, the evidences of a gardener. And this is to suggest that God *could* be seen. It then turns out that this is a mistake. A gardener may be elusive, an architect retiring, a watch-maker hard to find, but we know what it would be to see them and so confirm the guesses that it is they who are responsible for what we see before us. Now what would it be like to see God? Suppose some seer were to see, imagine we all saw, move upwards from the ocean to the sky some prodigious figure which declared in dreadful tones the moral law or prophesied most truly—our fate. Would this be to see God?

Wouldn't it just be a phenomenon which later we were able to explain or not able to explain but in either case the proof of a living God. The logic of God if there is such a logic isn't like that.

She: Indeed, indeed. The way to knowledge of God is not as simple as we might confusedly hope. An evil and adulterous generation seeketh after a sign and there shall no sign be given it save the sign of the prophet Jonah. And that is not an arbitrary decree but one by which God Himself is bound. What you call 'the logic of God' couldn't be simpler than it is without His being less than He is, for the simpler the possible proofs that something is so the simpler it is for it to be so.

He: What d'you mean?

She: Well, if we mean by 'a rainbow' only a certain appearance in the sky then it is easy to know at a glance whether today there is a rainbow or not. But in that case a rainbow is only an appearance in the sky. The moment it is more, that moment it's harder to know. If one who says 'There's a rainbow' means not merely that there is a certain appearance in the sky but that that appearance is linked with water and the sun, then the appearance is no longer by itself a proof that what he says is so. It may be a sign but it is not one from which he can read off the answer to the question 'Is there a rainbow?' as he could when by 'a rainbow' was meant no more than a certain appearance in the sky. When a rainbow is more than the appearance of a rainbow then that appearance is not a sign which makes it beside the point to look for the rest of what makes a rainbow a rainbow. The simplest people are sometimes very good at telling whether a storm is coming but the full proof, the full confirmation of what they reckon is so, cannot be less complex than all that makes a storm. Horses are quick to know whether one is angry, babies to know whether one loves them, but the full proof of what they feel is so cannot be less complex than is anger or love itself—as you say it is not merely that there *is* not some fool-proof proof of God. There *couldn't* be. But that doesn't mean that there are no evidences of God's existence; it doesn't mean that there are no proofs of his existence; nor that these are not to be found in experience; not even that they are not to be found in what we see and hear. One cannot see power but it's from what we see that we know that power is present when we watch the tube-train mysteriously move towards the Marble Arch, and the more we watch, the more explicable the mystery becomes, the more, without limit, the proof approaches a demonstration. Each day a thousand incidents confirm the doctrine that energy is indestructible: and if the present proof is not a demonstration that is not because the conclusion calls for reasons of a kind we never get. It is because the doctrine is infinite in its implications so that beyond any conceivable evidence at any time there is still evidence beyond that time—evidence for or evidence against—until no wheels are turning and time stops. In the same way, as the scroll of nature unrolls the proof of an eternal God prevails—or fails—until on the day of judgement doctrine, like theory, must become a verdict and all be lost or won.

III

He: I understand that you are now saying that the order and arrangement of nature proves the existence of God, not as the moving machinery of a mill indicates the flow of water beneath it, but as the behaviour of an electrical machine proves the presence of electricity because electricity just is such behaviour. The average man is invisible but we may know whether he is orderly or disorderly because his existence and nature are deducible from that of individual men. He is orderly if they are orderly because his being orderly just is their being orderly. But now if the existence of God is deducible from the fact that nature is orderly then one who says that God exists merely puts in theological words what others express in the words, 'In nature nothing is inexplicable, there is always a reason why.' And those who speak of God would not allow that this is all they mean. This is why I say that the question, 'Does God exist?' can not be answered by observation and also cannot be answered by deduction. And this is why I say that though it seems to be a question it is not. The statement 'God's in his heaven' may express a feeling but it is not something that could be true or false, because nothing would make it false and therefore nothing would make it true.

She: You make too little of a move in thought which from a mass of data extracts and assembles what builds up into the proof of something which, though it doesn't go beyond the data, gives us an apprehension of reality which before we lacked. The move from the myriad transactions of the market to the conclusion that sterling is stronger isn't negligible. The move from the bewildering and apparently disorderly flux of nature to the doctrine that all that happens happens in order is one which called for our best efforts and gave us a very different apprehension of nature. Perhaps it took Spinoza a long way towards God.

Still it *is* very true that those who speak of God don't mean merely that nature is orderly. Nature would be orderly if it were nothing but an enormous clock slowly but inevitably running down. But then I am not saying that if there is order in Nature that proves that God exists. The fact that a machine is electrical is not deducible from the fact that its behaviour is orderly. If there were no order in its behaviour it couldn't be electrical but there could be order in its behaviour without its being electrical. It might run by falling weights. It is the fact that the order in its behaviour is of a certain character which makes the machine electrical. It doesn't need winding but from time to time it stops or goes more slowly just when the fire goes out—that's what makes it electrical. The mere fact that Nature is orderly would never prove that Energy is indestructible. What makes this true is the fact that the order in nature is of a certain character. It might have been of a different character but, as it is, each day confirms the doctrine of the conservation of energy.

The order of nature might have been of a character which would make it fair to say, 'It is all in the hands of someone who made it and then fell asleep' or, 'It's all in the hands of someone who arranges the little ironies of fate.' For all I have said to the contrary it may be of this character. For I am not trying to prove that God does exist but only to prove that it is wrong to say that there could be no proof that he does or that he does not.

He: But surely this comparison of the logic of God with the logic of Energy isn't a legitimate comparison.

She: I don't know whether it's legitimate or not. I am making it.

He: Yes but—well, it's like this: I understand you when you say that just as those who speak of the existence and properties of Energy don't deduce all they say from the fact that the procession of events in nature is orderly but from the particular character of that procession of events, so those who speak of God don't deduce his existence and properties merely from the fact that the procession of events is orderly but from the particular character of that procession. But surely the question 'Does God exist?' is very different from the question 'Does Energy exist?' I don't mean merely that the questions are different like the question 'Is there any milk?' is different from 'Is there any wine?' Those questions are very unlike because milk is very unlike wine. But they are very like in the sort of procedure which settles them; that is, the logic of milk is like the logic of wine. But surely the way we know of the existence of energy is very different from the way, if any, in which we know of the existence of God. For one thing, people have spoken of knowing the presence of God not from looking around them but from their own hearts. The logic of God may be more like the logic of Energy or of Life than at first appears but surely it is very different.

She: It is different. One can't expect to bring out the idiosyncrasies in what you call 'the logic of God' by a single comparison. The way in which we know God Who has been called 'the Soul of the World,' 'the Mind of the Universe,' might also be compared with the way one knows the soul or mind of another creature. It is clear that one couldn't find the soul behind the face of one's neighbour or one's cat as one could find at last the elusive and even ghostly inhabitant of the house next door. Because of this people have said that when we speak of the consciousness of another this is a way of speaking of those sequences of bodily events which are the manifestations of consciousness, just as when we speak of energy that is a way of speaking of the manifestations of energy and when we speak of a procession that is just a way of speaking of what makes up the procession. Here again this comparison is dangerous unless it is accompanied by a warning. For it neglects the fact that though one who has never tasted what is bitter or sweet and has never felt pain may know very well the behaviour characteristic of, for instance, pain, he yet cannot know pain nor even that another is in pain—not in the way he could had he himself felt pain. It is from looking round him that a man knows of the pain, of the love and of the hate in the world, but it is also from his own heart.

He: Yes, but what I mean is this. Even though we couldn't see energy because it isn't the sort of thing which could be seen we know very well what to look for in order to know of its existence and where it flows, we can measure it and deduce the laws of its transmission and conservation. Even when we ask of someone, 'Is he really pleased to see us?' we know what to look for to prove that the answer is 'Yes,' and what to look for to prove that the answer is 'No.' We may ask him and beg him to tell us the truth, and if we are not satisfied we may await developments, watch for further signs, and these may, in your words, approach more and more a demonstration. But with the questions 'Does God exist?' 'Is this what He approves or that?' there is no agreement as to what to look for, no agreement as to what the character of the order of events must be to count in favour of the answer 'Yes' or in favour of the answer 'No.'

She: Not *no* agreement. If there were *no* agreement that *would* make the question meaningless. But it is not true that there is no agreement. One could describe a future for the world which were it to come would prove the triumph of the Devil. Hells, it is true, are more easily described than Heavens, and Paradise lost than Paradise regained. Descriptions of heaven are apt to be either extremely hazy or to involve too much music or too much hunting. And this isn't a joke, it may spell a contradiction in perfection. But it's not true that we haven't a clue about the kingdom of heaven. Every description of what appears to be heaven and turns out to be hell makes plainer the boundaries of heaven. We don't know what would be heaven and this shows itself in the fluctuating logic of heaven, that is to say in our feeble grasp of what it is we do want to do with the words, 'Will the kingdom of heaven come?' 'Does God exist?' But this doesn't prove that there isn't anything we want to do with them. An artist may not know what he wants to do, and only come to know by doing first one thing which isn't what he wanted to do and then another which also isn't what he wanted to do. But this doesn't prove that there wasn't anything he wanted to do. On the contrary in finding what he didn't want to do he may find at last what he did. In the same way with words, finding out what one didn't mean, one may find out at last what one did mean.

Now with regard to God and the Devil and whether there is any meaning in asking whether they exist: Freud so far from thinking these questions meaningless says in the last of the New Introductory Lectures: 'It seems not to be true that there is a power in the universe which watches over the well-being of every individual with parental care and brings all his concerns to a happy ending. On the contrary, the destinies of man are incompatible with a universal principle of benevolence or with—what is to some degree contradictory—a universal principle of justice. Earthquakes, floods and fires do not differentiate between the good and devout man and the sinner and unbeliever. And, even if we leave inanimate nature out of the account and consider the destinies of individual men in so far as they depend on their relations with others of their own kind, it is by no means the rule that virtue is rewarded and wickedness punished, but it happens often enough that the violent, the crafty and the unprincipled seize the desirable goods of the earth for themselves, while the pious go empty away. Dark, unfeeling and unloving powers determine human destiny . . .' Something about the facts, Freud feels, is brought out by saying not merely that often men do evil things but by saying too that 'dark, unfeeling and unloving powers determine human destiny.' It's preposterous but we know what he means— not clearly, but obscurely. Others have spoken in the same way. St. Paul says, 'that which I do I allow not: for what I would that I do not; but what I hate, that do I.' Euripides makes Helen say to Menelaus:

> . . . And yet how strange it is!
> I ask not thee; I ask my own sad thought,
> What was there in my heart, that I forgot
> My home and land and all I loved, to fly
> With a strange man? Surely it was not I,
> But Cypris there!

He: It's all very well for her to say, 'It was not I.' The fact is she did it.

She: There is evasion in such words as there has been ever since Eve said, 'The serpent beguiled me,' ever since Adam said, 'The woman that thou gavest me she gave me of the tree.' There is an evasion and confusion and inappropriate humility perhaps in one who says, 'Yet not I but the grace of God that dwelleth in me.' And yet is it all evasion and confusion? Is it for nothing that we speak of someone as not having been himself, as never having been able to be himself. We speak of compulsive acts, compulsive thought, of having been possessed. Possessed by what? A demon evil or good or both good and evil. And why do we speak so? Because we come on something done by Dr. Jekyll which is out of order, out of character, inexplicable, if it was Dr. Jekyll who was in control. It is in an effort to understand, to bring order into the apparently chaotic, that we find ourselves saying preposterously, 'It wasn't really Dr. Jekyll, it was Mr. Hyde—or the Devil himself.'

He: But there is no need to speak of the Devil here. It is just that there was more in Dr. Jekyll than appeared.

She: Not just that. There was more than there appeared in the man who called about the gas meter and left with the pearls. But that's different. *We* were taken aback when we found he'd gone with the pearls, but *he* wasn't. It was all in order as far as he was concerned. But in those cases of multiple personality, for example in that case Dr. Morton Prince studied, the one personality, Miss Beauchamp, was horrified to learn of the lies which Sally, the other personality, told. Miss Beauchamp couldn't have told such lies and still be Miss Beauchamp.

He: Yes, but Sally was just a part of Miss Beauchamp's unconscious. There were in her desires and thoughts which she didn't allow, as St. Paul says, which she didn't know, to translate St. Paul's Greek still more literally.

She: I am not denying that we can explain the seemingly inexplicable and grasp the order in what seems like chaos with the help of the conceptions of the unconscious, of the Super-ego, of the id, of internal objects, of ghosts that are gone whenever we turn to see them, of currents hidden in the depths of the soul. But if the logic of God and of the Devil is more eccentric than it seems, so also is the logic of the Super-Ego and the Id and the Unconscious. Indeed what makes us speak of the unconscious and the good and the evil in it, the wine of life and the poison of death so mixed, is closely connected with what makes us speak of a hidden power for good—God—and a hidden power for evil—the Devil. For when we speak of the thoughts and acts of Mr. So-and-So as 'coming out of his unconscious' we are often inclined to say that they are not altogether his, that he is compelled, driven, helped, possessed by something not himself. When we recognize the unconscious in the soul we no longer find adequate the model of objects with definite shapes, and we begin to think of the soul as the energy continually flowing and transformed. For example Natasha in *War and Peace* though she loves Prince André Bolkonsky is fascinated by Prince Kouragine. His fast horses stand at the gate and it is nothing in her that prevents her flying with him. It was after Bolkonsky had heard of all this that his friend Peter Bezukov visited him and told him that Natasha was very ill. Bolkonsky replied that he was sorry to hear of her illness and—Tolstoy says—an evil smile like his father's curled his pinched lips. He said, 'Then Prince Kouragine did not after all consent to give her his hand.' Peter replied, 'He could not—he is already married.' Prince André laughed evilly—again reminding one of his father.

Here I feel the presence of evil, evil that has flowed from the father to the son. Anger against Natasha was justified if you like. But that's not what I am now thinking about. Whether anger was or was not justified—in that laugh we feel evil, an evil that we can't place altogether in Prince André. We feel inclined to trace it also to his father. But then when we come to the father it doesn't seem to lie altogether in him either. He was the man who a little before he died accused the daughter who loved him of 'endless imaginary crimes, loaded her with the bitterest reproaches, accused her of having poisoned his existence . . . dismissed her from his presence, saying she might do whatever she pleased, that he would have nothing more to say to her, and that he never would set eyes on her again.' And this was only the climax of what had gone on for years. This wasn't out of character. Or *was* it? For later he is dying. He makes a desperate effort to speak. 'I'm always thinking of you' he says, and as she bows her head to hide her tears he strokes her hair and says, 'I called you all night.' 'If I had but known,' she says. Dark, unfeeling, and unloving powers determine human destiny.

Or is this going too far? Is it evil and unloving power only that determines human destiny and directs the course of nature? Or is there also at work a good and loving power? It has been said that once at least a higher gift than grace did flesh and blood refine, God's essence and his very self—in the body of Jesus. Whether this statement is true of false is not now the point but whether it's so obscure as to be senseless. Obscure undoubtedly it is but senseless it is not, beyond the scope of reason it is not. For to say that in Nero God was incarnate is not to utter a senseless string of words nor merely to express a surprising sentiment; it is to make a statement which is absurd because it is against all reason. If I say of a cat, 'This cat is an abracadabra' I utter a senseless string of words, I don't make a statement at all and therefore don't make an absurd statement. But if I say of a cat which is plainly dead, 'In this cat there is life' I make a statement which is absurd because it is against all reason. The cat is not hunting, eating, sleeping, breathing; it is stiff and cold. In the same way the words, 'In Nero God was incarnate' are not without any meaning; one who utters them makes a statement, he makes a statement which is absurd and *against* all reason and therefore *not* beyond the scope of reason. Now if a statement is not beyond the scope of reason then any logically parallel statement is also not beyond the scope of reason. For example, the statement, 'Your house is well designed' is not beyond the scope of reason. It may be obviously true or absurdly false or obviously neither true nor false, but it's not beyond the scope of reason. The statement, 'My house is well designed' is logically parallel to the statement, 'Your house is well designed.' The statement, 'My house is well designed' may be absurdly false or neither true nor false or obviously true. But like the parallel statement about your house it is not beyond the scope of reason. The statement 'In Jesus God was incarnate' is logically parallel to 'In Nero God was incarnate.' The latter we noticed is not beyond the scope of reason. Therefore the statement 'In Jesus God was incarnate' is not beyond the scope of reason.

And we may come at the same result more directly. Consider the words 'Was there someone, Jesus, in whom God was incarnate?' These words call first for investigation. Was there such a person as Jesus is alleged to have been? Was there someone born of a virgin? Was there someone who rose from the dead? Was there someone who said all or some or most of the things Jesus is alleged to have said? Did someone speak as this man is said to have spoken? These things settled, we have only started. How far does the rest of experience show that what this man said was true? Did what Jesus said reveal what we hadn't known or what we had known but hadn't recognized? Was there someone, Jesus, who was God incarnate? The question calls for investigation but it also calls like every other question for thought, reflection, reason. He made himself the Son of God. 'Preposterous presumption' the priests said, but was it the truth? The facts agreed upon, still a question is before the bar of reason as when, the facts agreed upon, still a question comes before a court. 'Was there negligence or was there not?' To such a question maybe the answer is 'Yes,' maybe the answer is 'No,' maybe the answer is neither 'Yes' nor 'No.' But the question is not beyond the scope of reason. On the contrary it calls for very careful consideration and not the less when what's relevant is conflicting and not the less because what's relevant is not enumerable because there's not a separate name for every relevant feature of the case and an index to measure its weight. In a cat crouched to spring burns the flame of life. There are signs we can mention—nothing moves but, very slightly, the tail and there's something about the eyes but what? She springs. Still the proof of life eludes language but it's there, was there, and will be there, in the moving picture before us. Was Jesus God incarnate? The law in this matter is not as simple nor as definite nor as fully written out in statutes as we might wish it could be. The question is large, slippery, subtle. But it is not true that nothing is more relevant to it than another, so that nothing supports one answer more than it supports the other. On the contrary every incident in the life of Christ is relevant to this question as every incident in the life of Nero is relevant to the same question about him. To both much more is relevant. For an affirmative answer to either implies the existence of God. And to this question every incident in the history of the world is relevant—whether it is the fall of a sparrow or the coming of harvest, the passing of an empire or the fading of a smile.

Here ends this talk about how in the end questions about God and the Devil are to be answered.

The statement 'There is someone who feeds the cattle upon a thousand hills, who can match the powers of evil and lift up the everlasting doors' is not one to which what is still hidden from us in space and time is all irrelevant. But it seems to me it is not only this that makes the question, 'Is that statement true?' a hard one. It is also the fact that this question calls upon us to consider all that is already before us, in case it should happen that having eyes we see not, and having ears we hear not.

The consideration this question calls for cannot be conducted by a definite step by step procedure like that of one who calculates the height or weight or prospects of life of the average man or the Bengal tiger. Nor is it a question which though it has no answer 'Yes' or 'No' may yet be considered on perfectly conventional lines like the question before the court 'Was there or was there not neglect of duty?' For the statement

'There is one above who gives order and life amongst disorder and death' when taken on perfectly conventional lines is as preposterous as the statement that the sun doesn't move though we see it climb the sky. Nor are the new lines on which the statement is to be taken firmly fixed as they are with 'We are turning to the sun at n m.p.h.' And yet in spite of all this and whatever the answer may be the old question 'Does God exist?' 'Does the Devil exist?' aren't senseless, aren't beyond the scope of thought and reason. On the contrary they call for new awareness of what has so long been about us, in case knowing nature so well we never know her.

Nothing in all this makes less of the call for critical attention, whatever sort of statement we are considering. Nothing in all this makes less of the need to get clear about what we mean by a statement, to get clear as to what we are comparing with what. Just this is called for, just this done, in that statement so obvious yet so preposterous, 'My dear, it's the Taj Mahal.'

CHAPTER FIFTEEN

MAPPING THE LOGIC OF MODELS
IN SCIENCE AND THEOLOGY*

by Frederick Ferré

My purpose in this paper is to show that the notion of the "model,"
which has received considerable attention and stimulated much controversy among scientists and philosophers of science, should be recognized
as of central importance to theologians and philosophers of religion. In
order to reach my goal I shall have to survey and attempt to make at
least roughly intelligible a domain for which there exist few charts and
within which there is as yet little agreement on boundaries, trail mark-
ings, or compass directions. To do a really comprehensive job, such as is
urgently needed, will not be possible within the limitations of an essay;
but if the existence and fertility of the territory can be established and
if a few major landmarks can be plotted with reasonable accuracy, even
a large scale logical map may prove useful.

I

Models and Theories

The term "model" has one fairly common use, found most frequently
among social scientists and psychologists, that is more or less equivalent
to "theory." One word becomes a virtual synonym for the other. Such a
rough and ready way with language, however, will not satisfy our present
needs. It not only conflates what can usefully be distinguished but also
may subtly beg important questions by leading us precritically into what
will later be seen as a particular view of models and their logical role.
Some preliminary formal analysis of "model" is required to set off
models from theories without prejudicing later material analyses.

*Used with permission from *The Christian Scholar*, Vol. 46, No. 1, Spring 1963.

One such formal description of "model" and "theory" is offered by Ernest Nagel, who distinguishes between (1) the "abstract calculus" which provides the logical skeleton of a theory, (2) the "rules of correspondence" which connect the implicitly defined statement-forms of the theory with experience, and (3) the "model" which serves to *provide an interpretation for the abstract theory.*[1] Equipped with these distinctions, Nagel proceeds to use "model" and "interpretation" interchangeably:[2] the statement-forms of a theory's abstract calculus remain devoid of intelligibility until provided with a sense, and that which provides this sense for the theory is its "model." (Nagel should not be misunderstood to be speaking *temporally*. The theory does not necessarily stand first a naked skeleton of statement-forms, later fleshed out by a model. These are stages of analysis, not of development.) But useful as this proposal for the use of "model" and "theory" can be shown to be in many respects, Nagel's analysis has the unfortunate consequence of making every theory separated from a "model" (in his sense) merely a theory-*form*; and once again substantial questions are obscured by making a "model" (i.e. "interpretation") of *some* kind necessary, by definition, for every "theory" that is fully to be a theory.

R. B. Braithwaite avoids this danger by maintaining that the distinction between a model and a theory is properly located in the relative epistemological priority of those higher-level formulae of the calculus that contain theoretical terms.[3] A model and a theory, for Braithwaite as for Nagel, utilize the same formal calculus-skeleton; but for the model it is the *initial* formulae of the calculus that are epistemologically prior (i.e. intuitively clear to us) whereas for the theory it is the *derived* formulae of the calculus that possess this priority, the initial formulae gaining interpretation in reverse order from the order of logical dependence.[4] Given Braithwaite's terminology it is logically possible that a theory may stand in full independence from any model, since it is not a logical necessity, *prima facie* at least, that epistemological and logical priority must parallel one another for the provision of an adequate interpretation for the statement-forms of a theory's calculus. But, on the other hand, it is also perfectly conceivable that operating with the same terminology one might discover reasons for insisting (as Braithwaite does not) that models and theories are somehow essentially linked together by logical, epistemological, or psychological bonds.

Because of the initial neutrality of this formal analysis of the relation of models to theories, I shall make use of it in what follows. A model, let me repeat, is not itself a theory but fits to some extent, or is believed to fit, the same abstract calculus as does the theory; the difference between them resides in the fact that a theory draws the meaning of its initial (or "abstract" or "theoretical") formulae from the meanings of the lower level formulae that have been deduced from those logically prior but epistemologically secondary initial formulae, whereas a model presents the meaning of its high level formulae somehow directly.

Views of Models

Just what it is that makes for this "direct presentation" of meaning—what "models" are, not formally and abstractly but concretely and "in the flesh"—has been the subject of sharp debate and, I am afraid, of much needless misunderstanding. I shall now offer, as data which will have to be drawn together into some kind of order, a sampling of substantive views on this subject.

One familiar and frequently influential view of models has taken them to be essentially mechanical contrivances designed to illuminate, by their working, the meaning of a scientific theory. Lord Kelvin, it is said, complained that he could not frankly consider himself to "understand" a physical theory unless he could build some such mechanical model to illustrate it.[5]

Another view considers models as primarily scale reproductions (larger or smaller) of an object or type of object being studied. The relation between the planets, their sizes, satellites, relative orbits and orbital speeds, and so on, are often shown by a scale model at a planetarium. If it is a working scale model, the theory (for instance) explaining apparent planetary retrograde motion can be made vividly intelligible; but whether or not a scale model also "works" (à la Kelvin), much of value may be learned from it.[6]

Others may mean by "model" only a mental picture of some kind. The late Arthur Pap, for example, comments: "It is a natural tendency of the human mind to think of physical reality as something that can be pictured, on the analogy of the objects of common-sense experience. As a result, physical theories are intuitively satisfactory only if they gain pictorial content through *models*."[7] Supporting Pap's view that models are something essentially picturable are such men as Sir James Jeans, to whose views we shall need to return before long, and the great physicist P. A. M. Dirac who is quoted by Schrödinger as having said in conversation: "Beware of forming models or pictures at all."[8]

A fourth view, cited by physicist and philosopher Henry Margenau, is that models are best understood as "auxiliary concepts"[9] which are more useful for the purposes of theory-construction than of description. This position, Margenau says, holds "that science, released from the bondage of sensory experience, no longer describes reality but makes 'models' of reality which serve only the purpose of explanation and calculation."[10] Such a view, premised on "release" from sensory experience, would seem to involve the "*un*picturability" of models and thus to depart sharply from Pap, Dirac, and Jeans.

Margenau is not alone, however, in recognizing a use of the term "model" for referring to what cannot be pictured. A fifth usage finds "model" equivalent to "analogue," and thus applicable to wholly formal and unpicturable domains of thought. The British philosopher Mary B. Hesse, for example, notes that Riemann's non-Euclidean geometry functioned as an important model for Einstein's general theory of relativity. In light of this and many other similar cases the term "model" may even

mislead: "Sometimes the models used in physics are purely mathematical
in character, and this is why the word *analogue* is generally preferable
to *model*, because the latter may seem to imply something mechanical
or at least picturable."[11] With this position[12] we have moved far
from Kelvin or Dirac, for whom "model" (for better or for worse) *should*
"imply something mechanical or at least picturable."

A sixth conception of "model" finds the essential question not in the
issue of picturability or non-picturability but in the capacity of a model
to focus language drawn from one domain of discourse onto another and
less familiar domain. Max Black supports this view of what he calls "theoretical models" and declares: "the heart of the method consists in *talking* in a certain way."[13] It is this general sort of model with which we
shall be largely—but not exclusively—concerned in the present essay.

Let us, finally, bring to a close this sampling of views on the meaning of "model"—that elusive companion to a theory that somehow brings
epistemological familiarity (for good or ill) to the abstract logical structure
of pure theory—by noticing a striking use of the term by Stephen Toulmin. Toulmin, in his latest book on the philosophy of science, discusses
those broadest understandings that men may have concerning the natural
order. In any such view, Toulmin says, we find some elements that are
taken as simply self-explanatory, basic truths that simply "stand to reason" and on which all other explanations are based. "Such models and
ideals, principles of regularity and explanatory paradigms, are not always
recognized for what they are; differences of opinion about them give rise
to some of the profoundest scientific disputes, and changes in them to
some of the most important transformations of scientific theory . . ."[14]
"Model," here, has obviously come to mean something vastly different
from Lord Kelvin's "rude mechanical models,"[15] Margenau's "auxiliary concept," or Hesse's mathematical isomorphism.

Has this brief excursion revealed nothing but ambiguity and equivocation? Or can we, as map-makers, hope to lay hold of some principles of
projection with the help of which we may discover form and intelligibility
within the logical terrain we have now surveyed? Our next task must be
to develop, if possible, such cartographic tools as may be applicable to
this pursuit.

II

The differences of opinion and usage which we have noted may on inspection be seen to fall into three classes. First, there is a class of questions concerning a model's degree of concreteness—whether a model
must be of a sort to be actually built or may only be pictured or, perhaps, merely be conceived. This class of questions is directed at discovering what I shall call the *type* of a model. Second, there is a class of questions concerning a model's degree of inclusiveness—how much a model
may be supposed to represent: a single entity, a general species of thing
or event, or still wider domains of thought. Here the questions revolve
around what I shall name the *scope* of a model. A model's scope, it will

be noted, does not necessarily depend on its type or *vice versa*. Third, there is a class of questions concerning a model's degree of importance— how highly valued should models be: are they indispensable, dangerous, or may they "be taken or left alone"? This sort of query is concerned with what I shall label the *status* of a model. Judgments of status may, or may not, vary with different attributions of type and scope. Let us now put these distinctions to use in an attempt to sketch in an orderly way the major features of the landscape before us.

Mapping Models in Terms of Type

Some models, as we have seen, may be of a type that permits their being built in the laboratory or the shop. Mechanical models and scale models have already been mentioned. Some scale models are supposed to work, as certain models of steam or gasoline engines; some scale models fortunately do not, as, for instance, the huge model of a locust used in zoölogy lectures. Working models, likewise, may or may not be true to scale. The logically important function of the scale model is to permit spatial relationships to be read off in true proportion; the logically significant function of the working model is to illustrate a process and to permit temporal elements to be read off in true succession. In those cases where one has a scale model that also works, one is given a representation of both spatial and temporal relations. In other, commoner, cases when one has a model either built to scale or built to function mechanically, but not both, the temporal and the spatial proportions of the model, respectively, are logically irrelevant. This notion of "relevance" and "irrelevance," as we shall see throughout the present study, is of critical importance for any logical analysis of models.

Still another kind of model of the type that permits construction may be neither a working model nor a scale model. We are all familiar with the models constructed out of little balls and dowel to illustrate various sorts of molecules and their structure. These models are neither expected to "work" (as in a model steam engine) nor to be true to scale. At the same time, however, they "work" *logically* by offering an epistemological immediacy to the theoretical term "molecule" which, as a term appearing only in the higher level formulae of the calculus-skeleton of the molecular theory, would apart from a model of this or of some other kind have needed to have had its meaning derived much more indirectly.

At this point we find ourselves approaching a type of model which fulfills its function of offering epistemological vividness to that which it represents merely through mental images. It is clear that any model which can be built may also be pictured. The reverse, however, is not so obviously true. Some picturable models may defy construction. Cosmologist Fred Hoyle's "steady-state universe," for example, may with a stretch of imagination be crudely pictured in the "mind's eye": a spheroid blob surrounded by absolutely nothing, in which hydrogen endlessly pops into existence in the center at the same rate at which constantly accelerating galaxies around the edges twinkle out of existence. But such a model could not even conceivably be built in the laboratory shop!

There may, indeed, be some difference of opinion as to whether Hoyle's model can even be a mental picture. Sidestepping this controversy, which is not really important to the typology or to the thesis being presented in this paper, I am brought directly to the most inclusive type of model, within which all previously mentioned types must fall. Here we permit the term "model" to apply to anything that manifests the formal characteristics of a model and *can merely be conceived*. It goes without saying that all models that can be built or pictured must be conceivable; it is not the case that all conceivable models can be pictured or built. It is no doubt on some such ground as this that there are those[16] who warn against taking "picturability" as a defining characteristic of models. That warning is well taken.

Within this most inclusive model-type we find a constrast between "substantive" and "formal" models.[17] The latter group will contain, for example, such models as are drawn from pure mathematics, where, as has frequently been the case in mathematical physics,[18] "the mathematical formalism of one theory can serve as a model for another theory with a more inclusive scope of application than the original one."[19] Here, too, we may find many of Black's "theoretical models," in which a "way of speaking" is of the essence. But theoretical models will not fall exclusively or even for the most part within the class of "formal models." Many of the ways of speaking which serve as models for one domain will be drawn from other, familiar, domains of life and discourse. And all these "substantive models," in contrast to formal models, will be such *because* they have drawn from domains of familiar "filled" experience rather than formal relationship. All constructable or visualizable models are, of course, of the substantive variety, and it is argued by some that all substantive models are at least visualizable.[20] Is this the case? *Most* substantive models will, indeed, be picturable, but an interesting issue is raised by the question whether this is true for *all*. Erwin Schrödinger, for example, urged (some years ago) that irrelevant details simply be eliminated from substantive models of science, and he asserted that this process of selective elimination could be accomplished "without leading to the consequence, that no visualizable scheme of the physical universe whatever will prove feasible."[21] But he went on immediately to acknowledge that one of the first "irrelevancies" to such important theoretical entities as electrons will be "the property of possessing this or that definite color, though common to all perceptible objects . . ."[22] Can the electron be "visualized" as colorless? We can hardly understand the question and still answer affirmatively, but if our answer is negative we shall be forced to admit that at least some substantive models defy our *imagining* if not (*pace* Berkeley) our *conceiving*.

This, however, is a puzzling conclusion, if a model's logical function is somehow to represent something with an epistemological vividness greater than that possessed by the theory! To what extent are we any longer "using a model" when we merely conceive the unimaginable? Is Schrödinger supposing that the *model* of the electron is without color (and thus unvisualizable), or, as seems more likely in context, does he take the model qua model to be fully equipped with some color but "read" or interpreted in such a way that the color aspect of the imagined model is deliberately ignored or suppressed as logically irrelevant? Once again we note the importance of our conventions of interpreting what is relevant, an importance that is underscored by Schrödinger who warns us that "it will be necessary to acquire a definite sense of what is *irrelevant* in our new models and schemes, before we can trust to their guidance with more equanimity and confidence."[23]

The understandings of "model" encountered in our initial sampling have proved to be far from mutually exclusive, at least with respect to type. Instead of spending our energies arguing with Kelvin against Hesse or with Black against Pap, we have discovered certain logical relations of inclusion and subordination among different concepts of model. In place of sheer diversity we have found some degree, at least, of underlying order. Whenever we encounter some use of "model" we shall do well to locate it as precisely as we can within the framework of types we have begun to construct.

Mapping Models in Terms of Scope

A second framework which may be provided our growing logical map of models deals with the extent of a given model's field of application.

At one extreme we find models with scope limited to a single entity like the city of ancient Troy, or the *Friendship Seven*, or the projected North Campus. In these cases the model may serve the function—when correctly interpreted with respect to its logically relevant features—of permitting measurements or manipulations, as well as an immediate mental grasp of the subject matter, which would be difficult or impossible to obtain from the original. It is noteworthy that models of this restricted scope usually have the highest proportion of logically relevant features. A model that represents the *Queen Elizabeth*, for example, will properly be interpreted as offering a great many more "relevant" details than a model representing, say, Cunard liners or twentieth century steamships in general.

In this way we move from models with scope limited to simple entities to models with a scope that is representative of a general class of entities. It is worth noticing that models with general rather than particular scope may in fact also be models of a single entity. A model of the *De Witt Clinton*, for example, may—depending on the context of its "reading," that is, the conventions of its interpretation—stand for the whole class of early steam railroad trains rather than the *Clinton* alone. But, on the other hand, a model with general scope may deliberately be fashioned so as to be unlike any particular member of the class of entities modeled, like the composite airplane appearing on some air mail postage stamps. This practice has the logical effect of emphasizing that the model is not to be interpreted as representing uniquely any single entity of the class within its scope—and thus that a large number of particular features of the model (e.g. the exact angle of slope of the rudder, the position of the cockpit windows, the length of fuselage relative to wingspan, and the like) are logically irrelevant.

It will be evident that my examples, although not drawn from science, have a bearing on the use of models in scientific inquiry. An astronomer may find a model of the moon useful as a model of particular scope, but he may in another context use the same model as representing simply "satellite"—in which case many features of the model that were logically relevant in the first use will become irrelevant in the new "reading." Even more obviously, an astrophysicist who utilizes Bohr's model of the sodium atom to help in his explanation of certain absorption lines in a spectrogram will not "read" his model as having unique reference to a particular atom. He will, instead, consider a great many features of his model as logically irrelevant—including not only (as Schrödinger mentioned) the color he may imagine the electrons to have, but also (as quantum theory insists) the fact that his model's electrons in their "orbits" all may have simultaneously determinable velocity and position.

Widest of all scope, at least for scientific models, is possessed by those models mentioned by Schrödinger as visualizable schemes "of the physical universe" or distinguished earlier by Toulmin as explanatory paradigms for the whole natural order. Models of this breadth of scope are no longer interpreted as representatives of limited classes of entities or events but as "conceptual archetypes"[24,25] for the synthetic organization and the synoptic "seeing" of all that is within the purview of the natural sciences. Once again, however, very simple and particular (as well as esoteric or abstract) phenomena may be chosen to function as models of this most comprehensive sort. Aristotle's model for a "self-explanatory" dynamic principle, drawn from particular common-sense experiences of objects "naturally" at rest when not being pushed or pulled,[26] undergirded much of his thought and significantly, even spread its influence as far in time, space, and subject matter as to the first two of St. Thomas Aquinas' Five Ways of proving the existence of God![27]

Mapping Models in Terms of Status

Any model, such as Aristotle's, that can function in dynamical explanation and in theological speculation is bound to stir philosophical controversy. Controversy, however, surrounds the entire territory we have been engaged in charting. There are those who insist that models are dangerous, others who consider them helpful but inessential, and still others who defend their employment as both rational and crucially important. A final set of conceptual guidelines will be provided for our logical map by an examination of the arguments stated by various sides of this dispute and by our own evaluation of the merits of the cases presented.

The physicist Dirac, we remember, warned Schrödinger against "forming models or pictures at all." And Sir James Jeans advances a case against models which would support that warning. It is perfectly possible, if a model is formally defined as an epistemologically familiar interpretation of a theory's abstract system of logical relations, for *more than one* such model to be found that would perfectly "fit" a single theory. But then, Jeans says, it would be impossible to choose between these models since, *ex hypothesi*, each is unable to be faulted "in the only property by which it could be tested, namely the power of predicting phenomena."[28] The models, however, may be mutually incompatible, though each fits the formal structure of the theory being interpreted. "Neither model could, then, claim to represent reality," Jeans concludes, "whence it follows that we must never associate any model with reality, since even if it accounted for all the phenomena, a second model might appear at any moment with exactly the same qualifications to represent reality."[29]

Why, if models are thus deceptive, have many physicists sought them and worked with them? Jeans explains that pictorial representations come more naturally to human minds than abstract mathematical formulae because "our mental faculties have come to us . . . from fishes and apes."[30] The pressures of survival would have naturally selected for mental traits "more suited to deal with concrete facts than with abstract concepts, with particulars rather than with universals; minds which are more at home in thinking of material objects, rest and motion, pushes, pulls and impacts, then in trying to digest symbols and formulae."[31] Our simian heritage must be overcome, however, for the sake of progress. Physicists may make use of many cognitive techniques: "but the final harvest will always be a sheaf of mathematical formulae."[32] To suppose otherwise is to be deceived by the Neanderthal in modern man. "Beware of forming models or pictures at all!"

Taken together with this case against models and this description of human mentality, it is especially revealing to note Jeans' repeated warnings that "knowledge of reality" or "understanding" of the "loom of things" is impossible for human beings. Apart from the concrete pictures and ideas drawn from sense, he seems to be saying, cognitive satisfaction is not to be had. The "sheaves of mathematical formulae" will be of use in describing our past observations and in predicting future observations, but they are of little use in *understanding*. "We see," Jeans says, "that we can never understand the true nature of reality."[33] Try as we may "to replace unintelligible universals by intelligible particulars,"[34] we shall always fail. Intelligibility tantalizes but always escapes us. Models would serve to provide understanding and intelligibility if only they could be trusted, but—alas!—this is forever beyond our reach.

But is it? Jeans' case against models, though a powerful warning against an uncritical abuse of models, is nevertheless an overstatement in need of modification. The first assumption—that the only way of

choosing between models is in terms of their predictive power—is open
to serious question.[35] Even if this assumption were established, however, it would not follow that *just because* more than one model could
be formulated for a theory, *neither* model could "claim to represent
reality." One of these models might still be supposed to "represent
reality" to the exclusion of its rivals, just as an honest man at a Liar's
Convention might continue to tell the truth though every one of his assertions is countered by a host of incompatible ones. Jeans himself later
modifies his stand when he comes to recapitulate his argument. Instead
of denying models the logical right even to *claim* to represent reality
because of the possible plurality of predictively indistinguishable models,
Jeans merely notes that in this situation: ". . . we should have at least one
perfect model which did not correspond to reality. Thus we *could never
be sure* that any model corresponded to reality."[36] From the outright
denial that a model can represent reality to a warning against undue confidence in the representative power of models is a significant step. It is
in this connection interesting to note that Jeans' earlier conclusion,
"whence it follows that we must never associate any model with reality . . .,"
is not repeated in his later statement of the argument, whence it would
not any longer follow. Instead, a more moderate conclusion is drawn:
"In brief, we can never have certain knowledge as to the nature of
reality."[37]

With this more temperate view, Jeans very nearly approximates the
position of those who, like R. B. Braithwaite, argue that models may
have their uses but that they had better be used cautiously and with the
steady awareness that a model, like alcohol, is a potentially dangerous
luxury. Braithwaite acknowledges that "to think in terms of [a] model
is . . . frequently the most convenient way of thinking about the structure
of [a] theory . . ."[38] But this convenience consists primarily in permitting us to think about a theory without at the same time having to ex-
pend the effort of thinking explicitly about the symbolic structure in
which the theory is expressed. Since the theory's formal structure is
"given" immediately and easily along with the concrete structure of any
model that "fits" it, "the use of models allows of a philosophically un-
sophisticated approach to an understanding of the structure of a scientific
deductive system."[39]

The perils of unsophistication, however, lurk close at hand. Braithwaite is quick to distinguish two such perils which may be serious enough
under some conditions to militate against the use of models at all. They
are, first, that "the theory will be identified with a model for it . . .,"[40]
and, second, that someone will be misled into "transferring the logical
necessity of some of the features of the chosen model on to the theory,
and thus of supposing, wrongly, that the theory, or parts of the theory,
have a logical necessity which is in fact fictitious."[41] Both dangers,
if I may express them in terms that I have introduced earlier, reduce to
forgetting that the model is a model and thus to taking certain of the
model's "logically irrelevant" features (empirical or logical) as "logi-

cally relevant." "Thinking of scientific theories by means of models is always *as-if* thinking," as Braithwaite says. But as long as this is kept in mind, even Jeans is ready to accept some limited use of "pictorial representation." "Although we can never devise a pictorial representation which shall be both true to nature and intelligible to our minds, we may still be able to make partial aspects of the truth comprehensible through pictorial representations or parables. As the whole truth does not admit of intelligible representation, every such pictorial representation or parable must fail somewhere."[42] The main trouble with nineteenth century physics, it turns out, is not (as we might earlier have gathered from Jeans) that models were used *at all* but that the mistake was made "of treating the half-truths of pictorial representations and parables as literal truths."[43]

Even half-truths, however, are better than no-truths—if we can decide which "half" is which! Granting, as Braithwaite says, that "the price of the employment of models is eternal vigilance,"[44] what in general shall we look for to help us exploit the value of models without falling prey to their irrelevancies? There is little use in ordering us to keep our eyes peeled without at the same time describing the colors of friend and foe. Here Jeans, in a far mellower mood than before, becomes explicit. Models can be compared with maps, he says; and just as two-dimensional projections can never tell the *whole* truth about a three-dimensional object, so models are limited to telling partial truths. But maps can be faithful to *aspects* of reality (even though distorting other aspects) and we can, if we are careful, *use a map only for the purposes suited to it*, avoiding the misleading consequences which would follow from taking its logically irrelevant features as logically relevant.

The model of "light as a wave" and the model of "light as a particle" each contains partial aspects of truth, Jeans says. "Neither of these can of course tell the whole truth. In the same way, an atlas may contain two maps of North America drawn on different projections: neither of them will represent the whole truth, but each will represent some aspect of it. An equal area projection, for instance, represents the relative areas of any two regions accurately, but their shapes wrongly, while a Mercator projection represents the shapes rightly, but the areas wrongly. So long as we can only draw our maps on flat pieces of paper, such imperfections are inevitable; they are the price we pay for limiting our maps to the kind that can be bound up in an atlas. The pictures we draw of nature show similar limitations; these are the price we pay for limiting our pictures of nature to the kinds that can be understood by our minds."[45] The important thing, then, is to be aware of which features of a model are functioning, in context, as relevant and which are not; we need to keep in mind, that is, what *kind* of map we are using. It may be that many features will be relevant; it may be that they will be few. In any case we are warned that no sweeping *a priori* assumption that reality must resemble our models will be permitted. Resemblances of many kinds there may be between model and the reality modeled, but "the only resemblance required is that of formal structure."[46]

If a model can be depended upon for no more than formal or structural resemblances, and if a theory, unaccompanied by model, can provide this structural resemblance without raising the danger of subtly introducing irrelevancies and falsehoods into our conceptions of things, might we not be better off without models, despite their limited usefulness as intellectual conveniences? If there were no further logical considerations, this "take them or leave them alone" attitude toward models might be the most rational one to adopt. But there are further points of considerable importance to take into account before drawing any final conclusions about the proper status of models.

A model may be regarded not only as a labor-saving device, with Braithwaite, but also as a heuristic tool of no mean value. One must not overlook the usefulness of models at every stage of the theoretical enterprise. First, models may be of incalculable help in the original process of *suggesting* and *formulating theories.* As Ernest Nagel points out, offering copious historical backing for his claim, "a number of outstanding scientists have been quite explicit about the important role models play in the construction of new theories."[47] But this is only the start of the model's heuristic usefulness. Once a theory has been formulated and its main assumptions clarified with the aid of a model, it still remains for these *assumptions to be explored,* and the model may in this connection *suggest new questions* to be asked about the theory and hint at *new domains* for the theory's application. Nagel offers a good example of this process: "In the historical development of the kinetic theory of gases . . . the model for the theory suggested questions about the ratios of molecular diameters to the distances between the molecules, about various kinds of forces between the molecules, about the elastic properties of molecules, about the distribution of the velocities of the molecules, and so on. Such questions would perhaps never have been raised had the theory been formulated as an uninterpreted set of postulates. But in any case, these questions led to the deduction of a variety of consequences for the theory, some of which served as hints for reformulating experimental gas laws and for recognizing new ones."[48] More even than thus suggesting ways of extending the power of the theories "embedded in them," models may also be useful in offering ideas for *relating theoretical concepts to empirical ones.* Another example or two will help to illustrate this function: "Again, the interpretation of optical theory in terms of waves propagated in a medium invites the association of theoretical expressions referring to the amplitude of waves in the model with the intensity of the illumination; the wave interpretation also suggests the linking of theoretical expressions referring to the interference of waves with the dark lines (or absence of illumination) observed in certain experimentally generated patterns of light and shadow."[49]

But these heuristic functions, important as they are, do not exhaust the logical usefulness of models. There is no longer, I hope, the danger that the employment of models will be contemptuously considered merely

"a prop for feeble minds . . . or a convenient short cut to the consideration of deductive systems . . .,"[50] but it still may not be fully recognized
that models sometimes, as Max Black says, are "not epiphenomena of
research, but play a distinctive and irreplaceable part in scientific investigation. . . ."[51] In what way can this claim be defended?

First, beyond its purely heuristic functions, a model may "contribute
to inclusive systems of explanation"[52] not merely in terms of the
limited domain of a single theory but in terms of its power to relate that
theory plausibly to our whole conceptual account of reality. In this way
a well chosen model may link *widely divergent domains of understanding* in a freshly intelligible way, substituting coherence and unity for
fragmented and partial explanatory systems. Another way of putting this
would be to say that a good model, as a "speculative instrument,"[53]
has the function of helping us "to notice what otherwise would be overlooked, to shift the relative emphasis attached to details—in short to
see new connections."[54]

Second, can this function be shown really to be an "irreplaceable"
part of scientific investigation? Our answer to this will depend on
our view of the essential purposes of science itself. If, with Jeans, we
conclude that "we can never understand what events are, but must
limit ourselves to describing the pattern of events in mathematical
terms . . .,"[55] and that "the study of physics has driven us to the
positivist conception of physics,"[56] in which the functions of science
are reducible to prediction of phenomena, then the importance of models
beyond their heuristic powers will be minimized. But if, as I believe, the
aim of science is not merely prediction but also *understanding*, then it
will turn out that "science progresses, not by recognizing the truth of
new observations alone, but by making sense of them."[57] For this,
models are needed to supplement theories serving as bare techniques
for predicting. Even Jeans recognizes the presence of this wish for "making sense" of observations—while denying any possibility of its fulfillment—when he notes: ". . . we not only wish to predict phenomena, but
also to understand them. Thus it is not surprising that philosophy and
science alike have found this [predictionist] mathematical description
unsatisfying . . ."[58] Grant science the function of making sense of
phenomena, illuminating data, searching for understanding of reality,
and models achieve a cognitive status of their own which defies replace-
ment by the abstract calculi of theoretical constructs. Only at the price
of shrinking science from what it is—a humane and imaginative attempt
at rigorous understanding of wide domains of being—into a cramped
technique for anticipating impacts on the senses, can one suppose that
models are "disreputable understudies for mathematical formula."[59]

We are well warned, by those who consider the status of the model
to be primarily a dangerous incitement to metaphorical thinking, against
approaching the use of a model literally, expecting the wrong things from
it; we are also well warned, by those who look at models as primarily
convenient luxuries, against adopting models uncritically being lured off

into pseudo questions by logical irrelevancies. But we are now prepared to proceed, vigilantly but aware that models can add great power to our cognitive pursuits, with the knowledge that, risky or not, models put a tool in our hand for understanding what, without models, may remain opaque. And for the sake of understanding as best we can—within all our human limitations—we should perhaps be willing to take even serious risks.

III

I shall assume for the purposes of this essay that theology, like science, is interested in understanding—as far as may be humanly possible—the reality in which men find themselves. This is not, of course, an uncontroversial assumption; there are those who deny that theology is even *concerned* with cognitive questions, quite part from her success or lack of it in answering them. Against this point of view, whether resting on philosophical or theological grounds, 1 have elsewhere[60] argued at some length, but I shall not repeat those arguments here. Instead, let me simply note that a faith unconcerned with cognitive issues is emasculated. It is well for theologians to remind their critics (and their churches) that faith is not reducible without vastly important residue to cognitive assent given various propositional elements; but this salutary warning against the *reduction* of faith to "mere belief" must not be confused with an *elimination* of belief from faith. Without the retention of some element of belief, the theologian is required to abandon any pretense to interest in truth or falsity; he is forced to give up any chance of giving point or justification to his attitudes, emotions, utterances, or behavior; and he is condemned, as a purveyor of one more item of personal taste, to isolation from the determinative issues of life—toward which, ironically, his faith prompts him to speak with "the wisdom of serpents"—an isolation no less complete for its being self-imposed.

Assuming, then, that theology is not indifferent to truth about reality, it becomes relevant to ask whether there are models in theology as well as in science and, if so, how they should be related to other models on our logical map.

Finding the Models of Theology

If we continue to understand by "model" that which provides epistemological vividness or immediacy to a theory by offering as an interpretation of the abstract or unfamiliar theory-structure something that both fits the logical form of the theory and is well known, we shall find models in abundance within theology. In a very straightforward sense, every parable (as Jeans hinted in quite a different connection) is a model: " 'Listen! A sower went out to sow. And as he sowed, some seed fell along the path, and the birds came and devoured it. Other seed fell on rocky ground . . .' And he said to them, 'Do you not understand the parable? How then will you understand all the parables? The sower sows the word. And these are the ones along the path, where the word is sown; when they hear, Satan immediately comes and takes away the word which is sown in them. And these in like manner are the ones sown upon rocky ground...' "[61] Here is an epistemological vividness offered by imagery drawn from common experience, but imagery which is deemed appropriate because it shares a common logical structure with a theory that can be duly stated, independent of the model, to a few initiated disciples. "Here is how you may *think* about it, if you like...; but here is how it *really* is...," is a frequently repeated pattern, and not only in Western religions. The open and abundant use of models, analogues, similitudes, seems to be an entrenched part of the religious mentality.

But clearly labeled uses, as in parables, are not exhaustive of the uses of models within theology. Within Christian thought, for example, there has been a long established practice of searching the scriptures for covert models of theologically significant figures or events. The many "types of Christ," for example, allegedly found by fundamentalist and pre-critical—or, interestingly, by some of the very newest and most so-phisticated[62]—biblical scholarship are noteworthy here. Jonah's "three days and three nights in the belly of the fish," to choose but one crude ex-ample, has been taken as a model of Jesus' three days in the tomb. And in this sort of searching for significant models we may be discovering the quest for a unity and coherence in the biblical account as a whole which can bring together into a simple focus what might otherwise seem a sheer, vast multiplicity. Looking at one thing, and without in any way failing to see it in itself, many other things are seen as well. Finding or forming models in this sense of underlying patterns of structure within his religious tradition may help the believer see new connections within his data. And such "seeing" through models, by giving his theological be-leifs increased internal coherence, may strengthen the believer's sense of the intelligibility of his faith.

That this sense of intelligibility is illusory, however, apart from ad-ditional external relations of coherence between the cognitive context of faith and all established knowledge was one of the most important em-phases of the liberal theological movement of the nineteenth and early twentieth centuries; and it remains the one permanently valid contribu-tion of all "rational theologies," despite their many notorious defects. It is with respect to this domain of theological interest—interest in cognitive ties with all knowledge and in beliefs about reality that can be simply *true* or *false*, rather than "true within a certain 'language game'" —that we discover another sort of employment of theological models, most conveniently called the metaphysical use of models or, for short, "metaphysical models." When the Judeo-Christian scriptures set about representing the nature of ultimate reality, this enterprise is not ap-proached through abstract theory but through epistemologically vivid stories and anthropomorphically immediate images. Ideas drawn from one area of experience are put to work in another area—an area in which, we are explicitly warned, these ideas have no proper place. The keystone of the biblical ontological scheme, the concept of God, is beyond human conception: "His ways are not our ways, nor His thoughts our thoughts." But in spite of such reminders, the theoretical term "God" is constantly interpreted in terms of epistemologically vivid personal models. The very warnings against supposing our concepts of God to be literally represent-ative are themselves couched in the language of the model: the per-sonal *His*, the anthropomorphic attribution of *thoughts* to God. Even when, in the second of the Ten Commandments, the people of Israel are warned against making themselves *graven* images of God ("He Who Is," beyond images), or of forming "any likeness of anything that is in heaven above, or that is in the earth beneath, or that is in the water under the earth,"[63] the same commandment relies on forming *verbal* images of God and offering the epistemological "likeness" of human passions as a justification for this prohibition: ". . . for I the Lord your God am a jeal-ous God, visiting the iniquity of the fathers upon the children to the third and fourth generation of those who hate me, but showing stead-fast love to thousands of those who love me and keep my command-ments."[64] Models, and warnings that what we have to think with *are* models; epistemological vividness, coupled with vehement affirmations of human ignorance before ultimate reality as it is in and for itself—this is the ambivalent approach of biblical religion.[65]

The dominant attitude of biblical faith is not nescience, however, but a sense of understanding. The models are *trusted* even when recognized as images and likenesses of a reality that stands beyond human powers of imagining or comparing. And for Christians, of course, the models of the Old Testament—however helpful or even essential—all take second place to what they believe to be the one supremely reliable model for God, Jesus of Nazareth. In looking at one thing, a human life of a cer-tain quality and with certain specifiable empirical characteristics, they are given a concrete interpretation of the abstract concept, "God," that is totally without the epistemological immediacy of the model. One of the tasks of the church, we may note, has been the difficult one of dis-tinguishing between what are properly to be taken as "logically relevant" and "logically irrelevant" features of this supreme personal image of ultimate reality. Their problem has been how rigorously to interpret the key epistemological statement of the New Testament: "He who has seen me has seen the Father; how can you say, 'show me the Father'?"[66] Every christological formulation that takes that statement seriously is, whether consciously or not, a study in epistemology and an exercise in model-reading.

Christian faith does not abandon the Old Testament, however, and because of this it has avoided the temptation to reduce the meaning of "God" to any single one of its models, including its supreme model. In-stead, the great numbers of epistemologically immediate images, stories, and anthropomorphic conceptions of scripture are blended together into a panoramic mosaic picture of reality including God, man, and nature. This is a picture shot through, as we have seen, with unifying strands

based on master models; it is a picture with a definite place for everything under the supreme sovereignty of a personal God; and it is a picture of the world which, if taken as literally descriptive either in terms
of the mosaic-bits which make it up or in respect of its "three storey"
world-picture as a whole, is unquestionably false—to the consternation
of Rudolf Bultmann and his "demythologizing" followers. But if this
composite picture, what we may call the biblical model of reality or the
biblical metaphysical model, is properly taken *as a model*, it may be
that the very *falsity* of its empirical pseudo claims falls into that "half"
of all such "half-truths" which *should be read as logically irrelevant*.
Perhaps, we may find, theological metaphysical models do not function
as rivals to the models of empirical science.

Mapping the Models of Theology

How shall we locate the models, particularly the metaphysical models,
of theology in terms of the triple conceptual framework we constructed
earlier? It will help to sharpen our understanding of them to plot their
position in terms of type, scope, and status.

First, as to type, it is clear that the models of theology are not of a
sort that *must* be constructed. We have already noted an explicit Old
Testament prohibition against such attempted constructions, and although this commandment is not felt by Christians to stand in the way
of religious art, the fact remains that the Jews have shown that biblical
models can function perfectly well without overt portrayal of this kind.
At the same time, however, the very existence of artistic representations
of biblical imagery in sculpture, painting, stained glass, and the like,
proves that we are not dealing with that type of model—at least in all
aspects—which logically defies pictorial representation. The vigorously
anthropomorphic Father God in Michelangelo's great "Creation," for
example, should not properly be an object of embarrassment to the theological purist; on the contrary, the rugged vitality of Michelangelo's
bearded patriarch is magnificently in keeping with a biblical logic which
glories in anthropomorphism. The purist who squirms at anthropomorphism in his religious conceptions might well listen to Feuerbach's crusty
truth: "He who dreads an existence that may give offence, who shrinks
from the grossness of a positive predicate, may as well renounce existence altogether. A God who is injured by determinate qualities has not
the courage and strength to exist."[67]

It might, however, be misleading to leave the impression that all
"determinate" qualities are visualizable ones. "Picturing" language is
sometimes rather loosely used. Sometimes it is said that one can "picture
how Harry must have felt." But if more is meant by this than that one
can visualize facial expressions, gestures, and the like, associated with
certain feelings, the metaphor of the "mind's eye" is being stretched
rather far. Theological models, likewise, may be considered of the essentially "picturable" type only by an extended metaphor. The emotions of
jealously or love cannot be pictured, strictly speaking, but they can be

imagined. And in this sense we shall classify the bulk of biblical meta-physical models as substantive-conceptual in type.[68] Within this type, as we saw earlier, there may be models open to imagination but not to visualization, models open to visualization but not to construction, and models open to construction as well as to conception and visualization. All the important models of biblical religion are to be found here, from the clearly labeled parables of Jesus to the overarching composite biblical model of reality as a whole, despite the presence in the Bible of some models which may be considered "formal" (note the importance of the numbers "seven" or "three") but which are definitely subordinated within the substantive mosaic biblical model taken as a unity.

Next, turning from type to scope, we see at once that although there may be models of different degrees of appropriate extension within the-ology, the key metaphysical model of reality possesses the widest possi-ble degree of application and relevance. There is nothing in principle, beyond the scope of the biblical model of nature, man, and God. The function of this model, indeed, would seem to be that of laying down guidelines for what may be counted as being real! Therefore anything counted by Christians as real will—must, a priori—fall within the scope of this model.

A consequence of this unlimited scope of the biblical metaphysical model[69] is the notorious unfalsifiability of theological concepts.[70] It would take us too far afield from models to the workings of theological theory itself to explore this issue in detail, but it may quickly be seen that a model which is taken to include, in principle, all real or possible events, cannot be disproved by any real or possible event that comes to pass. It has already, in germ, accounted for anything that might occur, and accounted for it within an interpretative framework that cannot possibly be tested independently of the framework, since any test—and any outcome of that test—that is real or possible is already accounted for within the framework! The adequacy of the "fit" of theological models with respect to whatever structure reality as a whole may have, then, is not able to be tested through straightforward empirical criteria; and it is seriously questioned by many whether any tests at all are pos-sible. Max Black, for example, warns that the widest models may be-come "permanently insulated from empirical disproof," and that the con-sequence of this development is the model's becoming "a self-certifying myth."[71] But it is not necessarily the case that "open to empirical dis-proof" or "self-certifying myth" are, as Black here assumes, the only viable alternatives. To explore this question further here is impossible, since any methods of testing models—including metaphysical models—are inseparable from the theories with which the models are associated, and this additional question must remain beyond the reach of the present study.[72]

Touching even briefly on this falsification controversy, however, brings us inevitably to the question of the status of theological models. What importance or value do they have?

Such a question always demands the counter-question: "Value *for what?*" To begin most narrowly, the biblical metaphysical model provides theology with the possibility of offering intelligible interpretations for its lesser parables and models. We have noted earlier that a parable is of the form: "Here is how you may think about it, if you like . . .; but here is how it *really* is . . ." What is it, though, that the interpreter of the parable must put in place of his parabolic imagery? He is forced back upon more imagery, perhaps of wider scope and different emotional impact than before, but imagery none the less. Jesus' parables of "The Kingdom" substitute homely likenesses for more august ones, but *likenesses* of one sort or another are not avoided: certain characteristics drawn from a mustard tree or a pearl of great price are used to bring into vivid focus certain others drawn from the human experience of living in great societies under the reign of kings. Of course this divine "King" will be "ruler" of all creation who will be "just," "merciful," "slow to anger," "aware of and concerned about his lowliest subject," and so on—he will be far superior to any king actually experienced and his Kingdom will be far more wonderful than any earthly kingdom ever known—but the dependence on some form of the personal root model will remain vital to the interpretation of any lesser model or figure of speech. In terms of the intra-theological interpretation of theological parable, then, we discover that the metaphysical theological model has an essential status.

This point must be generalized, however; for not only are the models of theology essential for interpretation of theological discourse within the language using community but—at least equally important—these models are necessary for the expression of religious beliefs to the world at large. Apart from concepts intelligible to human minds, theology remains empty of meaning to friend and foe—as well as to the theologian himself! And it is in the *models* of theological theory, not in abstract theory itself, that all intelligible theological ideas are rooted. Let us briefly, without plunging deeply into the nature of theological theory as distinct from models, consider why this must be.

First, it might be supposed that theology could rest content with giving its theoretical terms ("God," "Christ," "the world," and the like) merely *implicit* definitions, that is, definitions reflecting the logical relations of these terms within the abstract calculus of the theory. To this we may reply that implicit definitions of this kind can always be provided within an uninterpreted formal system, but such definitions remain purely formal. On the basis of implicit definitions it is possible to construct well-formed formulae of the system in question (e.g. "God was in Christ reconciling the world to Himself"), but this turns out to be no more than the manipulation of empty tokens. The apparent intelligibility of such formulae is due to the model by which we habitually interpret these terms. Shorn of its model-evoking terms, the resulting formula (e.g. "A was in B relating C asymmetrically to A") would more accurately reflect the emptiness of a theology attempting to depend on nothing but implicit or syntactical definitions.

But, second, the theoretical terms of a scientific theory may be given a meaning indirectly and without a model by the expedient of our working back from the theory's lower level experimental formulae to the higher level theoretical formulae of which the former are logical consequences. May this not be done in theology? No, it may not; and the reason for the theologian's inability to define his higher level formulae indirectly in terms of the particular observation-statements they entail and exclude is the fact, briefly noted above, that theological systems cannot be falsified by any observation-statement. If they cannot be thus falsified, they cannot be supposed to entail any particular observation-statements; for if they did so entail only particular abservation-statements, the empirical discovery of such statements to be false would be tantamount, by *modus tollens*, to a falsification of the theological system. It may be argued that the theologian's difficulty is due to the fact that his system entails *every possible* observation-statement. But this, if so, would have the same net logical result, with respect to the present question, as if his system entailed *no* observation-statement, since no particular empirical meaning can be derived for the system in either case, and that which means nothing in particular is no better off than that which means nothing at all! Theological models provide the particularity of concept that would otherwise be missing from theology.

Even the theologian's technical vocabulary is not so independent of his model as he might think. Is. "God's transcendence" under discussion? An analyst need not look far before he finds the thinly disguised spatial metaphor that underlies this term. Everywhere the model peeps through, and it is more difficult than many realize to be rid of it and still to *say the same thing* that was intended before. "Transcendent? That means above the universe. Above? Well, not really above, but *beyond*. Beyond? No, not in space—but simply not exclusively in the universe. *In* . . .?"

Is this merely a difficulty, or is it a logical necessity that without his model the theologian simply cannot say what he wants to say without a change of meaning? That is, is it a logical necessity that the theologian must depend on the model? I have been trying to show that models are necessary in terms of the cognitive enterprise of the theologian, and I think the case is sound. But whether or not I have been correct in my argument so far, the injection of non-cognitive dimensions of meaning into the question should tip this balance quite independently of the previous logical considerations. For it is without doubt the imagery of the models in theology which evoke the communal adoration, obeisance, awe, devotion, ecstacy, courage—the emotive and conative dimensions of faith that constitute it *religious faith* rather than philosophical speculation or metaphysical system-building. I am not claiming that imagery alone can support such non-cognitive elements—courage without *belief* that courage is appropriate in the situation is something less than courage!—but it is precisely because the models of faith are taken as trustworthy, that is, believed to be in some sense true, that their non-cognitive functions are possible. Toward a theory without the vividness and immediacy provided by the biblical model, however, such responses could never be expected; and without the language of the model, having the power to bring together and to intertwine domains of personal value and of ontological plenitude in emotional as well as cognitive relation, distinctively religious dimensions of meaning could not be expressed by the believer.

The status of metaphysical models in theology, then, is essential, since it turns out that the presence of these models is a necessary condition[73] of theological meaning and belief. But to what extent, we may still ask, is theology itself essential? Models may be of the greatest importance to theology, but of what importance is theology to us?

There can be no simple answer to this question, and a full answer would be too much to undertake here. I shall make only two brief and unsupported points. First, theology is at least no worse off, in epistemological principle, than rival metaphysical systems. Every metaphysic relies, no less than the theological metaphysic, on its own model; and in its long history the personal model of biblical faith has proved itself not only highly evocative, non-cognitively, but also an interpretative tool with claims to real cognitive power. Second, it must be acknowledged that metaphysical beliefs are indeed useless in connection with the scientific enterprise of solving empirical problems or with prediciting and controlling the world. Thus, if human life can be lived to its full entirely with reference to the anticipation and the manipulation of one's environment, then metaphysics—and with it theology on its cognitive dimension—is without importance and the status of metaphysical models may be reckoned low. *If*, on the other hand, man is more than a tool-user and a problem-solver, *if* his yen for understanding first principles and his thirst for searching out the most nearly intelligible and the most nearly reliable notion of the ultimate nature of things is inexpungeable —*if* these characteristics are constitutive of man (and these are not questions invulnerable in principle to empirical testing, though the tests would be extremely difficult and time-consuming), then theology, as one candidate for metaphysical truth, is potentially of the greatest possible importance. And if there are those who find full contentment in tool-using and problem solving, for whom the vast speculations and unsettleable disputes of metaphysicians are only a waste of precious time, they are asked to be tolerant toward those others to whom these questions seem the very stuff of life. Grasshoppers, as well as ants, must live as best they can.

IV

We have now reached the point in this study where I can bring the models of science and theology into a single focus. In order to make this possible I have attempted to impose some definite form on the protean concept of "model" in general, with particular emphasis on the fields of science, wherein the notion is most often encountered; and I have attempted to chart the location and logical character of models for the field of theology, wherein they are seldom explicitly acknowledged at all. Now, taking readings from the conceptual map with which we have provided ourselves, let us attempt to determine the distances, relative positions, and topographical relations of these models, which, in both fields, we have descovered to be useful *instruments for understanding*.

Reading off Common Features of the Models in Science and Theology

There are certain features shared by scientific and theological models by virtue of their being models that no longer need detailed reviewing here: e.g. that any model *models something else* to better or worse effect, that any model is offered *within a context* and *for a purpose*, that these purposes even for the same model may not always be the same in different contexts, that different purposes lead to different characteristics of models being taken as "logically relevant" or "irrelevant," that models have heuristic value in formulating theories, that any use of models involves certain risks, and so on. More interesting now are certain particular consequences of these general constitutive characteristics of models as they make themselves analogously felt in the two fields.

James Clerk Maxwell, working scientist, made some perceptive comments on scientific models (he calls them "physical hypotheses") which, with certain significant exceptions, could almost be echoed in somewhat modified language by a working theologian. I shall reproduce his words, quoted by Max Black, as a basis for discussion. "The first process therefore in the effectual study of the science must be one of simplification and reduction of the results of previous investigation to a form in which the mind can grasp them. The results of this simplification may take the form of a purely mathematical formula or of a physical hypothesis. In the first case we entirely lose sight of the phenomena to be explained; and though we may trace out the consequences of given laws, we can never obtain more extended views of the connections of the subject. If, on the other hand, we adopt a physical hypothesis, we see the phenomena only through a medium, and are liable to that blindness to facts and rashness in assumption which a partial explanation encourages. We must therefore discover some method of investigation which allows the mind at every step to lay hold of a clear physical conception, without being committed to any theory founded on the physical science from which that conception is borrowed, so that it is neither drawn aside from the subject in pursuit of analytical subtleties, nor carried beyond the truth by a favorite hypothesis."[74]

First, then, a model *simplifies* the data at hand "to a form in which the mind can grasp them." And if this is important within a branch of science, how much more pressing still must be the importance of this possibility for a theology which hopes to bring meaning and order to the "scheme of things entire"—including not only all the data and all the conclusions of all the sciences but also all the realms of value, obligation and aspiration felt by men! The theologian, like the scientist, is justly grateful for his model.

But both, second, need to be wary since models permit this simplification by requiring their users to "see the phenomena only through a medium." A model may be useful—may even be indispensable for many purposes—but it is not the same thing as what it models. A model filters the facts. And the temptation to forget this because of the values of the model can become great, great enough to deprive the user of the model of appropriate humility before his own intellectual powers and before the realities mediated by his model. Both scientists and theologians frequently stress the virtues of humility and the serious consequences to those who become "wise in their own conceits." And it is interesting to note that the greatest among scientists and theologians have been more prone to take these warnings seriously in their own work than have their lesser followers or men in the street. The creative scientist is usually well aware of how far his models fall short of exhausting his subject matter, and the sensitive theologian is sharply conscious of the truth in the ancient *via negativa* which stands over against all his affirmations, however needful and trustworthy they may be.

This means, third, that the reliance upon models in either of these fields demands that we learn how to employ an epistemologically immediate conception "without being committed to any theory founded on the [domain] from which that conception is borrowed." The physicist must not permit himself to become *committed* to the point by point relevance of the theory of wave-dynamics, when he is studying the behavior of light, even though the theory is fully established in its own domain. He must remember that the conception of the wave is still a borrowed conception and that however fruitful it may be in its new application it remains a model. Conversely the theologian needs to resist supposing that because elements in the models he uses have a domain in which they would properly be taken as empirical propositions (e.g. "the bush was burning, yet it was not consumed") he needs, *ipso facto*, to be committed to the primitive theories and physical conceptions reflected in that domain. A well confirmed theory in one domain may prove a very good—or a very poor—model in another domain; and, likewise a poorly confirmed or even a positively disconfirmed theory may find new life as a model in another domain. The logic of a conception used as a model must be distinguished from its logic—its usefulness, degree of confirmation, truth-value, and so on—when it is used in its own proper domain. Both theologians and scientists will gain maximum value from their models, then, when with the benefits of *simplification* from seeing their subject matter *through the medium* of a model, they combine a conscious *freedom from commitment to* any theory grounded in the model's original domain.

Lurking behind our use of models, whether as scientists or as theologians, there may be some question as to the degree of actual correspondence between our model and what it models. This is no less true for theologians than for scientists. Jeans, we have seen, discourages the scientist from expecting such correspondence; Braithwaite, agreeing, asserts that "thinking of scientific theories by means of models is always *as-if* thinking . . .,"[75] and Toulmin adds, "to think that A *is* B is one thing, to think of A *as* B is another. . . ."[76] The relation, as we have seen, between model and subject is not identity. Still, as Black points out: "we pin our hopes upon the existence of a common structure in both fields."[77] May the "structure" hoped for in common be more than *logical* structure alone? May scientists and theologians hope for some kind of imaginatively accurate representation of this subject matter through their models? In some cases the answer is plainly negative, when there are convincing grounds in principle that prevent even conceiving such a model without contradiction. A familiar case of this sort in science has to do with the theoretical impossibility of producing an imaginative model that can be supposed to correspond to the electron.[78] And a similar theological case would be with respect to the theoretical impossibility of "visualizing accurately" and *ex hypothesi* invisible God. In other cases, where there are no reasons to judge one way or the other, it would be foolhardy to make an assertion either way. Certainly one's sense of the explanatory power of a model is enchanced by one's supposition that it may be "quite a lot like" that which it models, but where there are no grounds there can be no cognitively relevant judgment.

In still other cases, however, it may be possible to test a scientific model against its original. Nothing stands in the way *in principle* of observing directly the molecules of gases that are now modeled as little elastic pellets like billiard balls. Perhaps more powerful electron microscopes will one day permit a point for point comparison of billiard balls and simple molecules. Then the scientist will know just how accurate or how inaccurate his models have been. And he will need his billiard ball model far less than before. At this point, however, we take leave of the features shared by scientific and theological models and begin to notice points of divergence between them. These similarities have perhaps been instructive; the divergences may be no less so.

Reading off Divergent Features of the Models in Science and Theology

Previously, in examining the status of theological models, we noted the dependence of theology on its models—particularly on the key composite biblical model of ultimate reality—for the very statement of distinctively theological dimensions of meaning and belief. The model, we say, is a *necessary condition* of theological theory. This dependence, not shared by scientific theories, leads to a consequence which was not pursued earlier. Cognitive assent cannot be given to theological theories alone, stripped of their models, as can be done (in principle at least) for scientific theories which in Maxwell's earlier-quoted words "may take the form of a purely mathematical formula" rather than the form of a "physical hypothesis" or model. Any act of cognitive assent to theology's claims will have a necessary reference to theology's model of reality. But cognitive assent to a claim, P, incorporating P into one's scheme of things, is equivalent to affirming that P is *true*. Thus, since every theological truth-claim has a necessary involvement in the key theological model, the *model* in this sense must be judged true or false if any theological statements at all are judged true or false. This is not usually supposed to be the case with respect to scientific models, which are termed "fruitful" or "misleading," and the like, but not "true or false." Theological models, however, are of the essence for theology, and any attempt to withhold the notion of truth from these models is in effect a move to deny theology the right to deal in truth or falsity at all.

Theological models, however, cannot justly be judged with respect to truth or falsity apart from the theories that articulate them, interpret them, and relate them to other cognitive domains, i.e. that provide the conventions for "reading" them cognitively. Here we have moved out, once again, to the edge of the subject matter to be dealt with in the present study, but it will at least be noticed that if theories in theology are never intelligible or true *qua* theological theories without models, so theological models do not function (cognitively, at least) without some theory, however implicit or however crude.

A further difference which may be startling to those accustomed to the high rate of turn-over among the models of science is the remarkable resistance to change exhibited by theological models. The situation in this respect is reversed in the two fields. For science, models are altered, discarded, or replaced with relatively little compunction as knowledge increases and the demands of theory develop. The highest level theoretical constructions, however, are tampered with only when absolutely necessary—and then reluctantly, since altering the prime theories of a science can bring about a major scientific revolution that may sweep away the patient labors put in by many over long periods of time. For theology, theories on the interpretation and the linking up of models to other areas of thought are abandoned or replaced in the light of increasing knowledge far more readily than are the models themselves. And the highest level models, those at key positions within the overarching model of reality, are defended at all costs—defended most bitterly against the prophetic personalities who are usually the very ones who best succeed in altering the fundamental religious models—in the knowledge that a change in model signals a religious revolution that may sweep away that which has received the devotion of multitudes over the ages.

The logical characteristic which may account for this interesting reversal is the difference between the *scope* for scientific and theological models. Theological models, sharing the unlimited inclusiveness of all metaphysical models, are in a limited sense "above change." Their empirically unfalsifiable character makes of them not necessarily "self-certifying myths" in all respects (since theological models *do* change and religions *are* reformed—and abandoned), but it does free them from the kind of forced change that is both the despair and the glory of the sciences.[79] Just as a mountain of experimental data cannot move a mustard-seed of faith, so scientific conclusions and models of limited scope, cannot by themselves threaten or support theology. The science *versus* religion conflicts of yesteryear, on which we may now bring this study to a close, rested, most commentators now agree, on a mistake.

But what was the mistake and on whom did it rest? The answer to this question is not so simple or straightforward as is sometimes assumed, inasmuch as exclusive responsibility cannot be thrown onto either the scientist or the theologian and inasmuch as the mistake itself is less garish than are the colors in which it is sometimes painted.

Essentially, theologians and scientists both misinterpreted the logic of theological models, "reading" them as empirical assertions which could be (and were, on this interpretation, in fact being) disconfirmed in just the way appropriate to the assertions of astronomy, geology, or the like. Both must share responsibility for the error. But there are mitigating circumstances often unrecorded by modern analysts: the theories associated with theological models still tended to encourage just the error that was made, and it was only later, thanks largely, no doubt, to the way in which theological models refused to "stay falsified," but could endlessly bounce back from every scientific victory, that the logic of theological affirmations began to come clearer to all sides of the dispute.

To compound the situation, the logical status of the scientist's own assertions were also not altogether clear to either of the contending parties. Just as theologians needed to learn that their statements of universal scope were not designed to rival the function of the scientist's limited and empirically confirmable propositions, so scientists required a warning against supposing that their carefully controlled and empirically specific statements could be set to work as propositions having unlimited scope and in competition with theology's—*while remaining scientific statements*.[80] If a sentence bred in science's neatly fenced pasture wanders off to frolic in metaphysics' Elysian Fields, it had better expect to receive new brand-markings!

Here, then, is a more complex picture than is normally offered. Scientific models and theories can, it seems, be metamorphosed into world-hypotheses of unlimited scope and thus become genuine metaphysical rivals (or allies) of theological models and theories. And the latter, while not entailing any specific empirical consequences or permitting straightforward empirical falsification can never be indifferent to scientific conclusions, since they have as one of their most important cognitive functions the simplification and bringing into coherence of all knowledge.

It was a mistake for scientists and theologians to have battled so hard over, say, the theory of evolution. Yes, but it was a mistake with many levels to be untangled. Theologians were wrong to argue, *qua* theologians, for the immutability of biological species; but scientists were equally wrong to argue, qua scientists, that the evolutionary model, once scientifically established, could take the place of the God of theism.[81]

Both these questions must be argued with appropriate tools and on appropriate grounds. The concept of fixed species may be better or worse biology than the concept of mutating species, but to determine which is the case biological and paleontological arguments, not metaphysical ones, are appropriate; the model of a personal deity may or may not be better metaphysics than the model of an evolutionary universe, but to guide our choice metaphysical arguments, not biological or paleontological ones, are required.

These points may help to place in logical focus the tensions which still may be found between science and religion—enlightened men in both fields knowing that they *ought* not to have any conflicts with the "other side," and yet finding grounds for anxiety or relief in pronouncements made or conclusions published. To a certain extent it is legitimate and even essential for theologians to be concerned about the models and theories of the sciences. Not only is it theology's job to offer (ideally) a conceptual synthesis containing all such models and theories but it may be that new models of great scope being developed by scientists may offer cognitive support or challenge. Where there is a challenge it will usually be found that the challenger is attempting to replace the theological model with the claim to do the cognitive job of the biblical picture of reality but to do it more adequately. And when there is support it will usually be found that the model taken by the theologian as promising support will do so by providing the theological model with new theoretical ties to other domains of established knowledge, these new semantical connections thus increasing the power of the biblical model to do its cognitive job more effectively than before. When a new model appears in field-theory, for example, the theologian may adopt it as part of the interpretative net surrounding his model and may draw upon it to help explicate that primary model and to draw coherent relations between it and other bodies of knowledge. "Perhaps *this* is what Christian faith means by 'man's freedom,' " a theologian might say, "man's behavior and choices determined by a *field* of forces responsibly controlled but not mechanically compelled. . . ." As such the scientific model (no longer used scientifically in any sense) becomes subordinate to the key biblical model itself, but it may thus function for theology with considerable importance. Unfortunately, it may acquire such importance to the theologian that when scientists, who have in the meantime hurried on, tell him that the model is "on the way out" or that it is being replaced or radically altered in its own domain, the theologian may feel threatened and thus be tempted to argue against the scientists—far over his depths and floundering, but properly subject more to compassion than to ridicule. And so the weary science-religion conflict goes on.

My paper, for want of existing maps to follow, has had to make its own way through the underbrush. I hope that this initial exploration has not distorted its subject matter any more horribly than did the quaint old maps of Greenland or Africa now resting, peacefully, in antique shops. But even they, for all their faults, once served a purpose, until other expeditions and other catographers returned to correct their errors. Similarly, this venture will have served its main intended function if it can attract others to see—and to improve—for themselves. Maps, after all, are logically no more than models. And models, we have learned, are to be taken as sacred only in theology.

FOOTNOTES

1. Ernest Nagel, *The Structure of Science: Problems in the Logic of Scientific Explanation* (New York: Harcourt, Brace & World, 1961), Ch. 5.

2. Cf. *ibid.*, pp. 90, 95, 96, 107, etc.

3. R. B. Braithwaite, *Scientific Explanation: A Study of the Function of Theory, Probability and Law in Science* (London: Cambridge University Press, 1953), Chapter IV.

4. Cf. *ibid.*, pp. 89-90.

5. For a specific case, cf. Nagel, *op. cit.*, p. 114.

6. Cf. Max Black's discussion of scale models in his *Models and Metaphors* (Ithaca: Cornell University Press, 1962), pp. 220-221.

7. Arthur Pap, *An Introduction to the Philosophy of Science* (Glencoe: The Free Press, 1962), p. 355.

8. Erwin Schrödinger, *Science and the Human Temperament* (translated by J. Murphy and W. H. Johnston), (New York: W. W. Norton Co., 1935), p. 160.

9. Henry Margenau, *The Nature of Physical Reality. A Philosophy of Modern Physics* (New York: McGraw-Hill Book Co., Inc., 1950), pp. 44-46.

10. *Ibid.*, p. 45.

11. Mary B. Hesse, *Science and the Human Imagination* (London: SCM Press, Ltd., 1954), p. 138.

12. Cf. also Max Black's excellent discussion of analogue models and mathematical models in Black, *op. cit.*, pp. 222-226.

13. *Ibid.*, p. 229.

14. Stephen Toulmin, *Foresight and Understanding: An Enquiry into the Aims of Science* (Bloomington: Indiana University Press, 1961), pp. 42-43.

15. Sir William Thompson, quoted in Black, *op. cit.*, p. 229.

16. Cf. pp. 11-12 above.

17. Nagel, *op. cit.*, p. 110.

18. Cf. *ibid.*, p. 111.

19. Nagel, *op. cit.*, p. 111.

20. Cf. *ibid.*, p. 110.

21. Schrödinger, *op. cit.*, p. 165.

22. *Ibid.*

23. *Ibid.*

24. Stephen C. Pepper, *World Hypotheses* (Berkeley: University of California Press, 1942).

25. Black, *op. cit.*, p. 241.

26. Toulmin, *op. cit.*, for a fascinating treatment of this subject.

27. *Summa Theologica*, Q. II, Art. 3.

28. Sir James Jeans, *Physics and Philosophy* (New York: The Macmillan Co., 1943), p. 10.

29. *Ibid.*

30. *Ibid.*, p. 9.

31. *Ibid.*

32. *Ibid.*, p. 15.

33. *Ibid.*

34. *Ibid.*, pp. 174-175.

35. Stephen Toulmin argues to good effect on this question in Toulmin, *op. cit.*, *passim*.

36. Jeans, *op. cit.*, p. 175, italics supplied.

37. *Ibid.*

38. Braithwaite, *op. cit.*, p. 92.

39. *Ibid.*, pp. 92-93.

40. Braithwaite, *op. cit.*, p. 93.

41. *Ibid.*, p. 94.

42. Jeans, *op. cit.*, pp. 15-16.

43. *Ibid.*, p. 16.

44. Braithwaite, *op. cit.*, p. 93.

45. Jeans, *op. cit.*, p. 176.

46. Braithwaite, op. cit., p. 91.

47. Nagel, *op. cit.*, p. 108.

48. Nagel, *op. cit.*, p. 113.

49. *Ibid.*, pp. 113-114.

50. Black, *op. cit.*, pp. 235-236.

51. *Ibid.*, p. 236.

52. Nagel, *op. cit.*, p. 114.

53. I. A. Richards, cited by Black, *op. cit.*, p. 237.

54. *Ibid.*

55. Jeans, *op. cit.*, p. 15.

56. Jeans, *op. cit.*, p. 15.

57. Toulmin, *op. cit.*, p. 81.

58. Jeans, *op. cit.*, p. 174.

59. Black, *op. cit.*, p. 236.

60. Cf. my *Language, Logic and God* (New York: Harper & Brothers, 1961), Chap. 12; also K. Bendall and F. Ferré, *Exploring the Logic of Faith* (New York: Association Press, 1962), Chs. 2 and 4.

61. Mark 4:3ff. (Reviser Standard Version).

62. Cf. Ronald W. Hepburn's critiques of this form of theological interest in models in "Demythologizing and the Problem of Validity," *New Essays in Philosophical Theology* (New York: Macmillan & Co., 1955), and "Poetry and Religious Belief" in *Metaphysical Beliefs* (London: SCM Press, 1957).

63. Exodus: 20:4.

64. *Ibid.*

65. Analogous things could be said, I believe, about other major religious traditions of the world, but defense of such a thesis must remain beyond the scope of this paper.

66. John 14:9 (Revised Standard Version).

67. Ludwig Feuerbach, *The Essence of Christianity* (translated by George Eliot) (New York: Harper & Brothers, 1957), p. 15.

68. It should not be assumed that such a classification necessarily holds good for all metaphysical models. Aristotle's hylomorphic metaphysical system, for example, may utilize the formal-conceptual model of the grammatical relationship between subject and predicate. The application of my remarks to the whole field of metaphysical construction cannot, however, be made in this place.

69. In contrast to their multiplicity of types, all metaphysical models, theological or otherwise, share this characteristic of unlimited scope. I would, indeed, wish to argue that such scope is the key defining characteristic of metaphysical models, providing both the necessary and the sufficient condition of their metaphysicality.

70. Cf. Antony Flew's "Theology and Falsification" and subsequent discussion in *New Essays in Philosophical Theology, op. cit.*, or my treatment of this question in *Language, Logic and God*, Chap. 3.

71. Black, *op. cit.*, p. 242.

72. But cf. *Language, Logic and God, op. cit.*, and *Exploring the Logic of Faith, op. cit.*, especially Section 10 of the latter, for a suggested method of testing a metaphysical model-cum-theory.

73. But not a sufficient condition, since a model must be provided with relations to other domains of interest and knowledge and must be explicitly affirmed before it can be considered to be functioning fully theologically. It is perfectly possible, for example, that an important biblical model—or even the key biblical model of reality itself—may be contemplated aesthetically or otherwise entertained in thought without being given a full

theological employment. The missing element, in these cases, is the "theory" or "conceptual synthesis," concerning which space forbids me to deal in this monograph.

74. James Clerk Maxwell, quoted in Black, *op. cit.*, p. 226.

75. Braithwaite, *op. cit.*, p. 93.

76. Stephen Toulmin, *The Philosophy of Science* (New York: Harper & Bros., 1960), p. 165.

77. Black, *op. cit.*, p. 238.

78. Cf. Norwood Russell Hanson, *Patterns of Discovery* (London: Cambridge University Press, 1958), especially Chapter VI, "Elementary Particle Physics," for a clear discussion of the logical grounds of this impossibility.

79. My remarks about the *experimental* unfalsifiability of theological models should not obscure the requirement that the cognitive dimensions of theology eventually stand exposed to *some* forms of critical evaluation (that is, broadly speaking, to "verification" or "falsification"). These forms or methods will have the character of metaphysical testing in general, wherein the model-cum-theory's power to make coherent sense out of all empirical fact is one vastly important component. In this extended sense, then, even metaphysical world views are "falsifiable"; but this is "falsification" of a different kind than is being spoken about in most current discussion. The true "falsification" of a metaphysical position is more like an erosion than an explosion—a gradual process in which the inadequate metaphysical view is not disproved but, rather, is quietly abandoned.

80. Cf. Stephen Toulmin's excellent article, "Scientific Theories and Scientific Myths" in *Metaphysical Beliefs, op. cit.*, for a discussion of scientific propositions gone astray.

81. Cf. Julian Huxley's *Religion Without Revelation* (London: Max Parrish, 1957, revised), Ch. IX, for a book that is well written and thoughtful but none the less an excellent specimen of this mistake.

CHAPTER SIXTEEN

ON UNDERSTANDING MYSTERY*

by Ian Ramsey

It is by this time well known that contemporary empiricism represents a
challenge to Christian belief. What needs to be said, however, and indeed
emphasized, is that this challenge needs often to be welcomed, first for
setting squarely before us problems of crucial importance which otherwise we might not notice or even seek to bypass if we did; and second,
since contemporary empiricism encourages us to loiter over our language,
to be alert to its variegations, to see how we use that language in various
ways to do different jobs of work, this approach is likely to be a great help
as we turn to that most complex and peculiar language in which in a
vast variety of ways a religious man expresses himself. I believe that contemporary empiricism may revitalize our faith and our doctrine and make
what seem so often to be the dry bones of theological discourse live. At
any rate, those are the convictions which lie behind this lecture, and
they will prepare you I hope for what follows, not least because I begin
my lecture precisely with one of those valuable challenges of which I have
just made mention. In a recent paper on the *Hiddenness of God and
Some Barmecidal God Surrogates*, Dr. Robert C. Coburn, of the University of Chicago, rightly remarks that the concept of God is "both exceedingly complex and exceedingly peculiar."[1] A particular example of this
complexity and peculiarity occurs, he would say, in those "innumerable
pieces of religious discourse" where talk about God displays two features
not obviously reconcilable. On the one hand, talk about God is about
"something with quite determinate humanly intelligible characteristics."
God is for instance "a supremely powerful, perfectly righteous, all knowing person, who created and controls the spatio-temporal order in a provi-
dential way." The particular puzzle arises, however, because talk about
God is *also* of "something whose characteristics are totally beyond our

*Used with permission from *Chicago Theological Register*, Vol. 53, May 1963.

grasp, something ineductiably unknowable and wholly incomprehensible."
Here, says Coburn, is "a very fundamental problem."[2] How can we
justly talk of God as being both hidden from and open to our comprehension? How do we combine mystery and understanding? How do we
understand a mystery?

Now it is true, as Coburn reminds us, that some believers would give
and have given short shrift to the question. There are those who have
in Coburn's words, "italicized God's hiddenness at the expense of his
openness and then retreated into holy silence";[3] those who have held,
in the words of another philosopher, Thomas McPherson, that religion
"belongs to the sphere of the unsayable."[4] And at the other extreme,
are those who have produced, says Coburn, "a more or less readily understandable but somehow religiously uninteresting philosopher's
God,'"[5] and I think we ourselves might go even further and say religiously scandalizing philosopher's God. Now Coburn recognizes that the
sanction of the Church, however, has most often been accorded to those
whose views have avoided both these extremes, those who have somehow tried to reconcile God's hiddenness with God's openness. But the
broad argument of Coburn's paper is that these attempts "are easily as
preplexing as the difficulty of difficulties they ostensibly surmount."[6]
Can I hope for better success? At any rate let me try.

Two points become clear from Coburn's discussion, though I shall
put them largely in my own way. First, if religious language is used
literally, if religious language is descriptive through and through, then
the only possibility of mystery arises from there being some inaccessible
facts. This indeed is a sense of "mystery" which even scientific inquiry
could and does allow. Lord Rayleigh and others in 1892 no doubt spoke
of the "mystery" of the atomic weight of nitrogen, when samples of
nitrogen prepared in different ways, and in each case with every possible
precaution, yielded different values for the atomic weight of nitrogen.
But this mystery disappeared once Sir William Ramsay discovered the
presence in atmospheric nitrogen of the inert gas argon. When Ramsay
and Rayleigh announced the discovery of argon in August 1894 the mystery had disappeared. Here is mystery used as a synonym for temporary
ignorance about the facts. In this case we might speak of a two-year mystery. Now I think it is quite clear and for two reasons that this sense of
mystery is of no help whatever for religious belief. First, to preserve ultimate mystery, we should have to talk of facts which were permanently
inaccessible. But what could be meant by talking of facts which are
permanently, indeed logically, inaccessible to everybody? If any facts are
logically inaccessible they will never, logically never, be talked about.
And the sooner we cease trying the better. The alternative is to suppose
that the mystery of religion will sooner or later, like the mystery of the
atomic weight of nitrogen in 1894, lie open for everybody to see, believers
or not. But then the topic of religious belief is no more than observable
facts and, being in no sort of way transcendent, is in no sort or way religious. So let us agree with Coburn that religious language can hardly

be literal and do its job of understanding mystery.

Now the second move. If, however, religious language preserves a reference to mystery by somehow not being used literally, there are at least two different difficulties. First, it is objected, if religious language is not used literally, what becomes of its factual claims? What sort of fact is it that can only be talked about in some slanting kind of way? What sort of fact is it which eludes direct statement? It is "far from obvious," claims Coburn, that "the notion of facts which elude direct statement" makes sense. Indeed I think Coburn would say that all these attempts to avoid the literal use of religious language, if they are intelligible at all, either compromise factual claims or prove unavailing by having to make in the end the very kind of link between language and fact which they set out to avoid. Or perhaps both. As for the first alternative, which makes no pretense to possess factual claims, claiming that religious language merely expresses this or that way of looking at things, we may readily agree that of all religions Christianity cannot give up its factual claims by regarding its Bible or doctrines as, say, no more than encouragements to or mnemonics for a worship which then will be no more than the family at play, a sort of make believe with jolly social possibilities. This is something not too far from C. B. Martin's picture parody of what he thinks worship is.

On the other hand, suppose a more subtle attempt ot preserve the factual reference is made by supposing religious language to be used metaphorically. Now on such a view, an assertion like "God is a person" might be supposed to work, to take Coburn's own example, like "Mrs. Q is a duck" or, as I heard someone say the other day, "General de Gaulle is a mule." The trouble is that if those metaphorical assertions claim to be in any sort of way a "statement of fact" we must still suppose, says Coburn, and rightly, that they fulfil both what he calls the "referring condition" and the "descriptive condition."[7] In short, without going into all the complexities, God, like Mrs. Q or General de Gaulle, must be somehow identifiable, and there must also be a number of literal descriptions, however few, which God shares with persons, as Mrs. Q presumably shares either her waddling or her cackling with the ducks, and De Gaulle his stubbornness with mules. But, says Coburn, and I think we are bound to agree, "God can neither be indicated demonstratively nor described in such a manner as to be uniquely related to a demonstratively identifiable particular."[8] Second, does anybody know of any literal description which God satisfies and shares with all of us? It is clear, I think, without pursuing the matter further, that we shan't answer Coburn's difficulties, we shan't meet his challenge, unless we are able to elucidate a "notion of facts which elude direct statement,"[9] unless in other words we are able to broaden Coburn's empiricism in some intelligible way. So our problem becomes: What can be meant by claiming that something is mysterious if, as we agree, it is not to be understood in terms of the inaccessibility of facts, and yet has got to have some sort of factual reference? In other words, in what sort of situation do mystery and understanding meet? What sort of "facts" elude in principle exhaustive description and yet permit us some measure of understanding? What is my recipe for a wider empiricism?

My answer begins with, though plainly it must not finish with, ourselves—each one of us. None of us need doubt that an enormous amount can be said about himself in descriptive language, that an enormous number of facts in Coburn's ordinary sense can be predicated of all of us. These are the facts about our age, our height, our hair, our eyes, our health record, and so on—all those facts indeed in which passport officers are interested and which are the very bread and butter in the lives of immigration officers and insurance agents; and there are those facts about our behavior responses, our complexes, our learning abilities, in which the pyschologists will be interested. There are also the facts about our social life and our families and our budgets in which the sociologist and economists are interested; facts about our digestion in which the biochemist will be interested, and so on. Further, it is to those experts that I go to clear up any "mystery" about my age, or my behavior, or my purchasing ability, or my digestion. For it is all a matter here of further inquiry and greater competence, of knowing more facts, of greater expertise. But is each of us then in principle no more than what the passport officer, the insurance broker, the psychologist, the sociologist, the economist, the biochemist, and so on, can report about us? Are we no more in principle than what is referred to by such a very variegated cluster of important and true and far-reaching assertions? The answer in principle is "No." Why? Well notice what the claim that it *was* sufficient in principle would imply. It would imply that a first person assertion about myself could be replaced without loss by that admittedly enormous but nevertheless finite cluster of *third-person* assertions, assertions about objects. But if that were ever true, it would objectify the subject and it would deny the very subject-object distinction which is the basis of all talking, all language, and all experience. Now it is true that "He has blue eyes" is subject-predicate in character, but a mere glance at it makes it evident that nevertheless it is a third-person assertion through and through, even though it is subject-predicate in character. And as a third-person assertion it is wholly about objects, despite its subject-predicate structure. Indeed, its logical incompleteness can be recognized the moment we reflect that every third-person assertion is enclosed in invisible quotes. So that "He has blue eyes" needs setting within a wider sentence frame such as "I have written for your consideration: 'He has blue eyes,'" *or* "I am telling you: 'He has blue eyes,'" *or* "I am saying: 'He has blue eyes.'" Now, I am not denying that, on occasion, we all of us use first-person assertions which give "I" no more genuine self-reference than you give to "He" when you use it of me. And undoubtedly that kind of point would make the whole story very complicated. But for our purpose, all that need be recognized is that there is a subjectivity which each of us realizes for himself which is not, and logically could not be, exhausted by any number of third-person descriptions, however far they went and however various they were. Here, then, is a "fact"—my own existence as I know it, in its full subjectivity—which eludes, and in principle, any exhaustive direct description. How then is it revealed, and how do we come across it? "Revealed" indeed is the right word, for in fact it is disclosed to us, it breaks in on us at some point or other as the descriptive story is ever more fully built up. Here is something whose possibility I think we may recognize from various illustrations. For example, we must all have played those party games where clues are given and the winner is the one who "sees," from the fewest clues, what is being talked about. On the basis of the fewest clues, the disclosure occurs; the winner sees the point of the story. Let us see how the same game goes in the case of self-disclosure. Suppose B comes up to A one day and says: "I am looking for a man who is age 23, black hair, blue eyes, 5'9", weight 162 lbs., Passport EA 24607, suffers from chronic catarrh, can't eat shell fish, earns $7,800 a year, has a wife and two children, and so on." Now A could perfectly well understand all that B said and never, as we say, realize that it was himself. Even though the description fitted every time and even though with the help of the passport officer, the bathroom scales, the mirror, a doctor, a sociologist, an economist, a biochemist, and so on, the picture was better and better filled in, at no point would we be *compelled* to conclude "It is I." It could always be no more than an interesting character study of my perfect double. If, however, at some point we declare, "It's I," it means that at that point, as those pictures are enumerated, the light dawns, we jump to it, a disclosure occurs, and we recognize the inquiry to be for ourselves: "Thou art the Man."

That which each of us knows, when he most significantly comes to himself in this way, is nothing at which we can satisfactorily point, it is nothing which can be "indicated demonstratively." There is no demonstratively identifiable particular which is I. Whatever particular fact is selected for rough and ready identification purposes, e.g., as on the passport, color of eyes, height, even what is called in those documents "distinguishing marks"; whatever fact is selected, it is not logically impossible for somebody else to share it—even the so-called "distinguishing mark." As A. J. Ayer himself admits—a point to which I return presently—there is no particular which could unambiguously identify a person. On the other hand, what each of us realizes himself uniquely to be is something which facts in Coburn's sense may contrive to disclose. By my argument has been that what they disclose is something which is all of these facts and more, and it is *not* a more that will ever be covered by more of the facts. For it is a subjectivity for which no set of third-person descriptions, of what are technically public "objects," no matter how many or varied, can ever be exhaustive currency. Here is a fact that eludes direct statement.[10] But it is a fact as indisputable a fact as my own subjectivity.

Let me elucidate this subjectivity a little further. There might be, in principle, circumstances when, from the point of view of my identifiable description, my existence to you may be exceedingly problematical. We might imagine, for instance, that by some extraordinary freak of space and time, when I am leaving this room, I suddenly disappear and at the same spot appears General Robert E. Lee of the Civil War. Now from the point of view of identifiable descriptions, I should certainly be an exceedingly great puzzle. Even if I said, "But I am Ramsey," the identification difficulties would be immense. But the important point is that, all the time, no matter how bewildered you were, I have *no doubt whatever at any time* that I am the same person.

Contrariwise, suppose, to give another example, that someone believed that a completely satisfactory set of identifiable characteristics had been listed, guaranteed to isolate me on any occasion. He would certainly have made a great mistake. Because there would always be in principle the identical twin, he who is born an identical person in some counterpart earth which the course of evolution has thrown up. Or as A. J. Ayer himself points out, there is always at least the logical possibility that history could quite literally repeat itself.

I need neither complicate the examples nor take them further. My point is that in the disclosure he has of his own subjectivity, each of us has a notion (and it is a "notion" in a sense very close to that technical sense in which George Berkeley used the word) of what eludes direct statement, or what eludes expression in descriptive terms. Each of us in his own subjectivity has a paradigm of mystery, and it is irreducible mystery because the subject will never be exhaustively objectified.

Now with that background, let us pass to the case of God, in order presently to say how we shall understand mystery, and talk intelligibly about the mystery of God. My suggestion will be that the mystery of God arises and is safeguarded precisely because God discloses himself in situations which objectively match those of whose subjective features I have just been speaking. Indeed, I would suggest—and let me emphisize, since my task at the moment is primarily one of giving meaning to religious assertions that on the face of it are questionably intelligible, I need no more elucidate a visible possibility—I am going to suggest that such awareness of our own subjectivity, of our own subjective transcendence, arises along with and matches an awareness of objective transcendence, a cosmic disclosure, when the universe, as we'd say, "comes alive." We may recall, for instance, that David in the presence of Nathan came to himself *subjectively* when there bore down on him objectively, through the parable or model that Nathan used, a moral challenge.

In this way, and to this degree, but no further, I can agree with those who, following Kierkegaard and other existentialists, stress the significance of what is called "the realization of one's existence as a self" or (another favorite phrase) "choosing oneself" or rather "receiving oneself," "coming to oneself as an inward action of the personality," and I agree when these existentialists go further and argue that this significant and "authentic life" will be matched by "a word from God."[11]

Suppose, then, that this is the situation in which language about God is grounded, the kind of fact that subjectively and objectively eludes any exhaustive descriptive account, which eludes direct statement, which combines hiddenness and openness. How do we contrive to talk about it? To what conclusion do these suggestions lead about that "peculiar and complex language," which occurs in "innumerable pieces of religious discourse"?[12]

My broad answer will be that a religious assertion which embraces the comprehensible and the incomprehensible, which does justice to and is currency for both the hiddenness and the openness of God, which speaks of a disclosure in part mysterious, does so by incorporating words or phrases whose logical behavior I called elsewhere that of "models" and "qualifiers," respectively. Let me illustrate and develop that distinction by reference to two examples: (1) "God is a necessary being," or its synonym, "God necessarily exists." (2) "God is infinitely loving." Now in these examples, I call "being" and "loving" models; I call "infinitely" and "necessarily" qualifiers. Why and how I call them that, I will explain. It will always be tempting to someone who is all too literate in theology to suppose that the assertion "God is a necessary being" has a *logical* behavior precisely like its many *verbal* kinsmen, for instance, "Churchill is a remarkable being." Similarly, it will be supposed that "God is infinitely loving," works like its verbal synonym, say, "Wendy (or Jim) is wonderfully loving." In this way it will be supposed that "necessary being" describes some brand of existence, that "necessary existence" takes its own place alongside the "shadow existence" of a Labour Cabinet in Britain, the "crowded existence" of a city artery at the rush hour, "future existence" on the moon and so on. Now if that parallel is made, objections cluster fast and furious. Some like Professor J. N. Findlay would remark that "necessary" can characterize nothing but propositions like those in mathematics and symbolic logic, and can never characterize things so that "necessary being" is a mere noise.[13] Others will emphasize that every existent we know is contingent—it could have been different. So God must exist as we can suppose nothing else to exist. The implication is that talk about God as a necessary existent is absolutely vacuous. Those are certainly difficulties into which we get when we either neglect the function of qualifiers and say in isolation "God exists" or "God is loving," or misread their logic regarding them as descriptive of some sort of quality, some brand of existence, some brand of love. What is the alternative? The alternative, I would suggest, is that we look at the assertion "God is a necessary being" as we ought to look at *all* assertions about the mystery which is God. First we shall look for one word on which everyone will agree; one word which can be understood descriptively, something to give an intelligible route into the disclosure of mystery, something to enable us to be as articulate as possible about it afterward. Here is the model. It is like all models at least in this regard, viz., it is something about which we are reasonably clear by which to understand something which is very problematical.

Now in the sentence "God is a necessary being," the model word here is "being"—and I take it in its universally admitted sense, to de-

scribe anything, say, a melon or a house; there need be, on this view,
nothing esoteric about "being." Now suppose we start with a melon on a
dining table on a particular evening. Clearly, this is not a necessary
being. It may be indeed the first time we have had melons for twenty
years. So the qualifier "necessary" will direct us, starting here and now
with this melon, to seek situations displaying less and less contingency.
For instance it might be said that while a melon obviously would not
always grace a college dining table, meals would. But there are times
when there are no meals on the table. So when we talk about a college,
and in that context "Here's a melon" is more contingent than "Here is
a meal," which is itself more contingent than "Here's a table." But is
not the dining hall more necessary than the table it contains? The city
though might exist without the college; the state without the city. But
the country could be here without this state, and so on. In this way, the
qualifier "necessary" pushes us along and along, to generate an ever
broadening perspective, to embrace and to pass beyond more and more
models for being. It is the party game again. And the hope is that as
this pattern is developed and increased, at some point a disclosure will
occur, the universe will "come alive." In the words of David Hume and
despite all his criticism of the argument from design, "something will immediately strike us with a force like that of sensation."[14] Now if this
disclosure occurs at the level of the word "country," if we "see" and
"jump to it" when we have got that far, people will begin to speak of
"my country, right or wrong," or across the water they will start to sing
"There will always be an England." And they may well then make a religion out of their patriotism. But the religious man would claim that
as and when the disclosure occurs, "God" is the word appropriate to
what is objectively disclosed, where "God" is a word about which this
can be said, that the assertion "God necessarily exists" stands as an ultimate posit, or presupposition of all the tales I have told of any being.
Put differently, just as we move by an informal inference, that is, by an
inference within a particular context, from "Here is a melon" to "Here
is a meal" to "Here is a dining hall" to "Here is a college" to "Here is
a state," and so forth, the claim is that in the same sort of way our inference will culminate in "There is God," when God is the end of our
inference spread. With that sort of logical map work, that kind of placing for the word God, we could then say that God declares himself to us
as each of us to ourselves when each of us knows his own subjectivity.
We speak of there being "one God," as some, like Gilbert Ryle, would
speak of "one world." Here is some final key concept, one ultimate presupposition. I would suggest, incidentally, that it is by reference to a disclosure as the ground for belief in God that people have said that "God
is the one true subject," or that "God is not one object among others."
We do not demonstrate God any more than we demonstrate ourselves.
He is no object any more than we are wholly objects. We know God in
his disclosure of himself.

In order to show that there are countless routes to disclosures, and that qualifiers may proceed by either inclusion or exclusion, let us now take a house as a candidate for necessary being. This may seem very plausible because as the builders say, "All contingencies have been overcome; here is the bill." But this house, which is of wood, might have been of brick, or it might not have been there at all. Once it wasn't. Still, someone might say, there has always been a hill there. But there was not before the Ice Age. Well, wasn't there at least soil? But perhaps not this soil—only perhaps certain basic elements like carbon nitrogen, oxygen or phosphorus; or it may have been just some fundamental particles, or whatever the infinite divisibility of space might yield . . . and that means (you see) endless possibility of playing the game forever. So we see how we might continue the tale, develop whatever model we choose for being, and in whatever way the word "necessary" suggests, until we reach the point at which a disclosure is evolved, when everything collapses into immediacy, if I may pilfer a phrase from Hegel. Thus the logic of "God is a necessary being" can be most reliably expressed as

$$\text{necessary (being)} \rightarrow \downarrow \text{ "God."}$$

Here "necessary" has the logic of an operator, a directive, an imperative, so that the assertion is not altogether unlike

$$n \rightarrow \infty \left(\frac{n}{n+1} \right) \rightarrow \downarrow \text{"1" .}$$

I do not think that I need now spend long on the elucidation of "God is infinitely loving." Here is another assertion with both descriptive and imperative force. "Loving" is the model: bearing, enduring, hoping, trusting, redeeming, caring for, and so on, which "infinitely" would develop along the lines of 1 Cor. 13:7. Beareth *all things*, endureth *all things*, always unwavering, unyielding, untiring in reconciliation, we must build out that picture till it discloses God. When we know what the phrase "infinitely loving" refers to, we know God. Our position indeed concurs with what P. T. Geach says rightly about Aquinas. For Aquinas as indeed for me, the phrases "God," "the Power of God," "the Wisdom of God," and so on, all have the same reference. The logic of God is as odd as that.

In this way, then, God is known as disclosing himself, and religious discourse works to "show" God in this way. Religious assertions thus in part conform to the logic of descriptives, but in part, because of the qualifiers they control, they also display the logic of directives and imperatives, and they are inexpressible in descriptive language. Indeed, the qualifiers gear into models, they intersect with models, like operators or directives gear in the terms in which they relate. Suppose you are in some hall and there at the back is written on the wall the word "Exit." Now "Exit" is in part a very good descriptive word. But supposing you see the word "Exit" on an absolutely blank wall, with blanks on either side, you remain rooted to the spot. Before you can do anything, there needs to be an arrow added or some doors below. So it is with "loving" or "being." Qualifiers have to be added if they are going to take us to

God, if they are to prepare us for a disclosure.

Which leads me, by way of conclusion, to the first of five corollaries.

1. "God is loving," "God exists," are therefore logically incomplete, as we might say of any third-person assertion about ourselves that it was logically incomplete. Qualifiers are needed for logical completion, so that we more aptly say that God is infinitely loving, God necessarily exists. We don't even say that God is our Father. When we are wise we say that God is our Father Who art in Heaven, and there is qualification enough in that phrase. The first need of a religious assertion, if it isn't going to generate bogus puzzles and unnecessary difficulties, is to be logically complete.

2. It is to models that we must look when we want to be articulate about the mystery to which with the qualifiers they point, which with the qualifiers they enable us to reach. But the fact that we have but models, which never exhaust the mystery, models which inevitably provide only partial understandings, means that sooner or later, inferences from those models become precarious. We then need to balance one model with its associated context against another model with its associated context. Contrariwise, we will always look for more and more adequate models for talking about that mystery which is God. These will·be discovered as and when we grade our models and discover super models. Let me illustrate that distinction like this: It is as though we might have talked usefully about something in terms of an ellipse one day, a parabola another, a hyperbola another, a circle another, a pair of straight lines another, a point another. We might then discover a double cone as a super model. Here will be a far more reliable way of talking about what hitherto we have only talked about piece-meal. What we have talked of will be better talked about as a double cone. Similarly, what is talked of in terms of power, wisdom, love, models of one order may be better talked of in terms of the concept of person—a model of a higher order. And, again, we shall be the more reliably articulate about the mystery; the most coherent our discourse is, the more we complete cross-plottings from one model to another. For instance, in the case of God, the models of King and Judge and Power may all lead us to talk of "protection." And further and most importantly, at the outposts of our discourse we must connect that discourse with facts and observable behavior in the world around us. In this way there are various criteria which will test the reliability of our theological understanding about a mystery.

3. Not all qualifiers will be a single word. For instance consider those models contained in such sentences as "God is a Potter," or "The Lord is My Shepherd." Now here the logic is somewhat different and not straightforward. To say "God is a Potter," or "The Lord is My Shepherd," we must suppose that God in fact disclosed himself, that the world became alive around the Potter's bench, or the Sheep Fold. But mystery may now be safeguarded, not this time by incorporating a qualifier as a word, though that might be possible, but more usually as in the Psalms and Hymns, by qualifying with other models in the single discourse.

Mystery is now safeguarded by recognizing that to talk adequately of the God who is disclosed on any occasion will need language culled from and growing out of all the models which arise in all the vast variety of circumstances God has been disclosed. So Jesus is spoken of as Shepherd, Prophet, Priest, my husband, Friend, and King. In this kind of way, we see piling up of models, each qualifying the next. This is a rather more rough and ready way of qualifying: by the jostling of models. Here is another less orderly, and more haphazard way of being articulate about a mystery. But it emphasizes from another direction the need to balance one model against another and to be literate only with the greatest circumspection.

4. Having once mentioned Kierkegaard, another reference at this point may not be entirely misplaced. Insofar as I have appealed to a disclosure, to something which breaks in on us, to a situation in which we pass beyond any and all the models we have developed to date, when (as *we* say) we "jump to it," there is involved what might be called logical leap, just as there is a logical leap between seeing "$1 + 1/2 + 1/4 + 1/8 + 1/16 \ldots$" and saying "2." So, like Kierkegaard, and Lessing before him, I too can talk of a leap. But for me there is no special reason whatever for thinking of that leap as a leap across what Lessing called a "grim broad chasm." For me, it can be pictured not only just as well but I think rather better and more consistently with the rest of our language about God, as a leap into the arms of a loving Father, as a jump to an embrace, an embrace which cannot be wholly and aptly described in terms of muscular grippings with appropriate organic sensations.

5. Let me finally illustrate my theme by reference to angels, in reflections which take their cue from Coburn. The word "angel" is, of all words, probably that one where there is almost an equal danger of making it too intelligible on the one hand or too incomprehensible on the other. To some people the word "angel" disappears in a fog of mystery; and to others the word is so intelligible as to be crude. For instance, the angels which walked up and down Jacob's Ladder did not fly (said the boy in his scripture examination) because like his hens they were moulting. "And how do angels get their jackets over their wings?" asked the down-to-earth coal miner in Warwickshire after listening to a lecture on Religious Symbolism. Here you see are people taking angel as a descriptive word and the question "Are there angels?" is on logical all fours with the question Are there Pygmies? or, are there Himalayan snowmen? But the wings on angels' backs are not supposed to be descriptive of what we see on hens in the farmyard. The wings on an angel's back have the logical function of qualifiers so that the picture of an angel symbolizes a particular encounter with God, and models it in terms of personal interchange. Because talk of an angel is talk of a personal interchange, we never speak of an angel whose model is like a businessman carrying a briefcase. In other words, the concept of an angel has to be grounded in a situation which discloses God through some particular kind of quasi-personal encounter. What these philosophical reflections suggest is that "The

Angel of the Lord" is a rather more reliable, because logically more complete, phrase to use of these situations. We have to be especially cautious
in talking about angels, lest being too articulate, we cease to be religious,
like the boy in the scripture examination. To ask whether there are angels
is really to ask whether God can be known in particularized circumstances.

Let me now complete my paper by brief reference to another philosopher who, like Coburn, writes in a very lucid and challenging fashion —
Paul Ziff of the University of Pennsylvania. In a paper called "About
God," which Ziff gave to a New York symposium in 1960,[15] he gives
his own account of the mixing of the intelligible and the incomprehensible
in discourse about God. It has to be understood, he says, by reference to
what he calls the Unproblematic Conditions and the Problematic Conditions which characterize God. To quote:

> Some unproblematic conditions are the conditions of being a being, a force,
> a person, a father, a son, a creator, spatio-temporal, crucified, just, good, merci-
> ful, powerful, wise and so forth. I class these conditions as unproblematical,
> because it seems clear to me that each condition is in fact satisfied or readily
> satisfiable by something or someone; furthermore, each condition is satisfied
> or readily satisfiable in a fairly obvious manner.[16]

> Some problematic conditions are the conditions of being omnipotent, omni-
> scient, eternal creator of the world, a non-spatio-temporal being, a spirit, the
> cause of itself and so forth. I class these conditions as problematic for this rea-
> son. If someone were to maintain that a traditional conception of God is unin-
> telligible, I should think he would base his claim on the prior claim that such
> conditions as these are fundamentally unintelligible.[17]

> All such conditions seem to involve some extreme form either of generaliza-
> tion or abstraction.[18]

Omniscient, he says, merely generalizes "the condition of being informed
or learned." Non-spatio-temporal being is an abstraction from the condition of being a. spatio-temporal being. He believes that such terms as
these are like the high abstractions of a scientific theory which of course
is only asking for trouble, as Ziff not surprisingly soon discovers. You will
have noticed, though, that this distinction between problematic and unproblematic conditions can in fact be alternatively and further analyzed
in terms of what I think is the more fundamental distinction between
models and qualifiers. But this means that on my view Ziff is wrong in
supposing that we have two brands of conditions, for models and qualifiers have not the same logic as this supposition implies. It is not a case
of what Ziff calls two conditions differing only in respect to the degree
of generalization. The difference between models and qualifiers is something far more radical than that. So I think that the distinction between
models and qualifiers not only illuminates Ziff's distinction, I think it also
shows where the problem as he expresses it, is bogus, and his account
mistaken. But it is true, as he suggests, that the problem of uniting the
intelligible and the incomprehensible is the problem of relating what he
calls the unproblematical and the problematical conditions which for me
becomes the problem of uniting models and qualifiers which I hope I
have done something to illuminate here.

The over-all lesson to be learned, then, is that if we want to understand language which claims to talk of a mystery, if we want to understand some piece of distinctive religious discourse, we must first pick out the words which are most straightforward and most obviously descriptive. We then look at the other words to see which of them act as qualifiers behaving logically like an imperative to direct us to a disclosure. Every complete religious assertion will thus use words descriptively and also specify a technique by which we may move from "what is seen" to "what is seen and more," from the expressible to the point where the expressible becomes part of the inexpressible. Religious assertions will certainly scandalize if descriptive assertions are taken as an ideal of understanding, or if the function of qualifiers is neglected or their logic misread.

The broad conclusion may be expressed alternatively by saying that we must recognize two sorts of "understanding." One arises when we use words descriptively; the other arises when we use words which, in Berkeley's phrase, direct us how to act, when we engage in activity directed toward that which we are descriptively familiar. We are thus like a musician who, on the one hand discursively understands his "score," but who also in keen devotion gives himself to the playing of it, responding to the disclosure which it has evoked. Theological literacy demands both kinds of assertions.

Now for a brief summary: The problem of understanding mystery is, I said, one of those problems with which contemporary empiricism usefully challenges us. Our response must be (a) to elucidate some meaning of "facts which elude direct statement" and (b) to say how this sort of fact can be expressed in language. A case could be made out for such facts, I said, if we considered an illustration which discloses my first-person subjectivity and contrast this with a similar disclosure of objectivity. As currency for such a disclosure, I considered expressions which incorporate models and qualifiers, and I tried to show the ways in which we can then be articulate about a mystery and how we may use the distinction of models and qualifiers to solve the problem of understanding mystery at it is put to us by Ziff.

FOOTNOTES

1. *Journal of Philosophy*, LVII, Nos. 22 and 23, October 27 and November 10, 1960, p. 689.

2. *Loc. cit.*; p. 694.

3. *Loc. cit.*, p. 694.

4. See his "Religion as the Inexpressible," in *New Essays in Philosophical Theology* (ed. A. N. Flew and A. MacIntyre), chap. vii.

5. *Loc. cit.*, p. 694.

6. *Loc. cit.*, p. 695.

7. *Loc. cit.*, p. 701.

8. *Loc. cit.*, p. 702.

9. *Loc. cit.*, p. 704.

10. See Coburn, *loc. cit.*, p. 704.

11. Cf., e.g., Reidar Thomte, *Kierkegaard's Philosophy of Religion*, pp. 48-49, and *The Witness of Kierkegaard* (ed. C. Michalson), p. 127.

12. Coburn, *loc. cit.*, p. 689.

13. See his contribution in *New Essays in Philosophical Theology* (ed. A. N. Flew and A. MacIntyre).

14. *Dialogue concerning Natural Religion*, Part III (Cleanthes).

15. *Religious Experience and Truth* (ed. S. Hook).

16. *Ibid.*, p. 198.

17. *Ibid.*, pp. 198-99.

18. *Ibid.*, pp. 200-201.

PART FIVE

THE
NEO-CATHOLIC
PERSPECTIVE

INTRODUCTION

The traditional Roman Catholic stance with respect to the relation between philosophy and religion is well known. It is based on the thought of Thomas Aquinas who has held near absolute sway within Catholic philosophical theology up until this century. At the heart of the Thomistic system is a dichotomy between the divine and natural realms of experience and reality. Aquinas was convinced that the relation between such concepts as faith, grace, and virtue on the one hand, and reason, nature, and law on the other, is best understood in terms of separate functions related according to a dualistic hierarchy. Thus he maintained that philosophy (reason) and religion (faith) are neither to be opposed to, nor synthesized with, one another. Rather, each is to be viewed as having its own function, and as complementing the other. Both reason and faith are gifts of God's creation and part of His divine economy.

The philosophical system which resulted from this foundational dichotomy—and the detailed argumentation to which it gave rise—came to be known as "scholasticism." There are two correlative assumptions which provide the limitations within which this system is worked out. The first is that the philosophy of Aristotle is in all important respects correct. The second is that the Christian Scriptures are the final authority on matters of faith. A good deal of scholastic energy has been expended in an effort to eliminate any disharmony that might arise among the implications of these two assumptions.

Within the last thirty years several major changes have taken place in the Catholic attitude toward the relation of philosophy and religion, thus providing some basis for the employment of the term "Neo-Catholic perspective." The first of these changes was the rising influence of existentialist thought among Catholic thinkers. The unrelenting search for personal meaning which characterized existentialist writers was acknowledged by many as a powerful ally against the materialism and positivism of the twentieth century. In addition, many Catholic thinkers came to feel that the confines of scholastic philosophy were too ingrown and intellectualized to do business in the contemporary world.

The Catholic "tribute to existentialism" became quite widespread and well-organized, especially among French and American Catholic thinkers. Some have even gone so far as to claim that Albert Camus, had he lived a bit longer, would have embraced the Catholic faith. Etienne Gilson and Jacques Maritain have argued that Thomas Aquinas himself was the first, and most consistent, existentialist. There still remains, however, a rather large amount of tension in such an approach, and it is generated by the difficulties of uniting a highly systematic Thomistic philosophy with a highly unsystematic existentialist posture. Most Catholic philosophers attempt to resolve this tension either by constructing an existentialist system, à la German existentialism, or by simply dropping the Thomistic rigor altogether, as with Gabriel Marcel.

More recently another change has taken place which contributes further to the development of a Neo-Catholic perspective. This change is a result of the influence of process philosophy, and is especially evident in the work of Pierre Teilhard de Chardin. The principal out-workings of this influence have been in the philosophy of science, and have for the first time given rise to serious Catholic contributions in this field. The focal issue has become the implications of the concept of evolution for our understanding of man's place in the world. A fascinating and complex system has begun to emerge which seeks to draw correlations between biological and anthropological science and ethics, metaphysics, and theology. Perhaps the key area of difficulty is that of working out the implications of a process philosophy for the understanding of the nature of God. The overtones of the possibility of a finite God cannot be ignored.

A third, and perhaps ultimately the most influential, change taking place within the Catholic monolith is that resulting from the pronouncement and recommendations of the Second Vatican Council. Although the primary implications of this Council are more specifically religious in character, it must be said that the spirit of exploration and tolerance which it loosed on the Catholic world has already begun to have its effects upon Catholic philosophic thought. To put it the other way around, one might argue that the exploratory and creative character of contemporary philosophical and theological thought gave rise to the spirit which made the Second Vatican Council possible. At any rate, it cannot be denied that there is a real Neo-Catholic perspective in the making.

A final area of Neo-Catholic concern which needs mentioning is that of developing a contemporary religious epistemology. This concern has at least two main emphases at present. The first is to dig deeply into the nature of the knowing experience in order to "understand understanding." This emphasis reflects the most recent work done in empiricist philosophy, phenomenology, and gestalt psychology, as well as showing a familiarity with the work of analytic philosophers and theologians. The chief goal of this emphasis would seem to be the overcoming of the dichotomies between the knower and the known on the one hand, and between fact and value on the other hand. It is felt by those involved in this enterprise that such dichotomies have too long held sway in epistemological discussions, and that, moreover, they systematically cause more difficulties than they purport to eliminate. Knowing is here seen as a holistic act involving the whole person—a synthesis of the objective and the subjective.

The second emphasis of Neo-Catholic epistemology is upon constructing an approach to metaphysics which provides for empirical controls. Many Catholic thinkers are impatient with the tendency, among both philosophers and theologians, to lapse into a form of metaphysical thinking which is in no way grounded in concrete experience. The new work is aiming at an understanding of human cognitive experience which will stress the role of mediation played by empirical experience in our awareness of "higher" dimensions of reality, such as the moral and the religious. Clearly, such an emphasis will also involve a more flexible concept of metaphysics as well.

The following selections have been chosen in order to provide an introduction to most of those themes discussed above. In addition to remembering that other themes are also present, the student should remember that these selections only provide an introduction to Neo-Catholic thought. It is well worth becoming better acquainted with.

Pierre Teilhard de Chardin's attempt to interrelate the concept and implications of evolution to Christian theology is by now well known. Because it is not possible to obtain permission to reprint his writings, an essay which seeks to expound his thought has been included in this section. E. R. Baltazar is an important Teilhard scholar, and in his essay he shows the relationship between evolutionary thought and process philosophy, and their combined influence on religion. Henri Bouillard's approach to the relation between philosophy and religion, while in some respects more traditionally Catholic than that of other authors included in this section, does reflect an updated interpretation of Thomistic thought. He is especially influenced by the work of Maurice Blondel. Perhaps the most influential of all contemporary Catholic epistemologists is Bernard Lonergan. He has systematically sought to plumb the depths of the knowing process by way of constructing a sound view of religious knowledge. In the essay reprinted here he seeks to relate this view to an understanding of metaphysics. He does this through an analysis of the thought of several other writers in this field. An extremely versatile thinker, Michael Novak, has written novels and analyses of contemporary culture as well as having made first-rate contributions to the philosophy of religion. His essay in this section forms the culmination of his attempt to come to grips honestly with both belief and unbelief. He finds them both within himself, as a "man come of age."

CHAPTER SEVENTEEN

TEILHARD DE CHARDIN:

A PHILOSOPHY OF PROCESSION*

by E. R. Baltazar

One of the most remarkable trends in recent Roman Catholic theology—a trend exemplified most notably in the work of the late Pierre Teilhard de Chardin, S.J.—is the effort to move away from the static categories of classic Aristotelo-Thomism and to consider man in terms not of "essence" and "nature" but of uniqueness and subjectivity, time in terms not of substance but of process. Such an approach does not issue in subjectivism, declares E. R. Baltazar, because process is the basic and objective structure of being. "Personality is not for the sake of nature, but nature for personality. . . . The basic flaw in the scholastic solution to the problem of nature and supernature was to relate grace to nature instead of to personality."

*Used with permission from *Continuum*, Chicago, Illinois, Spring 1964. Reprinted in *New Theology* No. 2, The Macmillan Co., New York, New York, 1965.

The validity and worth of the philosophy of procession[1] can be demonstrated by its ability to solve what may be considered as the central problem of human thought—the relation between reason and faith, nature and supernature, finite and infinite, immanent and transcendent, and now, in a new form, evolution and Incarnation. What is necessary, first, is a conversion from the Aristotelian to the Teilhardian or biblical philosophic pattern of thought. This attempt is not novel or original, since it is but an attempt to express modern man's new way of looking at reality on all the levels of his constructions and systematizations.

Aristotelian philosophy, as we know, was not a creation that was independent of its milieu. It was in fact a philosophic expression of the science of the day which aptly illustrates the maxim: as the physics so the ontology. The ancient view of the universe was Ptolemaic: the earth was the center and the sun and other heavenly bodies revolved around the earth. This geocentric pattern was reproduced in the classic view of man as the center of the world, with the lower forms of life about him. He was a microcosm, i.e., a universe on a small scale. Aristotle's genius was to integrate these views and give philosophic expression to them in a philosophy whose basic category is that of substance and whose dynamism, act and potency, is egocentric. Substance is the ultimate substratum which is no longer predicated of anything else;[2] it is a dynamic principle of identity, activity and organization;[3] it exists of itself and not in another and is the substratum of accidents.[4] We thus have a Ptolemaic view in which substance is the center and the accidents are the satellites. It was, in this context that the medieval theologians integrated theology. As F. Crowe, S.J., notes: ". . . medieval theologians took over Aristotelian philosophy, which had already integrated the mathematical and physical sciences, and added theology to obtain a coherent and closely-knit view of the universe."[5] Again we have a Ptolemaic view of truth where the truths of faith (substantia fidei) were located at the center together with philosophic metaphysical truths, and outside were the contingent and particular truths of science, related to the universal truth as instances. The emphasis in theology became from henceforth the timeless and unchanging nature of Revelation, and the self-assigned task of theologians was to be champions and defenders of the timelessness and immutability of dogma. In line with this view, too, the theologians assumed the right to say what philosophy and science can or cannot do since they possessed the universal truths of reality.

Today we have moved far from this classic and medieval world-view. There has been a conversion in outlook. First on the geophysical level the conversion has been from the Ptolemaic to the Copernican; on the biological, from the Aristotelian eternal species to the Darwinian; on the physical from the Newtonian and Euclidean fixed and mechanical explanation of matter to the Einsteinian view of relativity and the conversion of matter to energy; and on the philosophical and theological levels there has also been a conversion but not as definitive as those in science. Thus there has been a shift in our view of man from the static, objective approach in terms of his nature to the dynamic, subjective approach in terms of his personality; in philosophy in general, there has been a movement from the idealistic and metaphysical to the empirical, phenomenal and existential. In theology there is a movement back to the Bible, a movement from treating theology as timeless truths to considering the mysteries as a history of salvation, as particular and contingent events, or even developing processes.

If we single out the main characteristic of modern thought it is its historical rather than timeless view of reality. This has been achieved progressively and is true on all levels. The conversion on the scientific level has already been accomplished: the Copernican, Darwinian, Einsteinian outlooks give us an integrated view of the physical world. There has been a shift from egocentricism to a centering in the opposite: from the earth to the sun, from the past to the future, from matter to energy. There has been a shift from the static and timeless to the dynámic: the earth in orbit, matter as energy, fixed species as evolving. However, on the philosophic level no comparable conversion has yet been made. The works of the empiricists, phenomenologists and existentialists are admirable but partial, and the only attempt that can be called a philosophy in the sense of being a synthesis is that of Teilhard's *The Phenomenon of Man*. The philosophy implied in this work has not been formalized, however; and before theology can attempt a conversion from the timeless to the historical, philosophy must furnish a framework.

The process of conversion is not going to be easy, due to the conditioning of centuries. Aristotelian philosophy is a philosophy based on common sense observation just as the Ptolemaic and Euclidean views of physical reality are based on common sense; and this explains their persistence and appeal, as is evident from the Galileo case. Those who opposed Galileo took the frame of reference of common sense observation as an absolute frame of reference, and within this context Galileo was truly wrong. But his opponents were also wrong in considering this context as some kind of an absolute. Indeed, from common sense observation, the mountains and valleys are models of changelessness; the species of plants and animals are eternal and immutable. But the reason for this is that the time scale of our frame of reference is so small that within that scale no changes are perceived. But if we take a very long and wide time scale, and thus change our contextual situation, then we are able to see that everything is process. What we called permanent in what may be termed the two-dimensional setting (2-D) of common sense observation, is really process in a three-dimensional (3-D) frame of reference.

One may conclude then that substance is process. There is no contradiction here unless one takes the statement out of the context of 3-D. But even with this 3-D distinction, it is apparent that the notion of process is not correctly understood. Thus a distinguished Thomist has written:[6]

I do not question that St. Thomas made no systematic use of the idea of development or evolution in the modern sense of these words. But for one thing, that idea itself is neither enlightening nor fertile except in the context of an ontological analysis, of reality. . . . to enclose a metaphysic in a compartment of history is not a way to give evidence of a sense of history; and it is no more proof of philosophic sense to think that there is nothing more in a metaphysic than the scientific imagery which in a given era permitted it to exemplify itself in the plane of phenomena, which plane never confined it.

It is clear from the above passage that evolution or process is relegated to the category of the phenomenal or accidental as opposed to the metaphysical or substantial. And having made this identification, what applies to phenomena, namely, that they cannot enclose a metaphysic, is also applied to evolution. Again we find the identification of evolution with activity in the following observation:[7]

The subject is the reality which is principal . . . the power of operation is a complementary reality, secondary, subordinated, the principle of evolution of the individual, the principle of the "accidental" order, or the order of "secondary" perfection. It exists by the subject, in the subject and for the subject.

The same view is held by Louis de Raeymaeker who asserts that evolution is an activity of the universe.[8]

What these statements represent is an attempt to hold on to the 2-D frame of reference and then try to assimilate process or evolution in it. The 3-D statement that reality is evolving, or that substance is process is made to mean that first we have substance or a subject and from it proceeds process as an activity. The reason for this is that in 2-D, substance and accident are comprehensive categories, so that any being within that context is either substance or accident. Accidents inhere in or proceed from substance; and process is placed in the category of accident. A conclusion which seems well supported by observation: eating, talking, typing, etc., are actions and they proceed from the subject or substance and are contained in it as the effect in the cause. Process is movement, hence logically it is seen as an activity of substance, and consequently, evolution or process is seen as proceeding from substance. The fallacy however is in identifying process with activity, relative to the 2-D context.

With regard to any given concrete being, one can look at it from a 2-D or 3-D frame of reference. Thus one can look at a being here and now, abstracting from his birth and death, and this would be a 2-D frame of reference. But one can look at it from a greater time scale which includes birth and death, and this would be in 3-D. Now in 2-D one can observe activities like talking, singing, typing, etc., and they do indeed proceed from substance; but can one say that birth proceeds from substance? To say so would be tantamount to saying that this substance gives birth to itself which is a contradiction. One is driven to conclude that birth cannot be assimilated within the 2-D context, for birth is not an accident that inheres or proceeds from substance, because the substance in question does not yet exist. It does not stand out from that which precedes birth; to say otherwise would be like saying that the chicken laid the egg from which it would develop. Substance proceeds from birth and is therefore contained in birth. Now birth is not just a first event:

substance is continually born to the next moment, and hence substance is always in the context of process. Similarly with death. Death is a complete cessation or it is a rebirth. If it is a rebirth, then substance is contained in it. If it is a cessation, then in like manner, death contains substance, and not the other way around. Substance does not perdure in such a way that death inheres in it as an accident, for death means and presupposes the non-existence of substance. It is death that contains substance as the subject contains the predicate. As long as we abstract from birth and death, the 2-D category of substance-accident is all-comprehensive. But when it takes birth and death, which are the alpha and omega of process, into consideration, then it is unable to assimilate them and attempts to do so only at the cost of distorting the facts. It is more nearly true to relate substance to birth than birth to substance. What is true of our analysis is true for all beings, because all beings come to be by birth. Nothing comes to be simply an adult.

Let us consider another concrete example to illustrate how process does not proceed from substance. A seed corresponds perfectly to the Aristotelo-Thomistic notion of substance: self-enclosed, well-defined, able to exist of itself. Now, if one literally translates the substance-accident category with respect to the seed, so that process is an activity of the seed, then this would have to mean that the seed left alone is able to germinate itself, grow itself, flower and bear fruit, all by itself, i.e., without help from the "ground" (soil, moisture, heat, etc.). Given this example, one can see that the process of the seed does not proceed from the seed. What causes germination is the *union* of the seed with its "ground." It is the ground that germinates the seed, that makes it grow, matures it and lets it flower and bear fruit. Process is this continuous vital union of seed and "ground." That this *union* cannot be within the seed is obvious for it is the seed that is within the process and *is* the process, since this union is successively the seedling, the plant, the fruit. We have reached here the first stage in our conversion of the notion of substance. Thus the center of substance is process. In the example of the seed, it is not the seed that stays put, and the ground comes toward it; it is the seed that tends toward the ground. The ground is the center and the seed roots itself in it.

The second stage in this conversion is the destruction of the notion of substance as having its own act of "to be." Again, let us consider an example from the world of nature. If we look at a plant, abstracting from its rootedness in the ground, the plant seems to have its own act of "to be." But a little consideration is sufficient to show that it is the union of the plant with the ground which is the very existence of the plant. Uproot the plant and it is dead. Clearly there is no proper act of "to be" separate from the ground. All the things that we see and call substance, i.e., as having autonomous existence are really the result of *union*. Existence is not something locked up within a being or substance; this is merely the impression we get in 2-D. We see a dog move around and we say it has its own act of "to be," for it has a different existence from that of another. That observation is true in 2-D, but in 3-D, no object or substance in this universe can be understood apart from the evolutionary unity of the universe in which it is situated and from which it takes its meaning and existence. Outside of this context, it has no meaning. God is not an Aristotelian God that thinks of essences, dog, cat, man, etc., and who then puts them together to form a world. Although common speech and our common way of thinking abstract from the evolutionary context, we cannot argue from our common way of thinking to the way reality is. It is ideal to think of a single object as having an existence apart from the world; but existence is sharedness. All things are born into a world. They are not simply born, for without a "world" there is no existence. The foetus in the womb is born to the womb; its existence is continued union with the womb. When it is born, it is born into another world, and its existence is precisely this union; death being a separation from its world. The existence of what we call substance is always existence-with. *To be* is always to-be-with. Being is always being-with-another. Thus the very notion of substance as self-enclosed, as self-subsistent, as the principle of its own activities is simply a construct. We cannot define substance apart from its essential relatedness to a world.

What is true of the analysis of individual beings is true of the universe as a single evolutionary unity. The universe is a process: it is born. Yet we impose upon it the category of substance. The naturalistic evoluntionists, unconscious of the philosophic pattern of their thoughts, think it to be scientific to consider the universe as self-sufficient, as able to evolve itself. But this is comparable to saying that the seed left alone can germinate itself, grow itself, and bear fruit; and in effect it is to say that the seed is its own ground, the foetus its own womb, the egg its own hen. And yet this absurdity is preferred to admitting that the universe needs a "Ground," and this "Ground" directs it, brings out its potentialities and leads it to fulness. The universe does not contain its process like some monad or self-enclosed seed, for such a view would be a metaphysical contradiction. As Corte notes of Teilhard: "to him and men of his way of thinking, evolution demands the continuous action of creative wisdom more imperiously than does fixity (of species), for we are clearly concerned with an evolution which has a purpose, a *directed* evolution, an evolution which itself suggests that once it has reached its summit, which is man, it has nothing more to do but to stop and leave man himself the task of following it through in the order of reflective consciousness."[9] Divine creativity, therefore, is not finished; the universe through man, participates and cooperates in its own creation. It in fact is a grander and more nearly true view of God's omnipotence that he can make a creature to create himself. In what sense after all is man an image of God if he is not able to create like God?

The final result of the preceding kind of analysis would be a new ontology. The notion of being would be converted from being as substance to being as process; from being as an island, to being-with-another; for existence is a sharing, is a union. The shift in perspective may be illustrated by the example of the seed alone by itself and the seed in union with the soil, for being is not the being of the seed alone, but being-with-the-ground. Since the being of the seed is not true being, when left alone the seed dies. Hence its being is a being-towards-death. We cannot build ontology on being-towards-death. The being-towards-the-"ground" is being-towards-life: and on this alone is true being founded. Thus the paradox which Aristotelo-Thomism with its philosophy of common sense cannot see is that not everything which exists is being. Being is being only when it is *born* to *its* world; and outside it, there is no being, only death. This truth is the primitive datum of ontology. Being is union-with-a-world, not substance. The biblical view of reality is founded on this view of being: being is covenanted; creation is covenanted; man is covenanted. As regards man, he is ordained towards God as his "Thou," or "Ground," and outside of this union he is nothing. This covenant, which is a bond of union, is the basic and central category of the Bible. As Johannes Pedersen notes:[10]

> For the Israelites, one is born of a covenant and into a covenant, and wherever one moves in life, one makes a covenant. . . . if the covenant were dissolved existence would fall to pieces, because no soul can live an isolated life. It not only means that it cannot get along without the assistance of others; it is in direct conflict with its essence to be something apart. It can only exist as a link of a whole, and it cannot work and act without working in connection with other souls and through them.

Through the preceding analysis we had come to this same conclusion. There is therefore need of conversion from the category of substance to the category of relation or process. But anyone cognizant of Aristotelian categories will know that *relation* is the most ignored and most maligned of all. It is labelled as a "debellissimum ens," i.e., as the weakest of beings, and the borderline between being and non-being. It is *substance* which has claimed principal recognition as the basic category; and so the goal of a new ontology is to restore to *relation* its birthright.[11]

Process or relation is not a passing thing, it is not accidental. Destroy process, and separation or death results. It is coterminus or coextensive with existence. "Rootedness" or "union" is existence itself. Again the Israelites have the same view: ". . . annihilation of the covenant would not only be the ruin of society, but the dissolution of each individual soul."[12] Process is also necessarily the basis of epistemology, of truth. It is only in process that being unfolds, reveals itself to itself and to others. To say that the essence of the seed is seedness is pure tautology. There is no revelation of being here, but concealedness. Substance then has no meaning in itself apart from its ground or world, for meaning is based on true existence and this is attained only in the union of substance with its world. To define is to relate, not to cut off and isolate. In 2-D individualization is freedom from essential dependency, so that to be united essentially is to lose one's individuality. This view is the basic philosophy of individualism. But deeper reflection will show that union differentiates; and this is the lesson of evolution. As Teilhard notes:[13]

> In any domain—whether it be the cells of a body, the members of a society or

the elements of a spiritual synthesis—*union differentiates*. In every organized whole, the parts perfect themselves and fulfill themselves. Through neglect of this universal rule many a system of pantheism has led us astray to the cult of a great All in which individuasl were supposed to be merged like a drop in the ocean or like a dissolving grain of salt. Applied to the case of the summation of consciousnesses, the law of union rids us of this perilous and recurrent illusion. No, following the confluent orbits of their centres, the grains of consciousness do not tend to lose their outlines and blend, but, on the contrary, to accentuate the depth and incommunicability of their *egos*. The more "other" they become in conjunction, the more they find themselves as "self."

The law that individualization is to be in union may be again illustrated by the example of a plant. The more it is rooted in the ground, the greater its growth, its differentiation, its fulness; and if we move to a higher level, we observe that the "I" becomes truly a personality when it is united with its "Thou," and the greater that union, the greater the personalization.[14] Outside the inter-personal union, we have an individual but not a person.

Existence, selfhood or individuality, and meaning are all therefore to be found in the context of union or process. The Aristotelian notion of substance as autonomous, existing in and for itself, having an essence or meaning apart from any relation to the whole (evolutionary whole) is as philosophical as the observation that the sun sets and rises is scientific. The true philosophic view is that "all around us, as far as the eye can see, the universe holds together, and only one way of considering it is really possible, that is, to take it as a whole, in one piece."[15] "The distribution, succession and solidarity of objects are born from their concrescence in a common genesis."[16]

The third and last stage in the conversion of *substance* is the elimination of the view that substance (or nature) attains its end by its own powers alone. The end of being is *fulness* by a process of growth; but growth always presupposes a "ground," and hence it is through *union* that the end of being is attained. The plant attains its end not by its own powers alone but more fundamentally through rootedness in its ground; the foetus attains its birth through vital union with its womb; the feminine attains fulness through union with the masculine; and the "I" attains full personality through the powers of the "Thou" cooperating in fruition.[17] Being attains self-sufficiency only in union. Being, then, is not "proud"; the basic attitude of being is "gratitude." There is no being that can say: I stand alone.

Since *substance* tends to its "other" in order *to be* and be *true*, the dynamism of being is not a having but a giving. The conversion is from the dynamism of act and potency to the dynamism of love. "Love" in the popular conception is a sentiment or an emotion, but it is in its natural dynamism and evolutionary significance that it is considered here. In this sense, Teilhard observes:[18]

> Considered in its full biological reality, love—that is to say the affinity of being with being—is not peculiar to man. It is a general property of all life and as such it embraces, in its varieties and degrees, all the forms successively

adopted by organized matter. In the mammals, so close to ourselves, it is easily recognized in its different modalities: sexual passion, parental instinct, social solidarity, etc. Farther off, that is to say lower down on the tree of life, analogies are more obscure until they become so faint as to be imperceptible. ... If there were no internal propensity to unite, even at a prodigiously rudimentary level—indeed in the molecule itself—it would be physically impossible for love to appear higher up, with us, in "hominised" form. By rights, to be certain of its presence in ourselves, we should assume its presence, at least in an inchoate form, in everything that is.

The universe then is in the framework of love rather than that of justice. The Aristotelian view of nature would put a claim, exigency, and title in nature for its natural end. This view is correct if nature attains to its end alone, for then it must have the necessary means to attain that end, and God cannot create a being in vain. Therefore, it is claimed, God owes it to Himself to give the means by which the creature attains its end. The relation is one of justice. In line with this view, nature is seen as an objective potency which fulfills itself by receiving acts or perfections which realize its potencies. But this dynamism is relative to, and for the sake of, the deeper dynamism of being which is in union. Being in its essence is a gift. Being must first be a *we* before it can become an *I*. The seed must die to itself and give itself to the ground before there is new life. This pattern and dynamism is repeated throughout the whole hierarchy of being up to the Infinite Being.[19] And thus the biblical view conforms to this analysis of the dynamism of being. The whole of reality from the lowest to the highest is *covenanted*. The universe is seen as feminine and its perfection is to be found in that covenant which is conceived as a marriage between Yaweh and all creatures. The whole of Christian spirituality conforms to this view that it is in giving that we receive.[20] The life of the plant exemplifies the pattern for being. It is in a state of constant rootedness which is a state of constant surrender, a constant giving of self; but it is only in this dynamism that it truly possesses itself.

Since being tends towards the other in order to be, being is not in itself but in the other. Its *presentness* is not being; its *future* is the place of being and truth. In the whole Greek tradition of philosophy, the present is the region of being; the future is non-being. This Greek view is, again, based on common sense observation. The present is the center of organization where we relate the past and the future to the present. We say, "my birth" or "my death," thus relating the past and future to the present. Again, ordinary speech refers to the future as coming; we speak of the "coming" week, month, year, etc.; we consider ourselves in the present as stationary. But the problem is whether the present is stationary or whether it is in orbit. For the Greeks, reality is seen as substantially finished. Thus present reality is being or substance and the future is purely accidental. It is this view that is integrated into the Ptolemaic and Aristotelian theories. But today, when reality is regarded as evolving and tending towards fulness and transformation in the future, then the weight of being is in the future. The Omega is the Future-Universal which is also Hyper-Personal,[21] the irreversible culmination of the movement of synthesis,[22] The Centre of centres where the universe fulfills itself.[23] The Bible expresses this philosophic view in its own language as the movement of creation, represented by man himself, towards the *Land*. The word "Land" has various levels of meaning: Jerusalem, the Holy Temple, Christ and the Church, Faith, Heaven. But on all these levels, there is a common symbolism, namely that *Land* is Truth (the land of truth), Being (the land of salvation flowing with milk and honey). Being is in a journey; man is a wayfarer; we are tentdwellers.

For the Greek tradition, time is the place of opinion, of change, of non-being. Truth is in the unchanging and permanent. True knowledge is accordingly substantial or metaphysical knowledge because substance is the principle of permanence in being. The methodology for the attainment of truth and being is a flight from time by a metaphysical separation from temporality or by abstraction. All this is logical if we start with the presupposition that present reality is substantially finished. But in an evolving universe, to stay put is to die. Permanency is falsehood; process is truth. The reason is that the domain of being and truth is the future, and the only way to attain the future is to be in time. To be outside time, then, is untruth; while to be in time is truth. Instead of assimilating time into substance and so destroying its reality, we should bring substance into time, make it process, and thus restore to time its reality.

With this new view, there is now a metaphysical basis for involvement in time. In the past, the early Christians, in accordance with Hellenic philosophy, had no reason to involve themselves in time, since time was protrayed as the region of flux, error, change, non-being. There was, as a result, a physical retreat into the desert, into the monastery; a retreat into the region of the mind and the idea. Christians shunned public duties and civil affairs; and the ideal man was the thinking and contemplative man; thought was placed before action. Philosophy became a thinking philosophy and more and more withdrew from dealing with existential problems; theology likewise became a thinking theology, a textbook theology, instead of a history of salvation.[24] Our inheritance from the past resulted in a cleavage and a split in man: the duality of thought and action. Thought is substantial; action phenomenal. But in a non-Hellenic context, being as process is at once *existence and unfolding*; to act is to grow in being and be revealed to oneself.

For the Hebrew, time has always been the region of truth. Timelessness is likened to a barren woman and this state is untruth, death. To have time is to be true and it is likened to a woman with child.[25] Time was salvific for it is in time that God works his saving acts. Time matured and ripened Israel, the spouse of Yaweh, so that she gave birth to Christ, the Fulness of Time (Gal. 4:4). In the Christian dispensation, it is through liturgical time with its seasons and cycles that the Mystical Body grows to the *Pleroma Christi*. It is in time that the truth longed for by all nations is revealed. Thus we see that biblical epistemlogy is the complete opposite of Greek epistemology, and this resulted ultimately in a cleavage between bibilical thought and scholastic theology. It is in time that we see the universal who is Christ. To the Greeks this was a stumbling block: a universal could not apear in time, for time is the place of the contingent and particular. They therefore could not see Christ as God.[26]

Aristotelo-Thomism approached man wholly from the side of his nature.[27] Man was seen as an essence or being-as-object. But such a notion does not reveal the deepest in man, his uniquencess and subjectivity; for to apprehend being-as-object is to apprehend it as a thing.

The major problem however, is how to approach man as subject without being subjectivistic. It is the position here that subjectivity and uniqueness can be approached through the categories of process, namely of birth and death. Subjectivity is not attained through the dynamism of act and potency for then the person does not give itself. To know the subject one must catch it in the act of giving itself, and that act where the subject is given in its uniqueness is the act of love. The highest act of love is sacrifice or a form of "dying": that is, physical death or an act of faith where one dies to one's self-sufficiency and surrenders oneself totally to the "Other." It is in this act of immolation that the "I" is united with the "Thou" and through this union, the new "I" is born. And thus in the Bible, the categories of birth and death are the deepest of categories. On them are built the central mysteries of the Faith: the Incarnation and the Redemption. The categories of birth and death are eminently the categories that reveal being as subjective and personal.

There is no subjectivism here because *process* is the basic and objective structure of being. On the level of man, process takes on the categories of birth and death (commitment, immolation, sacrifice, suffering, love, hope, faith). The "I" is in process of birth; but to be born, there is the need of love, and love means a dying, a sacrifice. There are thus two levels in man: the level of the objective: nature; and the level of the subjective: personality. Personality is not for the sake of nature, but nature for personality. And the dynamism of nature which is that of receiving is for the sake of giving. Thus, man is not perfected by individualism but by love. The basic flaw in the scholastic solution to the problem of nature and supernature was to relate grace to nature instead of to personality.

FOOTNOTES

1. We prefer to call this philosophy that of *procession* rather than that of *process* in order to express the *verbal* rather than *substantival* character of reality. What is given here of the new philosophy is a sketch.

2. *Metaphysics*, V, 8.

3. *Sum. Theol.* Ia, Q. 4, art. 2 & 3; Ia. Q. 2, art. 3.

4. I *Sent.* d. xxiii, q. Ia. I; II *Sent.* d. xxxv, q. 2, a. 1 ad. 1.

5. Cf. "On the Method of Theology," *Theological Studies,* 23 (1962), p. 638.

6. Jacques Maritain, *Existence and the Existent* (New York: Pantheon 1948), pp. 45-46.

7. Fernand Van Steenberghen, *Ontology,* trans. Martin Flynn (New York: J. Wagner, Inc., 1952), p. 127.

8. Cf. his *Introduction to Philosophy,* trans. Harry McNeill (New York: J. Wagner, Inc., 1948), p. 49.

9. Nicolas Corte, *Pierre Teilhard de Chardin* (New York: Macmillan Co., 1960), p. 85.

10. Johannes Pedersen, *Israel, Its Life and Culture:* I (Copenhagen, 1926), p. 308.

11. There is an inherent contradiction in scholastic theology in that in its philosophy, relation is the weakest of categories and yet this weakest of categories is used to portray the highest of beings, namely the Divine Persons in the Trinity. It is true however that, scholasticism prefers to treat of the Godhead under the category of substance and its attributes under that of relation. And yet the central mystery of our Faith is the Mystery of the Holy Trinity. But the primordial mystery and the heart of the mystery is the *Eternal Procession.* This Being *is* an eternal procession. In the Godhead, process is the central category, not substance. The former category is revealed in Scripture, not the latter.

12. Pedersen, *op. cit.,* p. 308.

13. *The Phenomenon of Man* (Harper: New York, 1959), p. 262.

14. The greatest union possible according to Catholic theology is the eternal procession in the Godhead. So infinite is the union that the result is a differentiation into subsistent relations or personalities.

15. *Phenomenon,* p. 44.

16. *Ibid.,* p. 217.

17. The whole economy of faith and salvation is built on a metaphysics of process or interaction where finite reality is "I" in relation to God as "Thou." Opposed to this is the Aristotelo-Thomistic view where revelation is seen as an "It" which is accidentally related to man taken as "substance" or human nature.

18. *Phenomenon,* p. 264.

19. In the eternal procession in the Trinity, the dynamism is that of Love. As St. John says: God is Love. It is an eternal procession of love where one totally gives of Himself to the Others.

20. There is a cleavage, as many have observed, between theology where perfection is the *reception* of grace as perfective of nature and Christian spirituality where perfection is in union, in giving. The first is a dynamism of act and potency, the second, of love. This cleavage can be healed with the view of being as including the dynamism of love.

21. *Phenomenon,* p. 260.

22. *Ibid.,* p. 270.

23. *Ibid.,* p. 294.

24. Crowe, *op. cit.,* p. 637.

25. Claude Tresmontant, *A Study of Hebrew Thought* (New York: Desclée Company, 1960), p. 26-29.

26. *Ibid.,* p. 80.

27. Robert Johann, S.J., "Towards a Philosophy of Subjectivity," *Twentieth Annual Convention of the Jesuit Philosophical Association* (1958), p. 19.

CHAPTER EIGHTEEN

THE NATURE OF APOLOGETICS*

by Henri Bouillard

1. Definition and function

Christian apologetics, in the classical sense, is the theoretical and methodical exposition of the reasons for believing in Christianity. It is not to be confused with the psychology of conversion; it does not describe the diverse routes taken by souls on their way to the Christian fold; its proper object is to state the reasons for Christian belief. These it sets out in the form of a general theory in which all essential questions are systematically reviewed and the findings given as universal a bearing as possible.

Christian apologetics differs, therefore, from the act of the apostolate, which consists in placing before certain individuals or groups considerations likely to appeal to them, recognizing and resolving any difficulties, and suggesting to them the attitude of mind that will enable them to see things in a clearer light. The apostle's art, it may be assumed, is acquired by actual experience rather than academic teaching. On the other hand, what can be taught is the theory of the credibility of Christianity, the rational justification of the act of faith.

Now the rational justification of faith should, of its very nature, be of value to every human soul, Christian or not. True, Maurice Blondel insisted that its business was "to say something that will carry weight with those who do not believe." We should not, however, take this to mean that our theoretical exposition of the reasons for our belief is intended solely for the conversion of non-believers. It is also of concern to those who believe, for it brings out one of the essential characteristics, one of the permanent conditions, of faith. And that is the conviction that not only is the Christian faith reasonable but—what is far more—that it is

---

*Used with permission from *The Logic of Faith*, translation by M. H. Gill and Son Ltd., Sheed & Ward, Inc., New York. New York, 1967.

compelling, imperative. The credibility of Christianity always goes hand in hand with the Christian faith—not that the Christian is continually preoccupied with it, but in the sense that it is always available for recall when he or others may need it.

The process of reasoning whereby one becomes satisfied that Christianity is credible and becomes convinced that one not only *can* believe but *must* believe, is not by any means peculiar to the non-believer in course of conversion. It can also take place in the mind of the believer, without any suggestion that his mind has been troubled by pre-existing doubts. A sound exposition of the reasons for the faith that is in him offers the committed Christian a means of re-affirming his faith. It rids him of that inferiority complex which so many Christians feel when confronted by non-believers. It enables him to take his stand solidly and surely in an atheistic environment. More important still, it gives him a better understanding of his faith, because it brings him back to its secure foundations. From this point of view, indeed, apologetics would be better described as fundamental theology. Later on, I shall have occasion to say more about this. For the moment I would point out that apologetics would justify its existence even if it proved completely ineffectual in influencing non-believers.

But is it true, as some allege, that apologetics never succeeds in converting anybody? Admittedly, some books on Christian apologetics are not very helpful. They are so unconvincing that even believers find them unsatisfactory. They are superficial and burke the real problems; they lack method and handle their material so inadequately that the conclusions which emerge are quite incapable of satisfying an exacting mind.

On the other hand, there are also treatises on apologetics that can well be classified as outstanding; these continue to exert a profound influence. If we take inspiration and example from them we may hope that what we say will carry weight with non-believers.

Let us be very clear, however, as to how, and within what limits, apologetics can have any efficacy at all. A neurotic patient needs something more for his cure than a course of reading in psychiatry. No more does the study of a treatise on Christian apologetics suffice to bring men to Christ. By and large, the theoretical treatise only indicates in a general way an attitude of mind for adoption. It does not inevitably bring about the act by which this attitude is effectively adopted. That is not to say it is of no use; without the indications given by it, the reader would not know the road to take.

I have used the word "attitude." That is the right word, seeing that what is in question is the Christian faith. For the faith is not just the acceptance of a certain number of dogmas. It is the movement of the soul towards God, personal adherence to Christ, willingness to live as a Christian in the bosom of the Church. The intellectual assent that precedes conversion is itself an entirely voluntary act, an act of perfectly free choice; it is not necessarily compelled by the force of any argument.

No reason for believing dispenses with the act of believing. All apologetics, like all preaching, here meets the limit of its efficacy. But if it is true that faith is in accordance with reason, then we cannot believe without reason. And that is where apologetics comes into its own.

2. The sure basis of our faith

To understand more exactly the role and range of apologetics, we must call to mind the grounds on which our conviction of the truth of our faith is based. The First Vatican Council, after surveying the corpus of traditional doctrine, declared that we believe, not because we should ever be able to apprehend the intrinsic truth of the Christian message by the light of our natural reason, but because of the authority of God who reveals it. The question, therefore, is how we can be certain that the Christian message is God's revelation?

Can the fact of revelation be proved by historical arguments? If it is true that God reveals himself through the mediation of certain historical personages, undoubtedly historical knowledge of those personages plays a part in assuring us of the truth of our faith. But it is no less clear that this alone is not a sufficient basis on which to build our belief. What is involved here is not the question of knowing whether a historical demonstration supplies real evidence, or just a probability, or—more often than not—a discreet conviction. For—and let us make no mistake about it—the divine reality as such is not dependent on the mere opinion of a historian.

God is God. He is the Totally Other, incommensurable with intramundane realities. He dwells in an inaccessible light. We cannot know him, then, except through himself. If we discern him in the world about us and in our own souls, it is because he chooses to manifest himself there. If we perceive him in certain historical figures, it is because he chose to reveal himself through them. And we have no means of knowing that he really and truly reveals himself except his own revelation.

How does that revelation manage to make itself felt, we are bound to ask? How does it impose itself on us, on each of us, penetrating to the very core of our spiritual being? We can only answer that it brings conviction with it. We have the certitude that God reveals himself from the very fact that he does reveal himself to us, to each of us believers.

Revelation, in fact, does not simply consist of the objective reality of Christ and the Church, or of the objective tenor of the Christian message. There is no revelation independent of the souls that receive it. A revelation that was not received by anyone would be a misnomer. Revelation is always made to someone. Let us recall Christ's words to Peter after Peter's avowal at Caesarea: "Blessed are you, Simon Bar-Jona! For flesh and blood has not revealed this to you, but my Father who is in heaven" (*Matt.*. 16:17). It was the heavenly Father who revealed the supernatural character of Jesus to the prince of the apostles. It is God himself who is the revealer, and he reveals himself to the believer in the very act of faith which he determines and evokes.

In theological teaching this idea is commonly presented in a some-what different form. The determining factor in believing is described as the light of grace, as the holy Spirit shedding his light upon our souls and drawing them to God—the *instinctus interior Dei invitantis*. But this is sometimes interpreted too imaginatively, as if man were faced with a revelation independent of all perception, to discern and accept which he would be favoured with a supernatural light, which would let him see the revelation, and a supernatural impulse which would urge or draw him towards it. In reality there is no objective revelation beyond that which is apprehended by human souls, and the divine light in the soul is nothing other than that of the revelation received. The Word that God pronounces in Jesus Christ reaches the believer's soul through the me-dium of the holy Spirit. And the light of faith is this very Word in so far at it is apprehended by the believer.

God reveals himself to each of us in the heart of the act of faith which he determines and evokes. Our consciousness of this revelation has the quality of a direct, personal intutition; it is an intimate experience, a supernatural perception analogous to mystical knowledge. Today this is admitted by many theologians. And it is this experience of God that constitutes the sure basis of our faith.[1]

But we should beware of illuminism. I have said that the divine rev-elation brings conviction with it and that our certitude in its regard comes from our direct apprehension of it. By this I mean that it imposes itself upon us *per se* in the course of an experience personal to each of us. We must stress, however, no less strongly, that God always reveals himself through an intermediate agency, under the sign and veil of things distinct from him; we always know him in an indirect way, through signs.

Because God is infinite and we are infinitely beneath him, we cannot apprehend him in himself; we can only know him through his works. The natural knowledge that we can have of him consists of what we can discern of his manifestation of himself in the world and in the human soul. Knowledge of God by faith consists in recognizing him in the his-torical signs of his actual revelation. Whoever says revelation says mani-festation by signs. By signs we mean not alone miracles of the physical or moral order but the totality of divine action that constitutes the his-tory of salvation, the totality of creatures that God has selected and sanctified so that they may be the signs of his presence and the instru-ments of his action, in the history of mankind. The sign of signs is the human reality of Jesus Christ.

But the attestation of God in Jesus has been the object of both expec-tation and commemoration. The Jews, whose Messiah he was, had looked forward to his coming, while the Church, inaugurated by the faith and preaching of the apostles, has never ceased to commemorate him. And so we may say that God's attestation in Jesus—the period during which the signs of Christian revelation are manifest—stretches, in unbroken continuity, back into the history of the people of Israel and forward into the history of the Church. It is always through those signs, and therefore indirectly, that the believer encounters the divine revelation.

But note that these signs are not the middle term in a line of reasoning that would inevitably lead to the conclusion that God has actually revealed himself. They are the place or juncture in which we experience, the transparency (so to speak) in which we perceive, the revelation God is making to us. The point at which they mediate is the point of immediate contact between God as he reveals himself and the surge of faith that rises to meet him in the revelation. We do not reason from the signs to the revelation; we read the revelation in the signs.

But while we read the revelation in the signs, our perception of it is none the less obscure. Indeed the historical personages who bear witness to God screen him also from our sight. In order to reveal himself, God abases himself. Even the humanity of Christ implies an abasement of God and hides his real being. And how much more does it hide the human reality of the Church which can present such an equivocal aspect to the nonbeliever! In all the things that God uses as signs in revealing himself, he veils himself even as he reveals himself. One can remain blind to his revelation. One can even be scandalized at having to acknowledge the Absolute in a human—all too human—reality. We are sure, perhaps, that we have him in our grasp at last, only to find that he has again eluded us. In the words of St. Thomas Aquinas: "The revelation made to us in this life does not tell us what God is, and so our union with him is like union with an unknown Being."[2] In other words, God, even in revealing himself, remains a mystery, and it is as a mystery that he discloses himself to the believer.

Revelation, then, does not lend itself to being attested as an evident fact; we can only recognize it by agreeing to regard it as the mystery that it is. In a very real sense I perceive God revealing himself in a way that does not dispense me from believing he is revealing himself. To discern the reality of the revelation and to discern the duty to believe in it, are, therefore, both one. Through the signs I apprehend the revelation as *credendum*. The act by which I apprehend it is an act of submission and the experience is an act of obedience.

Because one can fail to understand the signs of revelation and because, in fact, many do not understand them, it will be well to inquire at this stage what conditions need to be fulfilled in order that the signs may be understood.

First, we may remark that the signs would have no meaning for anyone if the mystery they were supposed to make known had no intrinsic relation to human existence. But, as it happens, their purpose is to impress on us that communion with God is our supernatural end, and this, according to patristic and medieval tradition, revived in our own day, is the object of an immanent human desire. This means that Christ and the Church offer us communion with the living God as the answer to the question of the meaning of human existence. We can, indeed, read God's revelation in the signs to the precise extent of our capacity to read in them also the revelation of the meaning of human existence.

Now what are the conditions that enable us to understand the signs in this sense? The message which the signs bear stipulates that we must render ourselves receptive to communion in the divine life. If we would accept that life we must agree to love it more than our own natural pleasure, and, above all, to renounce all hankering after self-sufficiency in the finite field of our own activity. Anyone who would pretend to self-sufficiency in his finiteness could only reject the notions of supernatural life and revelation. For such a person, consequently, the signs of revelation would not be signs at all but either disconcerting, or else quite unimportant, facts. To anyone who has felt the yearning for the infinite but lacks the courage to accept the self-sacrifice demanded, revelation, though he might long for it, is not for him. Nor do the signs convey anything to him, because to understand them would be to apprehend revelation. But when a man has come to understand that the absolute to which he and all mankind aspire is only to be found in the death of the individual to himself; when he is ready to practise the self-abnegation that will lay him open to God's action, then the renunciation and submission imposed by Christianity will actually appear to him as a sign of its truth. He would have none of a God who would not make such demands of him. Because he is ready to welcome communion with God, he understands the signs by which it is mediated.

One, therefore, only discerns the truth of Christianity by adopting a religious attitude of mind. Such an attitude, however, is oriented in the opposite direction to that of a certain natural human bent, and so it can be adopted and maintained only by a free effort of the will. Thus it transpires that the truth of Christianity can only be discerned if one freely chooses to discern it.

We must be more precise. The religious attitude in question is not any attitude whatever. It is a Christian attitude, and that is so even if the person who adopts it is not yet fully converted; for it is an attitude that is already within the ambit of the Christian faith. In the case of a professing Christian such an attitude shows the faith itself in operation. And with that we reach the point in our reasoning where we find that the truth of Christianity is discernible only when viewed in the attitude of faith. And the firmer and fuller this attitude, the more discernible that truth will be.

But are we not guilty of reasoning in a vicious circle if we say that intellectual perception is actually conditioned by the very attitude it sets out to justify? That will be the view only of those who harbour the delusion that knowledge and liberty, intellect and will, category and attitude, are pairs of unrelated terms. In reality each term of each pair is always conditioned by its partner. We find this confirmed whenever we delve deeply enough into the works of the human intellect. Scientists who have reflected on their work have been led to remark that to understand the theories of mathematics and physics involves a certain amount of subjective acceptance.[3] It is the same with philosophy. In his *Logique de la Philosophie*, Eric Weil, when he comes to list pure attitudes by categories, observes that the transition of one category to the next is "free," and even, in a sense, "incomprehensible."[4] That is to say, man cannot be *compelled* to go beyond the position he has taken up. Even the philosopher must be allowed full liberty to express himself!

That is all the more reason why full rein should be given to that intellectual perception whose function it is to ordain and govern man's existence. How could we ever grasp divine revelation, designed to move us to the very depths of our being, if we do not open our minds and hearts freely and lovingly to the divine invader?

It must not be thought, however, that there is nothing more to be said in dialogue with those who refuse to adopt the attitude that would allow them to see the light. If, in the realm of thought, a man cannot be compelled to shift his ground, he may be shown that he has, in fact, already done so without noticing it. An analogous possibility presents itself in the religious sphere. The non-believer can be shown how, in fact, he already accepts part at least of what he says he rejects, or he might very well be reminded that something within him sits in judgement upon, and perhaps condemns, his attitude of rejection.

3. The apologetical treatise

Now that we have taken a good look at the foundation on which our conviction of the truth of our faith is firmly based, and at the conditions under which that foundation can be perceived at all, we are in a better position to define the role of apologetics more precisely.

For one brief moment, perhaps, it might have seemed that we were engaged in the process of rendering any attempt at such a definition utterly futile. If it is true that my faith is founded on a personal perception of the divine revelation that compels my recognition, of what earthly use is it to discourse on the reasons for my belief? In the language of the theologians, if the motive of faith is the object of supernatural perception, what would be the relevance of any other motive or estimate of credibility or attempt at rational justification?

But we hastened to add that divine revelation is indirect, mediated by the agency of historical personages, who are its signs. There is, then, good reason for presenting these historical figures just as they appear in history.

We said that these figures conceal at the same time as they reveal, and that the revelation they bring is never so clearly perceived that we are dispensed from believing it. It is, therefore, proper that we should understand why we are under obligation to believe.

Finally, we noted that the perception of revelation and the discernment of our duty to believe were conditioned by a certain religious attitude. There is, accordingly, good reason for stating why we should adopt that religious attitude.

This brings us back to the part played by motives and estimates of credibility, and by rational justification of the faith. Where the faith is lived peaceably and without interference, and perhaps in the case of certain conversions, reasoned judgements as to the credibility of the faith, much less their explicit formulation, are scarcely to be looked for. They remain implicit in the conviction that the faith is true. But, in any event, the certitude is there, potentially, and can be formulated. Now apologetics consists precisely in making explicit in an analytical study, based on universally valid principles, the spiritual act whereby the divine revelation is discerned in historical Christianity.

In so far as such a study is analytical, it presents, in the form of a theoretical analysis, what is commonly apprehended by the individual as a synthetic perception. Inasmuch as it is of universal import, it must include some ideal, formal plan of its subject.

How are we to set about planning a work of this kind?

We have said that God's revelation would have no meaning for us if it was not also revelation of the meaning of human existence. In order to demonstrate our duty to believe, we must, therefore, show that the Christian faith is the indispensable condition for the fulfilment of our human destiny. No apologetic is of any value that does not deal somehow or other with this point. It would be useless to enumerate miracles and prodigious events if the Christian phenomenon of which they form part could not be convincingly established as the answer to the question of our existence.

Such a demonstration must take nothing for granted that it has not first established. It will start, accordingly, from the most radical negation, and rise progressively, stage by stage, to the most abundant affirmation.

The most radical negation consists in refusing to admit that existence presents any problem at all, because existence can have no meaning, and can therefore raise no problem. This is the nihilist attitude, very widespread these days, and current in several variations. For example, it is contended that existence is absurd or fundamentally precarious, that it has no meaning other than that one chooses to give it, that the profound is only to be discovered in the superficial. These theses merit discussion, if only to show up the internal contradiction they contain.

Once it is admitted that man's existence has a meaning, there will be the temptation to look for it in human activity itself, on this side of the absolute, in an atheistic humanism. Man's existence, it will be suggested, will be fulfilled in his work, in mastering nature with the aid of science and technology, in organizing society on a purely human basis so that man shall recognize nothing superior to mankind and nothing more compelling than human ends. Supreme wisdom will then consist in being conscious of the plenitude of man's achievement. This idea, with its variations, will also have to be discussed. But there is no reason to quarrel with the idea that man finds fulfilment in his own work. The question is whether he can find total fulfilment in it; whether he can realize his true end and destiny in it when he has within his reach a means of access to something that surpasses all his mere humanity could ever achieve. We shall have to show also that in the heart of atheistic humanism there is a yearning for the Absolute that tends to well up and overflow.

We could then go on with our analysis of the human condition at the lowest stage. On the one hand, we have the finiteness of man, who has been thrown into the existent world, condemned to be free in spite of himself, doomed to evil, suffering, frustration and death. On the other hand, we should never be aware of this finiteness if we did not have within us something that would enable us to transcend it. Within us, indeed, the presence of "the one thing necessary," the divine presence, asserts itself. We must give heed to it. We shall have to show that it confronts every man with an inevitable choice—either to ignore this presence of the Absolute Being within us or to open our hearts to him. The negative choice will deprive man of the source of his existence; the positive choice, therefore, is imperative. It will mean submission of oneself to the Absolute who is the source of our existence. This submission implies self-abnegation, and consists, in the long run, in acknowledging that our fulfilment, or rather our encounter with the Absolute—for it is the same thing—can only be given us by the Absolute himself.[5]

Such a dialectic obviously leads up to the idea of a supernatural as yet vague and undetermined. And now we come to a most important point. This vague, undetermined idea of a supernatural, immanent in every soul conscious of itself, paves the way for the clear, definite idea of the supernatural offered by Christianity. This point cannot be stressed too strongly today when many of our contemporaries find the very idea of a supernatural utterly meaningless. The dialectic that brings out the idea of a supernatural is an invitation, also, to adopt a religious attitude. And this religious attitude, which is already an adumbration of the Christian attitude of faith, is necessary, as we have said, for discernment of the divine revelation.

When it has been shown what our relationship to the Absolute is, and what it ought to be, it remains to demonstrate that Christinity is the historical definition of that relationship. By virtue of this the Christian faith will appear as the condition necessary for man's fulfilment.

To give direction to this demonstration it is useful to bear in mind two things. In the first place, as historicity is an essential quality of the human being, it should be no matter for surprise that man's relationship to the Absolute should be defined in contingent historical events. In the second place, Christianity thinks of itself as a history of signs that have a very special significance. It is founded on a connected sequence of events and a doctrine that declares what they signify; and it is an integral and indissoluble whole. Of these events one is regarded as central and decisive, and around it all the doctrine is disposed. That event is the appearance of Jesus Christ. The Church proclaims Christ and aspires to live by him. It must be shown that the answer to that yearning for the Absolute which every man feels within him is that remarkable organic *ensemble* which is the Church.

This faces us with a twofold task: on the one hand, to show that Christianity views itself as a coherent *ensemble*; on the other, to show that this *ensemble* provides the means of solving the various riddles of man's relation to the Absolute, and enables man to order his life in accordance with that relationship. On one side, we have understanding the faith; on the other, understanding by faith ("faith" being used here in its objective sense of "content of the faith"). The first task is mainly one for dogmatic theology; the second is more proper to apologetics. Both, however, aim at bringing out the rational element in Christianity.

Both of these tasks, it can easily be seen, are complicated in the extreme. True, nobody is required to perform them in full in order to have a rational faith. But it is necessary for the Church as a religious organization in society that these tasks shall be performed, because the Church should be able to render a full account of the faith. Theologians, at least, ought to know and be able to explain, for example, that the dogma of the Trinity is not an algebraic conundrum; it was formulated in order to clarify what the New Testament tells us about Christ, and it enables us, besides, to solve the enigma presented by the idea of a solitary God with no life of his own. Theologians ought to know also, and be able to explain, the human signification of the dogmas of original sin and the redemption, of the eucharistic symbol and the like. In short, they ought to know and be able to explain the *ratio fidei*. In this way they will demonstrate that Christianity, that is to say, Christian life in the bosom of the living Church of Christ, is the historical definition of man's relation to the Absolute.

This demonstration will have established the necessity for man to adhere to Christianity, recognizing it to be God's revelation. But it does not dispense man from freely taking the step demanded by the faith. As we have already said, no reason for believing dispenses from believing. And it is only by experiencing the faith that man can experience the certitude of divine revelation. Apologetical demonstration will, at least, have established that it is not reasonable to refuse experience of the faith.

Furthermore, it is important to note that not only at the end of the demonstration, but also at each stage of its development, free consent is required. The presence of "the one thing necessary" must be freely acknowledged. The inadequacy of atheistic humanism must be freely acknowledged. The nihilist attitude must be freely renounced. Every thesis on the meaning of existence can be contested. But it is important to remember that if the truth cannot be known without being recognized, the truth, none the less, passes judgement on those who fail to recognize it. The need to carry on the dialectic of everyday life does not do away with the need—the spiritual need—immanent in that dialectic.

You by this time will have detected the Blondelian hallmark on my treatment of this whole subject. As a matter of fact, I do not think anybody has improved on Blondel's definition of what apologetics ought to be in our contemporary world. True, his work has its obscure patches and it is, in quite a number of respects, outdated. But it has dealt with the crucial point so well that we can still learn something form it.[6]

Moreover, no profound knowledge of the history of Christian thought is needed to make one realize that Blondel's work is nourished entirely on traditional fare. St. Augustine, St. Anselm, St. Thomas Aquinas and Pascal have worked on analogous lines, each to meet the particular requirements of his own age.

And what is more, as Blondel himself has pointed out, this method is based on St. Paul. The apostle knew that, while the Jews wanted miracles, the pagan Gentiles set store by wisdom, and it was as divine wisdom that he presented Christianity to them. How does he set about explaining why they ought to believe in Christ? Early in the epistle to the Romans he tells them that the requirements of God's law are already written on Gentile hearts, and that Gentile consciences bear witness to it.[7] He offers adherence to Christ as the authentic means whereby they can recognize God. This is the very procedure I have already pointed out when I said that it must be shown that Christianity gives us the historical definition of man's relationship to the Absolute.

4. "De Christo legato divino"

I have now indicated the broad outlines of a logically planned manual on apologetics which would, at the same time, be based on universal principles and related to our contemporary situation. How would such a work compare with the classical treatise "De Christo legato divino" (Christ, God's Envoy), still current in the seminary curriculum?

In the form familiar to us, this treatise is a work that has developed from sixteenth-century origins. Its earliest titles were "On Christian Revlation" or "On the Truth of the Christian Religion" or "On Revealed Religion." Almost from the start, it is to be found sandwiched between two other works, one on religion in general (which became, in the seventeenth century, a treatise on natural religion and the necessity of revelation) and the other on the Catholic religion and the Church of Christ, designed to prove that the Catholic Church was the only one of the various Christian denominations that complied with the intentions of Christ. The object of the treatise on the Christian religion—the *De Christo*—was to demonstrate the truth of that religion from the intrinsic merit of its teaching and the external signs of its devine origin, namely, Christ's miracles and the fulfilment of the prophecies. In short, it was an elaboration of the arguments given in the gospels themselves.

In the course of the nineteenth century, the treatise seems to have been shaken to its foundations; thenceforward its main preoccupation was to make them firm and secure once more. On the one hand, the spread of atheism to a large section of the population did away with the only background against which the gospel arguments had any rational meaning at all. On the other hand, historical criticism, in which rationalism was now prevalent, appeared to have demolished the gospel arguments by calling in question the historical value of the gospels themselves. A twofold task, therefore, seemed imperative. First, the theoretical bases of the treatise had to be consolidated, more attention being paid to the phenomenon of atheism, and more insistence being placed on the possibility of supernatural revelation, of miracles and the like. After that it became the chief function of the treatise to establish, by the use of the historical and critical method, that the gospels were true accounts of what had happened, that they depicted Jesus as, in fact, he had been, that he had really performed the miracles attributed to him, and so on.

All this involved so many complications that the future Cardinal Dechamps felt it necessary to suggest a simpler method: the initial emphasis should be placed on the signs accrediting the divine origin of the Church and from this there should be a gradual transition to Christ as preached by the Church. This method was eventually adopted, but only in part, and the *De Christo* treatise thus modified, retains its place in the curriculum. It continues to go directly to the gospel texts, treating them as ordinary historical documents, and to seek out there the person of Jesus of Nazareth, what he said and what he did, just as it was heard and seen by those that heard and saw him and—often enough—went their way unconvinced. It was hoped that this objective historical approach would in time develop into an effective method of justifying faith in Christ.

But, lo and behold! as the twentieth century went on, first the Protestant, and then the Catholic exegetes became conscious that the gospels are not strictly neutral, strictly literal, historical documents, not exact accounts of what Jesus said and did. A theological idea and intention animate them throughout. They do not report what an objective eye-witness would have remembered about Jesus. They give us, instead, in a highly specialized literary form, Jesus Christ, Jesus Messiah, Jesus Lord, as the faith of the original Christian community believed him to be, commemorated him in their worship, and preached him. It is only through the faith of these earliest Christians and by way of the literary *genre* proper to the gospels, that we can arrive at a historical knowledge of Jesus. The work of discernment is exceedingly delicate, its details are often controversial, and it must always be carried out with due regard to the very specialized nature of the gospels.

Seen in the perspective of contemporary scriptural exegesis, it is obvious that the *De Christo* treatise must be given a new look, and that its tenor and argumentation must undergo some modification. It is for the exegetes to say what requirements in the matter of criticism the apologists must now live up to, and also what fresh resources are now available to them in this regard.[8] It is our business as apologists to say how that treatise, duly renovated—or remade—by the work of the exegetes, falls in with the concept of faith we have had in mind, and how it can be inserted in the proposed apologetical work already outlined. To tell the truth, when the necessary repairs and alterations have been carried out, the venerable treatise will be much more at home there than it is now.

The object of the Christian faith, indeed, is not the figure of Jesus laboriously reconstructed by the historians; it is the figure of Christ preached by the Church, Christ in whom the Church lives, moves, and has her being. The Church, of course, realizes that the Christ of faith is identical with Jesus of Nazareth and that Jesus of Nazareth lived among men and is a historical personage. But the Church is concerned with Jesus considered as the Christ, the Holy One of God, revealed by God. Now we have already seen that there is no revelation that is not revealed to somebody. The revelation manifested in Jesus implies not only the presence of God within him but also the recognition of that presence by those that were witnesses of his life. Accordingly, it is in the faith of the apostles and the original Christian community that God's revelation of Jesus to humanity was made effective. The Church has never failed to realize this down through the ages. On the one hand, indeed, she holds that the history of revelation was brought to a close not by the ascension but by the death of the last of the apostles. On the other hand, it has always considered itself as "apostolic," that is to say, as perpetuating the faith of the apostles. A correct view, therefore, of the relation between revelation and faith puts us in the same perspective as contemporary exegesis of the New Testament: we know Jesus only through the faith of the original Christian community.

But, while the Church presents Christ to us as he appears in the faith of the earliest Christians, she realizes full well that this faith is bound up with the historical reality of Jesus. If historical criticism were to establish that Jesus had conceived himself and his mission differently from what the gospels tell us; if it were to be proved that his message had quite another meaning, that the accounts of his miracles were all literary fabrications, that the fulfilment of the Scriptures in Jesus was only a fancy of the first Christian believers, then Christian preaching would have started out from a fiction and the divine revelation would not be a historical event but a legend. The Church would all along have misconceived her own origin and her preaching would embody a permanent error. It is, then, of the most vital importance to demonstrate that this is not so. Today that is the essential task of *De Christo legato divino*, a task all the more necessary at the present time when a good many non-believers accept the findings of radical criticism, and when even the faithful are disturbed by them.

By itself the treatise *De Christo* would not appear to have the apologetical force so badly needed these days. Neither the miracles of old nor the paradoxical fulfilment of the ancient prophecies would carry much weight with our non-believing contemporaries. Mention of the sanctity of Jesus would be likely to move them only if they were to see Christian sanctity, in imitation of Jesus, openly flourishing in our own time. Likewise, the gospel message that is likely to arouse their interest is the Church's contemporary teaching of the doctrine of the New Testament, rather than the message of Jesus reconstructed by historians. And the *De Christo* alone, in present circumstances, can have little effect in furthering recognition of Christianity as the historical definition of man's relation to the Absolute.

None the less, the venerable classical treatise, suitably modified as we have said, has an essential role in such a demonstration. For it is of very great consequence indeed to establish that Christianity is not under a delusion as to what it is, when it proclaims and prizes beyond measure its attachment ot the historical figure of Jesus.

This last-mentioned and most important point cannot be established by the historical and critical method. In theory, of course, that method, being scientific, ought to afford results that would be valid in the eyes of every historian, Catholic, Protestant, or uncommitted. But it is all too true that, on a good many important points, even on some essential points, exegetes have been led, by their belief or unbelief, to different conclusions. Are we to despair, then, of ever reaching conclusions, by the scientific historical method, that will carry general conviction? Must we admit that the work to which we devote our lives is only capable of convincing the convinced?

Contemporary theories of historical knowledge, for example, those of Raymond Aron, H. I. Marrou and others, show very clearly that such knowledge necessarily comprises a subjective element. The French Revolution is not depicted in the same manner by a royalist and by a republican. We need not be surprised, then, if the history of Jesus is not reconstructed in the same manner by a Catholic, by a liberal Protestant and by a non-believer.

But let us not conclude from this that historical knowledge can never be objective, that is to say, can never arrive at universally valid results. Raymond Aron once said that objectivity in history is defined by the dialogue of historians. The objective then emerges as what is accepted by the generality of historians who take one another seriously. There are, indeed, many things on which historians have reached agreement after dialogue.

Agreement of this kind is what we ought to envisage in the historical exegesis of the New Testament. If Catholic exegetes were to be alone in maintaining, even in the name of historical method, standpoints universally and definitively rejected by other exegetes, they would be placed in a delicate position. It might very well seem to those around them that they were not speaking in the name of historical science, but in the name of their faith. Their failure to say something that carried weight with incredulous minds would mean that their work would have no apologetical impact.

It is of great consequence that those who teach the *De Christo legato divino* should take care not to pin their faith on the apologetical efficacy of statements universally contested outside the Catholic world. Even if they set store by them, let them not base apologetical argument on violently controversial material. Let them rely rather on what is accepted by the generality of serious exegetes. Let us never confuse what we can, or ought to, admit among ourselves, with what we can establish by scientific historical method. In this way only can we say something that means something to those who do not believe. If, by confining ourselves to this rigorous procedure, we should succeed in getting our message across to others, they, too, may eventually come to accept by faith what we ourselves accept in faith.

We have seen how conviction of our faith is born of a vague experience of revelation that is itself implicit in the faith. We have seen, too, how this can be made explicit in an apologetical work capable of helping souls along the road to faith.

It will have been observed that the work we have outlined utilizes both the reflections of the philosopher and the labours of the historian. It brings out, on the one hand, the structure of the reasoning process implied in the act of faith, and, on the other hand, the historical event from which Christianity springs. These are two tasks that must be undertaken if we are to demonstrate that Christianity is the historical definition of our relation to the Absolute.

In so far as it concerns the faithful, it would be better if, as I have suggested, the manual of apologetics we have been planning here were to be described as a manual of fundamental theology. The reason should be now clear. It would supply the fundamentals to which dogmatic and moral theology must always return. For it would enshrine the true sense of dogma and the logical basis, the rationale, of Christian life.

FOOTNOTES

1. Cf. Roger Aubert, *Le Problème de l'acte de foi (3e edition)*, Louvain 1958, 721-34: "La perception surnaturelle du motif de foi". Also *ibid*, 587-644.

2. S. *theol.*, Ia, q. 12, a. 13, ad I.

3. See, e.g., J. L. Destouches, *Principes fondamentaux de Physique théorique*, I, 113-4.

4. E. Weil, *Logique de la Philosophie*, Paris, 1950, 345.

5. This is a paraphrase of the classical thesis maintaining that, once God's existence is admitted, we are under the duty to show our faith in him by adopting a religious attitude, and to lay ourselves open to his action, whatever it may be, including an actual experience of divine revelation.

6. See our *Blondel et le christianisme*, Paris, 1961.

7. *Rom.* 2:15.

8. See *Bulletin du Comité des Etudes (de la Compagnie de Saint-Sulpice)*, no. 35 Octobre-Decembre 1961, 311-26.

CHAPTER NINETEEN

METAPHYSICS AS HORIZON*

by Bernard Lonergan

Fr. Coreth, ordinary professor of metaphysics at the University of Innsbruck, has given us not only a text by a professor but also a work by a philosopher.[1] The professorial hand is evident in the abundant *Zusätze* that in finer print recall historical antecedents and the contemporary setting. The philosophic mind is revealed in the sweep and subtlety of an argument that develops a unified understanding of being through a study of the being of man, the being of things, and the being of God.

The great merit of the work, in negative terms, is its clean break from the Wolffian tradition. By being is meant, not what can be, but what is. By general metaphysics is understood, not a study of some prior realm of possibilities, but an understanding of actual existents. There is analogy not only of being but also of the transcendentals, and as the being of the subject grounds the account of the being of things, so the self-realization of the subject in inquiring, knowing, and willing grounds the account of the unity, ontic truth, and ontic goodness of things. If there is no omission either of the analysis of the finite existent or of the categories of material being, still the fact that the first analogate in our analogous knowledge of being is human existence inevitably is reflected in an account of personal being, of morality, community, historicity, and religion. In brief, the transition from being as what can be to being as what is has been carried through in its full implications. When being is the existent, when our knowledge of being is analogous, the object of the science of being has to be the set of existents, and the unity of the science can be only analogical.

Still, however familiar are these premises, and indeed however classical is Fr. Coreth's doctrine, the result is a new look. For Fr. Coreth is not merely breaking from the Wolffian tradition but also implement-

*Used with permission from *Collection: Papers by Bernard Lonergan*, Herder & Herder, New York, New York. Originally published in *Gregorianum* 1963.

ing the insights of Fr. Joseph Maréchal. In this, of course, Fr. Coreth reserves the right to go his own way. As he points out (p. 12), what has come from Fr. Maréchal is not a school but a movement, not a set of ready-made opinions repeated in unison by members of a uniform group, but a basic line of thought that already has developed in various manners and still continues to do so.

The substance of Fr. Coreth's development can best be approached through a consideration of his method. This he deduces from the assumption that metaphysics is the *Gesamt- und Grundwissenschaft* (total and basic science): it is total, for being includes everything; it is basic, for it accepts no presuppositions that it itself does not justify. Its method, accordingly, will have to be a mediation of immediate knowledge (pp. 68 f., 233). Though a subordinate use of synthetic-inductive and analytic-deductive procedures is granted (pp. 88 ff.), still such mediate knowledge cannot meet the main issues, for it has presuppositions (pp. 61 ff.). On the other hand, immediate knowledge in its immediacy will not do, for simply to assert the evidence of one's fundamental metaphysical views only provokes the answer, *quod gratis asseritur, gratis negatur* (p. 67). It remains that the main method in metaphysics is a mediation of the immediate. There exists a latent metaphysics, present and operative in all our knowing; it is the metaphysical *Ureinsicht* (primitive insight) in its immediacy; but it has to be thematized and made explicit, to be brought out into the open in accurately defined concepts and certain judgments (pp. 68 f.). The main task of the metaphysician is not to reveal or prove what is new and unknown; it is to give scientific expression to what already is implicitly acknowledged without being explicitly recognized (p. 93).

The proper tool in this mediation of the immediate is the rejection of the counterposition. Explicit judgments can contradict the latent metaphysics that they presuppose; but one has only to bring this contradiction to light, for the explicit judgment to be evident nonsense, and for its opposite to be established (p. 68). Such a procedure Fr. Coreth names transcendental method: its basis lies, not in the content of the judgment, but in the conditions of its possibility (p. 69); and he does not hesitate to assert that "transcendental method, as we understand it, is not only the fundamental method that is demanded by the nature of metaphysics as basic science; it is also, one might venture to say, the integral method that takes over all other methods which, standing in isolation from one another, are insufficient, takes them over and, while respecting their legitimate concerns, raises them to a higher unity."[2]

Such a tool, clearly, needs a point of application, and this Fr. Coreth finds in the concrete, conscious, active reality of the subject asking a question. To doubt questioning is to involve oneself in a counterposition, and so questioning is beyond the doubter's capacity to doubt coherently. Presuppositionless metaphysics, accordingly, begins from questioning: not from the appearance of it, nor from the concept of it, nor from judgments about it, but from the performance, the *Vollzug* (pp. 77 ff.). Linking such performance with conditions of possibility is the *Auslegung* (explicitation) in a sense carefully differentiated from that of Husserl and Heidegger (pp. 76, 91 ff.).

After the foregoing, merely introductory, discussion of method, the argument proper beings. No doubt, the proper place to begin is at the beginning, but some say one issue and others say another is the proper beginning. So there is a question about the beginning and, indeed, no matter where one starts, one starts from some question. For Fr. Coreth, then, questioning itself is the beginning.

What is the condition of the possibility of questioning? In other words, what is the essence of questioning, what is found in every question to constitute it, not as question about this rather than about that, but simply as questioning? It is claimed that the condition of the possibility of any and all questions is an awareness that goes beyond the. already known to an unknown to be known (p. 130).

What is this awareness of? At least, it is of the questionable, for if nothing were questionable, there could be no questions. But, further, the questionable is unrestricted: to propose a limit to questioning is to raise the question of the legitimacy of asking questions beyond the limit; and raising this question is already beyond the limit. In other words, to limit questioning lands one in a counterposition. Finally, as the questionable is unrestricted, so it is somehow one. For the condition of the possibility of questioning is always the same, going beyond the already known to an unknown that is to be known; it follows that the questionable, of which questioning is aware, must be as much one as the awareness that constitutes questioning.

Still, what is it that is questionable, unrestricted, one? It is being. Being is the questionable: it is the great unknown, that all our questions are about (quid *sit*? an *sit*?) and never exhaust; it is unrestricted, for apart from being there is nothing; finally, it is one for, despite all other differences, every instance of being is.

But we say "is" and "is not" in such different ways: we say there "is" a moon; but we also say there "is" a logarithm of the square root of minus one. In brief, there is a realm of absolute and unrestricted validity in which things "are" *simpliciter*, and there are other realms in which they "are" indeed but still are merely logical, merely mathematical, merely hypothetical, merely phenomenological, and so on. Which is the realm that is the condition of the possibility of asking questions? Plainly, we ask questions with respect to all realms, but the realm of being that is the condition of questioning is the one that must be presupposed for there to be the others. When one states that a statement is merely logical, one means that really and truly it is merely logical. It follows that one cannot suppose that all statements are merely logical, for then it would be merely logical that they are merely logical, and it would be impossible to say that any really and truly is merely logical. The same holds for the merely hypothetical, the merely phenomenal, and any other restricted or qualified realm. By the same stroke any and every form of idealism is excluded. The possibility of questioning is being, and this being is being in its unqualified sense, *An-sich-Sein* (being-in-itself). "From this it follows that there never is and never can be a closed 'inner area' of transcendental subjectivity, for subjectivity in its very perform-ance is already 'outside' in the realm of being-in-itself in general which transcends subjectivity. Performance is constituted in its nature and its possibility by its horizon, but the horizon in which subjectivity realizes itself is always the horizon of being-in-itself in general."[3]

Now we might continue to follow Fr. Coreth's argument. We should learn that questioning not only is about being but is itself being, being in its *Gelichtetheit* (lucidity), being in its openness to being, be-ing that is realizing itself through inquiry to knowing that, through knowing, it may come to loving. This being of the questioning questioner is the latent metaphysics from which explicit metaphysics is derived; and in explicit metaphysics it is the primary analogate through which other being as being is understood.

However, as we cannot reproduce the book, it will be more profitable to locate it. If the more obvious location would be in the German philo-sophic tradition, with which Fr. Coreth has the familiarity of one born on the spot, it will be more helpful, I think, to turn to the contempor-ary scholastic milieu, to which Fr. Coreth also belongs. Accordingly, I shall select for purposes of contrast Prof. Gilson's *Réalisme thomiste et critique de la connaissance (Paris, 1939)*. It is true, of course, that that book is not the whole of Prof. Gilson, and that Prof. Gilson is not the only opponent of Fr. Maréchal. It remains that Prof. Gilson's book is still influential (*Theological Studies*, 22 [1961], p. 561) and that our pur-pose is not a survey of contemporary scholasticism but an introduction to Fr. Coreth's thought. Our question is, then: In what manner do Kant, Prof. Gilson, and Fr. Coreth differ?

First, then, it is to be noted that the operative moment in Fr. Coreth's use of transcendental method cannot occur in a Kantian context. For that operative moment lies in a contradiction not between content and content but between content and performance; but a Kantian context is a context of contents that does not envisage performances. Thus, there is no ex-plicit contradiction in the content of the statement, We are under an il-lusion when we claim to know what really is. On the other hand, there is an explicit contradiction in the reflective statement: I am stating what really and truly is so, when I state that we are under an illusion when-ever we claim to know what really and truly is so. However, the content of the explicitly contradictory statement adds to the content of the first what is found implicitly in the first, not as content, but as performance. Now to bring to light such contradictions is the operative moment in Fr. Coreth's use of transcendental method. But such an operative moment cannot occur in a Kantian context for, while Kant envisages an *Ich denke* (I think) as a formal condition of the possibility of objective contents be-ing thought, still he cannot find room for a concrete reality intelligently asking and rationally answering questions. In brief, phenomena appear, but they do not perform; and transcendental conditions of possibility within a transcendental logic do not transcend transcendental logic.

If the point has been explained, it will be well to apply it. Kant, then, acknowledges the need of the concept of noumenon as a *Grenz-begriff* (limiting concept): such a concept is of no use to him in knowledge of things, for he knows no noumena; but the same concept is essential to him, if he is to state the limitations of our *Anschauung* (intuition), if he is to state that we perceive not noumena but phenomena (*Kritik der reinen Vernunft* [=*K. R. V.*] B 310 f.). Now Fr. Coreth would not claim that this passage in the *Kritik* is contradictory, for a passage is just a sequence of contents. He would claim that it is contradictory when the performer is added. For what the performer wants to assert is that really and truly our *Anschauung* is not of what really and truly is and, none the less, that we cannot know what really and truly is. This contradiction lies, not in the content uttered by the mind, but in the mind that utters the content, and not in a formal entity that merely thinks thoughts, but in a concrete intelligence that by its performance means and by its uttered contents denies that we know what really and truly is so.

Secondly, if now we turn to a comparison of Prof. Gilson's position with Kant's, the differences appear massive. Kant is a critical idealist; Prof. Gilson is neither critical nor an idealist. But so radical an opposition does not preclude all similarity, for Prof. Gilson's door to his real world is perception, and Kant's door to his world of appearances is *Anschauung*.

For Kant, the judgment that seven and five are twelve is synthetic and *a priori*. Still it is only *a posteriori*, by an empirical *Anschauung*, that Kant knows five books in one pile on his desk, seven in another, and so necessarily twelve in all. Moreover, this function of *Anschauung* is universal. *Anschauung* is the one means by which our cognitional operations are related immediately to objects (*K.R.V.*, A 19, B 33). Judgment is only a mediate knowledge of objects, a representation of a representation (*K.R.V.*, A 68, B 93). Reason is never related right up to objects but only to understanding and, through understanding, to the empirical use of reason itself (*K.R.V.*, A 643, B 671).

Of the pivotal importance of empirical *Anschauung* in his system, Kant was fully aware. It was his refutation of Pure Reason, for concepts and, along with them, principles can refer to objects and so can possess objective validity only through *Anschauung*. Of themselves, no matter how *a priori* they may be, they are the mere play of imagination and understanding (*K.R.V.*, B 301). But what condemns pure reason, by the same stroke condemns realism. For the only *Anschauung* we enjoy is sensitive; sense does not know noumena; and so our concepts and principles have no reference to noumena. Human cognitional activity is confined to phenomena.

Prof. Gilson is equally convinced that perception is the one manner in which cognitional activity attains objectivity. He differs from Kant, not on the question of principle, but on the question of fact. He maintains an immediate realism and, as he very acutely remarks in his *Realisme thomiste*, "Kant himself maintains an immediate realism with regard to the existence of a Kantian external world."[4] Accordingly, there are two questions. What is Prof. Gilson's fact? Does this mean that the whole issue turns upon a fact?

Prof. Gilson's fact is not the exact opposite of Kant's. Kant asserts that sense does not apprehend noumena, and Prof. Gilson is far from asserting that sense does apprehend noumena. His assertion is that over and above sensitive perceptions and intellectual abstractions there exists an intellectual vision of the concept of being in any sensible datum. Moreover, he adds, it is the concept of being, seen in this manner, that is predicated in perceptual judgments of existence. Thus, "the apprehension of being by intellect consists in a direct *vision* in any sensible datum whatever of the concept of being."[5] Again, "When the concept of being is abstracted from a concrete existent perceived by the senses, the judgment predicating being of this existent attributes being to it . . . as 'seen' in the sensible datum from which the concept of being was abstracted."[6] So much for the matter of fact.

But how does it come about that Prof. Gilson differs from Kant on a question of fact and not, as Fr. Coreth, on a question of principle? The reason is very simple. Prof. Gilson does not advert to Fr. Coreth's principle and, indeed, could not admit it without changing his own principles.

For Prof. Gilson idealism does not necessarily involve a contradiction. He denies flatly that he ever held critical idealism to be contradictory (p. 160, note). He asserts that, once Berkeley's starting point is admitted, one cannot find a contradiction from one end of his work to another (p. 195). He maintains that, if one starts from critical premises, then one may conclude to existence, but the concluded existence will be merely a postulate or merely a predicate (p. 183).

Now, if idealism is possible, there exists the problem of the bridge. Abstract concepts of *l'être en général* and of existence are one thing. Concrete, actual, extramental existence is another. To think the former is one thing. To know the latter is another. There has to be some ground, some principle, some evidence, if idealism is to be rejected, if it is to be claimed that we not merely think about immanent objects but also know extramental realities (cf. p. 185).

Further, the needed ground, principle, evidence cannot be reached by a deduction. If the premises are understood in a realist sense, then realism is not proved but presupposed. If the premises are understood in a nonrealist sense, then the conclusion has to be understood in the same sense, and so realism is not concluded. Realism must be immediate truth.

Moreover, this immediate truth cannot be anything proper to intellect, any innate knowledge, any *a priori*. When Prof. Gilson adduces the axiom, *nihil in intellectu nisi prius fuerit in sensu*, (there is nothing in the intellect unless it was previously in the senses), he claims that it is to be taken with absolute universality and that it is to be applied with full rigor. No exception is to be admitted, not even for being and the principle of contradiction (p. 200).

It follows that realism is possible if and only if we *preceive* reality. Some ground for it is needed, for idealism is possible. That ground cannot be a deductive conclusion. It cannot be innate or *a priori* knowledge. Therefore it must be *a posteriori*. On this point Prof. Gilson is explicit in a manner calculated to leave no loop-holes. "Thus, no matter what way we may put the question to realism, no matter how profoundly we may inquire of it, How do you know a thing exists? its answer will always be: By perceiving it."[7]

However, if Prof. Gilson agrees with Kant in holding that objectivity is a matter of perception, if he differs from Kant in holding that *de facto* we have perceptions of reality, one must not think that he attempts to refute Kant by appealing to a fact that Kant overlooked. Prof. Gilson's realism is dogmatic; the course he advocates is ". . . the blunt reaffirmation of the dogmatic realism whose validity was denied by Kant's critique."[8]

This does not mean that Prof. Gilson has no reasons for being a realist. He was a realist before he began philosophy. His study of philosophy, so far from leading him to abandon realism, has only confirmed his original convictions. For him the history of philosophy moves about an axis, and the axis is sanctioned by a Herodotean law of compensation. This axis is realism, and its sanction is that "When a man refuses to think as a realist where he ought to do so, he condemns himself inevitably to think as a realist where he ought not to do so."[9]

Prof. Gilson's dogmatism, if I understand him, is that the whole is prior to the parts, that realism is a whole, prior to its parts, and so incapable of being assembled by starting from some part and step by step adding on the others. We have already noted the proof that realism cannot be proved deductively. But the opposite procedures of advancing inductively or constructively, if not demonstrably impossible, certainly bristle with difficulties. In any case, Prof. Gilson does not attempt them.

His fact of intellectual perception is not conceived independently of his Thomist system. It is not investigated simply in terms of psychological introspection and analysis. On the contrary, Prof. Gilson does not believe metaphysicians should attempt to do psychology (p. 125). He asserts a general osmosis between sense and understanding, but leaves it to psychologists to work out the details (p. 207). He indicates the area in which the perceptual judgment of existence is to be found, but he makes no effort to survey, explore, and work out a detailed report (p. 225). Prof. Gilson's fact is not a manifest datum, accessible to anyone, by its sheer givenness imposed on any and every philosopher. On the contrary, its givenness is vague and its accessibility is restricted. And even were its givenness precise and its accessibility universal, that would not prevent the Kantian from placing the perceived existence in the category not of noumena but of phenomena. "That is why in the last analysis you do not accept any part of realism unless you accept it whole and entire."[10]

Thirdly, to complete our circle of comparisons, we must now turn to Prof. Gilson and Fr. Coreth. Here we are met with massive similarities, and it is the difference that requires clarification. For both are realists: they acknowledge the real existence of minerals, plants, animals, men, and God. Both are immediate realists: though Fr. Coreth mediates this immediacy, still for him no less than for Prof. Gilson realism is immediate truth. In both immediate realisms an *a posteriori* component is recognized: neither attempts to restore the Pure Reason that Kant undertook to refute. Not only are both Thomists, but also both are quite convinced of the priority of metaphysics, over everything in general and over cognitional theory most particularly. Finally, as realism for Prof. Gilson is a whole, as his thinking deals with philosophies as wholes, so too for Fr. Coreth the priority of the whole over the parts is cardinal.

The basic difference is that, while Prof. Gilson's immediate realism cannot be mediated and so is dogmatic, Fr. Coreth's immediate realism not only can be but also is mediated. For Prof. Gilson realism is a whole that one must accept or reject, and with this Fr. Coreth agrees. For Prof. Gilson realism is a whole that cannot be assembled step by step with every step guaranteed as alone rational, and with this Fr. Coreth flatly disagrees. His transcendental method is essentially the method for explicitating the whole: for transcendental method ascertains conditions of possibility, and the first and foremost of all conditions of possibility is the whole itself.

Let us attempt to get clear this point about a philosophy as essentially a whole. Aristotle and Aquinas distinguish the expert and the wise man: the expert orders everything within a restricted domain; the wise man orders everything. Further, to call a congress of all experts representing all restricted domains does not secure the presence of a wise man, for none of the experts knows the relations between the restricted domains. Knowledge of the whole, then, is distinct from knowledge of the parts and it is not attained by a mere summation of the parts. The very fact that the expert restricts his domain implies that he also restricts the number of aspects under which he considers the objects within his domain; as the restrictions are removed, further aspects come to light; only when all restrictions are removed, do all aspects come to light; and once all restrictions are removed, there can be no ulterior and higher viewpoint from which new aspects come to light with a consequent revision and reordering of previous acquisition. So the unrestricted viewpoint is ultimate and basic: it is wisdom and its domain is being.

Now it is technically simpler to express the foregoing in terms of "horizon." Literally, a horizon is a maximum field of vision from a determinate standpoint. In a generalized sense, a horizon is specified by two poles, one objective and the other subjective, with each pole conditioning the other. Hence, the objective pole is taken, not materially, but like the formal object *sub ratione sub qua attingitur* (under that aspect which the activity specifically regards); similarly the subjective pole is considered, not materially, but in its relation to the objective pole. Thus, the horizon of Pure Reason is specified when one states that its objective pole is possible being as determined by relations of possibility and necessity obtaining between concepts, and that its subjective pole is logical thinking as determining what can be and what must be. Similarly, in the horizon of critical idealism, the objective pole is the world of experience as appearance, and the subjective pole is the set of *a priori* conditions of the possibility of such a world. Again, in the horizon of the expert, the objective pole is his restricted domain as attained by accepted scinetific methods, and the subjective pole is the expert practising those methods; but in the horizon of the wise man, the philosopher of the Aristotelian tradition, the objective pole is an unrestricted domain, and the subjective pole is the philosopher practising transcendental method, namely, the method that determines the ultimate and so basic whole.

Now, to connect the foregoing with a point made earlier, the fact of horizon explains why realism and, generally, a philosophy cannot be proved deductively. The reason is that horizon is prior to the meaning of statements: every statement made by a realist denotes an object in a realist's world; every statement made by an idealist denotes an object in an idealist's world; the two sets of objects are disparate; and neither of the two sets of statements can prove the horizon within which each set has its meaning, simply because the statements can have their meaning only by presupposing their proper horizon. Further, what is true of statements is equally true of the statement of problems and of the statement of solutions; problems and solutions are what they are only in virtue of the horizon in which they arise; they cannot be transported intact into a different horizon. So we arrive in general terms and on the level of principle at the type of point that was made in a specific form by Prof. Gilson when he claimed: "I have never maintained that critical idealism is contradictory. What is contradictory is critical realism or, more precisely still, wishing to pose the problem of critical idealism from the viewpoint of Thomist realism. My thesis says no more than that."[11]

However, if Fr. Coreth grants that statements have a meaning only within a horizon, how can he escape the dogmatism that Prof. Gilson believes inevitable? The asnwer is that he begins, not from statement, but from a performance, a *Vollzug*, asking questions. It is a performance that begins early in childhood and is continued even by an Aquinas until a higher form of knowledge supervenes. No doubt, that performance will be interpreted or overlooked in different manners when assumed within different horizons; but it is given to be interpreted or overlooked whether or not it is assumed. Nor can any doubt be entertained about the fact of the performance. To doubt questioning is to ask whether questions occur. The condition of the possibility of doubting is the occurrence of questioning. Fr. Coreth, then, begins from a clearly known, universally accessible, indubitable occurrence.

Now that occurrence is also the subjective pole in the horizon he is mediating. It determines its correlative objective pole, which like questioning is one and unrestricted. Its name is being; for being is one, since every being *is*; and being is unrestricted, for apart from being there is nothing.

Now the determination of the two poles is the determination of a horizon, and it is easy to see that Fr. Coreth's horizon is total and basic. It is total, for beyond being there is nothing. It is basic, for a total horizon is basic; it cannot be transcended, gone beyond, and so it cannot be revised.

But further for Fr. Coreth being is precisely what St. Thomas meant by being. For as intended in questioning, being is unrestricted. In that premise there is already included the conclusion that *esse de se est illimitatum* (being of itself is unlimited), whence it will follow that finite being is a compound of essence and existence and that every *ens* is an *ens* by its relations to *esse*.

From this it would seem to follow that being for Fr. Coreth and being for Prof. Gilson must be exactly the same. For Prof. Gilson also means by being what St. Thomas meant. It remains that this identification is not without its difficulties, for if the objective pole in Fr. Coreth's horizon is the same as the objective pole in Prof. Gilson's, the subjective poles are manifestly different.

Thus, Fr. Coreth would accept the principle, *nihil in intellectu nisi prius fuerit in sensu.* But he would have to distinguish, say, between the way there is nothing in a box and the way there is nothing in a stomach. When there is nothing in a box, a box does not feel empty; when there is nothing in a stomach, the stomach does feel empty. Human intelligence is more like a stomach than like a box. Though it has no answers, and so is empty, still it can ask questions.

Further, for Prof. Gilson being (p. 225) or the concept of being (pp. 215, 226) is "seen" in the data of sense. But for Fr. Coreth being is what is asked about with respect to the data of sense. So far from being seen in data, being, for Fr. Coreth, is what is intended by going beyond the data. For questioning goes beyond an already known to an unknown that is to be known: for Fr. Coreth the already known is the datum, and the unknown to be known is being.

Again, for Prof. Gilson, our knowledge of being is *a posteriori*: abstract concepts of being and existence are had by abstracting from sense; and to reach the concrete there is added to the abstractions his intellectual vision. But, for Fr. Coreth, being is an *a priori*, i.e., the intention of being in questioning bears no resemblance to sensitive or empirical knowledge. What is perceived, is not unknown, not to be known, but already known. But being as intended in questioning is the exact opposite of the object of perception: it is not already known; it is unknown; it is to be known. In other words, the analysis of questioning forces one to conceive human intelligence, not on the analogy of sense, but properly in terms of intelligence itself.

Moreover, we have seen that Fr. Coreth rejects the idealist's acceptance of idealism as contradictory, that Prof. Gilson regards idealism as
non-contradictory, that consequently he is left with a problem of a bridge
from a concept of *l'être en général* to an *existence concrète, actuelle,*
extramentale; and that, inevitably enough, this bridge has to be an intellectual perception of existence. This narrative, it would seem, enables
us to pick the exact point at which Prof. Gilson and Fr. Coreth part
company. Both agree that idealism is noncontradictory. But where Fr.
Coreth maintains that the idealist's acceptance of idealism is contradictory, and so eliminates the problem of the bridge, Prof. Gilson acknowledges a problem of a bridge and so arrives at his need for an intellectual
perception of being. Hence being can be *a priori* for Fr. Coreth, because
for him the idealist is involved in self-contradiction; but being must be
a posteriori for Prof. Gilson, because for him idealism is not self-contradictory.

Finally, there remains the question how Fr. Coreth and Prof. Gilson
both arrive at the same objective pole, being in the Thomist sense, when
their subjective poles are mutually exclusive. The explanation would seem
to be that, if Prof. Gilson does not thematize questioning, none the less
he asks questions and so intends what is intended in questioning; further, while Prof. Gilson asserts an intellectual perception of existence,
still he is careful to integrate this perception within the structure of
Thomist cognitional theory, and so is able to shift from a theory of being
as something seen in data to a theory of being as something affirmed in
perceptual judgments of existence. Hence, inasmuch as Prof. Gilson
asks questions and gives rational answers, his position concides with that
of Fr. Coreth, and as the subjective poles are the same so the objective
poles are the same. On the other hand, if Prof. Gilson were to operate
simply and solely with a concept of being that can be "seen" in any
sensible datum, not only would his subjective pole differ from Fr.
Coreth's but also it would be impossible for him to reach being in the
Thomist sense as his objective pole; for being as object of perception is
being in which essence and existence are only notionally distinct.

Fourthly, we have been comparing Kant, Prof. Gilson, and Fr. Coreth
two at a time; there remain a few questions that are best put with respect to all three at once.

First, then, despite his use of such terms as "transcendental" and
"*a priori,*" Fr. Coreth is completely in agreement with Prof. Gilson's
contention that ". . . what is contradictory . . . is wishing to pose the
problem of critical idealism from the viewpoint of Thomist realism."[12]
Indeed, Fr. Coreth excludes as impossible within his horizon not only
critical idealism but any idealism and along with them Prof. Gilson's
perceptionism. For him there can be no problem of the "extramental,"
of getting outside the mind, for as soon as a question is asked, being is
intended, being includes everything, and so everything already is within
the mind's intention: ". . . subjectivity in its very performance is already
'outside' in the realm of being-in-itself in general."[13]

Secondly, does Fr. Coreth perceive being or does he not? I think his answer would be that (1) being is not known without perceptions, (2) being is not known by perceptions alone, and (3) by the light of intelligence we know whether or not what we perceive is. In other words, he would not say with Prof. Gilson that we know being by perceiving it; and he would say with St. Thomas: ". . . what those words of Augustine mean is this, that we do not expect to derive truth entirely from the senses. We also need agent intellect's light; through this we attain to unchanging possession of truth in changing things, and distinguish the things themselves from their mere likenesses."[14]

Thirdly, Fr. Coreth would agree with Prof. Gilson's statement: ". . . the transcendental viewpoint of *a priori* conditions for the object of knowledge is ignorant by definition of the empirical problem of the existence in themselves of the objects known."[15] He would point out, however, that Prof. Gilson is speaking of Kantian thought; and he would indicate the two essential differences between his approach and Kant's. First, his transcendental inquiry is, not into the *a priori* conditions of cognitional objects, but into the *a priori* conditions of questions. Kant wrote an *Erkenntniskritik*: the conditioned is the objective pole, the condition is the subjective pole. Fr. Coreth is writing a metaphysics: his subjective pole, questioning, is the conditioned; and his objective pole, being, is the condition. Hence Fr. Coreth's transcendental inquiry is just the inverse of Kant's. Secondly, Kant's *a priori* is in the essentialist order and so, as we have seen, it is solely through *Anschauung* that it can have any objective reference or any objective validity; further, since this *Anschauung* is not of noumena, there cannot arise within the Kantian approach any question of the *existence en soi* of the objects known in Kant's world as appearance. But what follows from Kant's *a priori*, does not follow from Fr. Coreth's. Fr. Coreth's is being an unrestricted, the whole of all that is; within being there is already included *An-sich-Sein*. Not only does *An-sich-Sein* lie within Fr. Coreth's transcendental viewpoint, but also from that very fact it follows that Fr. Coreth's treatment of objectivity differs totally from Kant's and, indeed, from that of any perceptionist. For Kant cognitional operations can be related to objects only through *Anschauung*, so that perception has to be the constitutive principle of objectivity. For Fr. Coreth the constitutive principle of objectivity is the question: questioning immediately intends being; data are referred to being as what questions are about; answere are referred to being as answers to questions. Fr. Coreth's position on objectivity is the inverse of the Kantian position; it also is the inverse of the perceptionist position, which relates our cognitional operations to reality, not through the intention of being in the question, but through sense.

At the end of this attempt to locate Fr. Coreth's position within the scholastic context, I must note that my operation is not altogether in accord with Fr. Coreth's exclusion on an *Erkenntniskritik*, his aim of presuppositionless metaphysics, his projected inclusion within metaphysics of an *Erkenninismetaphysik*. The fact is, of course, that while I consider

Fr. Coreth's metaphysics a sound and brilliant achievement, I should not equate metaphysics with the total and basic horizon, the *Gesamt- und Grundwissenschaft.* Metaphysics, as about being, equates with the objective pole of that horizon; but metaphysics, as science, does not equate with the subjective pole. In my opinion Fr. Coreth's subjective pole is under a measure of abstraction that is quite legitimate when one is mediating the immediacy of latent metaphysics, but is to be removed when one is concerned with the total and basic horizon. In the concrete, the subjective pole is indeed the inquirer, but incarnate, liable to mythic consciousness, in need of a critique that reveals where the counterpositions come from. The incarnate inquirer develops in a development that is social and historical, that stamps the stages of scientific and philosophic progress with dates, that is open to a theology that Karl Rahner has described as an *aufhebung der Philosophie.* The critique, accordingly, has to issue in a transcendental doctrine of methods with the method of metaphysics just one among many and so considered from a total viewpoint. For latent in the performance of the incarnate inquirer not only is there a metaphysics that reveals the objective pole of the total horizon but also there is the method of performing which, thematized and made explicit, reveals the subjective pole in its full and proper stature. Still, it is difficult to disagree completely with Fr. Coreth, for in my disagreement I am only agreeing with his view that, what has come from Fr. Maréchal is, not a set of fixed opinions, but a movement; indeed, I am only asking for a fuller sweep in the alternations of his dialectic of *Vollzug und Begriff.*

FOOTNOTES

1. Emerich Coreth, *Metaphysik. Eine methodisch-systematische Grundlegung.* Innsbruck-Vienna-Munich: Tyrolia-Verlag, 1961, p. 672.

2. *Op. cit.*, p. 88: "Die transzendentale Methode, wie wir sie verstehen, ist nicht nur die fundamentale Methode, die vom Wesen der Metaphysik als Grundwissenschaft gefordert ist; sie ist auch, wenn wir so sagen dürfen, die integrale Methode, die alle anderen, isoliert genommen unzureichenden Methoden in ihrem berechtigten Anliegen aufnimmt und in eine höhere Einheit aufhebt."

3. *Op cit.*, p. 193: "Daraus folgt, dass es einen gescholossenen 'Innenraum' der transzendentalen Subjektivität in ihrem Vollzug immer schon 'draussen' ist beim Ansich-Sein überhaupt, das sie selbst übersteigt. Der Vollzug ist in seinem Wesen und seiner Möglichkeit konstituiert durch seinen Horizont; der Horizont aber, in dem die Subjektivatä sich vollzieht, ist immer schon der Horizont des An-sich-Seins überhaupt."

4. *Op. cit.*, p. 176: "Kant lui-meme ... soutient un réalisme immédiat de l'existence d'un monde extérieur kantien."

5. *Op. cit.*, p. 215: "... l apprehension de'l être par l'intellect consiste à *voir* [his italics] directement le concept d'etre dans n'importe quelle donnée sensible."

6. *Op. cit.*, pp. 225 f.: "... Lorsque le concept d etre est au contraire abstrait d'un existant concret perçu par les sens, le judgment qui prédique l'être de cet existant le lui attribue ... comme 'vu' [his quotation marks] dans le sensible donné dont il l'abstrait."

7. *Op. cit.*, p. 203: "Ainsi, de quelque manière et à quelque profundeur de plan que nous lui posions la question; comment savoir qu'une chose existe? le réalisme répond: en la percevant."

8. *Op. cit.*, p. 163: "... la réaffirmation brute du réalisme dogmatique dont la valeur a été niée par la critique de Kant."

9. *Op. cit.*, p. 228: "Lorsqu'un homme refuse de penser en réaliste où il faut, il se condamne inévitablement à penser en réaliste là où il ne faut pas."

10. *Op. cit.*, p. 224: "C'est pourquoi, en fin de compte on ne prend rien du réalisme tant qu'on ne le prend pas tout entier."

11. *Op. cit.*, pp. 160 f., note: "Jamais je n'ai soutenu que l'idéalisme critique est contradictoire; ce qui contradictorie, c'est le réalisme critique, ou, plus présciement encore, c'est de vouloir poser le problème de l'idéalisme critique dans la perspective du realisme thomiste. A cela se limite ma thèse ..."

12. *Op. cit.*, p. 161, note: "... ce qui est contradictoire, ... c'est de vouloir poser le problème de l'idéalisme critique dans la perspective du réalisme thomiste."

13. *Op. cit.*, p. 193, note: "... die Subjektivität in ihrem Vollzug immer schon 'draussen' ist beim An-sich-Sein überhaupt ..."

14. *Sum. theol.*, 1 q. 84, a. 6, ad 1 m: "... per illa verba Augustini datur intelligi quod veritas non sit totaliter a sensibus exspectanda. Requiritur enim lumen intellectus agentis, per quod immutabiliter veritatem in rebus mutabilibus cognoscamus, et discrenamus ipsas res a similitudinibus rerum."

15. *Op. cit.*, p. 177: "... le point de vue transcendental des conditions *a priori* de l'objet de connaissance ignore, par définition, le problème empirique de l'existence en soi des objets connus."

CHAPTER TWENTY

DECIDING WHETHER TO BELIEVE*

by Michael Novak

1. WHAT IS REAL?

Commonly, two reasons are given to explain why religious persons believe in God: they desire emotional security; they desire rational order. Religion is believed to originate in the feeling of emotional dependence, or in the eros of the necessary and the absolute. Yet neither of these reasons—which are not reasons at all, but only motives—is the reason for belief. For belief is rooted in the drive to understand. And understanding is neither emotional nor rational, neither emotive nor cognitive, in the sense in which these words are generally used in Anglo-American philosophy. A belief anchored in the hidden God does not bring emotional comfort, particularly in an intellectual climate that regards such belief as illusory. One's nonbelieving peers imply rather regularly that one is being dishonest, or at best lacks nerve. It is true, moreover, that God is silent; the moments of aridity and darkness are long; one does not see him in whom one believes. If belief brings "peace" or "emotional security," such peace is of a peculiar kind; and sometimes one would like to have some.

On the other hand, the drive to understand does not generate anticipations of rational order, necessity, cosmic harmony, or classical design. On the contrary, after a little experience, the drive to understand leads one to expect variety, many contingencies, an order that is often and at best statistical, probability schemes that perish in competition with other probability schemes in the evolution of human history. It leads one to expect surds and much that is unintelligible to men. One

*Used with permission from *Belief and Unbelief*, The Macmillan Co., New York, New York, 1965.

need not be a cosmic optimist, nor a rationalist, in order to believe in God. On the contrary, religious prophets often anticipate catastrophe, and the Christian symbol is the cross which involves a surd.

The decision to believe, made with authenticity, appears to have other roots than emotional weakness or monistic prepossessions. The decision to believe springs from a decision about what in human experience is to be taken as the criterion of the real. As each man is, so will he decide what is most real in human experience. According to that decision, he will shape his own identity. He will in ironic truth *realize* himself. An empty or a full life, nervousness or contentment, will later be the measure of his wisdom. It is a fascinating study to observe aging persons carefully, to see how they are reacting to choices made long years ago; or to observe the middle-aged, as they pass the crest of their accomplishments and begin to see, not what they will be when they mature, but what they have become. Sometimes there is suppressed terror, and sometimes peacefulness.

There are, commonly, many candidates for what is real in human experience. Nearly every person has at least three favorites: the one he speaks about conventionally, the one he cherishes as his serious conviction, and the one that reveals itself in his daily choices. These three are seldom unified. For some, "sincerity" is the most real of human experiences: sincerity regarding oneself and others, and the encounter with sincerity in others. But sincerity as a policy turns out to be an evasion of the basic question. For the basic question concerns what is real; and sincerity may or may not be based on what is real. If, for example, yesterday a woman told a man sincerely that she loved him, and today tells him with equal sincerity that she no longer loves him, she may not be being as sincere as she thinks she is. On the other hand, what she is being sincere about may be her present emotional state as it presents itself to her consciousness. But to be sincere about her present emotional state is only to be fickle. If what is most real to her are her present emotional states, the universe will, as it were, rotate on her as on an axis; and it is difficult to see how she will respond to other things or other persons as they are, rather than as they appear to her in her present emotional state.

The point is that emotional states can be recognized for what they are and discounted; there is no need for one to be imprisoned by one's moods of the moment, unless over the long run one likes it better that way.

Other persons may take "sense experience" to be most real to them. We may leave aside the problems of what exactly it is that sense experience presents to us—whether brute sense data, or whole physical objects, or *gestalt* configurations.[1] The radical question is how one is to interpret first awareness, insight, reflective judgment, and the drive to understand. For one appears to be drawing on all of these as one experiences, analyzes, argues, discovers, and justifies the fact that what appears to one's senses to be the case is in fact the case.[2]

Still other persons may take their own pragmatic purposes, or those of science or of the human community, to be the most real features of human experience: What counts is to realize oneself, succeed in a respectable career, be the best one can be in one's profession, have good friends, eat well, and take steps through political and social action to maximize the numbers of those who can share in such good things. Then equality of opportunity, fair play, justice, war on ignorance and disease, reform of the political, social, economic, and familial order become the ideals by which one lives. But, on reflection, it appears that to devise such purposes, and to discriminate among purposes, one requires a vision of what man is. And to decide what man is, is to make use of first awareness, insight, critical judgment, and fidelity to the drive to understand.

What appears in fact, then, to be real to those pragmatic persons whose nobility in thought and action one cannot help admiring is what is in accordance with their fidelity to understanding. Pragmatism, as many Americans understand it, is not crass, small-minded, confined to what is expedient.[3] It is a policy of fidelity to intelligence, with emphasis on the requirement that itelligence be not idle but "make a difference" in the world. That is real which meets the demands of inquiring intelligence. If it were not for those contemplative moments of artistic creation and enjoyment, of reflection, of love, even of idleness and wonderment—moments which recur with an insistence that forbids their rejection as valueless—one would be inclined to uphold the emphasis on that part of intelligence which solves the problems of the world; and one would resolutely turn aside from mysteries that cannot be solved by reference solely to sense experience.

It is not pragmatism as such, but the confluence of pragmatism with a narrow form of British empiricism which cuts short inquiry about God. A larger pragmatism allows no such turning aside from mysteries. For there are moments when one becomes aware that one is different from the objects of the world; moments when one wonders that anything at all is; moments when one respects another person whom one loves, respects her as she is and not as one would like her to be, beyond any of the requirements of self-interest or self-aggrandizement, and even at some cost to one's own self-image, desires, or plans. There are also mements when one is struck by the unconscionable importance of individual human personality in the world in which we live, an importance that makes such categories as "role," "function," "usefulness" seem inadequate and demeaning. The world, at least the human world, is not accurately to be understood on the model of an ant heap, however humane, nor as a machine of production, however just and equalitarian in its rewards and opportunities. To be a person is to be inadequately provided for by models drawn from inanimate nature. In world views projected from such models, the human person is a stranger, an alien, an outsider. The human world, on the contrary, is personal, and requires a model based upon intelligent subjectivity if it is to be understood. To conceive of the world as the proper home of intelligent subjects, to reject analogies drawn from the mechanical uses of human reason, or the merely reflexive activities of the mind, may run counter to present prejudice, but it is plausible.

As we have seen, first awareness is the base of man's difference from other things in the world. This first awareness unfolds as the dynamism of inquiry; inquiry issues in understanding; and this understanding does not satisfy the drive of inquiry until it has been authenticated by critical reflection. If this description accurately expresses man's cognitional life (if not, it can be amended through a more accurate use of inquiry, experience, understanding, and reflection), then the real is that which is authenticated not by mere extroversion but by a complicated and lengthy inquiry. That is real for man which he attends to, inquires into, understands to the extent he can, and with sufficient reasons accepts to be as he understands it. Nothing is known to be simply because it appears or because it gives rise to an insight, for fantasies may do as much. That is known to be real which is apprehended by the understanding, and affirmed to be as it is by virtue of the reasons which support that affirmation. We do not know what is real until we have attended to the data, understood them, and supported our understanding with reasons that adequately withstand objections. The real is not what we touch, taste, see, and feel, but rather what we approve in our touching, tasting, seeing, and feeling, when we reflect upon the conditions under which our experience is taking place, our hibitual successess and failures under such conditions, the present state of our sense organs, memory, and reflective powers.

What we affirm to be real when we say that a lamp is really out there in front of us is not that about the lamp which impresses our eyes and sense of touch.[4] It is that about the lamp which allows us to conclude that what impresses our eyes and our touch is intelligible as a lamp, and that what our eyes look at and our fingers touch is susceptible of inquiry and withstands reflection. Looking and touching enter into our verification of what is real; but looking can sometimes be merely "seeing things," and touches may sometimes be merely imagined. The real, then, is what is arrived at, not immediately by extroversion but mediately by reflection. The real is the intelligible, not in the first moment of understanding but in the second. It is that which is marked by the affirmation Yes to the question "Is that so?" Even among sensible things, the real is not what we look at or touch but what, with good reason, we claim to be seeing or touching, or to be able to see or touch if it were in our presence.

It seems, at first, odd to think of the real as the intelligible rather than as the tangible or the visible, especially when we are concerned with things as plain before our faces as lamps and rocks and trees. But reflection soon discovers the reason for this oddity. If I hold my hand in front of my face in perfect certainty that, in truth, my hand is in front of my face, one element in my certainty is my own first awareness;

another is my sense of being awake and in at least normal spirits and self-possession. So it is not the case that what is known as real about my hand's being in front of my face is constituted by my seeing its brute, raw presence out there; what is known as real about it is constituted by a judgment authenticating my qualifications for seeing it there at the present moment, and its own qualifications for being seen. We protect ourselves from illusions, hallucinations, and fantasies by submitting to critical reflection what we appear to touch, see, or hear. The real is not known by simply touching, seeing, or hearing, but by understanding and verifying: the real is not the tangible but the intelligible.

Old-fashioned textbooks often counsel the awakening of a skeptic to reality by kicking him on the shins. Yet this technique is useful, not so much because it brings about the raw confrontation of toes and shins, but because it gives a start to the skeptic's awareness. It calls on him to retaliate; therefore to make a decision; therefore to come to terms with his understanding and critical assessment of what is happening; and therefore to begin a new policy of heeding sensory stimuli as intimations of realities that are not to be ignored, but understood. Sense-knowledge is not the most real nor the most certain of human experiences, but it is the most immediately provocative.

But if the real is the intelligible, then in being faithful to understanding one is being faithful to what is real. This fact seems to reveal why what we understand to be the case sometimes makes a claim on us which appears to be inescapable. We may fail to act according to our understanding, and we may seek refuge from it in the contrary opinion of others, or in rationalizations of our own; but sometimes the truth of our understanding is borne inescapably in upon us, and, despite our evasions, we recognize it as true. The real as intelligible, then, is not just a figment of our imagination, though we may try to escape it as though it were, and no one else may blame us. Sometimes it makes claims upon us whose strength an open mind quickly attests, which even an evading mind cannot wholly escape.

The real as intelligible is the product of a decision: a decision to accept as sufficient the reasons which support one's claim to know. Such a decision is made with reasons, not arbitrarily. Yet it need not be absolutely final, but merely a completed stage in an endless pursuit of the unconditioned. It is a decision that fulfills the conditions of the present moment of inquiry in the ongoing dynamism of the·drive to understand. Further inquiry may call for revision in what is now taken to be real, yet those reasons which support the present claim, insofar as they are valid, will remain valid even in an extended or modified state of the question. Thus, development in knowledge has continuity, and the reasons supporting later stages include and subsume, as well as sometimes reverse, the reasons supporting early stages. There is a great deal of relativity in human knowing, since what one man decides are sufficient reasons for a claim to know may not be sufficient for another; and a later stage of human knowing may call for such serious revision of an earlier stage that some will be inclined to speak of "revolution," while others speak merely of "development."

The appeal, implicit or explicit, to first awareness, insight, critical judgment, and the dynamic drive of inquiry, however, remains constant in human knowing. And such an appeal constitutes human knowing as objective, not whimsical. It makes men the servants rather than the dictators of truth. Inquiry aims at what is real, not what is arbitrary; but the real is known only heuristically and partially: from a certain point of view, with certain purposes in view, within a given horizon or universe of inquiry.

The real, then, is the intelligible, and the dynamic drive of human intelligence is proportioned to it; that is to say, the universe in which we live seems to be such that within it fidelity to understanding is fruitful. When we are faithful to our drive to understand, we appear to act successfully, or at least more successfully than by any other program. For to try to determine what is real is to be prepared to act realistically. Faithful to understanding, a man appears to be more in harmony with other men and with things than in any other way; even love, apart from understanding, is destructive both of lover and beloved. Critical understanding is our access, limited as it is, to the real.

Unless these reflections are mistaken, to be faithful to understanding is in some way to be at home with other persons and with things; to cease being a stranger in the world; to end one's alienation. For understanding seems to be—in anticipation if not in realized fact—in harmony with the real. Our intentionality, unlimited and undetermined, appears to be one pole of a horizon of which the whole of the as yet unknown real appears to be the other. All that can be known as real is, by anticipation, present in the unstructured drive to understand; and the drive to understand hungers to understand all that can be understood. Even our capacity for sympathy with other persons can be extended beyond the bonds of family, history, and nation through appeal to a mutual drive to understand, a mutual fidelity to the demands of inquiry, a mutual respect for each other as each other is. Ideology demands conformity; but appeal to the drive to understand seeks community in diversity.

The real and the intelligible (the terms are convertible) appear to surround us, and to possess us rather than to be possessed by us. Through our senses and early experiences, the real is borne in upon our notice and, gradually, through out fledgling intelligence and knowing powers we appropriate it. Our minds are in some respects informed by the real as our lungs are stretched with air. Given a good start, we grow slowly in wisdom, detecting our own flights from the real, failing, and correcting our failures. Tragedy arises because we begin in ignorance, and yet cannot wait for wisdom before making choices and beginning to act. We are involved in unconscious patterns and surds in our actions before our understanding begins to be able to detect what we are doing. Struggling to come to self-knowledge, our lives have become dark and complicated beyond description before we are fairly under way.[5]

Still, our intelligence seeks the real as an arrow seeks its target; it intends to find, and to rest in, the real. We cannot be satisfied with illusions, nor with partial truths, nor with fantasies, except at the cost of diminishing our grasp of reality and inviting our own destruction. But when we follow this thirst for the real through to the end, does it lead us to God? It may be that the real ends where sense and imagination end; whatever cannot be reduced to corporeal sight or touch may not be real. The real may end where the uses of intelligence in the arts, the sciences, and the businesses of the world end. Belief in God may not be belief in the real, but belief in something beyond the real, and therefore, by definition, illusory.

We have not, however, acquiesced in the view that the real is the tangible or the visible. Quite apart from the question of God, this view does not seem to be tenable. The real is what, with reasons, we accept as intelligible and true to our experience. There is no other way of being united with the real; and the dynamic of inquiry, from experience to the first moment of understanding to the second moment of understanding, seems ineluctably to lead us in this way. It is difficult for many who are accustomed to think that they distinguish what is real from what is apparent merely by looking or by touching to agree that what is known as real is, not the tangible as tangible, but the tangible as intelligible. But reflection upon their own cognitional practice will show that not every sense experience is veridical, though, upon reflection, some are accepted as such.

The real, then, is reached through reflection; and what is real in things is that in them which withstands not only sensory exploration but also reflection. For we regularly discount appearances as deceptive or distorted because of departures from normal conditions, the refraction of light, an unusual distance or angle, the extraordinary condition of our own sense organs, or the like—departures which we recognize upon reflection.

If the real is the intelligible, then, it is not limited a priori to what we can experience with our senses. Our own intelligent subjectivity, for example, is not experienced through our senses, but rather the experience of our senses is possible because of our first awareness, and known to be veridical through inquiry and reflection.

Secondly, the unstructured drive to understand, by which we detect the limits of all our concepts and our rational systems, is not limited by what we can conceive or bracket in a rational system. The birth of a new theory, for example, is often first present in consciousness as a "glimmering," and expectation; sometimes only after long discursive effort is a new insight reduced to new concepts that can be related to familiar concepts, and a new rational system worked out to express it as the former could not. The drive to understand, since it is prior to concepts and systems, aims beyond them. At the limit, our unstructured drive to understand, then, does not merely anticipate a full, final concept or a rational system, a system to end all systems, in which the relations of every single event, or series of events, to every other is made clear. For the drive to understand is the appetite of an intelligent subject. When every scientific question has been answered, that drive will still seek another intelligent subject who responds to its anticipation of unlimited intelligence. Our drive to understand seems to be an exigence, not only for an understanding of all that can be understood but also for the source of such understanding and intelligibility. Its rest appears not to reside merely in an understanding of things, but also in intelligent dialogue with a person; not merely in seeing the point of theories, but in kinship of spirit with their authors. It will be well to recall several matters of ordinary experience.

The religious query seems to be a constant in human history. If our age is characterized by a widespread decision to declare the religious query illegitimate, it is possible that this decision arises from a preconception of what inquiry is, and of what is real. The quest for God is not eradicated; it is declared to lead off limits, and is ignored. "My soul," sings the Psalmist, "seeketh God as the hart panteth after water." In our generation, too, it seems true that many men seek God even though they have come upon no break in the wall by which to come into his presence, and even though that search is at present out of fashion.[6] Many others seem able to repress the question about God, and to live without suffering from his absence.

Yet not all are equally content in the belief that by such a choice they are doing justice to their drive to understand. For it does seem to be true that the drive to understand intends to reach the real, breaking through horizon after horizon in its effort to understand more accurately and fruitfully. And it is startling and repugnant to some minds to believe that an effort manifestly so fruitful and successful is out of harmony with the real; that is to say, is an accident, yielding no clue to the riddle of our destiny.

It would not be surprising that the universe were absurd. It would be surprising were there intelligent subjects who recognized it to be so, and yet seemed to be successful in coming to grips with it. Things seem to happen *as if* the real were the intelligible—not, surely, according to logical or classical expectations, but including surds and the unintelligible and the statistically probable in ways that men now detect. J. N. Findlay in defining his own atheism admits what he, with trepidation, calls a "god-ward trend" in things; "certainly there are *some* facts in our experience which are (one might say) *as if* there were a God."[7]

It is remarkable, for example, that men communicate with each other, from lasting and profound friendships, sometimes sacrifice themselves for one another, respect other persons quite differently from things, value creativity, build universities, and are incurably attracted by the ideal of fidelity to understanding. These facts are odd if the world of which these intelligent subjects are a part is radically absurd. It seems that in an absurd world there would be neither fruitfulness nor honor in being faithful to understanding. If the real is absurd, man's nobility doubles the absurdity by his failing to grasp the irrelevance of nobility and honesty. If man can *make* nobility and honesty relevant, the real is not quite so absurd as it seems.

If we observe what the nonbeliever does rather than what he says, we find that he acts as if understanding, friendship, honesty, nobility, and creativity are relevant to the real. If he believes that the real is without any meaning of its own, he creates his own values within it, as far as his power extends. But then his success at this project is a curious fact. Thus some nonbelievers appear to keep open the possibility of there being some sort of God, though they reject the conceptions of God they have encountered, and resolutely will not push their minds into the cold, unfamiliar darkness such an inquiry must brave. There is a strange fear of metaphysics in our generation, as though too many failures had broken our spirits.

Nevertheless, the finite answers to finite questions that preoccupy the workaday life of the scientist and the productive man do not exhaust the human drive to understand. For that drive, taken in its root and at its base, raises a different kind of question from any of those that occur in its ordinary problem-solving operations, in any of its efforts to predict and control. That question is whether the appetite of the intelligent subject is radically in harmony with the world, whether it is at home or in a strange land. The answer to that question is the first major step toward belief, or toward unbelief. For if the drive to understand is in harmony with the real, then the source of that drive and of the real may be one and the same. If the real is the intelligible, then there may well be a God.

Earlier, we came to think of God as the source of the intelligible and as an intelligent subject. These do not provide us with the content of a concept of God. For we do not understand what such a source, such a subject, might be like. But they do offer us a means of guiding what we may, and may not, properly say of God. Our earlier inquiry and our present one have now arrived at the same point: the real as the intelligible, God thought of as the source of the intelligible and of our intelligence, and our intelligence seeking its own identity.

Is there, then, a God? Have we evidence to support our belief that there is? It seems that we have one main line of evidence: all those things that seem to indicate that the real is the intelligible, and the insight which insists that, without an intelligent source, the intelligibility of the real is a mere accident and hence unintelligible. This, then, is the structure of the reflections that lead us to think belief in God is justified. The conviction that the real is intelligible, and the mere notion that God is both the source of the intelligible and the source of our intelligent subjectivity, lead us to *suppose* that that idea of God is true. Reflecting upon this supposition, and seeing its point, we conclude that there is a God, and that his existence and power explain why the real is intelligible, and why our drive to understand is as it is. This is the structure of the evidence and we will return to it in the next section.

Many, however, will choose to say at this point: "Yes, but the fact is that our science is only a more effective myth than, say, the Homeric myths;[8] we move from myth to myth; the world *itself* is simply unintelligible to us. And this is simply a hard fact to be swallowed by adults." They will add: "Yet the conclusion is not that we should despair. On the contrary, there are many tasks to keep us busy, and many incentives toward living a useful and satisfying life, without reference to a God we can in no way assure ourselves exists."

We may hasten to concede that "the world *itself*" is ever beyond our actual reach. But that our inquiries do not bring us to more effective and fruitful approximations of the real seems disproved by the success of those inquiries. We should not imagine that "world *itself*," or "objective," mean something out there now that we need to get a spiritual look at, in order to attain the real and the intelligible. Such a look is impossible. On the contrary, we need only detect that our drive to understand *seeks* the real, that the dynamism of inquiry heads toward the real, in order to say that the real is the intelligible. The "objective" is what in the context of reasonable discourse we are aiming at and what, at this stage in the heuristic dynamism, we now have good reasons to accept as fulfilling the conditions of critical inquiry. The "really, truly 'objective,' out there, independent of any human mind" is not accessible to us. It is appropriated only little by little, from approximation to approximation, as science develops and later inquiry corrects what earlier inquiry overlooked.

As to the incentives to be found for living "a useful and satisfying life," the decision for belief or unbelief appears to depend on one's threshold of satisfaction. Those satisfied by diversion and usefulness may choose one alternative; those in favor of trusting in their unrestricted drive to understand, beyond the limits of the conceptual, may choose the other. The key lies in who one is and what one expects from life; by belief or by unbelief one defines oneself. But it does seem that reflection on one's knowing activities favors belief. The exigence of our drive to understand does seem to be the intimation of the divine presence in us, the source of our restlessness, the occasion of our weariness with every finite diversion, every idol, every merely temporal achievement. One wants to be faithful to understanding quite totally—not to hold back for fear of the dark. Further, it sometimes seems as if unbelief represents a failure of nerve. One wonders what psychological pressures, what loves, what prior decisions, incline one toward unbelief, and away from fidelity to understanding, at the very moment when understanding makes its most basic claim.[9]

There are many reasons for unbelief—the problem of evil, the ugliness of religious organizations, rebellion against the injustices of a Christian civilization, conceptual difficulties, fears for personal autonomy, among others. But reflection upon our own cognitional activities seems to lead to the basic religious insight: the poverty of our own concepts and systems in the face of the exigence of our unlimited drive to understand. This drive seems to seek an intelligent subject, the source of the intelligibility of the real and the source of our own struggle toward the real. In that exigence we detect the invitation to believe, and thus to confer unity upon our inner life. For to respond Yes to this invitation confirms one's fidelity to understanding, reinforces it, and reconciles one to oneself, to others, and to the real. From the perspective of belief, so strong is this inner harmony, so clear the self-authentication of the drive to understand opening upon its fullest aims, that one cannot at first imagine a non-believer in harmony with himself.

On the other hand, one soon learns that fidelity to understanding is not a question of words. Many are faithful to understanding, yet do not believe in God. They refuse to reflect further on what it is to which they are faithful, perhaps because the name "God" has been cheapened on the lips of believers. The Jewish and Christian scriptures insist that God alone judges hearts and knows what is in man; our names are written in his sight, while we in the darkness grope to find out who we are.[10]

But since the God of believers cannot be seen, imagined, or conceived, the refusal of the nonbeliever to name such a God does not seem far removed from belief. The reality is more important than the words, and the reality in this case is fidelity to understanding. Believers and nonbelievers alike, faithful to this drive, appear to find harmony of spirit, a modicum of rest, and deep integrity.

2. INTO THE PRESENCE OF GOD

Time is required for the fact to sink deeply into our consciousness that the real is known through intelligent knowing rather than through mere sensory extroversion; through critical reflection rather than merely through taking a look. Once this simple and compelling lesson of reality is learned, however, the way to God is clearer and more straight. For if the real is the intelligible, two different lines of inquiry arise. One places the inquirer at the threshold of God's presence. The other prompts him to step forward into that presence.

The first line of inquiry is touched upon quite cautiously by J. J. C. Smart in an essay whose title is "Can God's Existence Be Proved?"[11] Professor Smart's answer to the question expressed by his title is at least a tentative No. He considers the three post-Cartesian arguments as they have been listed by Kant: the ontological, the cosmological, and the teleological. He exposes with no uncertainty the fallacies in the conception of a "logically necessary being." He argues successfully that the way taken by intelligence to God is not that of "logically necessity"; and, with him, we may accept the fundamentally Kantian rejection of this way. But when he has finished with the useless concept of a "logically necessary being," Professor Smart initiates the sort of inquiry which seems to us much more fruitful. In the last paragraph of his essay, he raises the meditative question to which we have already seen Wittgenstein advert: "Why should anything exist at all?" At first, Professor Smart

answers the question directly: "Logic seems to tell us that the only answer which is not absurd is to say, 'Why shouldn't it'?"[12] But then
Professor Smart reflects further:

> Nevertheless, though I know how any answers on the lines of the cosmo-
> logical argument can be pulled to pieces by a correct logic, I still feel I want
> to go on asking the questions. Indeed, though logic has taught me to look at
> such a question with the gravest suspicion, my mind often seems to reel un-
> der the immense significance it seems to have for me. That anything should
> exist at all does seem to me a matter for the deepest awe. But whether other
> people feel this sort of awe, and whether they or I ought to is another ques-
> tion. I think we ought to. If so the question arises: If "Why should anything
> exist at all?" cannot be interpreted after the matter of the cosmological argu-
> ment, that is, as an absurd request for the nonsensical postulation of a logically
> necessary being, what sort of question is it? What sort of question is this ques-
> tion "Why should anything exist at all?" All I can say is, that I do not yet
> know.[13]

Faced by the inquiry Professor Smart initiates so clearly, one may
be inclined to think that the desire to continue raising the question of
existence, and the awe which accompanies it, arise from the drive to understand. The reason we ask such a question seems to be our expectation,
even if not articulated, that the real is the intelligible. It does not make
sense to say that the real just happens; for then the real is radically unintelligible. It is an intelligibility whose source lacks intelligibility. Why
should anything at all exist? Professor Smart thinks that the answer which
is not absurd is "Why shouldn't it?" But, on the contrary, that is the one
answer which does seem absurd. For to take the position "Why shouldn't
it?" is to take the position "A reason for it is irrelevant; intelligence is
out of place here; existence is simply not to be explained, but taken as
a surd." Professor Smart's instincts are against this flight from understanding, and that seems to be why he is continuing his inquiry.

The search for a necessary being in rationalistic ontological categories,
then, is hopelessly misleading; for this reason we may concur with the
body of Professor Smart's essay. But when one comes up against the
question "Why should anything at all exist?" and agrees that to say
"Why shouldn't it?" is merely to evade, not to be faithful to, intelligence;
and when one is fortified by the firmly critical awareness that the real
is the intelligible; then one is brought up short before an awesome
possibility: Perhaps the real has an intelligible source—indeed, an intelligent source. "Why should anything at all exist?" "Whence comes the
real, which is all that is to be known?" In raising such questions, the
threshold from which one may answer "God" has been reached.

Two meanings of "real" are then involved. There is the real which
raises the question, "Why should the real exist?" There is, sceondly, the
real which is *intended by* the question: i.e., the intelligible and intelligent source which is an answer to the question. The gap between the
two realities is immense. They are not consecutive links in a chain. They
are as different as the data which raise the question and the answer
that resolves it. They are as related as the question requires. We do not

need to have caught sight of the intelligible and intelligent source in order to agree that it is the source. It suffices to agree that the real is radically intelligible, deriving from an unconceptualized but intelligible and intelligent source. In agreeing to this one is not bound to overlook the unintelligibles and the evils which also characterize the real. These surds present a subsequent but different dilemma: how can an intelligent source of a certain kind—omnipotent and good—allow them?

A formal argument for the existence of God is not of much use in the life of one who is trying to decide between belief and unbelief. For what is at stake is one's recognition of one's own identity, and there are many layers of point of view, inquiry, and new horizon to come through before one can understand the formal argument. Even so, to believe in God is not to accept the conclusion of a deduction. It is to accept the evidence that one discovers in one's own knowing and doing, indicating the presence of a God who remains unseen and even unconceptualized. It is, above all, to enter into a conversation with that God, not through words so much as through the direction of one's attention. Thus, talk of the "intelligible" and "the real" and "source," while indispensable as scaffolding, is not at the heart of the matter. Only if each one who inquires appropriates the way in which such words are being used, and laces it into his experience, does the inquiry get beyond the scaffolding and the poor words that serve as its signs. Only if those who share the inquiry carry with them their experience, and steadily reflect upon that experience, are they aware that what is at stake is not skill in verbal gymnastics, but fidelity to understainding and, through understanding, to experience.

At issue is an appreciation of the implications of our own drive to understand and our appropriation of the real. These implications cannot be usefully schematized, because individual human beings do not live by formal schemata. Each must travel the circles of self-discovery for himself, by those steep paths along which fidelity to understanding leads him. To begin such a search is already to have found God, even though the seeker, looking for an object—something to see—does not notice him. As Pascal suggests, to seek God is to be faithful to that drive to understand which has him for its final goal, and thus, in a significant way, is already to have found him. Even the believer can do no more than point toward a God whom he cannot see.

If we think of God, then, as the source of the intelligible, such as it is, and as the source of our intelligent subjectivity, then, if there is a God, the intelligibility of the real and our ability to know the real are related in their source. If our experience seems to indicate that the real is the intelligible—that fidelity to understanding, friendship, love, creativity, nobility, are relevant to the real world in which we live—then we seem to have found an indication that there is a God. For if there is a God, fidelity to understanding is not an ironic or a desperate or a Promethean way of life; it is the realistic way of life. The world may be cruel as well as beautiful, full of risks as well as comforts, the unintelligible as well as the intelligible, and of evil as well as good; but man is at home in it, at home as a pilgrim, perhaps, but not absurd, not isolated.

If, on the other hand, there is not a God, then the intelligible just happens; it is of itself unintelligible. And the fact that men can make realistic judgments, both in their knowing and in their doing, is an oddity. Every appeal to intelligence also makes an appeal to the drive to understand, to its intention of reaching the real, and to its competence in dealing with the real. It does not seem plausible that man's intelligence has no intelligible relation to the real, that it struggles for effectiveness in a world that is not susceptible of being dealt with by intelligence. Further, it seems implausible, though not impossible, that the real is indeed intelligible but it "just happens" to be so. One cannot bring oneself to see that there is a God by induction, or by deduction. One can only bring oneself to see, by reflection, what a consistent and thorough fidelity to understanding seems to indicate: (1) that understanding is not impotent in dealing with the world; and (2) that our understanding anticipates an intelligent subject as the source of its own drive to understand, and as the source of that drive's success in coping with the world.

Belief in God is rooted in reflection upon one's own intelligent subjectivity. But such reflection is not compelling, since not all men understand their own identity in the same way. It is only compelling in the sense that either fidelity to understanding operates "in the teeth of" the inscrutability and absurdity of the world, or it is a sign of the world's own intelligible dynamic. Much then, depends on one's spontaneous or acquired confidence in fidelity to understanding—as against, let us say, analogies from physics or mechanics—as a key to understanding the world. The drive to understand, it seems, points to God; we do not succeed in efforts to train our senses, imagination, or even concepts on him. To trust that pointing, or not to, is the question.[14] Some who habitually live by understanding, who struggle to move from horizon to horizon toward the real, will be inclined to credit understanding.

The second line of inquiry leads to this goal in a different way. Again it is required that one have come to see, implicitly or explicitly, that the real is not what is touched, seen, or heard, but what is understood and, on reflection, verified. A dagger in the air, a sound in the night, the touch of a mosquito on one's leg in the darkness, may be seen, heard, or felt, but they may or may not be understood and verified as real. What is touched, seen, or heard is at best a question for reflective intelligence, not a guarantee of what is real.[15]

Moreover, it is required that one reflect upon the dynamic movement of one's own act of understanding. For it occurs to some men that the finite things that they come to accept as real, the finite theories that they accept as true, and even the whole system of their common sense and scientific judgments do not exhaust their drive to understand. The more they reflect upon that drive to understand, the more they are let to wonder what, exactly, would respond to it and give it the full activity of rest. In this light, every finite proposal, and every extension of the finite to the infinite, seems inadequate. No one finite object, nor any infinite series of finite objects, offers to do more than to divert them, keep them occupied, and, finally, bore them. Moreover, the drive to understand is the appetite of an intelligent subject. There is a possibility that the full response to this drive is that of another intelligent subject. On such a supposition, the world in which we live is radically personal. A subject who responds to our intelligent subjectivity, as abyss cries out to abyss, would then be the source of the intelligibility of things, and also the source of that communication which in fact takes place between persons, through art, friendship, love, justice, rational discourse. On such a supposition, the world of human experience is not only, in spite of its appearance, "a bump on a bump"[16]—a tiny edge of consciousness on a tiny edge of animate life in a vast universe—but also the interpretive key to the rest.

One need not, in this supposition, assume that the divine is in the form of a man, or bounded by human limitations. One need only suppose that he is known indirectly by the unlimited, searching drive of our own intelligent subjectivity, and its rejection of all lesser objects offered in place of him. He is the response to our thirst for unlimited intelligibility and personal dialogue. Exactly what he is like, we need not and cannot imagine. Yet our approach to him is critical, since it proceeds through reflection upon our own unlimited drive to understand. Fidelity to that drive is necessary and sufficient for the rejection of idols, the correction of fanaticism, and respect for the human person, in oneself and in others.

To entertain the reflection that everything exists for reasons and in a manner known by an intelligible and intelligent source, or to think that finite objects do not exhaust the questions raised by our own nature, is not yet to have entered into conversation with God. It is only to have come to the threshold of his presence. At this threshold, for various reasons, many will turn back. The intellectual air here is too thin. There are enough things to do in our cities, our governments, our underdeveloped economies and health centers and schools, without opening such a difficult and energy-consuming line of inquiry.

But some men will think it in accord with their own identity to press further. Some will think that man is as naturally religious as he is social, political, economic, or artistic. Moreover, the religious sense is a sense that needs effort, practice, and exploration like any other. Its base lies in the unlimited drive to understand and it has the real for its horizon, so it requires the disciplining and harmony of all our other powers.

The step into God's presence is achieved in a fashion that can be described, but not accompanied by detailed instructions. One comes to trust one's own drive to understand. Then, quite simply, one begins to speak, even though God is hidden. If one's preceding reflections are correct, one stands already in his presence. Special words are not required; one can be speechless. For he knows us from before we were made; he knows our thoughts before we form them. Those infidelities to understanding that have escaped our attention have not escaped his. Far from destroying our drive to understand, or bending it down to the earth, he requires us to be more faithful than our own standards have yet insisted. He impels us toward more damanding honesty, more singular courage, more independence of our cultural milieu, a greater sense of community with other men who are caught in the same night, than we have yet practiced.

The terrifying thing about the discovery of God is that one comes to see that he has been there all the time. He is not dead; we have been dead. Even believers who neglect him, mumbling routinely through their prayers, will one day come upon this terror. To meet God face to face—quietly, wordlessly, wholly attentive—is no comforting experience. Moreover, the way in which this sense of the holy, of awe, of dependence, is described in books is partly misleading. For the uninitiated will think of the brute awe of standing before the Grand Canyon, or high in the cold Alps, or of the emotional dependence of the immature boy upon his mother or the dependence of his superego upon his father. But the encounter with God—with the living God and no counterfeit—is a chastizing experience. For it is accomplished not in the context of warm self-satisfying illusion, but in the nakedness of the self's critical drive to understand. In that light, one's inadequacies are only too plain. Standing in that light, nonetheless, one has the dignity of attempting to be faithful to oneself. One offers God one's ardent efforts to be honest. God is hidden, the self is naked and impecunious, but in this scorching light it is good to live.

Having entered God's presence, moreover, I cannot accurately say that I "possess God" or "have belief." It seems, rather, that God possesses me, that belief has surrounded me. This difference does not imply a loss of one's bearings, a mystical flight, a sense of being suspended in air. It merely represents what seems then to be the case, viz., that the dialogue between oneself and God is not initiated by the self; that when one is faithful to understanding one is responding to an attraction in the core of one's subjectivity; that God has done the calling, the guiding, the leading, and made it possible for men to respond, to be guided, to be led. It is not, however, as if God is separate from me and takes over my autonomy as a writer takes over a pen, or an artist a brush. It is rather that my autonomy, my separateness from things and from others, my full measure of responsibility to myself, my *own* drive to understand and commitment to my *own* understanding, are the very things that God respects, the very things through which alone I can authentically find him.

In possessing me, God does not dispossess me of myself; he invites me and he respects my response. He does not ask me to abandon my autonomy, least he leave me with nothing to offer him, and no way to find him. But I know with clear instinct that in being faithful to my own identity, I am faithful to him. In being intelligent, I am living by the light of his intelligence. In feeling the bite of objective honesty about myself, I hear his word. In respecting other persons, in loving them realistically, as they are, I do as he does. In creating, I share his fecundity. In him, it appears, I live, move, and have my being.

Yet is this nonsense and a myth? Perhaps. Not seeing God, one cannot help doubting, and worrying about conceptual difficulties. The hardened nonbeliever, who has considered a score of arguments, digested hundreds of books, and uncovered a thousand religious hypocrisies, will turn the skills of analysis upon such reflections as these. Sometimes he will almost convince me entirely, and always he will convince me in part. The drive to understand seeks relentlessly for intelligibility, and indeed for the response of an infinitely intelligent subject. Perhaps it does so in vain. But when I trust fidelity to understanding in my scientific work, in my writing, in my moral efforts, in my friendships and my loves, I am loath to distrust it in facing the riddle of existence. Understanding occurs. Love occurs. Respect for persons, and also friendships, occur. I am inclined to think that these are the significant occurrences in the universe, that, whatever the ravages of the unintelligible and the positively evil, these characterize the real, and that whoever trusts in understanding and in love is in harmony with the real. The God of intelligence and love draws men toward greater understanding, greater love. The dynamism of human development, however infinitesimal in the perspective of the universe, is the clue to the presence of God.

Nevertheless, children starve to death, and men of understanding and love are pointlessly murdered. Organized religion has often been the protector of an unjust social order. Conventional religion is largely false, delusive, and crippling. These are the reasons that most draw me toward unbelief. Reflection upon my own identity draws me toward belief.

FOOTNOTES

1. See, e.g., R. M. Chisholm, *Perceiving*, Cornell University Press: Ithaca, N. Y., 1957; Roderick Firth, "Phenomenalism," American Philosophical Association Suppl. Vol., 1952, *Science, Language and Human Rights*, pp. 1-20; and W. V. Quine, *Word and Object*, The M.I.T. Press: Cambridge, Mass., 1960, pp. 234-39, etc.

2. See Bernard Lonergan, *Insight, op. cit.*, chap. 8, pp. 245-70.

3. See Sidney Hook, *The Quest for Being, op. cit.*, pp. 227-28, for praise of a philosophy "wider and more precious than science." In this connection, see Henry David Aiken, "Sidney Hook as Philosopher," *Commentary*, 33 (1962), pp. 143-51; also, Morton V. White, "Beyond Positivism and Pragmatism," *Toward Reunion in Philosophy, op. cit.*, pp. 279-88.

4. See Lonergan, note 2, *supra*.

5. Lonergan, *Insight, op. cit.*, on "the scotosis of the dramatic subject," pp. 191-203.

6. Sidney Hook, for example, calls himself a "skeptical God-seeker." *The Quest for Being, op. cit.*, p. 115. In similar fashion, Wallace I. Matson has thought it worth expending the energy required to write his *The Existence of God*, though he does not understand why to some persons God matters more than anything else, and though he writes about the issue as would a visitor to a strange land, *op. cit.*, p. 245.

7. In *New Essays in Philosophical Theology*, *op. cit.*, pp. 74-75.

8. See W. V. Quine, *From a Logical Point of View*, *op. cit.*, p. 44.

9. See Chapter Seven, n. 11.

10. See Martin D'Arcy, "The Search for the Self" in *No Absent God*, Harper & Row: New York, 1962, pp. 72-84, esp. his reminder that God, according to St. John, knows each man by name (p. 75). See also D'Arcy's discussion of Ryle on the self, pp. 100-15.

11. In *New Essays in Philosophical Theology*, *op. cit.*, pp. 28-46.

12. *Ibid.*, p. 46.

13. *Ibid.* Smart, like Matson (*op. cit.*), seems to commit an historical error in assimilating the "five ways" of Aquinas to the "three traditional arguments" of later rationalistic thought. Nearly every key word in the discussion—"necessary," for example—has changed its meaning in the centuries intervening between Aquinas and Wolfe. For a start toward a more accurate historical view of Aquinas, see Edward Sillem, *Ways of Thinking About God*, Sheed & Ward: New York, 1961, and Thomas Gornall, S.J., *A Philosophy of God*, Sheed & Ward: New York, 1962. For an analysis of basic differences between Aquinas and Kant, see Joseph Marechal, *Le point de depart de la metaphysique*, Vol. V, *Le Thomisme devant la philosophie critique*, *op. cit.*, esp. pp. 564-97, and David Burrell, "Kant and Philosophical Knowledge," *The New Scholasticism*, 38 (1964), pp. 189-213, esp. pp. 206-13.

14. See Jean Danielou, *The Scandal of Truth*, Helicon Press: Baltimore, Md., 1962, pp. 1-7 and *passim*.

15. See my "A Key to Aristotle's 'Substance,'" *Philosophy and Phenomenological Research*, 24 (1963), pp. 1-19.

16. See the review by W. V. Quine of J. J. C. Smart's *Philosophy and Scientific Realism* in *New York Review of Books*, July 9, 1964. Quine writes (p. 3): "Physics investigates the essential nature of the world, and biology describes a local bump. Psychology, human psychology, describes a bump on a bump." Yet human psychology is the source of science, philosophy, and "scientific realism." It may also be the key to all else. At issue here is whether one takes physics or psychology to be the radical factor in one's own acts of understanding. At issue is one's interpretation of one's own identity.

12